Reconsidering Context in Language Assessment

This volume reconsiders the problem of context in language testing and other modes of assessment from the perspective of transdisciplinarity. Transdisciplinary assessment research brings together collaborators who draw on the strengths of their differing backgrounds and expertise in order to address high-stakes complex socially relevant problems. Traditional treatments of context in language assessment research have generally been informed by individualist cognitive theories within measurement and psychometrics. The additive potential of alternative social theories, including theories of genre, situated learning, distributed cognition, and intercultural communication, has largely been overlooked. In this book, the benefits of socio-theoretical reconsiderations of context are discussed and further exemplified in transdisciplinary research (TR) studies that investigate the use of assessment in classroom and workplace settings. The book offers a renewed view of context in arguments for the validity of assessment practices and will be of interest to assessment researchers, practitioners, and students in applied linguistics, education, educational psychology, language testing, and other related disciplines and fields.

Janna Fox is Professor Emerita of Applied Linguistics and Discourse Studies in the School of Linguistics and Language Studies, Carleton University. Her research interests include language assessment (test development, diagnostic and portfolio assessment); the consequences of assessment use on teaching, learning, policy and decision-making; and transdisciplinary partnerships in validation research.

Natasha Artemeva is Professor of Applied Linguistics and Discourse Studies in the School of Linguistics and Language Studies, Carleton University. Her research interests include social theories of learning and practice, genre studies, disciplinary and professional communication, forensic linguistics, and research ethics.

Routledge Studies in Applied Linguistics

Analyzing Discourses in Teacher Observation Feedback Conferences
Fiona Copland and Helen Donaghue

Learning-Oriented Language Assessment
Putting Theory into Practice
Edited by Atta Gebril

Language, Mobility and Study Abroad in the Contemporary European Context
Edited by Rosamond Mitchell and Henry Tyne

Intonation in L2 Discourse
Research Insights
María Dolores Ramirez-Verdugo

Contexts of Co-Constructed Discourse
Interaction, Pragmatics, and Second Language Applications
Edited by Lori Czerwionka, Rachel Showstack, and Judith Liskin-Gasparro

Second Language Prosody and Computer Modeling
Okim Kang, David O. Johnson, Alyssa Kermad

Reconsidering Context in Language Assessment
Transdisciplinary Perspectives, Social Theories, and Validity
Janna Fox and Natasha Artemeva

Evaluation Across Newspaper Genres
Hard News Stories, Editorials and Feature Articles
Jonathan Ngai

For more information about this series, please visit: www.routledge.com/Routledge-Studies-in-Applied-Linguistics/book-series/RSAL

Reconsidering Context in Language Assessment

Transdisciplinary Perspectives, Social Theories, and Validity

Janna Fox and Natasha Artemeva

Routledge
Taylor & Francis Group
NEW YORK AND LONDON

First published 2022
by Routledge
605 Third Avenue, New York, NY 10158

and by Routledge
4 Park Square, Milton Park, Abingdon, Oxon, OX14 4RN

Routledge is an imprint of the Taylor & Francis Group, an informa business

Library of Congress Cataloging-in-Publication Data
A catalog record for this title has been requested

ISBN: 978-0-815-39507-2 (hbk)
ISBN: 978-1-032-24484-6 (pbk)
ISBN: 978-1-351-18457-1 (ebk)

DOI: 10.4324/9781351184571

Typeset in Sabon
by Newgen Publishing UK

Access Appendix A at https://carleton.ca/slals/people/fox-janna/

Contents

Contributors

Peggy Hartwick, PhD, is an Instructor in Carleton University's School of Linguistics and Language Studies. Her research focuses on the affordances of digital tools and online learning contexts. She is the recipient of the 2015 Society for Teaching and Learning in Higher Education (STLHE)/ Brightspace Innovation Award.

Ana Lúcia Tavares Monteiro, PhD, works with the ICAO Language Proficiency Requirements at ANAC – Brazil, as a regulator, aviation English test designer, and interlocutor/rater trainer. She serves on international and national boards governing language proficiency testing in aviation. Her research interests include construct definition within the context of pilot–controller communications.

Acknowledgements

Reconsidering Context in Language Assessment was a natural outcome of our mutual engagement over the years with collaborating research partners who brought to bear their differing disciplinary, professional, workplace, and life experiences in addressing complex research questions of shared collective concern. Our ideas for a book on context in language assessment began to take shape early in 2016. We are grateful to Elysse Preposi, our Editor, for her generous input and ongoing support as those ideas come to fruition herein.

We thank our reviewers, Angel Arias, Peggy Hartwick, Ana Lúcia Tavares Monteiro, Josée-Anna Tanner, and Carolyn Turner, for their thoughtful, challenging, and sometimes humbling feedback, which deepened and clarified our thinking. This book would not have been possible without the thorough, systematic, and conscientious attention of our Research Associate, Ana Lúcia Tavares Monteiro. We thank her for her contributions to two chapters as co-author and her extraordinary insight and organizational talents. We are also grateful for Peggy Hartwick's contributions. Both Ana and Peggy shared their transdisciplinary, socio-theoretically informed research in illustrating hands-on practical applications of the ideas in this book. As such, they greatly increased the value of the book for teachers, graduate students, researchers, and others who are interested in language assessment.

We also wish to thank our graduate students who were actively engaged in the book's development. A special thank you to Chloe Grace Fogarty-Bourget, Tina Beynen, and Claire Reynolds for their methodical and thorough work as members of the meta-review Search Team, and for their contributions to several of our transdisciplinary research projects, particularly the engineering diagnostic assessment project. Our thanks as well to Kathryn Carreau, Angela Garcia, and Gillian Mclellan for their input on the salience and usefulness of social theories from the perspectives of doctoral students in applied linguistics, writing, discourse studies, and program evaluation. Such remarkable graduate students suggest a promising future for the many fields of inquiry concerned with language assessment.

Finally, we owe an enormous debt of gratitude to inspirational colleagues and mentors, such as Aviva Freedman, Anthony Paré, Ian Pringle, Tim Pychyl, Carolyn Turner, Liying Cheng, Lynda Taylor, Elana Shohamy, and Bruno Zumbo. Above all, we thank the patient and generous support of our families, who put up with our monk-like habits for extensive periods of time throughout the writing of this book.

Introduction

Theory, research, reflection, and action: What is this book about?

Janna Fox and Natasha Artemeva

> *... one begins with the assumption that the other has something to say to us and to contribute to our understanding. The initial task is to grasp the other's position in the strongest possible light ... based on mutual respect, where we are willing to risk our own prejudgments, are open to listening and learning from others, and we respond to others with responsiveness and responsibility.*
>
> (Bernstein, 1998, p. 4)

> *... ongoing dialogue permits no final conclusion. It would be a poor hermeneuticist who thought he [sic] could have, or had to have, the last word.*
>
> (Gadamer, 2003, p. 579)

> *There is a need to develop approaches to text analysis through a* ***transdisciplinary*** *dialogue with perspectives on language and discourse within social theory and research in order to develop our capacity to analyse texts as elements in social processes ... This is inevitably a long-term project which is only begun in a modest way in this book.*
>
> (Fairclough, 2003, p. 6)

Setting the stage: let the play begin

As long-time co-authors and collaborators, we have had the benefit of learning a great deal from each other. Years ago, we recognized that our differing backgrounds, both disciplinary and cultural, pre-positioned us to view and conceptualize the same complex problems from very different perspectives. One of us had an early disciplinary background in English literature which evolved into a focus on language teaching, high-stakes testing, classroom-based assessment, and curriculum (Fox, 2003, 2004, 2005a, 2005b). The other was originally trained for and worked in engineering for many years; later, her attention turned to writing and genre studies with a focus on disciplinary literacies and pedagogies in science, technology, engineering, and mathematics (STEM) disciplines (Artemeva, 2005, 2008; Artemeva & Freedman, 2015). Prior to our collaboration, in our individual work we had drawn on different bodies of research and

DOI: 10.4324/9781351184571-1

highlighted contributions from different theorists and researchers. We set up our studies, interpreted our findings, and explained outcomes of research in different ways. However, when we were brought together by a shared interest in an issue of mutual concern, it was our differences that supported dialogue, reflection, innovation, and new insights. Because of our differences, we have recognized the presuppositions and assumptions that are both explicit and implicit in how we frame our research, theoretically and methodologically, what we interrogate or explore within that frame, and how we describe, explain, or interpret what we find. Mining, recognizing, and reflecting on our differences has meant that our collaborations have strengthened our research outcomes by both deepening and expanding our own understanding of our home disciplines, as well as those of others, much as living in a different country increases our understanding of who we are as well as how others see and act in the world (Artemeva & Fox, 2010, 2011; Fox & Artemeva, 2011, 2017). In short, our collaborations expanded our horizons and led to learning.

There was so much more to be gained in working collaboratively. For example, engaging in research together, with a shared goal as our focus, sharpened and clarified the underlying theories that informed our individual work. Hereafter, we follow qualitative medical researchers and educators Reeves, Albert, Kuper, and Hodges (2008) in their understanding of theories:

> Theories provide complex and comprehensive conceptual understandings of things that cannot be pinned down: how societies work, how organisations operate, why people interact in certain ways. Theories give researchers different "lenses" through which to look at complicated problems and social issues, focusing their attention on different aspects of the data and providing a framework within which to conduct their analysis.
>
> (p. 631)

Even how we treat theory itself is deeply rooted in what we *believe* about the nature of reality (*ontology*), and how best to understand or know reality (*epistemology*). Johnson and Gray (2010) view such beliefs as "'small t' truths", which are "warranted" by knowledge or experience, or tacit "assumptions" (p. 87).[1] Beliefs carry with them implicit values of their worth (*axiology*) and inform what we do and how we act. Beliefs shape our worldviews, and within academic communities they are inculcated in relation to the disciplinary company we keep, and the shared conceptual positions and practices that define a discipline. We have the impression that when researchers engage in research, they may not typically take time to probe and reflect on these underlying beliefs and values, but they are inevitably implicit in every choice we make and action we take. The *methodology* we choose is "the broad inquiry logic that guides selection of specific methods", and arguably, "can be characterized as the mediator between conceptual [i.e., theory] and methods [i.e., practice] issues ... the point of integration between the two" (Tashakkori & Teddlie, 2010, p. 16).

However, theories are unstable. They are subject to change. They are interactive representations of what seems to be the case at a particular point in time – "a series of interconnected ideas that condense and organize knowledge" (Christ, 2010, p. 646). (The theory that the world was flat could not account for the largely anecdotal alternative evidence of early explorers that it was not.) Change comes about through growth in knowledge and understanding – by seeking out alternative, "plausible rival" (Cronbach, 1988, p. 13) evidence and explanations. Research should engender growth in knowledge and understanding. As researchers, our own explicit theoretical perspectives, along with our implicit or *taken-for-granted* assumptions and routinized practices, are clarified when we are challenged by different worldviews and concomitant practices. The potential for reflection, increased awareness, and learning is thus dramatically increased.

We did not have a name for our collective, collaborative research practices; however, we have come to understand they would best be characterized as *transdisciplinary* (cf. Fairclough, 2003; Moss & Haertel, 2016; Piaget, 1972). Such transdisciplinary research (TR), as Moss and Haertel explained, naturally evokes *methodological pluralism* – "the constellation of methods/methodologies that have come to be labelled 'quantitative' and 'qualitative'" (p. 127). With the emergence, development, and expanding use of mixed methods (cf. Creswell, 2015; Creswell & Plano Clark, 2011; Tashakkori & Teddlie, 2010), we became increasingly aware that treating quantitative versus qualitative research as distinct and dichotomous approaches limited and constrained research possibilities. Borrowing from Russell (1993; cf. Fox, 2003), we observed that these research approaches were not "separate static entities on opposing poles, but rather two limits which define a ... process" (p. 176): in this case, the TR process and the abundance of theoretically informed methodological possibilities it affords. As Smart (2008) pointed out: "methodology is method *plus* an underlying set of ideas about the nature of reality and knowledge" (p. 56). The methodology we choose is imbued with theories of why, what, how, who, when, and *so what*.

Over the years we have worked alongside many TR partners, within and external to the university (e.g., scientists, engineers, mathematicians, neurolinguists, psychometricians, test developers, policy and decision makers, managers, administrators, teachers, learners, test takers). We were drawn together through our mutual interest in complex problems. It is important to acknowledge that such transdisciplinary partnerships engage research partners in what are essentially *hermeneutic practices*, which Gadamer (1975) compared to a conversation: "in a conversation, when we have discovered the other person's standpoint and horizon, his ideas become intelligible without our necessarily having to agree with him [*sic*]" (p. 270). Engaging with other stakeholder partners involves coming to know their worldviews, conceptual stances, ways of being and doing, for the purpose of discovery, self-reflection, understanding, reconsideration, and learning. The goal is not reconciliation of differences or some kind of unsatisfactory synthesis. Gadamer argued, to advance learning and understanding through our practices, we need to locate ourselves in an *in-between* space – avoiding both artificial reconciliations and stubborn oppositions – recognizing instead that we are all limited by our own *situatedness* (cf. Lave, 1996) in time, culture, values, language. In the context of assessment (research and practices), policies, mandates, purposes, and agendas are inevitably at play in shaping decisions and outcomes. Arguably, these can be greatly improved through a broader transdisciplinary engagement of stakeholders, by increasing awareness, validating their participation in assessment research practices, and fostering more enlightened assessment use.

Our past TR experiences and our mutual recognition of the unresolved problem of *context* in language assessment research (e.g., Bachman, 2007; Chalhoub-Deville, 2001, 2003; McNamara, 2007, 2008; McNamara & Roever, 2006; Moss, 2016) prompted us to focus in this book on the relevance, meaningfulness, and usefulness of inferences drawn from assessment practices – decisions, actions, and consequences in *context* (Messick, 1989). This focus, as many of our intended readers will recognize, concerns *validity* and *validation research*, which collects and examines evidence in support of the inferences drawn from assessment practices. See the *Standards for Educational and Psychological Testing* (e.g., 1985, 2014), hereafter the *Standards,* jointly developed by the American Education Research Association (AERA), the American Psychological Association (APA), and the National Council on Measurement in Education (NCME). As we will discuss in the opening chapters of this book, understanding and conceptualizing context has remained a troubling, unresolved, and problematic challenge in language assessment validation research (cf. Bachman, 2007; Chalhoub Deville, 2001; McNamara, 2007; McNamara & Roever, 2006). We suggest that addressing this complex challenge necessitates a transdisciplinary approach. Transdisciplinarity opens up a myriad of theories, methodologies, and methods to interrogation, inspection, challenge, and discussion, which would support renewed considerations of context.

For purposes of discussion in the book, we have described certain disciplines of relevance to language assessment as either *language-centred* or *assessment-centred.* Some disciplines, those we have referred to as language-centred, have fully theorized context (e.g., writing studies, discourse studies, cultural studies).[2] Researchers in these language-centred communities have tended to draw on a rich repertoire of *social theories* to ground understanding and interpretation of social practices. In general, as Lave (1996) has explained, such socio-theoretical perspectives have considered practices to be embedded within and inseparable from the contexts in which they occur. She points out that "there is agreement that such phenomena cannot be analyzed in isolation from the socially material world" but urges socially informed researchers to further interrogate this assumption by reconceptualizing "*relations* between persons acting" and the material "social world of activity" (p. 5).

At the same time, other disciplines, which we have identified as assessment-centred, have largely been informed by cognitive theories (e.g., psychology, educational measurement, psychometrics). Researchers in such assessment-centred communities have tended to draw on cognitive theories to inform research on assessment. In general, cognitive theories tend to be premised on the view that actions, both observed or drawn from tests, surveys, questionnaires, etc., originate in what individuals are thinking. Such theories have conceptualized social phenomena in terms of mechanisms and processes internal to an individual: as traits or abilities that characterize human activity. As Kvale (cf. 1989, 1996) has explained, this theoretical perspective shapes "what is investigated and why" (1996), and thus, in "a test context, the what of evaluation is the student [test taker], and the why is the efficient prediction of his [*sic*] future" (p. 216). Context, when it is acknowledged, figures mostly in relation to factors in an environment which may undermine measurement of the ability in question: "If a test taker is expected to write for an hour while seated on an uncomfortable wooden chair we may also suspect that the score may not represent the learner's optimal ability to write" (Fulcher & Davidson, 2007, p. 25).

However, it is important to emphasize that there have been substantive contributions to theory and practice from researchers who were informed by different theoretical perspectives within each of these communities. For example, in writing studies, which we have identified as a language-centred community that has been largely informed by social theories, Flower and Hayes (1981, 2009) have elaborated what they referred to as the *cognitive process model of writing*, and much research continues to be informed by their work. On the other hand, in assessment-centred communities, such as psychology, there are significant streams of socially informed research. For example, *ecological psychology* (e.g., Barker, 1968; Gibson, 1966, 1979) is a school of psychology which in general explores the affordances of an environment in the interaction between an individual's perception and action and, as such, departs from mainstream notions of cognitive psychology. *Discursive psychology* (e.g., Potter, 2003; Potter & Wetherell, 1987) rejected the dominance of cognitive theories in mainstream psychology and social psychology (McMullen, 2011), and although there are many differing approaches within discursive psychology, in general, they examine discourse not simply as a representation of cognition (i.e., as an individual's attitudes, thinking, traits), but as the focus of research itself, as situated social action[3] – "as something people *do* rather than something people *have*" (p. 206; cf. Weber, 2019).

Further, in keeping with the overall purpose of this book, we would be remiss if we did not acknowledge what is referred to as *phenomenological psychology* (cf. Wertz et al., 2011) or *descriptive phenomenological psychology* (Giorgi, 2009) and the extraordinary efforts of Giorgi in challenging the conceptual stances and methodological traditions of mainstream psychology. Giorgi drew on the "transdisciplinary movement of phenomenology" (Wertz et al., 2011, p. 52) and encouraged psychologists to engage in research on first-person experience. He traced problems within psychology as a discipline to its attempts to study human consciousness (meaning making, thinking, feeling, knowing, doing) with natural science approaches. He argued that human experience was not consistent with the underlying assumptions and philosophies of natural science. Giorgi "played the leading role in adapting and systematizing the use of phenomenological methods for empirically based psychological research" (Wertz et al., 2011, p. 53).

Within validation research in general, including validation research within language assessment, cognitive theories have dominated research practice. Given our focus on context, and the rich and varied interrogation of context afforded by social/sociocultural theories, we have highlighted social perspectives. Arguably, within a TR agenda for assessment validation research, social theories offer an alternative, renewed, and refreshed understanding of context in language assessment, because they offer differing accounts of it in practice. Relying predominantly on cognitive theories to shape, inform, and account for assessment practices has offered a narrower and more constrained conceptualization of context. While writing this, we have sensed a turning point in the evolution of research practices and find growing awareness and evidence of transdisciplinarity in both the research literature of relevance to our own disciplinary and TR programs, and in the larger research ecology of which they are a part.

For example, writing research communities, informed by social/sociocultural perspectives, are implicitly reaching out to assessment-centred ones (e.g., Crusan & Ruecker, 2019), to explain the consequences of high-stakes testing on classroom level teaching and learning, by examining the role of such tests in "restricting the way in which writing is taught" (p. 201). Assessment-centred communities, which have largely been informed by cognitive perspectives, are elaborating *theories of action* (e.g., Bennett, 2010), which integrate social consequences in validity research. Kane (2013b) has reinforced the importance of interpretation and use in arguments for validity. Moss (2016, 2018) has long argued for the active engagement and collaboration of partners who use assessment information to shape decisions and actions with direct consequences in local contexts. She has highlighted the important and positive role test researchers can play in supporting informed interpretation and use of assessment information. Within the language assessment community itself, particularly with regard to testing in global education reform movements or GERM(s), researchers (e.g., Chalhoub-Deville, 2016; Shohamy, 2001) have long called for increased consideration of consequences and *theories of action*. Chalhoub-Deville (2016) proposed a "zone of negotiated responsibility" in which test researchers and decision and policy makers would "confer" (p. 467) with regard to the interpretation and use of tests and other modes of assessment (cf. Elder, 2021).

Each of these communities draws on a variety of meaningful and useful alternative theories and research approaches for studying social practices such as assessment. Again, we do not see theoretical perspectives as dichotomous, but rather take the view that the repertoire of cognitive, socio-cognitive (e.g., Weir, 2005), and social perspectives offers a wealth of relevant theories to shape and guide validation research practices. The issues relating to context and validity in assessment will arguably be best addressed when researchers from differing disciplinary communities, who share common interests in assessment and "are open to listening and learning from others" (Bernstein, 1998, p. 4), engage, dialogue, debate, differ, and thus move the validation research agenda forward.

Within a review of research related to writing studies, Tardy (2017), highlighted "the untapped potential of a truly transdisciplinary approach to language and language difference" (p. 187). A similar call is evident in Schissel and Arias' (2021) special issue on assessment innovations in multilingual contexts. They state that the special issue is in part a response to Leung and Valdés (2019), who urged applied linguists to better ground their considerations of assessment in local and situated social practices, where consequences play out for stakeholders *in situ*. At the same time, within the context of educational measurement and research on teaching, learning, and assessment, Moss (2016) argued for a TR agenda involving diverse educational stakeholders (e.g., teachers, curriculum developers, test developers, program evaluators, policy/decision makers). She pointed out that "the actual interpretations and uses of test scores [assessment outcomes] in context, are far more varied and nuanced than intended interpretation might imply" (p. 236). Use of data and information provided by such tests and other modes of assessment is affected by local purposes, capacities, student populations, resources, and so forth. She explained how a TR agenda could achieve more relevant and "robust" (Moss, 2016, p. 248) outcomes by incorporating "local capacity to support the actual interpretations, decisions and actions" (p. 236) that are the result of inferences drawn from assessment.

This book is a response to Leung and Valdés (2019), Moss (2016), Tardy (2017), and others who have called for a TR agenda which aims to contribute to more "robust validity theory for conceptual use" (Moss, 2016, p. 248). Such a research agenda necessitates the collaboration of stakeholders from disciplinary research communities that have not typically undertaken research together, as well as stakeholders outside the university who often have the largest *stake* in assessment outcomes and whose lived experiences are both relevant and useful.

As the framing quotes at the beginning of this introduction suggest, many within the language assessment community (e.g., Poehner & Inbar-Lourie, 2020a), and others outside it (cf. Addey, Maddox, & Zumbo, 2020) have recognized *context* as a *weakly theorized* (McNamara, 2007) and *persistent* problem (Bachman, 2007) in validation research. Given the "applicability gap" (Lawrence, 2010) that exists between assessment-centred and language-centred communities, transdisciplinary approaches that are oriented toward increased inclusion of social theories offer an alternative, useful means of addressing context in language assessment validation research. Arguably, this *gap* has impeded research on such complex problems and originated in "the compartmentalization of ... knowledge, the sector-based division of responsibilities in contemporary society, and the increasingly diverse nature of the societal contexts in which people live" (p. 125).

Our intent throughout has been to support the development of the mutual knowledge, understanding, and capacity of stakeholders (within and outside the university) as research collaborators who have a shared *interest* in the validation of assessment in the *diverse and varying contexts* of assessment use; and are open to alternative, rival (Cronbach, 1988), and differing perspectives. Such differences will at times challenge and conflict with known and accepted assumptions and practices, but they will also prompt new recognitions, learning, reflection, and innovation. This is the potential of a TR approach.

Because much of our research has been characterized by transdisciplinarity (cf. Artemeva & Fox, 2010; Fox & Artemeva, 2017), many of our collaborative research projects have involved research partners both within the university (e.g., psychologists, engineers, mathematicians, scientists), and external to it (e.g., policy makers, managers, medical practitioners, government workers, curriculum developers, high-stakes testers). As noted at the beginning of this chapter, this experience in large part has motivated us to write this book.

Intended readership: actors and audiences

Given the transdisciplinary approach we are taking, we have hoped to attract and engage readers from a broad range of different academic backgrounds, knowledge, expertise, and research experiences who share a common interest in assessment practices. As Moss and Haertel (2016) pointed out, following Bernstein (1998), "The initial task [for transdisciplinary researchers] is to grasp the other's position in the strongest possible light" (p. 232). In keeping with this foundational requirement, we anticipated that those readers who were *language-centred* (e.g., language teachers, writing researchers, graduate students in discourse, culture or writing studies) would most likely have more understanding of social or sociocultural theories and their concomitant methodologies/methods (e.g., case studies, critical discourse analysis, ethnography, narrative inquiry). On the other hand, they might have less familiarity with assessment-centred orientations and the evolution of practices within assessment-centred communities. However, readers who were *assessment-centred* (e.g., test developers, psychometricians, graduate students in educational measurement or psychology) would likely have more familiarity with inidividualist, cognitive theories and their concomitant methodologies/methods (e.g., experiments, large-scale surveys, systematic or randomly sampled observations) but have less familiarity with social theories. They might also be unaware of the array of theoretical perspectives that have informed evolving conceptions of language as a socially situated phenomenon, evident in practices, actions, and activity in relation to complex, diverse, and dynamic contexts of use. These recognitions have influenced the organization of the book as a whole, which is outlined below.

Overall organization: acts, scenes, and stage directions

Throughout *Reconsidering context in language assessment*, we have engaged with and described numerous research projects that were undertaken with collaborating TR partners, whose expertise and professional or disciplinary perspectives differed. In the discussions that led to the writing of the chapters in this book, the voices of collaborating authors are woven together, but at times one voice was dominant with regard to differences in investment, responsibility, and actual writing. To acknowledge this difference, we have distinguished co-authorship relationships at the beginning of each chapter. When co-authors contributed equally, as in this chapter, we have used "and" (e.g., Fox and Artemeva). However, when one author took the lead in all respects but benefited from the input, insights, and feedback of their co-author, we have used "with".

Taken together, the chapters in Part I provide a foundation for a shared, mutual understanding of the history, development, tensions, and debates within both assessment-centred and language-centred communities. They are offered as an initial staging point for a TR agenda involving researchers from both assessment- and language-centred communities in collaboratively addressing the complex problem of context in language assessment validation research.

Part I – Building foundations for transdisciplinary dialogue: new directions in assessment research

Part I of this book provides background, information, discussion, and reflection on ideas and research which have shaped and are shaping assessment practices in the present day. The four chapters which comprise Part I define and situate the key and complex terms in the title of this book (i.e., *context*, *language assessment*, *transdisciplinary perspectives*, *social theories*, *validity*) in relation to their historical, theoretical, and empirical evolution.

We viewed the chapters in Part I as differentially of use and interest to readers whose perspectives on assessment as a social practice have been rooted in and informed by their disciplinarity. Psychologists, psychometricians, and measurement specialists will find resonance with Chapter 2, on validity. They may disagree with the discussion, but they will recognize it as familiar. Conversely, language teachers and writing and discourse studies specialists will find resonance with Chapter 3. Although they may disagree with its emphasis and discussion, they will recognize it as familiar and in keeping with what they know, who they know, and what they do.

It is our intent and primary motivation for writing this book to encourage readers and researchers to read about what they do *not* already know; to explore other disciplinary perspectives with an open mind; to respectfully learn from alternative, differing worldviews, not as a challenge or affront, but rather as a potential for new insights, recognitions, heightened self-awareness, and self-reflection. Thus, we intended Chapter 2 – on changing conceptions of validity – for language teachers and writing and discourse studies specialists; and we intended Chapter 3 – on changing conceptions of language – for psychologists, psychometricians, and measurement specialists. The willingness to learn from those who view the world differently – to break down the disciplinary barriers and boundaries that divide in favour of learning, listening, and seeking to understand – could be an important catalyst for insight and innovation (and is a foundational requirement for TR agendas). Given the complexity of the problems we face, it has long been clear that reliance on old and well-worn disciplinary habits will not be (and has not been) able to address such problems effectively. We chose one such complex problem as the focus of this book: context in language assessment validation.

In sum, we view this book as a modest step in supporting TR agendas – which have been called for, for such a long time, in the literature. Where to begin? The answer to us was clear – with open, respectful understanding and learning from what disciplines outside our own are thinking and doing.

- **Chapter 1** focuses on defining TR itself. What is it? How does it work? How does it differ from other cross-disciplinary or interdisciplinary approaches to research? We would hope that all readers might begin here.
- **Chapter 2**, as noted above, focuses on validity. How have conceptions of validity evolved? What are the dominant theoretical perspectives and empirical traditions that have informed conceptions of validity? What are the current tensions and debates? Arguably, validity is the primary focus of assessment-centred disciplinary communities (e.g.,

psychology, educational measurement, psychometrics). We highlight the theoretical dominance of cognitive theoretical perspectives in assessment-centred communities, which have largely focused on cognition as individual thinking (underlying attributes, traits, abilities) and backgrounded or controlled for context in research. We intended this chapter for readers who may not be familiar with this rich history; readers from language-centred communities such as discourse studies, language teaching, writing studies; readers who conduct research on language, who use assessment, and engage in critiques of assessment as a social practice. Readers who are familiar with this history will note the emphasis on the consequences of assessment use – taking a close look at Messick (1989, 1998) *in his own words*.

- **Chapter 3** is focused on language. How have conceptions of language evolved? Why do theories matter in this evolution? What role have theories played within disciplinary communities in evolving conceptions of language (and, concomitantly, in how it is researched and assessed)? What tensions and debates have characterized this evolution? Arguably, language, as it has been variously defined within disciplinary communities that have it as a primary focus, has often been informed by social theories. Many of these social theories foreground context and see it as inseparable from and integral to language itself. Chapter 3 provides an overview of a few major conceptual schools of thought which have served as antecedents for numerous social theories. Included in Chapter 3 is a selective explanation of a number of prominent social theories that have frequently informed empirical research within language-centred communities. All of these social theories figure in the examples of TR projects included in Part II. We intended Chapter 3 for readers whose disciplinary interests align with assessment-centred communities and who may be *unfamiliar* with the evolution of conceptions of language and some of the social theories that could provide alternative perspectives in assessment research.
- **Chapter 4** is focused on the language assessment community itself. We argue that it has been precariously positioned between assessment-centred disciplinary perspectives on the one hand and language-centred disciplinary perspectives on the other. We present evidence from a meta-review of the literature that the preponderance of language assessment research has been informed by perspectives aligned with the inquiry traditions of assessment-centred communities. While recognizing seminal contributions of these traditions, we also discuss the implications of this dominance and highlight the thread of socially informed research in language assessment, which has shown modest increases in assessment publications in the past few years. Arguably, to address the complex issues of context in assessment practices, which has remained a persistent and unresolved problem for over three decades, a greater balance of perspectives (within an overall

transdisciplinary approach that welcomes alternatives) will move the research agenda forward. We hope all readers will be interested in reading this chapter.

An additional resource is provided for researchers, students, and others who are interested in following up on perspectives on context and social theories as they have been used in the assessment literature. Because of space limitations in this book, we have provided this resource at https://carleton.ca/slals/people/fox-janna/. This resource lists socially informed contributions to four prominent assessment journals (2004–2020), assembled for the meta-review. It includes additional summary tables by journal as well as annotations for selected papers.

Part II – Transdisciplinary research (TR) in practice: building connections

Part II provides three examples of empirical research in language assessment. Each example emphasizes the illuminating potential of social theories, and the essential role that TR practices played in research outcomes. We selected these examples to reflect a range of interests that are, in general, a focus of much language assessment research:

- **Chapter 5** describes processes of development and validation in a high-stakes, large-scale English language proficiency test of listening and speaking, used as part of a professional credentialing procedure for pilots and air traffic controllers. The chapter illustrates the role social theories and transdisciplinary partnerships played in defining and specifying the aural/oral proficiency *construct* (i.e., the web of theory, research, and experience that delimits and describes the dimensions and details of what needs to be measured).
- **Chapter 6** reports on the redevelopment of a diagnostic/analytic rating scale of writing afforded by the application of a social theory, Rhetorical Genre Studies (RGS) (e.g., Bakhtin, 1986; Miller, 1984), which is introduced and defined in Chapter 3.[4] The rating scale was developed as part of an assessment procedure that identifies students in need of additional academic support at the beginning of their undergraduate engineering program. The use of social theory deepened raters' collective interpretation of scale criteria, improved the quality of their training, and their understanding of the relationship between the scale criteria and the supplementary, individualized pedagogical support that was offered as the outcome of the diagnostic assessment. Additional support for readers new to RGS terminology is provided at https://carleton.ca/slals/people/fox-janna/.
- **Chapter 7** describes classroom-based assessment initiatives that were implemented in online learning spaces within English for Academic Purposes (EAP) classes. Social theories illuminate teaching and

assessment practices within these transdisciplinary initiatives, which were supplemental extensions of traditional, person-to-person classroom interactions prior to 2020, but became part of a fully online learning context as an outcome of the pandemic. In addition to describing research on the affordances of these online learning spaces, a post-pandemic reflection reveals more about their limitations and potential in language teaching, learning, and assessment.

Readers aligned with the empirical practices of assessment communities may be somewhat taken aback by these empirical examples. They do not conform to the generic expectations of readers who routinely consume empirical research. First, they highlight in detail the social theories that informed the research, speculate about other theories that might have offered an alternative perspective, and emphasize how theory shaped the research findings. It is our observation that the first thing a journal editor often suggests cutting is the theory that informed an empirical study. Within academic journals pertaining to assessment, there has been a general emphasis on the *how* (method) and the *what* (findings, discussion, and implications), but far less attention has been paid to the *why*. As a result, many students are generally predisposed to read for what and how. One of the generous students who read drafts of chapters in Part II asked, "why is there so much philosophy?" Second, the examples emphasize the important role played by transdisciplinary partners in assessment research (within and outside the university) who shared an interest and/or had a 'stake' in research outcomes. Stakeholders are most typically involved in research as participants – not as contributing partners as is the case in the studies described here.

Part III – Transdisciplinarity in practice: moving the research agenda forward

Part III concludes the book with a discussion of transdisciplinarity in practice. In keeping with the overall purpose of the book, the transdisciplinary projects discussed in the final chapter are unpacked and interpreted through the lenses afforded by social theories. Drawing on experience, the discussion explores why some TR projects produce positive outcomes and live up to their potential, and others do not.

- **Chapter** 8 examines transdisciplinary assessment research initiatives in practice. Three *narratives of experience* (Connelly & Clandinin, 1990) are viewed through the lenses afforded by the social theories of distributed cognition (Hutchins, 1995a, 1995b; see Chapter 3) and Communities of Practice (CoPs) (Wenger, 1998; see Chapter 3). In the first two cases, the original transdisciplinary potential of the assessment research initiatives was undermined as the research unfolded over time. In the third case, the transdisciplinary potential of the assessment research initiative was fully realized, involved ten years of successful engagement by collaborating stakeholders, and resulted in significant, positive educational outcomes beyond the initial horizons envisioned by the research partners.

The narratives of experience provide a resource for increasing awareness of and reflection on the viability of a transdisciplinary approach – how to *size it up* in advance, and what to do if issues arise in process. Resources to support engagement and strategies for troubleshooting are identified. In this final chapter of the book, readers are encouraged to take up the challenge of moving the field of language assessment forward by drawing more often on social theories (those reviewed in this book, or any of the others that were not included here) to inform, account for, and interpret research, and, by initiating transdisciplinary partnerships, address long-standing, complex problems, such as the role of context in language assessment.

The curtain rises: understanding resistance to transdisciplinarity and the challenges ahead

It is important to acknowledge that TR can be challenging. Working with TR partners heightens our self-awareness of our own disciplinary views. There is, as a result, some inevitable resistance to transdisciplinary practice.

The problem, as we see it, is the strength of our disciplinary lenses within disciplinary cultures and the concomitant filters they impose. For example, chapters in this book were circulated in advance to a number of generous colleagues who agreed to review them and provide feedback. We began by sending chapters which documented trends within validity or language to colleagues who have been focused on theorizing and researching validity or language for many years. Their reviews were extraordinarily helpful in improving the content and organization of Chapters 2 and 3. However, when we sent a chapter to a reviewer who did not affiliate with, or align disciplinarily with, the chapter's focus and content, the responses differed dramatically. One reviewer put it exceptionally well: "Why would I want to read this?" "Why did you think it would be of interest to me?" "Why should I be interested in this?" Or, "Well, I see what you're trying to do, but nobody from __________ (fill in the blank with whatever discipline you choose) will read this book!"

Transdisciplinarity can be a hard sell. Paré (2008) explains that our participation in disciplinary cultures shapes how we see ourselves and others, what we value in research, how we engage in it, and how we value the research of others. He identifies the many structures that impede transdisciplinary exchange: "Our institutions are structured against it – programmatically, economically, even architecturally; the hierarchical arrangement of disciplines makes real equality difficult; methodological variation can seem incommensurate" (p. 19). These structures have territorial and ideological roots (Becher & Trowler, 2001). And yet, if we can conquer our resistance to learning about alternative, rival descriptions, understandings, and conceptual stances, so much more is possible. As they say in describing theatrical performances, "we need to suspend our disbelief".

We do not have to agree with others. However, we need to understand, consider, and learn from them if we are to advance our research agendas and achieve the most benefit from them. This is a necessity for tackling the complex problems that engage our interest. So how do we begin? We argue that beginnings require new, transdisciplinary foundations and the initiation of many more open and respectful academic conversations.

Although in this book we have focused on the complex issue of context in language assessment validation, there are many complex problems that would greatly benefit from the transdisciplinary engagement of researchers with differing expertise and perspectives. It is disheartening to see the failure of research to address complex, seemingly intractable issues that have been the steady focus of one research community or another for decades. For example, within writing studies for at least 50 years researchers have been concerned about and critical of the *five-paragraph essay* in classroom instruction and assessment (e.g., Caplan & Johns, 2019). Many (e.g., Caplan & Johns, 2019; Hunt, 1994; Tardy, 2019) have considered that it is an artificial school invention which distorts and reduces writing to a formulaic template and serves none of the purposes writing is meaningfully used for – except as an artifact of writing for assessment (by a classroom teacher or unseen test rater). This *transactional* situation is often the case in test writing. As Hunt (1994) noted in describing such assessment-focused writing in a classroom:

> [the] essay was written on assignment by a student with no particular interest in the subject and with the sole aim of demonstrating the ability to invent or find and marshal, arguments ... It was read by a teacher with no particular interest in the subject, and with the avowed intention of assessing the mechanical fluency of the student's language and deciding whether she had successfully fulfilled the formal and stated requirement of the genre 'persuasive essay'. That teacher had no intention to 'respond'.
>
> (p. 216)

Unfortunately, high-stakes proficiency testing has inadvertently reinforced the use of the five-paragraph essay. It is often taught in test preparation courses as a technique for responding to essay questions (i.e., in paragraph one, state your position, focus, or thesis; in the three subsequent paragraphs, explain and support your position, discussing one argument per paragraph with supporting examples or other evidence; in paragraph five, conclude by briefly summarizing the above and restating your position). Only in classrooms and on tests do humans use writing in this way.

How does this relate to the focus of this book? Arguably, the necessary transdisciplinary conversations between writing test developers and writing studies theorists and researchers have not been sufficient, although Crusan and Ruecker (2019) have identified some integrated tasks on such tests that are marginally better. It is worth repeating that transdisciplinarity necessitates the involvement of and conversations with stakeholders in contexts of assessment use, who are affected by, undertake, and act upon assessment outcomes, data, and information, and whose decisions and actions have both short- and long-term consequences, intended and unintended. Incorporating and valuing their involvement in research on assessment practices will, as Moss envisions, build the "capacity to use data well" and increase the "value" (p. 248) of assessment practices. Moss identifies this as a "key challenge for validity theory in test use" (p. 237). This is the challenge of context and validity which is the central focus of this book.

We see evidence that this challenge is increasingly being met by TR collaborators such as Addey, Maddox, and Zumbo (2020). Drawing collectively on their different disciplinary backgrounds (i.e., educational sociology, cultural anthropology, measurement and psychometrics), they examined arguments for the use and interpretation of International Large-Scale Assessments (ILSAs). They explicitly acknowledge their agreement that validity is "a social practice" (p. 589) and draw on a social theory (i.e., Actor Network Theory, cf. Latour, 2005), in a refreshed and insightful view of Kane's (2006, 2013a, 2013b) argument-based, evidence-driven approach to validation (see Chapters 2 and 3). Addey et al. (2020) consider the "socio-material validation practices of assessment actors as they assemble validity" (p. 589) with the explicit goal of "creating a democratic space in which legitimately diverse arguments and intentions can be recognized, considered, assembled and displayed" (p. 588). It is this "democratic space ... for legitimately diverse arguments and intentions" which is central to our motivation and intentions for the present volume. This is the *transdisciplinary space* that Moss (2016) and Moss and Haertel (2016) so eloquently and thoroughly examine and define. This is the space and setting within which we situate this book.

Notes

1 In the process of transdisciplinary dialogue and research, certain words will generate a great deal of discussion and result in reflection and the need for negotiation in order to move forward. Although the word *belief* is often used in methodological discussions of epistemology and ontology (e.g., Johnson & Gray, 2010), in the process of writing this chapter, we disagreed on its use here and were fortunate to resolve the issue by drawing on their notions of "the 'small t' truths" or "warranted beliefs" (p. 87) or assumptions arising from practice and experience.

2 We have not listed linguistics, applied linguistics, or language teaching and learning as examples of language-centred communities here – although by any definition, they are language-centred. How they have theorized context, applied social theories, and regarded theory and its relationship to practice has varied greatly over the years. We discuss the evolution of conceptions of language within these language-centred communities in Chapter 3.

3 Here (and elsewhere in the book) we are guided by Max Weber's understanding of social action, wherein "By 'action' is meant human behaviour linked to a subjective meaning on the part of the actor or actors concerned; such action may be either overt, or occur inwardly – whether by positive action, or by refraining from action, or by tolerating a situation. Such behaviour is 'social' action where the meaning intended by the actor or actors is related to the behaviour of others, and the action is so oriented" (Weber, 2019, Chapter 1, para 1, Kindle edition).

4 Additional support for the Rhetorical Genre Studies (RGS) terminology used in Chapter 6 is available at https://carleton.ca/slals/people/fox-janna/.

Part I

Building foundations for transdisciplinary dialogue

New directions in language assessment research

1 The problem of context in language assessment

Validity, social theories, and a transdisciplinary research (TR) agenda

Janna Fox and Natasha Artemeva

In keeping with the focus of this book, rather than providing a traditional Abstract at the beginning of each chapter, we offer a brief, boxed note to situate the chapter within the overall context of the book as a whole. The notes generally highlight the purpose of the chapter and direct readers' attention to key information. This book is intended as a first step in creating a shared foundational background (which is extended and expanded in subsequent chapters) amongst readers who have differing disciplinary backgrounds (e.g., in applied linguistics, educational measurement, discourse studies, language teaching, psychology, writing studies), but who share a common interest in assessment practices in general, and language assessment in particular. In the present chapter, we provide initial working definitions of key words, which are of importance throughout the book. The chapter focuses on transdisciplinary research (TR) practices as a means of addressing complex problems such as context in language assessment validation research.

> *The social context of discourse and issues of discourse as social action are largely ignored. Instead discourse is mostly seen as the product of autonomous mental processes, or it is simply described as having particular linguistic features.*
>
> (Lemke, 1995, p. 21)

> *Understanding the roles of abilities and contexts, and the interactions between these as they affect performance on language assessment tasks, has remained a persistent problem in language assessment.*
>
> (Bachman, 2007, p. 41)

DOI: 10.4324/9781351184571-3

> *In standard works [on assessment] ... context has been theorized in terms of the demands it makes on individual cognitive attributes, but this has distorted the picture of the social context available to us.*
>
> (McNamara, 2007, p. 131)

> *How should different validity arguments and evidence be reconciled in situations where there are diverse stakeholders and multiple contexts of use?*
>
> (Addey, Maddox, & Zumbo, 2020, p. 588)

Context, orientations, and communities

As explained in the Introduction, the transdisciplinary agenda that has been set and the story we are telling here is a response to calls in the literature for more *robust* (Moss, 2016), expansive, substantive, and self-reflective considerations of *context* in assessment practices (cf. Chalhoub-Deville, 2001; McNamara, 2007; Moss, 2016). Readers who are familiar with discourse studies may wonder why we would frame this chapter with a 1995 quote from Lemke. As a well-respected colleague in discourse studies asked in reference to Lemke's comment, "Why frame the chapter in this way? This has not been the case for years!" And yet, much of the discussion in this book addresses the very issue that was of concern to Lemke in 1995, and remains a concern today, namely, the still unresolved problem of context in language assessment. As a starting point for discussion, the following observations are offered. These have guided the view of context that has been applied in this book, given the book's particular purpose and intent.

Disciplinary communities have distinctly different definitions of *context* (cf. archaeology, biology, politics, sociology), which speak to the theoretical perspectives that inform their research interests. For example, the *Oxford Dictionary of Philosophy* (2005) states that, "In linguistics, context is parts of utterance" that *surround a unit of communication*, and "may affect both its meaning and its grammatical contribution" (p. 77). However, a review of alternative definitions of context in online and print dictionaries reveals recurring patterns in how it is defined in more general terms. For example:

Context

1 "determines" (Holt Rinehart Winston, 1974, p. 126), "helps to fix" (Oxford English Dictionary, 1974, p. 184) or "throw(s) light on" (Merriam-Webster, n.d.) the meaning of an utterance, expression, passage or idea.
2 The "interrelated conditions", or the "environment, setting ... in which something exists or occurs" (www.merriam-webster.com/dictionary/context); the "surrounding circumstances, framework" (Holt Rinehart Winston, 1974, p. 126); "the situation within which

something exists or happens, and that can help explain it" (https://dictionary.cambridge.org/); "the circumstances in which an event occurs" (Oxford English Dictionary, 1974, p. 184).

We offer these definitions as evidence of the recurring patterns in their explanations of context. All of these definitions suggest that *meaning*, what we *construe* as "something", or as an "event", is embedded or situated in context which also affects it. An "utterance"/ "something"/ "event" is not only situated in context but is also at the same time affecting and forming the context. This complex reciprocal relationship is in keeping with our own understanding of context and is extended, expanded, and differentiated by the selected social theories considered in the book.

Orientations

Social theories and cognitive theories

As noted in the Introduction, we have applied the label *social theories* to the many theories that account for social phenomena, practices, and/or actions (e.g., teaching a class, writing a paper, conducting a study, taking a test). A few of these social theories are highlighted in this book. These social theories offer an array of differing orientations and accounts of context, and some are particularly useful in considerations of the actions and interactions of persons acting alone and with others (e.g., developing, validating, taking a test), and with the use of cultural tools (e.g., computers, test booklets, language, other semiotic resources). Given the purpose of this book, we have selected those social theories that are in keeping with our view of context 1) as "constituted *in relation* with persons acting" (Lave, 1996, p. 5), and 2) as the *surrounding* discourse, circumstances, situation, or setting within which social actions occur, from which they derive meaning, and which they, in turn, affect (cf. Weber, 2019).

Willis et al. (2007) provided a comprehensive overview of social theories within qualitative, public health research and concluded, "Social theories are complex, overlapping and … profound" (p. 443). This is a point to emphasize regarding the social theories and perspectives we have selected and highlighted in Part I of this book. These were selected because they offered particularly useful insights with regard to context in the social practices of assessment, but their rendering here should be taken as introductory and necessarily reductive. The intent is to offer to those readers who are less familiar with them a starting point for the consideration of alternative viewpoints and approaches in assessment practices. Evidence of their usefulness is illustrated in the transdisciplinary research (TR) projects described in Parts II and III. Further, we apply the same approach in characterizing *cognitive theories*. There is a wealth of different cognitive perspectives. However, within language assessment, the "individualist, cognitive bias of traditional psychometrics" (McNamara & Roever, 2006, p. 2) has been dominant. In this book, it is this particular view of cognition that we have selected for consideration.

Throughout this book we have emphasized the importance of theory in considerations of context. Within research, it is the theoretical lens (tacit or explicit) that bounds researchers' perceptions and accounts. Theory determines what researchers see (or do not see), their understanding as the research unfolds, and how they interpret and report their findings. Much of the discussion that follows in this book will extend, expand, and deepen understanding of context as it has been considered in theoretical and empirical literature that views language assessment as a social practice.

Assessment

We have intentionally used the term *assessment* to refer to all those practices (e.g., testing, interviewing, observing, surveying) which are put into play in order to gather evidence of relevance to a mandate and purpose. It follows, then, that assessment practices accumulate *evidence* (e.g., Messick, 1989; Kane, 2006, 2013a, 2013b) in keeping with:

- *why* it is needed (e.g., to inform a teacher's lesson planning; increase a student's self-awareness and goal setting; verify engineering or medical credentials; compare applicants for a job or for graduate school; authorize immigration or award citizenship status);
- *who* is being assessed (e.g., students with first language (L1) or additional/second language (L2) backgrounds; children or adults; applicants seeking a change in immigration status or employment opportunities);
- *what* is being assessed (e.g., development; needs; performance; achievement; proficiency; knowledge, skills, attributes); and,
- *how* best to collect and interpret such evidence (e.g., through tests, portfolios, interviews, questionnaires).

We foreground the *problem of context* in assessment with regard to considerations of *validity*. Put simply, we have defined validity as the degree to which the evidence elicited through assessment practices supports meaningful, relevant, useful, and appropriate inferences, actions, decisions, and consequences (Messick, 1989). Definitions of validity have evolved over time (see Chapter 2), and they remain the focus of ongoing discussion and debate (e.g., Newton & Shaw, 2014; Cizek, 2020). However, there is a long-standing consensus that validity requires theoretical and empirical support (i.e., *validation*) of claims regarding the inferences drawn from, and the actions taken as the result of test scores and other assessment practices (see *Standards for Educational and*

Psychological Tests [hereafter, the *Standards*], American Educational Research Association (AERA), American Psychological Association (APA), and National Council on Measurement in Education [AERA, APA, & NCME, 2014]). (See also AERA et al., 1985; Chapelle, 2021; Kane, 1990, 2006; Messick, 1989, 1998). Those who investigate the validity of inferences drawn from assessment practices are said to engage in validation research. "The process of validation involves presenting evidence and a compelling argument to support the intended inference and to show that alternative or competing inferences are not more viable" (Hubley & Zumbo, 2011, p. 219).

There is, as noted above, general agreement that inferences drawn from assessment practices require evidence to support them (e.g., Kane, 1992, 2006, 2010, 2013a, 2013b; Addey et al., 2020). Further, based on the definition above, validity *evidence* largely consists of:

1 *plausible*, technical evidence accumulated when an assessment is designed and developed for use within a *projected* or *intended* context(s); and,
2 *actual* evidence drawn from the *diverse and varying contexts* of assessment use.

Over the past three decades, the *Standards* have identified assessment use as a proper focus of validation research (although assessment in the *Standards* has almost exclusively been viewed as tests). Further, in keeping with Messick (1989), validation of assessment in use must consider the decisions, actions, and consequences, both intended and unintended, that result from the inferences drawn from assessment scores, processes, or outcomes (cf. AERA et al., 2014; Messick, 1980, 1989, 1998). Validation has been the disciplinary focus of many assessment-centred communities. Such communities are defined in this book, as having a main focus on assessment, particularly high-stakes testing (e.g., psychology, educational and psychological measurement, psychometrics). In general, their primary concern has been to collect evidence of the *plausible* validity of inferences drawn from tests, and to improve the technical quality of tests as a means of insuring *potential* use. Thus, a central issue for such assessment-centred communities since the 1980s (e.g., Cronbach, 1988; Messick, 1980) has been what Cronbach (1988) referred to as "contextualism" (p. 14), namely, the role of consequences, decisions, and actions in assessment and validation practices as they play out in *actual use* (cf. Chalhoub-Deville, 2001; Larsen-Freeman & Cameron, 2008a; Maddox, 2014; Norton & Stein, 1998; Moss, 2018). Within assessment-centred communities there has been ongoing tension and debate amongst researchers concerned with validation over whether the consequences of assessment decisions in contexts of assessment use should be a focus of validity research at all (e.g., Cizek, 2012, 2020; Yallow & Popham, 1983).

Communities

What's in a name?

Naming in the *in-between spaces* (Gadamer, 1975) of transdisciplinary practice can be challenging, where dialogue occurs in *conversations* between interlocutors with differing orientations. Naming often requires negotiation and compromise in relation to the overall purpose, goal, or intent of the transdisciplinary dialogue. For example, in this book we have applied *community* and *communities* in naming the general interests of certain disciplines. While it is not uncommon to find the word "disciplinary" as an adjective modifying the term "community", a review of the literature will illustrate that *community* is not a neutral or uncontested concept (e.g., Eraut, 2002; Gee, 2004; Harris, 1989; Williams, 1976) and its use is controversial for some. For example, Gee (2004) attacked the notion of *community* (as in disciplinary community, or community of learners) and suggested the more porous and flexible notions of a "semiotic social space" (p. 79) or "affinity spaces" (p. 83). In the end, we feared these notions might not readily be understood and so we opted for *community*, recognizing the limitations of this concept.

Thus, in keeping with the purposes of this book, for the sake of general comprehensibility, and for convenience, we have named collections of disciplines, fields, and sub-fields, which share a core interest in assessment as *assessment-centred communities* (e.g., psychometrics, measurement, psychology); and, we have named others, which share a core interest in language (e.g., applied linguistics, discourse studies, writing studies) as *language-centred communities*.

The distinction between groups of disciplines as communities that share differing core interests and are marked by differences in theoretical perspectives (i.e., cognitive and social) was helpful as a first step in a transdisciplinary approach that explores differences, understands them "in the strongest possible light" (Bernstein, 1998, p. 4), reflects on them, and learns from them.

Differing perspectives on context

As previously noted, assessment-centred communities have largely been informed by cognitive theories (McNamara & Roever, 2007), which have traditionally viewed "knowledge domains – or the given individual's mental models and cognitive structures – as the context of problem solving, thinking, and learning" (Engeström, 1996, p. 66). From this perspective, *context* resides within the individual. Historical, cultural, societal situations and local circumstances are reduced or simply disregarded (cf. Lazaraton & Taylor, 2007), what Lave (1996) referred to as one of the "paradoxes and silences of cognitive theory" (p. 11). Or, as McDermott

(1996) noted, this perspective has typically viewed cognition as "static" and context as "an empty slot" or "container" (p. 282). Conversely, language-centred communities (e.g., discourse studies, writing studies) have largely been informed by social theories, some of which view all human endeavour (e.g., thinking, knowing, speaking, acting) as contextually "situated" within the "socially material world" (Lave, 1996). Although the social theories highlighted in this book share this view in common, there are many different socio-theoretical perspectives on "relations between persons acting and the social world" (p. 5). Such is the case with differing cognitive perspectives as well.

However, the gap between perspectives of the assessment-centred communities and those of language-centred communities has grown over the years, and arguably, at times, given rise to disregard, distrust, and dismissal of some communities by others. Such differing theoretical perspectives have tended toward dualistic viewpoints and increasing disciplinary specialization has accelerated distance and fragmentation (cf. Lawrence, 2010; Somerville & Rapport, 2000). Lawrence (2010) warned researchers against the "applicability gap", which he traced back to "a lack of effective collaboration" in the face of increasingly "complex real-world issues" (p. 125). Language assessment researchers are caught in the middle of this gap as their disciplinary interests straddle those of both assessment-centred and language-centred communities.

Enter transdisciplinarity. The trends toward fragmentation and 'either-or' dualisms have been met by opposing trends, which have recognized the additive benefits of interactions across disciplinary specializations in addressing complex problems. According to Nicolescu (2006), the word *transdisciplinarity* first appeared in conversations amongst three distinguished and internationally renowned participants at a 1970 Organization for Economic Cooperation and Development (OECD) meeting, in Nice, namely: Jean Piaget, educational/developmental psychologist; Erich Jantsch, physicist and philosopher; and, André Lichnerowicz, mathematician. Subsequently, Piaget (1972) defined TR as a "superior stage", or useful extension of interdisciplinary research which is not "limited" by "interactions and or reciprocities" (p. 144) that support but also constrain research within disciplinary communities.

Transdisciplinary approaches require the collective, deeply collaborative, and respectful engagement of researchers, both within and outside academia, who share a common interest in a complex issue or problem, which is typically beyond the potential of any one group to address.

We offer this brief overview of transdisciplinarity as a place holder and starting point. A more substantive discussion of our use of the term is provided later in this chapter. Throughout we argue that the long-standing problem of context in language assessment validation research will best be addressed through a transdisciplinary approach.

Background

Having discussed the present volume's purpose, intended readership, contents, and overall organization in the Introduction, below we situate the volume within the key questions that motivated its development, and the research literature that informed it. We also provide a more detailed discussion of key concepts and terms we have applied, and examine the problem of *context* in language assessment validation research in relation to disciplinary research practices. We begin below by addressing three of the key questions that motivated our focus on context in language assessment.

> ***Three key questions***
>
> 1 What is the *problem* with context in assessment validation practices?
> 2 What is the potential of a transdisciplinary research (TR) agenda in addressing the problem of *context* in assessment validation?
> 3 What role do disciplines play in constraining and limiting innovation?
>
> Each of these questions is discussed in the following sections as a means of introducing the book as a whole.

Question one: what is the *problem* with context in assessment validation practices?

As noted above, conceptualizations of validity (cf. AERA et al., 2014; Messick, 1989, 1998; Zumbo & Chan, 2014) have generally identified types of evidence that are required to support the inferences drawn from an assessment practice. First, there should be plausible evidence to support the assessment's projected implementation, given its purpose and *intended* use. Second, but of equal importance, there should be evidence supporting its *actual* use, drawn on an ongoing basis, and evalutating the consequences of actions and decisions, intended and unintended, that result from assessment use (Messick, 1989). Clearly, the second type of evidence must be drawn from contexts of use, which are inherently complex and characterized by variability and a myriad of local influential features.

Within the larger validation research literature, researchers have tended to focus on *intended* uses of assessment and the plausibility of arguments and evidence that support projected assessment use (e.g., Chapelle, Enright, & Jamieson, 2008; Kane, 2006, 2016). They have generally simplified the role of context in *actual* assessment use, or treated it as *unproblematic* or outside their purview (cf. McNamara & Roever, 2006; Moss, 2016). Although consensus defintions of validity (e.g., Zumbo & Chan, 2014) have long recognized that the consequences and side effects of assessment (cf. Messick, 1989) must be taken into account in arguments for validity (cf. Kane, 2013a), "validation practices have been observed to lag behind validity theory" (Chatterji, 2013, p. 299). Further, the reluctance or inability to adequately or comfortably account for the consequences of test use have prompted some (e.g., Borsboom, Mellenbergh, & van Heerden, 2004; Cizek, 2012, 2020; Lissitz & Samuelsen, 2007) within measurement and psychology to suggest reducing such requirements for validity evidence. For example, Borsboom et al. (2004) argue that validation should be narrowed to a clearer, simpler, practical, and more effective approach that is "stripped ... of all excess baggage" (p. 1070). Here, it is the requirement for considerations of context – as the consequences, decisions, and actions that result based on inferences drawn from assessment use – that are referred to as *excess baggage*. Advocates for a narrower approach to validity propose instead, "a simple conception of validity that concerns the question of whether the attribute to be measured produces variations in the measurement outcomes". They argue that validity theory should be "based on ontology, reference, and causation, rather than epistemology, meaning and correlation" (p. 1069).

Fulcher (2015) observed that researchers who caution against broader conceptualizations of validity, fear "infect[ing] the purity of the link between a score and the mind of the person from whom it was derived" (Fulcher, 2015). Of course, this *purity premise* is questionable in itself, and depends on a theoretical worldview that is cognitive, *in the head* of an individual. Fulcher suggests that the current consensus conceptualization of "validity theory is capable of taking complex context into account while maintaining score generalisability for practical decision-making purposes" (p. 227). We agree. We argue, as McNamara (2007) has pointed out, the problem of context relates to the reliance on the theoretical perspectives that have dominated validation research: namely, the individualist, *cognitive* perspective (cf. "realist" in Messick, 1989; Lissitz & Samuelsen, 2007). This theoretical perspective is not useful in accounting for the consequences of assessment use. However, social theories provide particularly useful alternative perspectives for validation research which is focused on the consequences of assessment in diverse and varied, situational, circumstantial, social, and cultural contexts.

In their landmark book, *Language testing: The social dimension*, McNamara and Roever (2006) identified the "urgent and significant need" (p. 253) to better account for *context* in assessment practices.They argued that a key barrier to considerations of context was insufficient understanding of social theories and the contributions they could make in addressing the "problem" (p. 253) of context. They concluded that "the most productive and relevant of these [social] theories" were "relatively unfamiliar" (p. 253) to researchers who focus on what is considered to be the key issue in the development and use of assessment – *validity*.

The problem of *context* in assessment validation practices, namely the "obligation" (Cronbach, 1988, p. 6) to consider the *actions*, *social effects*, and *consequences* (cf. Messick, 1989, 1998) of the inferences drawn from assessment, remains largely neglected in mainstream validation research. As Chatterji (2013) pointed out, "While educational testing [assessment] is ubiquitous internationally today, the validity ... is frequently compromised in *test* [assessment] *use* settings by conditions and factors that are still largely undocumented and not well understood" (p. 1).

McNamara and Roever (2006) argued that although social theories could provide richly informed frameworks to account for the actions and consequences of assessment practices in contexts of use, they also "challenge many of the fundamental epistemological and ontological assumptions" (McNamara and Roever, 2006, p. 253) of the dominant disciplinary communities that have been concerned with assessment (e.g., psychometrics, educational measurement, psychology). As a result, they argued, validity researchers have failed to adequately address the problem of context.

In order to collect validation evidence, researchers set boundaries, define, and design validation studies. Theoretical perspectives shape what researchers choose to investigate, the questions they ask, the descriptions or explanations they seek, and the meanings they draw from findings. In this regard, Bachman (2007) observed, "While the different theoreretical perspectives ... are not mutually exclusive, they are based on different sets of values and assumptions" (p. 41). Further, as noted above, McNamara (2007) pointed out, "the social context theorized on its own terms has featured rather weakly in discussions of language [assessment]", and this, he argued, necessitates a "renewed discussion of the social context" (p. 131) in assessment practices.

Over a decade before McNamara and Roever's (2006) analysis of the problem of context, a similar recognition was registered by Moss (e.g., 1994; 1998), who prodded taken-for-granted thinking and practices in validation research, for example, by asking provocative questions such as, "Can we have validity without reliability?" Her question appeared as the title of a 1994 paper, published in the top-tier journal, *Educational Researcher* – a journal recognized for the dissemination of significant scholarly work of broad interest to research communities concerned with assessment.

In that article, Moss (1994) problematized the *a priori* notion that "without reliability, there is no validity" (p. 6). She focused on the largely unquestioned definition of *reliability,* which originated in measurement and psychometrics (e.g., the consistent quantifiable evidence of performance across tasks, test takers, and assessors/raters/scores). She pointed out that this psychometric definition was appropriate in considerations of large-scale, *standardized* assessment, wherein:

- test takers responded to the same (or comparable) items, or tasks on a test;
- time limits were defined and systematically enforced;
- performances were scored in relation to a fixed standard (scale); and
- raters, machine or human, were systematically trained, monitored and calibrated.

However, the definition was problematic in "less standardized forms of assessment, such as performance assessments" (p. 6) or in classroom-based assessment of portfolios, student writing, group projects, poster presentations, and so forth. She argued for an expanded definition of reliability which would accommodate diverse and alternative forms of evidence by incorporating *hermeneutic* interpretation. Such interpretation is characterized by a "holistic and integrative approach", which considers collections of evidence over time, and "privileges readers who are most knowledgable about the context in which the assessment occurs" (p. 7). Moss (1994) maintained that,

> By considering hermeneutic alternatives for serving the important epistemological and ethical purposes that reliability serves, we expand the range of viable high-stakes assessment practices to include those that honor [local] ... purposes and ... contextualized judgments.
>
> (p. 5)

The first section of this 1994 article by Moss was of particular relevance to the present volume. In this section, she recounted her experience with the journal's review process, explaining that the article ultimately appeared in print only because the editor overruled the evaluations and recommendations of the journal's peer reviewers. Her precient views contradicted and challenged the received disciplinary worldviews and expertise of the reviewers' notions of reliability and validity. Their reviews reflected the deeply ingrained disciplinary values and practices which were associated with traditional psychometrics, psychology, and educational measurement.

Her discussion of the review process highlighted the role of disciplinarity in academic research. How we define a research problem and conceptualize an approach pre-positions us to see, understand, and act. We do this in keeping with our formative experiences, knowledge, and ongoing, increasing expertise within a discipline. The way we talk, who we cite, the manner in which we express our ideas – all are reflective of our education and practice within a chosen disciplinary community (or communities). Haas (1994) illustrated the transition to disciplinary identity and identification, by documenting an undergraduate student's development as a biologist over the four years of her post-secondary education. Haas documented the student's evolving beliefs, values, knowledge of, and identification with members of her chosen disciplinary community.

The student was mentored into the disciplinary community through a myriad of interactions with other biologists, her teachers, fellow-students, their research, and their scholarly contributions (including the texts, topics, and activities she experienced). The pathway to her undergraduate degree was one of disciplinary enculturation as she encountered, experienced, resisted, and accommodated disciplinary ways of seeing the world, of processing information, and practicing or acting as a biologist within (and outside of) her disciplinary community. Haas explained, there were "not only changes in her reading and writing", there were also profound changes in her attitude toward and perceptions of her discipline: "her representations of the nature of texts, and her understanding of the relationship between knowledge and written discourse within her disciplinary field of biology" (p. 43).

Many research studies (cf. Artemeva, 2005; Artemeva & Fox, 2010; Bazerman 1982, 1988, 1994b; Russell, 1997) have investigated and documented disciplinary development, enculturation, membership, and transition to professional practice. Much of this research has examined disciplinarity through the analytical lenses offered by social theories. Arguably, the socio-theoretical perspectives that guided this research afforded comprehensive, meaningful, and useful accounts of what is essentially a social phenomenon. Social theories provided the heuristic foundation for the definition of research frameworks and concomitant methodological approaches; informed the questions that were asked, and the data that were collected; helped researchers make sense of what they found; framed their interpretations of findings; and prompted the future directions for research they proposed.

As members of disciplinary communities, we grow to understand (tacitly and explicitly) what signals disciplinary membership, what research is central to disciplinary interests, and whose ideas we recognize as contributions toward future directions for research. In the case of the 1994 seminal article by Moss, we have the editor to thank for recognizing its significant and novel contribution, which was outside the bounds of the received disciplinary views of the time. Such challenging and alternative ideas, including extra-disciplinary questions and comments, should be encouraged, because they can serve as catalysts for new learning. Recognizing and reflecting on differences creates opportunities for new and innovative thinking and is at the heart of a transdisciplinary approach. The goal is not synthesis (although it might occur to a degree in some cases). Rather, the goal is learning from our differences through productive dialogue. Such an approach "privileges difference and seeks practices that sustain dialogue and collaboration across different perspectives in addressing social problems" (Moss & Haertel, 2016, p. 232). In response to the question that framed this section, following Chatterji (2013), McNamara and Roever (2006), and Moss (1994), we view the lack of social theories and alternative social perspectives as a contributing reason for the unresolved problem of context in assessment validation research. We see the potential of a TR agenda to address this problem: to support understanding of "truly alternative points of view" and allow us to "learn more about the character and value of the positions we ourselves espouse ... [by] opening the door to critical enrichment and 'reciprocal refinement' of diverse perspectives" (Camic & Joas, 2004, p. 9).

Below we elaborate key distinctions we have drawn throughout this volume by defining and discussing differences in *disciplinary*, *cross-/multi-disciplinary*, *interdisciplinary*, and *transdisciplinary* approaches to research. We expand our discussion of transdisciplinarity and explain our premise that it provides a productive approach to addressing the problem of context in language assessment validation research.

Question two: what is the potential of a transdisciplinary research (TR) agenda in addressing the problem of *context* in assessment validation?

As Moss and Haertel (2016) have discussed in detail, there is a great deal in the literature regarding the role of *disciplinary*, *cross-/multi-disciplinary*, and *interdisciplinary* research. In contrast, the term *transdisciplinary* has only recently been foregrounded by researchers, often in calls for more research of this type (e.g., Addey et al., 2020; Mendes-Flohr, 2015; Tardy, 2017). Moss and Haertel (2016) report that a 2014 search of the *American Educational Research Journal* revealed only three articles in which the research approach was described as transdisciplinary. Further, it is important to acknowledge that there is no consensus definition of transdisciplinarity (e.g., Balsiger, 2004; Lawrence, 2010; Paré, 2008).

Defining transdisciplinarity

In order to clarify our own use of the term *transdisciplinary*, we begin by distinguishing it from other research practices, all of which share the same linguistic root: *disciplinary*.

As Figures 1.1a and 1.1b illustrate, we envisioned each of these different *disciplinary* research approaches as overlapping, dynamic research spaces, along a continuum of research practices:

- purely *disciplinary* (or mono-disciplinary) research (Figures 1.1a and 1.1b, #1) is characterized by membership within a bounded community of researchers, who share worldviews, knowledge, expertise, practices, etc.; novices/newcomers are mentored by experts/old-timers who practice the ways of seeing, doing, knowing, and thinking that characterize group membership;
- *cross-disciplinary/multi-disciplinary* research (Figures 1.1a and 1.1b, #2) occurs when two or more disciplinary communities present,

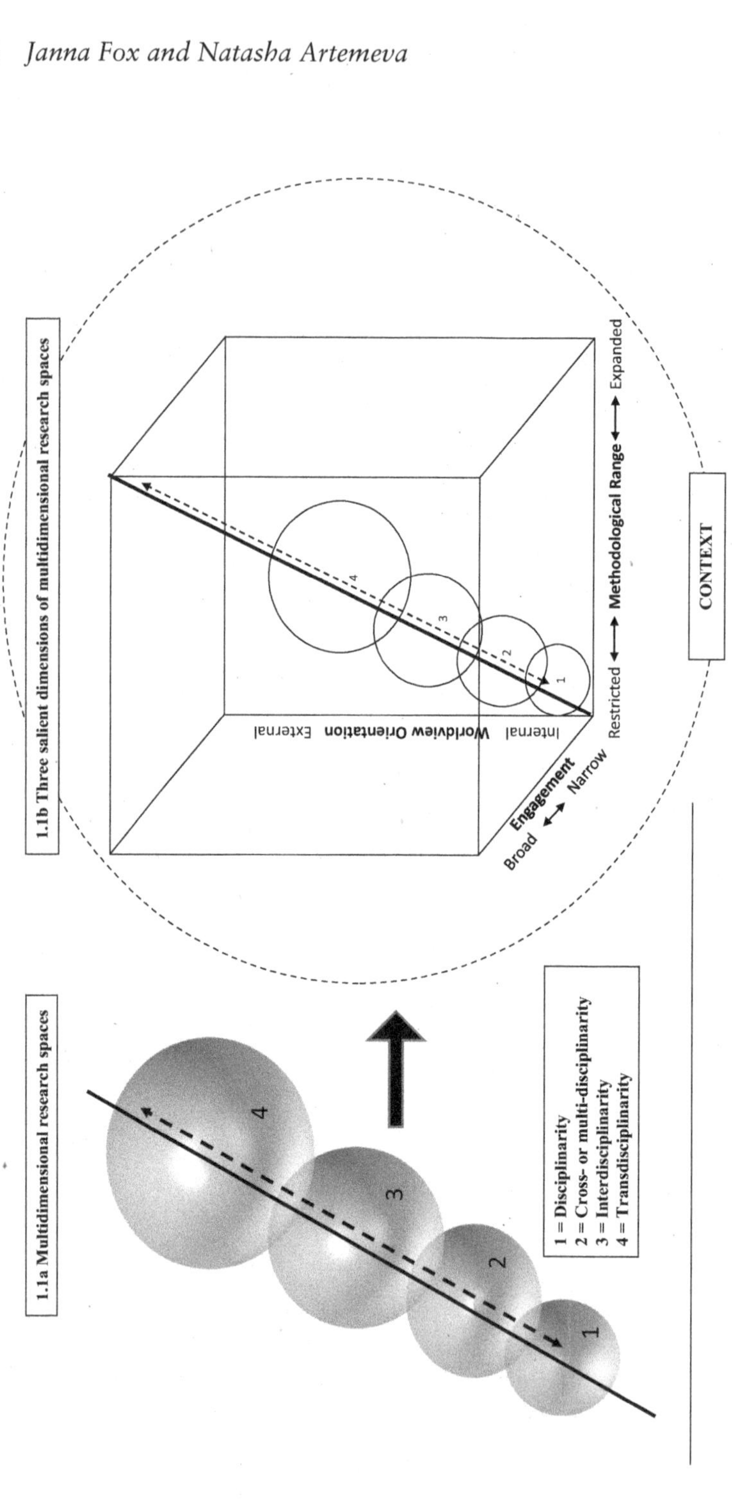

Figure 1.1a and 1.1b Conceptualizing three salient dimensions of multidimensional research spaces.

discuss, or debate a particular issue from differing, *juxtaposed* perspectives;

- *interdisciplinary* research (Figures 1.1a and 1.1b, #3) engages researchers from two or more disciplinary communities, who share a focus on the same issue and draw on differing disciplinary expertise to undertake a project and produce shared findings. Interdisciplinarity can involve "excursions into other fields" and result in nothing more than "rhetorical tourism", whereby, as Paré (2008) explains: we visit, we engage in research with others, and "we come back to our disciplinary colleagues to describe what we've seen" (p. 18). Conversely, interdisciplinary research can evolve into TR due to, for example, deepening collective understanding of other perspectives, expanding stakeholder participation, increasing research scope, etc.;
- *transdisciplinary research (TR)* (Figures 1.1a and 1.1b, #4) can and does occur amongst researchers from different disciplinary communities, but often engages stakeholders from outside academia as research partners. Transdisciplinary approaches offer a means of managing complexity by increasing the pool of knowledge, expertise, and insights productively brought to bear on a research problem. They "enable the cross-fertilisation of ideas and knowledge from different contributors that promote an enlarged vision of a subject, as well as new explanatory theories" (Lawrence, 2010, p. 126). Collaborators learn other ways of seeing, being, doing, and reflecting in addressing complex problems that are often beyond the scope of any one disciplinary or other group to address.

There are many dimensions which might define a TR space. In each case, characterizing a research approach is a matter of context, perspective, and degree. Transdisciplinary approaches are most useful in addressing a complex problem where a team can be brought together to consider the problem from multiple perspectives. Further, these projects are typically not short-term in nature; they often involve more time than traditional disciplinary research and arise more frequently within a program of research (comprised of multiple research projects). Their scope is typically larger, and the problems being addressed are typically more complex.

Research spaces are both dynamic and emergent. What begins as an interdisciplinary research project may devolve into a cross-disciplinary exchange or expand into transdisciplinarity (the former is a much more common trend than the latter) (cf. Paré, 2008). Dynamism is inevitable, given the interactions taking place as a research project unfolds. In disciplinary research projects, researchers are advised to *listen to what your data tell you*, and data do not always *speak* in the ways we have anticipated. However, the least complex or dynamic and most stable approaches to research are those which are disciplinary. Such approaches are defined by the *known territory* of the discipline, including practices which are recognizable and recurrent as accepted (at times, taken-for-granted) ways of framing, designing, implementing, analyzing, and interpreting research.

Figure 1.1a provides a rough conceptual illustration of the complex, multidimensional research spaces (Niglas, 2010) of overlapping and dynamic approaches, along a continuum from disciplinary to TR. In addition to scope, complexity, time required, and dynamism, we have found three dimensions were salient in distinguishing TR approaches from others, as they unfold within the context of research (Figure 1.1b), namely:

1 *methodological range* (from restricted to expanded)
Transdisciplinary approaches are characterized by increasing methodological breadth and an expanding range of methods used to address research questions. They avoid exclusive reliance on the range of methodologies and methods that are characteristic of one's home disciplinary community;
2 *worldview orientation* (from internally directed to externally directed)
Transdisciplinarity is characterized by openness to other, different worldviews; a conceptual stance that is outwardly oriented rather than inwardly directed to the shared disciplinary perspectives of one's own, home disciplinary community. We have highlighted some social theories which provide alternative social perspectives or worldviews in the present volume because they have been underutilized in considerations of context in assessment validation research. However, from a transdisciplinary perspective what is valued is alternative viewpoints – all of which provide additive benefit by generating dialogue, reflection, and learning; and
3 *engagement* (from narrow to broad)
Transdisciplinarity is characterized by collaborating partners both within and external to academic/disciplinary communities (e.g., pilots, government bureaucrats, administrators, software programmers). Shared, collective interest in a research problem is accompanied by balanced valuing of differing partners' perspectives and expertise, and encouragement of dialogue and mutual investment and/or ownership.

Transdisciplinarity in practice

In our view, a key feature of transdisciplinarity is the additive benefit of collectivity, collaboration, mutual acknowledgement, and recognition within or across theoretical and methodological practices. Below, distinctions with regard to the continuum of overlapping research approaches (Figures 1.1a, 1.1b) are discussed as they have played out in academic research contexts.

- *Disciplinary research* (see also mono-disciplinary) is *bounded* by implicitly (and, at times, explicitly) shared knowledge of content and practices within a research community. In other words, members of the community share ways of speaking, doing, and acting through received disciplinary discourses which engage with the contents, topics, and purposes that motivate and sustain group membership. Although interpretations may differ across members of a community, and tensions, disagreements, and debates may arise within the community, such differences are generally viewed as necessary for a discipline's development. Disciplines evolve and emerge in relation to interpretations over time.

Highly competitive disciplinary conferences set a theme, invite participants to submit abstracts for presentations, recruit peer reviewers who are recognized as disciplinary experts to evaluate the submitted abstracts, and generate a conference program shaped to the knowledge and interests of the disciplinary community. Academic journals also shape submitted articles through peer review in relation to readers' disciplinary communities.

Undertaking and presenting research to a disciplinary community, as the old adage suggests, is like *singing to the choir*. Each time a familiar piece of music is presented "to the choir" (e.g., with a new voice, nuance, arrangement, cadence), the choir's experience of the music deepens and increases. It learns new things, increases its knowledge, appreciates new directions – but its learning is constrained and informed by what was assumed and known before, and the choir's shared knowledge of choir music.

We find the *singing to the choir* analogy apt and have heard it often repeated by academic colleagues who have presented their research to groups of like-minded peers with the same or similar disciplinary backgrounds. Although their peers may affirm and appreciate their work, they also lament its limited impact as often stakeholders outside the bounds of the discipline, who might benefit from hearing the outcomes of their research, are generally not in the audience. When findings are disseminated, they appeal most often to the narrow disciplinary communities which gave rise to them.[1]

- *Cross-/multi-disciplinary research* involves the juxtaposition of different disciplines and their concomitant disciplinary traditions. To follow on the musical analogy above, within a single concert, a classical guitar recital may be followed by a jazz ensemble; or vocal numbers may include an operatic aria performed by an up-and-coming tenor, which is juxtaposed with a rap-group's hip-hop rendition of a hit song. It's all the same concert, but the individual contributions are not collective, collaborative, or interactive.

  Academic conferences which take a multi-disciplinary approach often juxtapose streams. For example, in a large conference with the theme of *Transitions to university*, one stream might offer papers on large-scale student satisfaction surveys and have sessions on innovative approaches to their analysis (e.g., sampling strategies in Structural Equation Modelling; new techniques in Differential Item

Function analysis). A second stream on student satisfaction might feature papers on the phenomena of attrition, with sessions on entering, undergraduate students' accounts of their first-year experience (e.g., *narratives of experience,* captured in stories told by newly arrived international students; or case studies describing engineering or business students' adjustment to university). Although there is shared interest in the common theme of transition, participants following or presenting in one stream might not choose to discuss or share knowledge and experience with those following other streams.

- *Interdisciplinary research*, on the other hand, involves collaboration and integration of differing theoretical and methodological traditions. To follow on our musical analogy, interdisciplinarity might be compared to an old/familiar song which is rendered new when a pop star sings it with a well-known operatic diva (or vice versa). What results is new and innovative, combining the strengths of two different traditions of music within the presentation of a single, familiar song. A famous example in the history of Western music might be the collaboration of two popular singers, David Bowie and Bing Crosby (e.g., *Peace on Earth/Little Drummer Boy*). The resulting musical version of *Little Drummer Boy* involved drawing on the distinct voices, personalities, and differing musical traditions of two well-recognized singers to spark something new.

Examples of such interdisciplinary collaborative approaches abound in the literature on interdisciplinarity within and across researchers from different universities (e.g., Franks et al., 2007). It is also evident in conference roundtables or symposia that draw participants from different disciplines to discuss, dialogue, and debate a shared issue of concern. The extent to which such symposia presentations engage with each other (e.g., in their conceptualizations of the issue under discussion, evident learning from each other's differences, identification of proposed alternative directions for research) is the extent to which they are interdisciplinary.

However, as Moss and Haertel (2016) point out, and as Abbott (2001) observed more than 20 years ago, "interdisciplinarity is old news" (p. 131). Over the intervening decades, there has been an abundance of literature on interdisciplinary research practices. In recent years, new interest in *TR* (e.g., Klein, 2007; Moss, 2016; Moss & Haertel, 2016; Pohl & Hirsch Hadorn, 2007, 2008; Smythe, Hill, MacDonald, Dagenais, Sinclair, & Toohey, 2017) has emerged, signalling the need for reinforced and expanded collectivity and collaboration amongst researchers with differing disciplinary, academic, professional, and other backgrounds, who share a common interest in researching complex problems, such as those that abound in research on social phenomena.

Moss and Haertel (2016) traced the initial description of *transdisciplinary* approaches in education research back to a 1972 report of the OECD.[2] In the opening pages of this chapter, Piaget's first use of the term *transdisciplinary* was acknowledged as part of the same OECD meeting and report. Leman (2007b), traced transdisciplinarity back to nineteenth-century research in musicology.

In the 1972 OECD report cited in Moss and Haertel (2016), interdisciplinary research was defined as a *range* of interactions among researchers from different disciplinary backgrounds, which could involve simply exchanging ideas, identifying problems, or communicating directions for research. Transdisciplinary approaches extended these notions of interdisciplinarity to the full engagement of researchers from different disciplinary backgrounds who "agree to design, implement, and bring to a consensus the results of a systematic investigation" (Bruhn, 2000, p. 58) and who take into account their differences and responsibly and respectfully acknowledge and learn from them. Over the years, TR has been identified as the most intensive and extensive kind of collaboration, interaction, and engagement in addressing complex problems, which are beyond the capability of a single group or disciplinary community to adequately address (cf. Klein, 1990; Klein & Newell, 1998; Leman, 2007a, 2007b), and which engages research partners beyond the walls of academia.

- *Transdisciplinary research (TR)* requires an environment which is characterized by dialogue, discussion, understanding, negotiation, and accommodation in addressing, designing, implementing, and interpreting research regarding complex problems. Such research draws on researchers who have been shaped by different disciplinary, professional or other experiences and whose expertise has privileged differing theoretical and methodological approaches. Rather than putting a new spin on an old, recognizable song, transdisciplinary practices can lead to a breakthrough genre – to innovation, recognitions, and new directions.

Leman (2007b) discussed the limitations of mono-disciplinary views within the history of music research, taking issue with "the so-called cognitive musicology approach which up until today, still offers a main scientific research paradigm to systematic musicology" (2007b, p. 1). He explained that the cognitive musicology approach had focused on quantitative measurement of empirical data, computer modelling, and hypothesis testing (quite as the assessment validation research tradition has done). Leman explained why TR is a "core necessity" in his view:

> The reason why a single discipline, be it music theory, psychology, sociology, acoustics, computer science, or even brain science is too narrow a basis to grasp the different ways in which people deal with music is that music is a highly multimodal phenomenon involving all human faculties and very different social and cultural contexts.
> (p. 1)

Leman's advocacy for transdisciplinarity parallels our own recognitions of the *core need* for this approach in the validation of inferences drawn from assessment practices in development and use. Collaborating and building on the sharing of disciplinary knowledge and understanding, will potentially generate what Karlqvist (1999) referred to as a kind of *meta-knowledge* (p. 379). Such meta-knowledge may increase meta-awareness and lead to more self-reflection, flexibility, insight, and innovation.

Some approaches to TR have reinforced the notion of non-traditional research partnerships that lead to positive outcomes which are in the interest of the *common good* (cf. Lawrence, 2010; Moss & Haertel, 2016; Smythe et al., 2017). Herndl and his colleagues (e.g., Herndl & Brown, 1996; Herndl & Wilson, 2007) have documented research partnerships with farmers, agronomists, economists, environmental scientists, teachers, experts in discourse and writing studies, etc. Such rich and illuminating partnerships were engaged, for example, in research regarding the persuasiveness of arguments for sustainable development and were guided by a shared collective recognition of the value of the research. Smythe et al. (2017) reported on research partnerships with colleagues from differing backgrounds within a large Faculty of Education who shared a common interest in "educational advocacy and to working alongside those who have been typically marginalised or disempowered in educational settings" (Smythe et al., 2017, Preface, Kindle Edition).

TR projects with expressed goals such as those in Smythe et al. (2017) share characteristics of *Participatory Action Research* (see Wicks & Reason, 2009; Wicks, Reason, & Bradbury, 2008). They typically engage multiple stakeholders as researchers (particularly those who are involved in or may be affected by research findings) in research design, implementation, and interpretation in order to work toward more useful, relevant, and just outcomes. (See also Wyman et al., 2010, for an example of Participatory Action Research in language assessment.) Approaches to TR that support data users (e.g., decision makers, teachers, other stakeholders) and data use (e.g., policy, educational activity, community development, resource allocation) generally share perspectives that are consistent with Participatory Action Research (cf. Moss, 2016).

Arguably, the problem of context in the validation of assessment will best be addressed through a TR agenda. Such an agenda would bring together researchers from differing disciplinary traditions, founded on differing theoretical premises and concomitant methodologies/methods, who nonetheless share a common interest in addressing this complex problem. If this shared goal is to generate knowledge, if learning is the envisoned outcome, a TR approach may offer new insights and "movement forward" (Lave, 1996, p. 28). This requires a research environment characterized by respectful recognition of differences. If this environment is established, then, through a process of argument (Strike, 2006), "meaningful discussions" (Biesta, 2010, p. 99), open-mindedness (Tardy, 2017), dialogue and critical, self-reflective engagement (Bernstein,

1998), new insights, new approaches, and learning are possible. Conversely, it has proved to be impossible to address the problem of context and consequences in assessment practices through mono-disciplinary approaches (cf. McNamara & Roever, 2006; Moss, 1994; Moss & Haertel, 2016), further discussed below.

Question three: what role do disciplines play in constraining and limiting innovation?

In the research literature, disciplinary barriers have been considered both *symbolic* (Lamont & Molnár, 2002), because they "generate feelings of similarity and group membership", or *social*, because they "are objectified forms of social difference" (p. 168), which define and institutionalize researcher identities, group membership, and practices. Whether symbolic or social, both have consequences in terms of foundational knowledge, material resources, opportunities, and potential, or actual social relationships. Disciplinary communities develop theoretical and methodological preferences, which over time becomed traditions – the way things are viewed, the way things are done, and what is valued. Theoretical preferences – worldviews and conceptual stances – are particularly important. As Larsen-Freeman and Cameron (2008a) explain:

> The theory that we choose to work with ... will dictate how we describe and investigate the world. It controls how we select, out of all that is possible, what to investigate or explain, what types of questions we ask, how data are collected, and what kinds of explanations of the data are considered valid.
>
> (p. 16)

For example, consider the keywords *validity* and *context* in relation to *assessment practices*. For readers and researchers associated with or educated within disciplinary communities that have traditionally focused on assessment (e.g., psychometrics, educational measurement, psychology), *validity*, as noted above, would be central to their academic concerns. However, the notion of incorporating *context* in validation research might be problematic, unless it was defined as a variable which was carefully delimited and controlled for analysis. Members of these disciplinary communities would draw on theoretical perspectives that generally considered cognition to be a property of an individual's thinking (cf. McNamara & Roever, 2006). Their focus would tend to be on the assessment of abilities, attributes, or underlying traits, viewed as properties of an individual and assessed in isolation from the circumstances, situations, or contexts within which they occurred – unless the context was operationalized as a treatment, condition, or other carefully defined variable. Most researchers would also acknowledge and cite the great validity philosophers of the past, who continue to shape validation practices today within these disciplines (e.g., Cronbach, Messick), or more recent contributors, such as Kane, Mislevy, Newton, and Zumbo.

For readers and researchers from a number of other disciplinary communities (e.g., discourse studies, writing studies, language teaching), the meaning of the word *validity* might need further clarification, or be rejected in favour of other terminology (e.g., *trustworthiness*)[3] (Lincoln & Guba, 1985) because of its association with measurement (Bryman & Teevan, 2005; Tashakkori & Teddlie, 2010). Further, the notions that assessment was a social practice occurring *in context* would typically pass without question, and the names of Cronbach and Messick would not even *ring a bell*. These communities would generally view assessment, like any other social practice, as inseparable from *context*. In other words, most *credible* research would inevitably involve substantial recognitions of context in some form, the application of one or more *social* theories, and reference to one or more social theorists. Scholars working within these communities would argue that, "Without a theoretical conception of the social world one cannot analyze activity *in situ*" (Lave, 1996, p. 3), and their research might reference such historic giants as Bakhtin, Berger, Luckmann, or, depending upon the disciplinary community for which their research was intended, Cole, Scribner, Gee, Engeström, or Miller (scholars whom psychologists, measurement specialists, or psychometricians might not recognize). As Moss and Haertel (2016) have explained the theoretical and methodological traditions of disciplines are "reflected in sustained, historically situated dialogue and mutual citation among those who locate their work in that tradition, and where the participants routinely acknowledge (embrace, revise, or resist) common understandings and practices" (p. 129). However, their expansive discussion of methodological pluralism, in the 2016 *Handbook on research on teaching*, provides compelling evidence of the benefits of "working knowledgeably across research traditions" (p. 234) within transdisciplinary programs of research.

The potential of such transdisciplinary programs of research has long been recognized. In the 1990s Lave (1996) reported on a conference that addressed *the context problem* (p. 4). It drew international participants from a wide range of disciplines (e.g., anthropology, cognitive science, communication sciences and disorders, communication studies, computer science, education, psychology, sociology), all of whom shared a concern about "conventional limitations on various approaches to the study of ... socially situated activity", with specific attention accorded to "context ... [which] our work often seemed merely to take for granted" (p. 4). The outcomes of that conference were anthologized in a subsequent collection entitled, *Understanding practice: Perspectives on activity and context*, co-edited by Chaiklin and Lave (1996).

The approach taken by the conference participants was transciplinary, although Lave did not define it as such. She introduced the book by describing the "spirit" that guided participation, namely, the valuing of *differences* (e.g., theoretical, methodological, interpretative), "motivated as little as possible by opposition" (p. 28). Rather, engaging with and valuing such differences introduced "multiple possibilities for interrogating social experience" and resulted in new and "positive" directions for research on social practices in context. Lave's account of this transdisciplinary approach illustrates the benefits of the collective, collaborative engagement of researchers from different disciplinary backgrounds, who share a common interest in a research problem and are guided by a willingness to learn from their differences, to listen to and come to understand such differences in "the strongest possible light" (Bernstein, 1998, p. 4).

Moving the research agenda forward

In the remaining chapters of Part I, additional background is provided as a foundation for a TR agenda in language assessment validation practices. Chapter 2 reviews the contributions of assessment-centred communities to the evolving conceptualizations of *validity* as the locus of concern in *assessment*. Chapter 3 examines the contributions of language-centred communities to the evolving conceptualizations of *language* itself and discusses implications for its assessment. Both communities are integral to *language assessment*, but their differing theoretical perspectives have led to an *applicability gap* (Lawrence, 2010). This gap is examined in relation to the importance of theory in research, the dominance of individualist, cognitive theories in assessment-centred communities, and the concomitant lack of awareness and application of alternative social perspectives in language assessment research. A selective overview of what social perspectives share is followed by some examples of the differing theoretical perspectives they offer (and further illustrated in the empirical research projects included in Part II of the book). At the end of Chapter 3 an example illustrates how increasing dialogue between scholars within assessment-centred and language-centred communities could address the conundrum of context in validation research and promote reflection, insight, and forward movement.

Chapter 4 provides evidence of the under-utilization of social perspectives in scholarly assessment journals, reporting on the outcome of a meta-review of the assessment literature from 2004 to 2020. There is, however, increasing evidence of a socially informed thread in language assessment research. The social thread of research in language assessment is examined and discussed.

In Part II, examples of transdisciplinary language assessment research are provided. These studies involved stakeholders with different backgrounds, expertise, and experience: *disciplinary* (e.g., engineering, mathematics, applied linguistics); and/or *professional/workplace* (e.g., pilots, test developers, computer scientists, teachers, students, raters). All were engaged in or affected by assessment. Following Moss, Phillips,

Erickson, Floden, Lather, and Schneider (2009), these transdisciplinary studies were the outcome of collective and collaborative *dialogue* which "foster[ed] mutual engagement – and opportunity for learning – across different perspectives" (p. 501). In our view, this approach is essential in addressing context and validity in language assessment validation research.

Notes

1 The *singing to the choir* analogy and other musical references are used as a convenient extra-disciplinary, rhetorical device and do not imply knowledge of musicology or expertise in disciplines related to it. For an in-depth history of music research and its transdisciplinary foundations, see Leman (2007a).

2 According to Leman (2007b), TR in musicology, as evidenced in Adler (1885), involved the intensive collaboration of researchers from a range of scientific disciplines who sought to "understand how people engage with music, and how music functions in perception, performance and as an aesthetic and social phenomenon" (p. 1).

3 Bryman and Teevan (2005) provide a useful discussion of the caustic conflict between advocates of qualitative and quantitative research traditions that arose in the 1980s and 1990s, popularly known as the period of the *paradigm wars*. The paradigm wars are further examined in Chapter 3.

2 Validity as an evolving *rhetorical art*

Context and consequence in assessment

Janna Fox with Natasha Artemeva

Chapter 2 selectively reviews the contributions of assessment-centred communities to evolving conceptions of validity, a principal focus of concern for such communities (e.g., measurement, psychology, psychometrics).This chapter will be most useful for our intended audience of readers aligned with language-centred communities (e.g., language teaching, discourse, writing studies), who may be less familiar with this rich history. In this chapter, pivotal contributions to our current understanding of validity as a social practice and rhetorical art (Messick, 1988) are reviewed. These contributions occurred within periods of considerable methodological turbulence that marked disputed theoretical perspectives and research practices. This overview of the assessment-centred communities' evolving conceptions of validity is followed in Chapter 3 by an overview of the contributions of language-centred communities to conceptions of language – the principal focus of language assessment. Building a foundation of shared mutual knowledge between these communities is essential for transdisciplinary programs of research which tackle complex issues such as the role of context in language assessment validation.

> *... if measurement is science and the use of measurements is applied (political) science, the justification and defense of measurement and its validity is and may always be a rhetorical art.*
>
> (Messick, 1988, p. 43)

> *Questioning Messick's (1989) theory of validity is a task akin to carving a Thanksgiving armadillo.*
>
> (Markus, 1998, p. 7)

The Introduction at the beginning of this book provided an overview of its purpose, organization, and contents. Chapter 1 emphasized the need for

DOI: 10.4324/9781351184571-4

transdisciplinary programs of research in addressing complex issues, such as the role of context in assessment practices. Two differing communities of particular importance to language assessment were broadly defined as assessment-centred (e.g., psychology, measurement, psychometrics) and language-centred (e.g., discourse studies, cultural studies, writing studies). Arguably, the need for transdisciplinarity is particularly evident in language assessment research – as this is a site of engagement by both of these communities.

In Chapter 2 the contributions of assessment-centred communities are highlighted in relation to the history of evolving conceptions of *validity* from the early twentieth century to the present day. Put simply, validity is generally considered to be the degree to which information drawn from a test or other mode of assessment is meaningful, useful, reasonable, and credible. V*alidation practices* (i.e., research which gathers evidence to support the development and/or use of a test or other modes of assessment) are undertaken in order to evaluate the validity of the inferences drawn from assessment. Cronbach (1988) invited us to consider validation as the collection of evidence in support of a "validity argument ... which must link concepts, evidence, social and personal consequences, and values" (p. 4). Messick (1988) defined validity as a "rhetorical art" (p. 43) – a complex *balancing* act (Messick, 1989), requiring different kinds of evidence for different types of inferences in relation to different purposes and audiences. The accumulation and interpretation of evidence – its nature, importance, sufficiency – determine how *meaningful* the inferences drawn from an assessment are, in what context, for what purposes, and to whom. Evidence is viewed through a theoretical lens (tacitly or explicitly), "where value assumptions frequently lurk" (p. 16). Meaning is attributed on the basis of "data, or facts, and the rationales or arguments that cement those facts into a justification of ... inferences" (pp. 15–16). It is this interplay of *fact*, *meaning*, and *value* that is at the core of arguments for validity, and may in part explain why Messick saw it as a matter of degree and *rhetorical art*. Although Messick's conception of validity continues to influence current *consensus definitions* of validity (Chapelle, 2021; the *Standards*, 2014; Zumbo & Chan, 2014), he provided only limited advice on how to engage in validation research. Kane (1992, 2006, 2013b) illuminated *how to proceed* by elaborating an approach to the collection of evidence in support of validity arguments. Because validation frameworks have been broadly and differently applied, with few examples in the literature and less guidance (cf. Chapelle, 2021), there is a general impression that they are intimidating and difficult to use.

However, as Chapelle (2021) points out, "Argument-based validity was developed as a way of managing the complexity of the process of validation, and it does so by incorporating important concepts introduced by previous generations" (p. 4). The history of such contributions will be familiar to those within assessment-centred (disciplinary) communities where *validity* has been a theoretical and empirical focus. Scholars accounting for *validation practices* have typically begun their books, textbooks, chapters, or articles with a description of the evolution of the concept of validity over time (cf. Chapelle, 2021; Cronbach, 1988; Fulcher, 2015; Messick, 1989; Zumbo & Chan, 2014). Students within assessment-centred communities are steeped in its history. Given the transdisciplinary research (TR) agenda of the present book, it was important to develop background familiarity, knowledge, and understanding of this history for our language-centred readers, who may have less familiarity with the history of validity and validation in assessment. This is the intent of Chapter 2.

There is a twist here, however, for those who know this history well. Our account of the evolution of conceptions of validity and attendant validation research practices is shaped by our focus on *context* as:

- a prevailing issue and source of debate in considerations of validity for over three decades;
- a concern that speaks to the historical times within which conceptions of validity evolved; and,
- an ongoing problem for assessment-centred communities, which have been dominated by "increasing disciplinary crystallization" (Johnson & Gray, 2010, p. 87), as evidenced in a tendency to rely on:
  - individualist, cognitive theories that have focused validation research on assumed, stable underlying traits, attributes, and abilities of individuals (including an individual's ability to use language); and
  - concomitant methodological practices, which control, reduce, disregard, or dismiss the role of context in validation research.

Background on validity – how it has been defined, why it is an issue, and why it is a concern in all assessment practices – is therefore central to the discussions which follow in Chapters 3 and 4. These chapters reinforce the argument that social theories should play an increased role in theorizing context and consequences and informing "alternative explanation[s]" (Cronbach, 1988, p. 14) of test scores or other assessment outcomes. Arguably, increasing the application of alternative social theories and perspectives will develop new insights regarding *actions* and *social consequences* of testing and other assessment practices (Messick, 1989, p. 13), as part of "a strong[er] program" of construct validation (p. 49).

Stronger programs of validation as the outcome of TR partnerships would address context from the alternative perspectives afforded by social theories, and expand possibilities while drawing on the contributions of Kane (e.g., 1992, 2006, 2013b) and Chapelle (2021) in clarifying complex pathways in building validity arguments. We view this as the essence of the *rhetorical art* that Messick (1988) alluded to. However, it is important to note that the ways in which social theorists and validity theorists write, speak, and engage is deeply disciplinary, and rooted in meanings and actions that are embedded within their disciplinary cultures. This is why transdisciplinary dialogue, exchange, and the sharing of expertise through collaboration is critical in building understanding and knowledge in order to move research agendas forward. Within assessment-centred communities, *moving the research agenda forward* would no doubt involve addressing current tensions and debates over validity and validation.

Newton and Baird (2016) point out that "Validity is the most important term in the educational and psychological measurement lexicon" (p. 173), and although some (e.g., Chapelle, 2021; Zumbo & Chan, 2014) have emphasized a core consensus on validity and validation practices, context (e.g., the consequences, decisions, and actions that result from test use) has long been at the centre of contentious debates. At the end of this chapter, we review the "tensions" (Newton & Shaw, 2016, p. 316) that have occurred in recent discussions of validity and validation within and across the disciplinary communities concerned with testing and other assessment practices. Ultimately, Moss's (2016, 2018) advocacy for a *transdisciplinary approach* suggests a way forward. She has consistently emphasized the value of alternative perspectives, and the need to build the local, contextual capability of assessment/test users to "use data well" (Moss, 2016, p. 248). It would appear that the timing is right (cf. Addey, Maddox, & Zumbo, 2020; Lawrence, 2010; Paré, 2008) for a transdisciplinary approach, as evidenced by increases in:

- clarity with regard to the rigour and usefulness of alternative/pluralistic research methodologies;
- pragmatism (i.e., less ideologically driven research);
- acknowledgement of complex, context-specific issues, including issues related to power and diversity;
- concerns regarding the relevance of assessment practices across local to global contexts of use;
- awareness of the limitations of narrow, disciplinary approaches to validation;
- awareness of alternatives (e.g., socio-theoretical perspectives, methodological pluralism) in the assessment literature; and
- recognition of the potential of transdisciplinarity in assessment validation research.

In sum, this chapter focuses on the contributions of assessment-centred communities: the past and present *state of play* in conceptions of validity and validation practices (evidenced by debates, dominant methodological approaches, and empirical research publications). By looking at the evolution of conceptions of validity over time and focusing on current debates, readers who are unfamiliar with such debates within assessment-centred communities may not realize the core issues that challenge them. Context and the consequences of high-stakes testing and other modes of assessment define much of this challenge.

Subsequently, in Chapter 3, we will discuss the contributions of language-centred communities to evolving conceptions of *language* over time. Chapter 3 may be of particular use to assessment-centred readers and others who are less familiar with this history and the concomitant contributions of language-centred communities, particularly those informed by differing social theories, in conceptualizing what it means to know and use language. In Chapter 3 we expand our discussion of the role of theories, explain why theories matter, and examine their influence within disciplines, fields, and sub-fields of relevance to language assessment. We then highlight the illuminating power and varying perspectives of a selective number of social theories in addressing the issue of context in assessment practices. This is followed in Chapter 4 with a discussion of the contributions of the language assessment community, with an emphasis on the social thread of research which has contributed to renewed considerations of context and validity in validation practices. Chapter 4 will be of use to all readers who may not be aware of this community's concerns for context and validity and its contributions to validation research, language test development, and classroom-based assessment.

With this background in mind, below we begin by providing a selective account of the evolution of validity in theory and research practices within assessment-centred communities.

The evolution of validity theory: validation as a social practice and rhetorical art

Past foundations: from shibboleth tests to correlation coefficients

To varying degrees, concerns over the social consequences of assessment practices – at both individual and societal levels – have inevitably accompanied assessment use. As the renowned sociolinguist Bernard Spolsky (1995) pointed out, scholars have long been aware of the high stakes and consequences of testing. He makes this point by referring to the Biblical *shibboleth test* (Book of Judges, 12, 4–6). This high-stakes, single-item pronunciation test was reportedly used by a victorious army to infer which returning soldiers had fought with them and which had not. Those who failed to correctly pronounce *sh*ibboleth (saying *s*ibboleth instead), met an untimely death.

Both historically and currently, shibboleth tests (based not only on pronunciation, but also on word choice, phrasing, written symbols, and so forth) continue to discriminate one person from another, one group from the next, on the basis of social, cultural, historical, or political distinctions. Such distinctions often result in profound personal and societal consequences, as McNamara and Roever (2006) discussed in their extensive account of historical and current examples of shibboleth tests. Kunnan (2018) provided another detailed historical discussion of language assessment in relation to societal needs and social consequences.

Recalling and reflecting on the socially informed meaning that surrounds and supports the inferences drawn from shibboleth tests is a good place to begin a discussion of the contributions of Cronbach and Messick, their reconceptualizations of validity to include the actions and consequences of inferences drawn from tests, and their early recognitions of testing as a value-laden social practice.

It is important to note, however, as McNamara and Roever (2006) have observed, that concerns over the social consequences of testing practices wavered in the face of "the triumph of psychometrics in the 1950s" (p. 2). This *triumph* was firmly rooted in the so-called *cognitive revolution* in psychology (e.g., Bruner, Goodnow, & Austin, 1956; Miller, 1956; Tolman, 1948) and the rise of cognitive theory and cognitive models of human language and language learning in psychology and linguistics (cf. Chomsky, 1957) (see Chapter 3 for additional details). Cognitive theory permeates the *epistemology* of the quantitative research tradition, quantitative research methodologies, measurement, and statistics. Put simply, Schwandt (1997) defines epistemology as how a group views "the nature of knowledge" and its "justification" (p. 39). Fulcher (2015) points out that what was true in the 1950s is still the case today: "The purely cognitive conception of language proficiency (and all human ability) is endemic to most branches of psychology and psychometrics ... [and] assumes that variation in test scores is a direct causal effect of the variation of the trait within an individual" (pp. 225). In other words, from the traditional cognitive perspective, *context* was a variable that needed to be controlled lest it undermine attempts to measure constructs of interest; and constructs were typically defined as an individual's stable underlying, traits, attributes, or abilities, observable in actions which were elicited by testing and other modes of assessment for research and evaluation purposes (cf. Bachman, 2007). As Chapelle (2021) points out, both Messick and Cronbach retained the notion of *trait* in their conceptualizations of validity. Further, most of their considerations of assessment were related to tests (rather than all modes of assessment). This remains largely the focus in the *Standards* today (cf. AERA, APA, & NCME, 1999, 2014). Nevertheless, Cronbach (1971) emphasized that inferences drawn from tests were "situation-bound" (p. 443), and there was a need for "situational specificity and ... local validation" (p. 81). Similarly, Messick (1989) argued for the evaluation of the "degree of generalizability for a measure" and the "scope ... of its ... applicability" (p. 57).

However, early *cognitive* (trait-based) perspectives led to narrow, largely atheoretical conceptions of validity, as evidenced by the observation of Guilford (1946) that "In a very general sense, a test is valid for anything with which it correlates" (p. 429). Angoff (1988) described this as a "purely operational" (p. 20) approach to validity, which required only that the test correlate with "some other objective measure of that which the test is used to measure" (Bingham, cited in Angoff, 1988, p. 20).

Although Cronbach and Meehl attacked this narrow conceptualization of validity as early as 1955, the operational approach of Guilford (1946) and Bingham (1937) continued to dominate (Angoff, 1988; Deville & Chalhoub-Deville, 2006). For example, it was common practice in the early 1980s for testing companies to publish test manuals in which validity evidence was summarized in a short passage which reported a single reliability (i.e., correlation) coefficient. Many mainstream measurement/psychometric books and textbooks continue to dedicate at least a chapter to this approach. However, decades earlier, Cronbach and Meehl (1955) argued that such validation practices were not "adequately conceptualized" (p. 281) and summarized "what qualities should be investigated before a test is published" (p. 281) in a landmark report of the American Psychological Association (APA) Committee on Psychological Tests (1950–1954).

Innovative recognitions: from construct validity (Cronbach & Meehl, 1955) to contextualism (cf. Cronbach, 1988)

Cronbach and Meehl (1955) stated that the "chief innovation" of the 1950–1954 American Psychological Association (APA) Committee on Psychological Tests was the identification and definition of the term "construct validity" (p. 281). They identified four types of validation studies, namely: predictive validity and concurrent validity [subsumed within criterion-oriented validation research], content validity, and *construct validity*. They defined a construct as "some postulated attribute of people, assumed to be reflected in test performance", or, in other words, "the attribute about which we make statements in interpreting a test" (p. 283). They explained that "Construct validation was introduced in order to specify types of research required in developing tests for which the conventional views on validation are inappropriate" (p. 299). Here *conventional views* is read as the purely operational approaches exemplified in the perspectives of Guilford (1946) or Bingham (1937).

This was a dramatic leap forward in the conceptualization of validity. Cronbach and Meehl (1955) signalled the advent of new requirements for multiple sources of evidence to support three different types of validity claims. This gave rise to what was known as the *tripartite view* of validity (which dominated validation perspectives in subsequent years), namely:

- *content validity*, based largely on the judgment of testing experts, who reviewed the adequacy of a test in representing achievement, performance etc., in a domain of interest;

- *predictive and concurrent/criterion-related validity*, based on empirical (typically statistical) evidence of the association between scores on a test and other criterion measures external to the test (e.g., other tests measuring the same construct for the same purpose; or subsequent performance measures which were predicted by the test); and
- *construct validity* (newly conceptualized and defined) as "making one's theoretical ideas as explicit as possible, then devising deliberate challenges" (Cronbach, cited in Kane, 2008, p. 78).

Over time, the implications of the requirement for multiple sources of evidence became clear, as ably summarized by Angoff in 1988, who foreshadowed the potential contribution of social theories, alternative worldviews, and methodologies. Angoff noted, "construct validity as conceived by Cronbach and Meehl cannot be expressed in a single coefficient. Construct validation is a process, not a procedure, and it requires many lines of evidence, not all of them quantitative" (p. 26).

Cronbach and Meehl (1955) attacked the atheoretical stance of the operational view, highlighting the need for specifying a "network of associations or propositions" (p. 299) in defining the constructs which tests measure. This *nomological network*, as noted above, required "reasonably explicit" (p. 300) specification of the theoretical and empirical basis for interpretation of test results. Kane (2008) viewed the emphasis on theoretical specification as a reaction against the prevailing and largely atheoretical times in which construct validity was first introduced. However, as is discussed below, there is ample evidence in Messick's work (e.g., 1988, 1989, 1998) that theories, and what some have called the philosophy of validity (Markus, 1998), are critically important to Cronbach and Meehl's (1955) position on validation.

Importantly, Cronbach and Meehl's (1955) report prepared the ground upon which Messick (1989) would build his philosophical treatise, arguing for a *unified* notion of validity – unified within the overriding or superordinate concept of construct validity. Although in 1955 Cronbach and Meehl were not prepared to assert the primacy of construct validity, arguably, they suggested that this might ultimately be the outcome:

> Without in the least *advocating* construct validity as preferable to the other … kinds (concurrent, predictive, content), we do believe it imperative that psychologists make a place for it in their methodological thinking, so that its rationale, its scientific legitimacy, and its dangers may become explicit and familiar.
>
> (p. 300)

In the section below we consider the elegant and comprehensive reconceptualization of validity initially developed by Messick (1980, 1989, 1995a, 1995b, 1998) but resting, we argue, on the foundations provided by Cronbach and Meehl, and reinforced by Cronbach's life-long contributions. We situate our discussion of context within Messick's (1989) philosophical elaboration of validity as a *unitary concept*, namely, his view that meaning drawn from test scores and other assessment practices is "embodied in construct validity [and] underlies all ... inferences" (p. 19). In other words, according to Messick, construct validity comprises all of the evidence, arguments, rationales, etc. that support the interpretation of assessment outcomes and their use: "construct validity binds the validity of [assessment] use to the validity of test interpretation" (p. 21).The centrality of construct and Messick's and Cronbach's references to the social consequences of testing are of particular interest in the present book. As Messick (1989) put it:

> for a fully unified view of validity, it must also be recognized that the appropriateness, meaningfulness, and usefulness of score-based inferences depend as well on the social consequences of the testing. Therefore, social values and social consequences cannot be ignored in consideration of validity.
>
> (p. 19)

Cronbach's (1988) view was quite similar, as evidenced by his advice to a "community" (p. 14) of *validators* in psychology, education, and the testing industry:

> The bottom line is that validators have an obligation to review whether a practice has appropriate consequences for individuals and institutions, and especially to guard against adverse consequences (Messick, 1980). You (like Yallow & Popham, 1983) may prefer to exclude reflection on consequences from the meanings of the word validation, but you cannot deny the obligation.
>
> (p. 6)

Over 30 years after his 1955 landmark publication with Meehl, Cronbach (1988) directs us to McGuire's (1983)[1] notion of *contextualism* as a way forward. Contextualism takes an all-embracing, all-inclusive "stance toward theory for recognizing the existence and utility of a wide variety of formulations to generate insights into the contents and determinants of experience and behavior" (McGuire, 1983). McGuire viewed a contextualist epistemology as "an appropriate meta-theory for psychology", which he considered was in need of methodological reform in "both process and product" (p. 8). He argued that too much focus in psychology was placed on the testing of hypotheses without an essential, concomitant focus on the generation of the hypotheses themselves. He supported the notion of "empirical confrontation" as a means of "discovery" (p. 13) (cf. Lave, 1996; Moss & Haertel, 2016).

In directing us to McGuire's meta-theory, Cronbach identifies a source for his own thinking, and articulates: 1) what was to become a central argument of Messick's (1989) treatise on validity; 2) what remains a core tenet of current validation practices today (cf. Chapelle, 2021; Chapelle, Enright, & Jamieson, 2008; Kane, 2013b); and 3) what is central in our consideration of context through the alternative perspectives of a selective number of social theories and an array of methodologies (see *methodological pluralism* in Moss, 2018; Moss & Haertel, 2016) in keeping with a TR agenda. For example, note Cronbach's (1988) prescient advice to measurement and testing professionals with regard to inferences drawn from test scores and other assessment practices:

> The advice is not merely to be on the lookout for cases your hypothesis does not fit. The advice is to find, either in the relevant community of concerned persons or in your own devilish imagination, an alternative explanation of the accumulated findings, then to devise a study where the alternatives lead to disparate predictions. Concentrating on plausible rivals is especially important.
>
> (p. 14)

Social theories and alternative methodologies can provide a useful source of information in clarifying and explaining not only the boundaries of *plausible* inference in the process of test development, but also in delimiting the boundaries of inference in the contexts of *actual* test use. Or, as Cronbach noted, *alternative rivals* illuminate tensions in the ecology of test development and use.

The game-changer: Messick's (1989) unified view of validity (Philosophical Conceits and the progressive matrix)

Messick clearly shared Cronbach's (1988) admonishment of those who would ignore or fail to seek evidence of the "unanticipated consequences of legitimate score interpretation and use" (Messick, 1998, p. 42). Messick acknowledged his "long-standing intellectual debt" (1989, p. 13) to Cronbach, and Cronbach's influence on his work. In a footnote at the bottom of the first page of his seminal treatise on validity, Messick (1989) mentions the feedback of many luminaries (e.g., William Angoff, Robert Guion, Warren Willingham) who provided input on multiple drafts of his manuscript, but he singles out Cronbach and Guion for their "thorough, sometimes humbling and often mind-stretching comments on the big issues as well as important details" (1989, p. 13). Since publication (over 30 years ago), Messick's definition of validity and his requirements for validation have arguably dominated discussion across communities concerned with testing and other assessment practices. As Fulcher (2021) noted, "recently proposed validity models are little more than a footnote to Messick" (p. 37). However, Messick's conceptualization of validity also remains at the centre of current debates (Cizek, 2012, 2020; Newton & Baird, 2016; Weideman, 2012). Core principles of Messick's (1989) comprehensive definition of validity are incorporated in the often quoted excerpt below:

> Validity is an integrated evaluative judgment of the degree to which empirical evidence and theoretical rationales support the *adequacy* and *appropriateness* of *inferences* and *actions* based on test scores or other modes of assessment ... validity is a matter of degree, not all or none. Furthermore, over time, the existing validity evidence becomes enhanced (or contravened) by new findings, and projections of potential social consequences of testing become transformed by evidence of actual consequences and by changing social conditions. Inevitably, then, validity is an evolving property and validation is a continuing process.
>
> (p. 13)

We will not dwell on a discussion of this definition. As noted above, such discussions have been a common and recurring feature of almost all publications on validity and validation since 1989. However, below is a summary of key points that are of particular relevance to this book.

Key features of Messick's (1989) definition of validity

- validation is a matter of judgment and degree based on accumulated evidence, which is theoretically informed, empirically supported, and value-laden;
- validity is a unitary concept, that is, of one kind, *construct validity*, which is supported by multiple lines of inquiry;
- inferences drawn from test scores or other assessment outcomes, resulting actions, and social consequences must all be taken into account in weighing validation evidence;
- validation is ongoing, and responsive to changing social conditions; it proceeds in relation to evolving constructs; and
- the extent to which we may draw inferences from assessment depends on a clear evidential understanding of the boundaries within which the inferences apply.

A section of Messick's (1989) treatise on validity, *Philosophical Conceits* (pp. 21–34), is of particular interest to a transdisciplinary program of validation research. In this section Messick argues for a complex, dynamic framework of inquiry in order to locate the boundaries of inference derived from assessment scores or outcomes. Drawing on Churchman's (1971) analysis of the work of five prominent philosophers (i.e., Leibnitz, Locke, Kant, Hegel, and Singer),[2] Messick (1989) examines the basic tenets of key inquiry systems in the history of science. Each of these five philosophers espoused a different theory of knowledge or epistemology – with differing worldviews and assumptions. In his discussion, Messick favoured a Singerian (1959) inquiry system, because it "starts with a set of other inquiring systems (Leibnizian, Lockean, Kantian, Hegelian) and applies any system recursively to another system, including itself" (Messick, 1989, p. 32). He argued that the Singerian approach would lead to methodological richness and avoid the "shortsightedness" (p. 33) of non-recursive reliance on a single system of inquiry.

Some (e.g., Cizek, 2020) have considered Messick's explication of and advocacy for a Singerian approach to validity inquiry as an impractical, unnecessary, and "embarrassing" (p. xiv) philosophical "excursion" (p. xiii), which has exacerbated the disconnect between theory and practice in validation research. Cizek blames Messick for this disconnect: "Validity theory and practice have never recovered" (Cizek, 2020, p. xiv). We disagree. We argue that Messick's endorsement of a Singerian approach is consistent with a transdisciplinary program of validation research, which opens up possibilities for "the critical enrichment and 'reciprocal refinement' of diverse perspectives" (Levine, cited in Camic & Joas, 2004). Camic and Joas (2004) argue for more active engagement with "truly alternative points of view", because engagement and dialogue lead to increasing recognitions and self-awareness about the "character and value" (p. 9) of our own points of view.

As noted above, although Messick's (1989) ideas continue to dominate discussions of validity, he provided only limited guidance on how to proceed. He illustrated his unified validity framework in what later came to be called a *progressive matrix*, which he stated was meant to sort out what he self-critically observed as the "untidiness" (Messick, 1989, p. 21) of his core ideas. However, Messick's (1980, 1988, 1989) early representations of the progressive matrix did not help clarify or crystallize his ideas. Later, tabular representations of the progressive matrix in, for example, Chapelle (2021, p. 10), Kunnan (1998, p. 2), or McNamara and Roever (2006, p. 13) have incorporated editorial changes that influence somewhat different interpretations of the matrix. Such changes suggest the confusion and at times conflicting understandings the matrix has prompted over the past 30 years (cf. Chapelle, 2021; Cizek, 2012, 2020; Kunnan, 1998; Markus, 1998; Moss, 1998, 2016; Popham, 1997).

Messick titled the progressive matrix "Facets of validity" and represented it as both a figure (1988, Figure 3.1, p. 42) and a table (1989, Table 2.1, p. 21). The matrix linked "sources of justification" to "functions or outcomes" (Messick, 1988) in validation practice, in order to arrive at an overall "appraisal" or "evaluative judgment" of the validity of inferences drawn from an assessment (p. 42). Messick used solid lines to separate the four central cells in the matrix. These solid lines of columns intersecting rows may have suggested distinctive differences between the four cells. It is interesting to examine how these core cells of the matrix were amended in some later adaptations (e.g., Chapelle,

2021; Kunnan, 1998) to reinforce Messick's (1989) extensive written descriptions of the matrix, which accompanied its representations. Messick explained that distinctions between the cells of the matrix were "fuzzy because they are not only interlinked but also overlapping" (p. 20). He (1989) reinforced the view that the *construct* is the unifying, overarching "whole of validity" (p. 21), which populates all of the cells in the matrix. He emphasized the *progressive* nature of the matrix "by having the contents of each cell include the contents of all previous cells" (Moss, 1998, p. 59). Messick (1989) explained,

> The validity of descriptive interpretation is based on construct-related evidence. The validity of decision-making uses is based on construct-related evidence as well, with the proviso that evidence be included bearing on the relevance and utility of the test for the specific decision. Thus, the validation of a descriptive interpretation versus a decision rule is viewed in this framework as being more hierarchic, or part-whole in nature than dichotomous.
>
> (p. 21)

Messick's own description of the progressive matrix reinforced the integration and embeddedness of the cells within a unified validity framework, as "hierarchic, or part-whole in nature" and not "dichotomous" (p. 21).

It is important to note that Messick conceptualized validity in broader terms than had traditionally been the case. He argued that validation must take into account not only plausible evidence arising from descriptive interpretations of assessment use, but also evidence arising from actual use. However, some (e.g., Cizek, 2020) have viewed Messick's requirements for differing sources of validation evidence, particularly evidence "bearing on an intended inference" which must be considered alongside "evidence regarding consequences of test use", as "incompatible" (p. 85). Cizek (2020) argues that distinctive differences in such sources of evidence preclude the possibility of arriving at an overall evaluative judgment in developing a validity argument.

Shortly before his death in 1998, Messick contributed to a special issue of the journal *Social Indicators Research*, which focused on *Validity Theory and the Methods Used in Validation* within the social and behavioural sciences. The special issue was introduced with a short obituary prepared as a tribute to Messick by the guest editor (Zumbo, 1998, p. vii). Messick had died only a few weeks before its publication.

The special issue is interesting for a number of reasons. First, it may include Messick's last words on the interpretation of his validity perspective. Second, it provides evidence of the dominance of Messick's perspective on validity from 1998 to today, across disciplinary communities, as six of the seven prominent contributors to the section on validity focus on Messick (the exception being the contribution from an economist).

Most of these contributors continue to actively engage in discussions of Messick and validity today (e.g., Keith Markus, Pamela Moss, Stephen Sireci, Bruno Zumbo). Of particular relevance to the present chapter is Markus's 1998 response to Messick (1989), wherein he interprets Messick's conceptualization of validity as an "incomplete synthesis" of the "tension between the evidential basis and the consequential basis of test interpretation and use" (p. 8). Markus asserts that "In order to complete the project of a unified theory of validity, there is a need to synthesize the evidential and consequential bases of test interpretation and use" (p. 31).

Messick's (1998) response to Markus's assertion is that such tension is to be expected as part of validation practice. He restates the view that validity arguments should be based on an ongoing evaluation of evidence arising from multiple sources. This evidence may be conflicting, may pose "a tension that must be carefully negotiated in the validation of test interpretation and use" (p. 38), but then the validity of inferences drawn from a test is a matter of degree. Messick asserts, *synthesis* is not the goal. The goal is to amass sufficient evidence of the construct – "the unifying force that makes validity coherent" (p. 39) – in order to warrant test inferences and use. In the process of validation, much is to be gained by fully considering alternative, and differing sources of evidence. As Lave (1996) noted, "differences offer multiple possibilities for interrogating social experience" (p. 28), by prompting self-reflection and awareness. This notion is central in Messick's advocacy of a Singerian inquiry system in validation research and central to a TR agenda as well (cf. Moss, 2018).

Messick (1998) also takes the opportunity in his response to Markus to argue against those who would reduce and simplify validation by simply ignoring or dismissing the consequences of test use. In his view, consequences must be considered, because they directly affect "the adequacy and appropriateness of interpretations and actions based on test scores" (p. 39). In the same year, Kunnan (1998) related a meta-review of validation studies in language assessment to Messick's progressive matrix framework. He concluded that "the list of studies in the Consequential Basis section compared to the list in the Evidential Basis section is smaller and more recent; it is here that the yawning gaps lie" (p. 6). Arguably, such gaps (cf. Kane, 2013a, 2013b) continue today, as does controversy over Messick's view of consequences and actions in test validation research (e.g., Borsboom, Cramer, Keivit, Scholten, & Franic, 2009; Cizek, 2020; Markus & Borsboom, 2013; Newton & Baird, 2016).

Before taking a closer look at current trends in discussions of validity, we consider below the dramatic shifts in research approaches that occurred in the decade after Messick's death. Messick's 1989 treatise on validity foretold these trends in his comprehensive discussion of:

1 validity as *inferences* drawn from a test or other assessment practice (rather than a property of the assessment itself);

2 the multiple sources of evidence required to support a validity argument (including the decisions, actions, and consequences of assessment use) as part of a unified validity framework;
3 the importance of alternative (rival) inquiry systems in validation processes;
4 the centrality of construct as the principal focus of all validity evidence;
5 the ongoing, evolutionary, and progressive character of validation;
6 the value-laden nature of theory and methodology in inquiry; and
7 the need for "multiple perspectives to offset the preemptiveness of value commitments" (p. 87).

Of particular importance to current considerations and trends in validation are Messick's (1989) endorsement of: 1) Toulmin's (1972) notion of argument and "rational bets" (p. 246), as a systematic and dynamic way forward; 2) Shapere's (1964) critique of Kuhn's (1962) notion of paradigms, their development and collapse; and 3) Lakatos's (1970) notion of a *research program* in validation inquiry – multiple studies, taking place over time, and throughout the life of a test and/or other assessment practices. All of these figure prominently in current discussions of validity and validation practices (cf. Addey et al., 2020; Chapelle, 2021).

Revolution and evolution: validation in turbulent times

Messick (1989) wrote and published his treatise on validity at the height of intense (and often acerbic) debate, raging within the research communities of the day, and generally known as a period of the *paradigm wars*.

These so-called 'wars' were rooted in

> contrasting epistemological and ontological positions that characterize quantitative and qualitative research and their various synonyms. At the level of epistemology, there is the issue of desirability of a natural scientific programme for social research, as against one that eschews scientific pretensions and the search for general laws and instead emphasizes humans as engaged in constant interpretation of their environments within specific contexts. This contrast is one that is frequently drawn up in terms of a battle between positivist philosophical principles and interpretivist ones.[3]
>
> (Bryman, 2008, p. 2)

Such *battle lines* were drawn by advocates who espoused staunch, *paradigmatic* (Kuhn, 1962, 1970) positions (e.g., Guba & Lincoln, 1989), metaphorically consistent with Kuhn's (1970) notion of *scientific revolutions*. Kuhn introduced the idea of paradigms as "universally recognized scientific achievements that for a time provide model problems and solutions to a community of practitioners" (p. viii). He argued that a new paradigm promises "success" (p. 23) in addressing problems of interest to the community. He explained that at the outset such a paradigm is largely "incomplete" (p. 24). However, through scientific endeavour it is "discoverable" (p. 23) and subject to "further articulation and specification under new or more stringent conditions" (p. 24). The process of articulation, specification, and discovery gives rise to "particular coherent traditions of scientific research", or what Kuhn referred to as "normal science" (p. 24). However, a "crisis" occurs when scientists fail through *normal science* to solve a problem; that is, when they are "confronted with anomaly [and] … the proliferation of competing articulations" (pp. 90–91). In the face of such "discontent" (p. 90) and the "growing sense … that an existing paradigm has ceased to function adequately" (p. 92), a *scientific revolution* ultimately occurs, "in which an older paradigm is replaced in whole or in part by an incompatible new one" (p. 92). Kuhn's interpretation of dramatic paradigmatic change in scientific development was exerting broad influence when Messick was writing his seminal chapter on validity.

Consistent with Kuhn's allusions to crisis and revolution, the tenor and rhetoric of the paradigm wars contributed to a hardening of dichotomous, oppositional positions. Such positions, imbued with sets of values, beliefs, norms, assumptions, and received procedures for conducting and interpreting research, were associated with accepted and respected practices of different disciplinary communities. As noted above by Bryman, qualitative and quantitative research methodologies and methods were linked directly to divergent, dualistic, and incommensurable theoretical positions (e.g., positivist versus interpretivist or constructivist worldviews).[3] This led to what was known as the *incompatibility thesis*, namely, "that it was inappropriate to mix … [qualitative and quantitative] methods due to fundamental differences in the *paradigms* (e.g., *positivism, constructivism*) underlying those methods" (Teddlie & Tashakkori, 2010, p. 336).

Greene and Caracelli (1997) explained that during this period, allegiance to a paradigm was linked to "a particular orientation to social inquiry, including what questions to ask, what methods to use, what knowledge claims to strive for, and who defines high-quality work" (p. 6). Rigid paradigmatic views discounted the possibility of appropriating or learning from alternative inquiry systems and methods. Such views were informed by and linked to distinct differences in *ontology* (what is deemed to exist), *epistemology* (the nature of knowledge; its definition; conceptual stances), *methodology* (principles and procedures for inquiry; research approaches), and *axiology* (what is valued as ethical and useful). Further, disciplinary communities directly and indirectly exercised power in controlling social inquiry. As Oakley (1999) explained:

> We pay attention to what other social scientists are doing, to fashions in both methodology and topic – the things it is considered proper for social scientists to study; we are affected by research funding

> and publishing opportunities, by the material resources available to support our work, by intraprofessional rivalries and difference, and by politics – both in its commonly understood sense and as applied to power relations between academics and those who take part in research. Apart from what we do, there is the whole issue of how others construct our work. And this is only some of what goes on. In short, it is a very *complicated business*.
>
> (p. 247) [Emphasis added]

In the late 1980s and early 1990s this "complicated business" led to the fractious and divisive debates of the paradigm wars, which centred on the use of quantitative or qualitative research methods – and hinged on arguments regarding the value of these differing research traditions (see the notion of *sovereign territories* in Becher & Trowler, 2001). Proponents of one or the other tradition recruited members who often exhibited fierce allegiance to their school of thought and actively challenged the merits of those with whom they did not agree. Bryman and Teevan (2005) point out that because the notions of validity and reliability originated within assessment-centred communities (i.e., educational measurement, psychometrics) that other communities, who were aligned with opposing traditions of research, rejected their use. For example, Lincoln and Guba (1985) argued for *trustworthiness* as a more appropriate concept, which encompassed credibility, transferability, dependability, and confirmability – each of which had a parallel in measurement and psychometric conceptualizations of validity and reliability (Bryman & Teevan, 2005, p. 27).

It is to his credit, that in the midst of the paradigm wars, as noted above, Messick (1989) aggressively recommended the application of multiple inquiry systems as part of a disciplined, recursive, and self-reflective validation process. He argued that "the recognition and systematic application of multiple perspectives is beneficial in a variety of ways, because it tends to broaden the range of values, criteria, and standards deemed worthy of consideration" (p. 87). In accordance with the contributions of Lakatos (1970) and Shapere (1964), he asserted that the process of scientific development was better characterized as gradual and evolutionary, rather than revolutionary and cataclysmic.

In the "positivistic climate" (Messick, 1989, p. 22) of the day, validation research typically conformed to a *paradigm package* (Tashakkori & Teddlie, 2010), which linked individual, cognitive worldviews to the quantitative research tradition. Given the dominance of this view, Messick's 1989 position on validity is all the more remarkable. After all, the height of the paradigm wars, according to Creswell and Plano Clark (2011), was in 1994, "with vocal advocates on both sides arguing their points at the American Evaluation Association meeting (Reichardt & Rallis, 1994)" (p. 25). In contrast, during this time, Messick argued for multiple inquiry systems, because of the rich explanatory potential they provided. He asserted that philosophies and methodologies evolve, "that validity conceptions are not uniquely tied to any particular philosophical position but rather, are congenial with aspects of multiple positions" (Messick, 1989, p. 30). In 1989 he foreshadowed the diminution of the paradigm wars; however, it would be another ten years before the drama would lessen and the debate become more amicable.

Staunchly ideological worldviews led to assertions that "research methods are permanently rooted in epistemological and ontological commitments" (Bryman & Teevan, 2005, p. 322). However, over time such views were increasingly disputed (cf. Rossman & Wilson, 1985). Teddlie and Tashakkori (2010) critiqued proponents of such rigid, ideologically driven positions as "purists" (p. 13) and rejected the *linkage* that was made between "assumptions (e.g., epistemology, ontology) and methodological traditions" (p. 13). The discussion of mixed methods research and more *pragmatic*[4] approaches to the use of different methodologies became more compelling (cf. Biesta, 2010; Greene & Caracelli, 1997; Morgan, 2007; Niglas, 2010; Stone & Zumbo, 2016). For example, Teddlie and Tashakkori (2010) advocated for the pragmatic, open, and flexible use of different methodologies, as this would allow researchers "to understand more fully, to generate deeper and broader insights, [and] to develop important knowledge claims that respect a wider range of interests and perspectives" (p. 6). Biesta (2010) viewed pragmatism not as a "philosophical position among others", but rather as a *conceptual stance* which positioned a research community to "acquire knowledge ... through the combination of action and reflection". He argued that pragmatic approaches gave researchers access to "a set of philosophical tools that can be used to address problems" (p. 97).

Purist definitions of a paradigm as an exclusive worldview linked explicitly to a methodological tradition was a concept described by Biesta (2010) as "unhelpful" (p. 98) and by Morgan (2007) as "exhausted" (p. 55). The advent of mixed methods approaches in research redirected the focus away from dichotomous, 'either-or' positions linked to specific methodological traditions (i.e., qualitative or quantitative), and advanced a more holistic approach, consistent with the concept of philosophical continua, characterized by multiple schools of thought and "a multidimensional model of research methodology" (Niglas, 2010, p. 224).

Arguably, Morgan (2007) provided one of the most detailed and thoughtful explanations of a *pragmatic approach* in social and behavioural research. At a time when mixed methods research was emerging as a productive and promising alternative, Morgan focused on methodology itself "as an area that connects issues at the abstract level of epistemology and the mechanical level of actual methods" (p. 68). Morgan moved beyond the traditional dualistic identification of two types of inferences which had been the focus of vitriolic debates during the paradigm wars, namely:

1 inductive inferences, linked to qualitative research approaches, which draw reasoned *descriptive* conclusions based on evidence from

observation, experience, analysis and synthesis of patterns emerging from data, *bottom-up*); and

2 deductive inferences, linked to quantitative approaches, which draw reasoned *explanatory* conclusions based on evidence arising from experimentation or logic that supports an *a priori, top-down* assumption or hypothesis).

Consistent with a pragmatic approach, Morgan identified other types of inferences, such as:

- *abductive inference,* or *explanatory* conclusions drawn from *redescription* or *recontextualization* (Danermark, Ekström, Jakobsen, & Karlsson, 2002);
- *intersubjectivity*, as opposed to the dualistic notions of subjectivity versus objectivity; and
- *transferability*, as opposed to the dualistic notions of context-specific/local versus generalizable/global.

These pragmatic concepts "supersede[d]" the traditional methodological "dichotomies" (Teddlie & Tashakkori, 2010 p. 14) and opened up new possibilities for expanding *philosophical breadth* (Biesta, 2010). Morgan placed "methodology at the centre of his pragmatic approach" (Teddlie & Tashakkori, 2010, p. 14) precisely because it linked theory (i.e., schools of thought and conceptual stances) with the actual methods used by researchers. Pragmatic approaches, like the one proposed by Morgan (2007), are of key importance in transdisciplinary programs of validation research.

Over the years, meta-reviews have documented evolutionary trends in research practices by classifying and counting the number of qualitative, quantitative, or mixed methods approaches reported in empirical studies and published over time in prominent, peer-reviewed journals. Such meta-reviews are useful sources of evidence with regard to changes over time. In the section which follows below, evidence from meta-reviews of changing methodological approaches is summarized. However, as discussed above, and as Moss and Haertel (2016), have pointed out, "while the terms *qualitative* and *quantitative* can be useful for characterizing 'methods', they underrepresent the rich range of methodologies ... glossing over [their] key differences and unique affordances" (p. 127). Important vestiges of the paradigm wars remain today as evidenced by the *applicability gaps* in language assessment validation research, and further discussed in Chapter 3.

The methodological turn: expanding philosophical breadth (1990–2010)

In 1997, Greene and Caracelli heralded "an era of methodological pluralism" (p. 5) and the advent of mixed methods in social science research.

They vigorously denounced the ideology-driven thinking of purists, who rigidly linked quantitative and qualitative research to fixed, dichotomous philosophical stances. However, it is clear from a review of the literature that qualitative research was neither well understood nor equally valued by researchers within disciplinary communities that engaged in testing and other assessment practices (e.g., psychology, educational measurement, psychometrics). For example, Wertz (2011) reports that, before the 1980s, a review of psychological databases using the search term *qualitative research* "yielded no hits" (Wertz et al., 2011, p. 76). Only terms containing phenomenology were present.

Wertz et al. (2011) also noted that by the 1990s a shift was slowly taking place as qualitative research approaches were attracting more attention. It may be that the vociferous debates of the paradigm wars clarified the rigorous, if ideological, traditions of qualitative research which were forcefully articulated by its proponents (e.g., Lincoln & Guba, 1985). Wertz (2011) examined the history of qualitative research traditions in other social science disciplines such as anthropology and sociology, and identified what he referred to as a "disciplinary revolution" (p. 83) from the 1970s to the 1990s. This period was marked by the growth of "various contextually sensitive, reflexive, self critical methods"[5] (p. 83). However, Wertz (2011) also documented the resistance of psychology to such methods. At the time of Greene and Caracelli's (1997) announcement, Krahn, Holn, and Kime (1995) reported that only 30 qualitative research articles were published in mainstream psychology journals from 1993 to 1997. However, by the late 1990s, like "its sister social sciences that [had] engendered a pluralization of research methods, psychology ... followed suit by developing and incorporating qualitative methods that allow[ed] greater expression on the part of research participants and a more responsive relationship with them in the practice of research" (Wertz, 2011, p. 101).

From the mid-1990s, an increasing number of meta-reviews of methodologies began to appear. For example, in applied linguistics, Lazaraton (e.g., 1995, 2005) carried out a number of such reviews. In 1995 she noted that although there was evidence of a "growing interest" (p. 456) in qualitative methods, quantitative research continued to dominate peer-reviewed publications. She reported on confusion over what qualitative research was, and noted that there were "no qualitative research methods texts written for and by applied linguists" (p. 458).

Similar trends were reported by Richards (2009), who examined research articles in 15 journals related to language teaching from 1998 to 2007. He noted, "even allowing for some latitude in what counts as qualitative research" (p. 151), fewer than 18 per cent of the research articles published in this 9-year period used qualitative methods. Although he observed that not all of the other articles were quantitative, the small percentage of qualitative research studies did not "suggest a narrowing of the gap between qualitative and quantitative studies" (p. 151). He concluded that although his review did not reveal any evidence of a dramatic increase in qualitative research publications, there was an important trend toward methodological pluralism. He concluded that "the most significant movement to emerge from QR [qualitative research] generally is a shift towards mixed methods research" (p. 167). He pointed out that the *Journal of Mixed Methods Research* was launched in 2007, signalling the increased importance of mixed methods approaches, which he predicted would be ever more prominent in future. His prediction was accurate (e.g., Cheng & Fox, 2013; Hashemi & Babaii, 2013; Turner, 2014).

The trend toward mixed methods research was important in terms of our consideration of context and the role that social theories can play in informing and accounting for findings in validation studies. As discussed in the opening pages of this chapter, Messick (1989) noted that the *rhetorical art* of validation argument required the *balancing* of different types of evidence for "Different kinds of inferences" (p. 15) (cf. Morgan, 2007). Lazaraton and Taylor (2007) also addressed the issue of *balance* in their support for the increased use of qualitative methods in test development and validation. They pointed out that "it has become increasingly apparent that the established psychometric methods for test validation are effective, but limited, and other methods are required for us to gain a fuller understanding of the language tests we use" (p. 126). Chapelle (2021) provides a recent, useful example of a *balanced* approach to the collection of different kinds of evidence marshalled in support of *different kinds of inferences* as part of a validity argument (see Chapelle, 2021, p. 114, p. 115, Table 7.2) further discussed below.

Current trends in validation (2011–2021)

In 2011, Wertz et al. published a seminal text which documented "the qualitative revolution" (p. 77) across many social science disciplines (e.g., anthropology, sociology, education). However, the revolution was far less evident in psychology. They note that although over 20 previous years the "qualitative movement" had gained "widespread attention" (p. 76), there remained ongoing "resistance" (p. 84) to qualitative approaches in psychology, educational measurement, psychometrics, and other disciplinary communities engaged in the validation of tests and other assessment practices. This resistance continues to some extent today (e.g., Cizek, 2020; Lissitz & Samuelsen, 2007).

A colleague who read a draft version of this chapter suggested that this was one of adverse effects of "neglecting transdisciplinarity". He suggested that this neglect can be traced in part to how students are trained: "Traditionally, psychometricians are rarely trained in qualitative approaches or are not directed/drawn/advised to expand their repertoire of data analysis and include QUAL[qualitative] inquiry. This is a systemic issue rooted in assessment-centred communities" (Arias, personal communication, April 2021). His observation was confirmed by a senior psychology professor, who acknowledged with some concern that qualitative approaches to research would no longer be taught to undergraduates in her large degree program. She explained that the professor who had previously offered courses in qualitative approaches to research was retiring, and her fellow faculty members did not see *any need* to continue to offer such qualitative courses. This appears to be a trend in many undergraduate psychology programs and may suggest ongoing disciplinary resistance to qualitative and mixed methods research within psychology.

As discussed above (e.g., Lazaraton & Taylor, 2007), qualitative approaches provide a critical empirical means of validation in contexts of use. They serve to highlight the actions and consequences of tests in local situations that define the limits or boundaries of inference (cf. Cronbach, 1988; Messick, 1988, 1989). Validation arguments focused solely on technical evidence of test quality tend to rely on quantitative, statistical approaches alone: a focus that is "internal to the test itself" (McNamara, Knoch, & Fan, 2019, p. 21). As McNamara et al. point out, such a focus may support arguments for *fairness,* but would not necessarily support arguments for *justice*. Examining the consequences of test use requires considerations of actions, decisions, or consequences of tests – of impact "on the lives of individuals and the societies in which they live" (McNamara et al., 2019, p. 21). Justice is best served through qualitative approaches, "through case studies, ethnographies, discourse analysis, policy and document analysis, and other qualitative methods" (p. 21). Resistance to qualitative methods in those disciplines (e.g., psychology, educational measurement) which most frequently engage in validation research has therefore been an important limitation.

Although Wertz (2011) documented resistance in psychology, there was evidence of increasing interest in validation within the discipline, along with a dramatic increase in published research studies on *construct validity* as the primary focus of validation evidence. This increased interest in validation was documented by Zumbo and Chan's (2014) meta-review of validation practices evidenced by abstracts published in peer-reviewed journals across a sample drawn from a range of social science disciplines (e.g., psychology, health, education) over a 50-year period (from 1960 to 2010). Using the PsychInfo database and the search terms *validity*, *validation*, *psychometric*, *measurement*, *assessment*, or *test*, they identified only 300 publications from 1961 to 1965 that focused on validity/ validation, whereas from 2006 to 2010 they identified over 10,000. They acknowledge that there had also been a dramatic increase in the number of journals and researchers during this 50-year period, which partially accounts for these remarkable findings; however, the results are still startling. They also found similar trends in validation studies published in other disciplines – although the greatest increases were in education and psychology.

Messick would no doubt be pleased with Zumbo and Chan's findings, as he would with the creation of the Messick Chair in Test Validity (ETS, 2008), instituted in honour of his work on validity and validation practices and occupied by Michael Kane since 2009. Kane's contributions have been paramount in recent discussions of validation, focusing as they have on how to undertake validation research within Messick's complex validity framework. As noted earlier, Kane drew on the thread in Messick's 1989 treatise, which singled out Toulmin's (1972) notion of the "rational bet" (p. 246), crudely defined here as a plausible conjecture of the consequences of an interpretation (and rival interpretations) of a test score, which is subject to evidence that either supports or refutes the interpretation(s). (See Kane, 2013b, pp. 11–12, for his explanation of Toulmin's model of argument). This is at the core of argument-based validation approaches (see also Chapelle, 2021; Mislevy, 2009). In Chapter 3, we further examine Kane's application of Toulmin's model with the benefit of Miller's (1994b) socio-theoretical perspective to illustrate the additive potential of some social theories. (See also Addey et al., 2020).

Kane's (2013b) notion of the interpretation/use argument (IUA) is defined as "all of the claims based on the test scores (i.e., the network of inferences and assumptions inherent in the[ir] proposed interpretation and use)" (p. 2). His IUA approach provided a hands-on practical application of Messick's framework in relating test performance to inferences, by requiring testers to spell out the interpretive/use claims they are making, and to collect evidence through research which either supports or refutes those claims.

Perhaps the most thorough example of an IUA approach is provided by Chapelle (2021), who extends Kane's (2006, 2013a, 2013b) contributions by detailing each step of an IUA process. She explains the *whats*, *hows*, and *whys* of the IUA approach, with systematic elaboration and examples. This followed on her earlier work in Chapelle, Enright, and Jamieson (2008), which described the validity argument for the development of the then new Test of English as a Foreign Language (TOEFL) internet-based test (iBT). However, whereas Chapelle et al., 2008 focused on a *plausible* interpretation of scores in the process of test development, in 2021 Chapelle addresses the issue Kane (2013b) acknowledged in considerations of his own work, namely, that interpretive arguments "may give too much weight to interpretations and not enough to uses" (p. 2). This issue is evident in Chapelle et al. (2008), who explain that the validity argument they are detailing relates to the first stage of test design and development only. They use the evidence accumulated in the process of test development to argue that the pre-operational TOEFL iBT warrants use. The interpretive argument regarding actual use is left to other researchers and other communities. They explain their position in the final chapter of their book: "An argument assumes an audience, and like the rest of the volume, this chapter is written primarily for the audience consisting of professionals in applied linguistics and measurement, who in turn will communicate it to other test users" (p. 119). Unfortunately, communication across *applicability gaps* that exist between language-centred, assessment-centred, and other communities is not particularly effective.

Ultimately, Chapelle et al. (2008) argued that the plausible inferences supported by evidence collected during the test development process would be validated in relation to data arising when the test was operational. On the one hand, we have a narrative of test design and development that spells out the types of evidence required to build a credible, plausible, design-validity argument; on the other hand, we have only half of the validity argument, because all of the evidence that is reported relates to a pre-operational test. In 2008, we were left without establishing the limits within which plausible inferences may hold in relation to actual use. In other words, we had no evidence of the consequences and actions of the test in use, and no understanding of the "exceptions [which] indicate conditions under which an otherwise sound inference may fail" (Toulmin cited in Kane, 2013b, p. 12).

Inadvertently, the approach played into the arguments of those who would narrow the scope of validation to the test itself (e.g., technical quality, content representativeness, reliability) (see Lissitz & Samuelsen, 2007) – a position which Kane (2008) rejected: "I am in favor of evaluating test-score interpretations and uses as they exist in context and in their full complexity" (p. 81). Later, Kane (2013b) reasserted that he would give "interpretations and uses equal billing" (p. 2). Further, he linked his advocacy for a broader definition of validity and validation practices – including those in actual contexts of use – to the breadth of interpretation. In other words, limiting validation to the pre-operational or plausible also limits actual interpretation and use of test scores.

In keeping with Kane's (2013b) concerns and advice, Chapelle (2021) subsequently highlighted the need for validation to include evidence that "(1) test scores are useful for certain decisions, and (2) their use results in overall positive consequences for test users and for society" (p. 38). Given these requirements for validation, she provides a comprehensive overview of the validation process, guided by specific questions, actions, and evidence (see Chapelle, 2021, Figure 7.3, p. 116), which allows the validator to build an IUA-based validity argument for inferences regarding "utilization" and "consequence implications" (p. 38). What is particularly notable is Chapelle's discussion of what she refers to as the *sociocultural milieu* of test development and use (which she traces back, as we have done in this chapter, to major contributors to conceptions of validity; see Chapelle, 2021, Chapter 7, pp. 102–120). Further to Cronbach (1988), Kane (2013b, 2016), and Messick (1989), Chapelle cites Swales' (1990) notion of "sociorhetorical communities that form in order to work towards sets of common goals" (p. 9) as her source for socio-theoretical conceptions of the milieu or context of assessment practices.

She explains (as Swales, 1988, 1990 had done) how such communities maintain and derive coherence through the use of discourse – which she defines as the spoken and written language that is understood and used by such a community to address and achieve its goals. Chapelle points out that arguments for validity are *refined* over time as the data drawn from assessment use clarify the meaningfulness of inferences in relation to who is being assessed and in what circumstances.

In 2014, Zumbo and Chan suggested there was a consensus on validation, summarizing some of the "core perspectives on validity seen in the current literature ... [which] are meant to guide the practice of validation" (p. 5). They list the following practices, amongst others: argument-based validation approaches (e.g., Cronbach, 1988; Kane, 2013b); theoretically informed conceptualizations of validity (Cronbach and Meehl, 1955; Cronbach, 1988); the progressive matrix as a framework to guide validation practices; and the centrality of construct in considerations of validity (Messick, 1989). Chapelle (2021) also emphasizes *consensus* views of validity and validation, and draws attention to the supporting role played by the *Standards* (e.g., AERA et al., 1999, 2014). She points out that the *Standards* have articulated the consensus view of members of professional communities and associations who have been most directly concerned with validity and validation (the communities we have referred to as assessment-centred). She notes that the current *Standards* (2014) place renewed emphasis on use and consequences in their definition of validity (still focused on tests – which are only one mode of assessment) as "the degree to which evidence and theory support the interpretation of test scores for proposed uses" (AERA et al., 2014, p. 1). Evidence drawn from test use and consequences is highlighted as one of five core validation sources (i.e., along with logical rationales/expert judgment of test content; test takers' response processes; statistical testing of the internal structure of the response data; and relationships to other variables – including convergent and discriminate evidence).

Chapelle (2021) argues that although there have always been discussions and debates amongst communities which are concerned with validity and validation, Messick's influence is evident in the emphasis placed on consequences, which is reinforced in both her own work and in Kane's (2016), as well as that of other scholars (e.g., Lenz & Wester, 2017; Shepard, 2016). As Shepard (2016) points out, the evolving definitions of validity and validation in the *Standards* (e.g., 1999, 2014) have acted as a "touchstone" (p. 268) over the years, against which those who argue with it, must nonetheless begin by acknowledging it. Like Chapelle (2021), Shepard (2016) states that the *Standards* provide *the* consensus definition of validity and validation practices:

> A century of disagreement about validity does not mean that there has not been substantial progress. This consensus definition brings

> together interpretations and use so that it is one idea, not a sequence of steps. Just as test design is framed by a particular context of use, so too must validation research focus on the adequacy of tests for specific purposes.
>
> (p. 268)

However, there is also evidence to suggest that tension and debate has increasingly begun to characterize current scholarly considerations of validity and validation practices (e.g., Cizek, 2020; Lissitz & Samuelsen, 2007; Newton & Baird, 2016; Newton & Shaw, 2014). For example, while Newton and Shaw (2014) discuss the view that a consensus exists, they also identify critical sources of disagreement such as:

1 the *scope* of validity studies, with disagreement centring on Messick's (e.g., 1988, 1989) requirement for consideration of the decisions, actions and consequences of the inferences drawn from test scores and performances; and
2 the *focus* of validity studies, that is, "what validity should apply to" (p. 180).

These alternative views are discussed below.

Disagreements over consequences and context: scope and focus in validation research

In 2016, Newton and Baird pointed out in an editorial framing a special issue on validity that it is not only "clear that the controversy over consequences still looms largest" (p. 174), but also evident that validity scholars within psychology and educational measurement cannot even agree on a common definition for validity. Newton and Baird (2016) surmised that "the crux of the debate is whether the meaning of the word *validity* should extend beyond plausibility to appropriateness; or indeed, whether it should extend beyond truth to plausibility" (p. 174). *Truth*, in this instance, refers to the technical quality of a test or other assessment practice (see also *fairness*, discussed in Chapter 4). Proponents of a return to technical quality alone (e.g., Borsboom et al., 2009; Cizek, 2020; Markus & Borsboom, 2013) in test validation reject *worth* (e.g., the consequences, ethics, impact of assessment use; also discussed in Chapter 4) as a proper focus of validation.

Within the language assessment community in scholarship that was nonetheless aligned with assessment-centred perspectives, McNamara et al. (2019) took a definitive position. While underscoring the critical role of test quality as an issue of *fairness* in arguments for validity, they emphasized the importance of consequences and test impact as an issue of *justice* (i.e., worth). They maintained that the concepts of fairness and justice go hand in hand in any consideration of validity:

> the question of whether or not the use of a test is just is not exhausted by simply investigating and improving test quality, important as that is. In addition to the question of the capacity of the test to generate information about individual candidates that is useful for making decisions about them, there is the broader question of the use of tests for decision-making purposes in the first place.
>
> (p. 6)

As noted above, McNamara et al. (2019) explained that considerations of justice are best "revealed through ... qualitative methods" (p. 21), which are typically informed by socio-theoretical schools of thought and conceptual stances.

McNamara et al. (2019), Messick (1989), and the *Standards* (AERA et al., 2014) have asserted that evidence of fairness alone does not adequately address issues of justice. Further, evidence of one is incomplete without evidence of the other. Validation researchers can choose from the extensive array of methods informed by differing philosophical and methodological possibilities (cf. Biesta, 2010), but evidence of both *fairness* and *justice* is required for validity arguments. However, this view would be rejected by those who have suggested that investigations of assessment use relate to broader questions of "utility" not validity (see Geisinger, cited in Newton & Baird, 2016, p. 175). They have argued that validity should be more narrowly defined, as a "very basic concept", which was "correctly formulated" as it was originally explained: "a test is valid if it measures what it purports to measure" (Kelley, cited in Borsboom, Mellenbergh, & van Heerden, 2004, p. 106). From this point of view, by increasing the psychometric or technical quality of assessment (i.e., tests), test developers and validators directly increase the validity of inferences drawn from test performance, regardless of contexts of use. Further, proponents of this view maintain that such evidence should be the primary (if not sole) obligation of test developers and test validation researchers. They contend that informed by cognitive theories and guided by an abiding focus on underlying traits of an individual, "the crucial ingredient of validity involves the causal effect of an attribute on the test scores ... [which] implies that the locus of evidence for validity lies in the processes that convey this effect" (Borsboom et al., 2004, p. 1062). They explain that

> Psychometric techniques and models have great potential for improving measurement practice ... but only if they are driven by a substantive theory of response processes. We think that, with such theory in hand, the problem of validity will turn out to be less difficult than is commonly thought.
>
> (p. 1070)

Whether Borsboom, Mellenbergh, and van Heerden (2004) are correct in their assertion is an unresolved matter open to research, discussion, and dialogue. Their conceptualization of response processes is limited by its sole reliance on cognitive theories and quantitative inquiry systems; so much more, we argue, could be learned if social theories and an array of alternative inquiry systems were engaged as well – particularly with regard to the role of context in defining the *boundaries of inference* that are meaningful, useful, and appropriate (Messick, 1989) in contexts of assessment use.

Although marked by differing and sometimes conflicting perspectives, there is consensus that considerations of fairness are an essential part of test validation. Borsboom and Markus (2013) advise us not to ignore *truth* in the quest to amass evidence. However, truths that arise from alternative theoretical frameworks, their concomitant methodologies, and evidence of *worth* in considerations of the consequences of assessment use should neither be ignored.

Both Cronbach (1988) and Messick (1988), citing the work of Frederiksen (1984), highlighted the need for test developers to draw validation evidence not solely on the basis of *truth* (technical quality) but also on the basis of *worth* (the consequences of tests in use). For example, they noted that although multiple-choice test formats used to measure educational achievement have excellent reliability, they also have been shown to lead to narrowed curriculum and "to increased emphasis on memory and analysis in teaching and learning at the expense of divergent production and synthesis" (Cronbach, 1988, p. 40). The most recent *Standards* (AERA et al., 2014) have also emphasized the importance of investigations of assessment use in validation research. Assessment users, policy and decision makers, have an ethical responsibility to monitor and investigate the consequences of assessment use, but so, too, do assessment professionals (e.g., test developers, validators). Cronbach (1988) referred to this as an *obligation.*

As Gafni (2016) argued, and as Newton and Baird (2016) asserted, "validation practice is often far from adequate and sometimes simply not conducted at all" (p. 176). Still, conscientious assessors/testers have followed the advice of Cronbach (1988), Messick (1989), and others to engage in strong programs of validation research throughout the life of a test or other mode of assessment, in order to provide ongoing evidence of usefulness.

In Chapter 4 we discuss this issue again in relation to the contributions of language assessment research to considerations of validity and validation. Most of this research has been aligned with the theories and practices of assessment-centred communities. However, we highlight the emergent social thread in this research which is best positioned to address complex issues of context and consequences in testing and other assessment practices.

Newton and Shaw (2014) suggest there is a continuum of views on validity. On the one hand there is the ultra-conservative position, which takes a narrow perspective on validation and evokes validity positions reminiscent of the 1950s (e.g., Borsboom, 2005; Borsboom et al., 2009; Markus & Borsboom, 2013). The emphasis at this conservative end of the continuum is on the technical excellence of tests. In other words, the priority is on measurement quality, which is rooted in causality. At the other end of the continuum is the liberal perspective (e.g., Moss, 1998, 2016), which "fully embraces the idea that it is insufficient, if not irresponsible, to evaluate tests from a purely scientific or technical perspective" (Newton & Shaw, 2016, p. 181). There is no resolution to these dualistic perspectives proposed by Newton and Shaw (2014). Later Newton and Baird (2016) highlight ongoing tensions between proponents of these differing perspectives in discussions and debates over validity – its definition, its role, and the evidence one should collect as part of a process of validation. Messick (1988) would no doubt appreciate this debate. The framing quote at the beginning of this chapter summarized his position: "the justification and defense of measurement and its validity is and may always be a rhetorical art" (p. 43). Messick's focus was on inferences drawn from the social practices of assessment, and the quality of that evidence collected in support of differing inferences. There is little doubt that he would continue to argue for the necessity of incorporating evidence of decisions, actions, and consequences drawn from assessment use. He viewed such evidence as central in arguments for validity, and consistently articulated this position throughout his professional life. Decisions, actions, and consequences are only evident in contexts of actual assessment use.

So, what is the way forward?

Renewed arguments for disciplinarity: addressing the "regrettable consequences" (Cizek, 2020, p. xiv) of Messick's writings

As history attests, and as summarized above, it is not surprising to find evidence of divergent directions and ongoing debates with regard to validity and validation practices. There continue to be articulate arguments against Messick's (1989) unified validity framework and the requirement for evidence of consequences of test use in validation research. For example, similar to Borsboom et al. (2004), Cizek (2020) has proposed an *integrated approach*, which would avoid what he viewed as the "incompatibility of combining evidence regarding test score meaning and test score use into a single concept" (p. xii). Cizek (2020) has provided a detailed roadmap for accumulating evidence to support the *intended* meaning of test scores and justification for their *intended* uses. He focused on what he referred to as a comprehensive approach to *defensible testing*. He finds that Messick's (1989) conceptualization of validity was *flawed*. For example, 1) it was too "abstruse" and plagued by "tortured . . . philosophical ruminations" (p. xiii) (a reference to Messick's (1989) *Philosophical Conceits* (pp. 21–22); 2) it lacked hands-on practical procedures or guidelines for validation practice, and thereby led to "anemic validation efforts" (p. xii); and 3) it created the "impossible demand" (p. xiii) for evidence of both score meaning and score use.

However, Cizek emphasized that the most substantive "flaw" in Messick's unified validity framework was that "all sources of evidence ... must be *synthesized* and evaluated as a whole" (p. xiii, emphasis added). As discussed above, over two decades ago, Markus (1998), like Cizek (2020), also highlighted *synthesis* as an issue in Messick's theory. Unlike Cizek, however, Markus focused on what he considered was the "core of Messick's theory" (p. 8): the *Philosophical Conceits*. Further, Messick (1998) was personally able to respond to Markus's concerns regarding synthesis. Messick noted, "a complete synthesis [of evidence] is unlikely" (p. 38); rather, he pointed out, "the relation between the evidential and consequential bases of validity [would remain] ... a tension that must be carefully negotiated in the validation of test interpretation and use" (p. 38). Messick (1998) warned against attempts to "resolve the tension ... by simply eliminating consequence as a legitimate aspect of validity" (p. 39). Rather, as he explained in his so-called "ruminations" (Cizek, 2020, p. xiii) in the *Philosophical Conceits*, a Singerian approach would recognize "the potential value of recursively applying the alternative perspectives of multiple inquiry systems" (p. 38) in validation practices. The interaction of multiple inquiry systems would illuminate "the value bases of scientific models" and increase access to "convergent and discriminant arguments" (p. 36). Such thinking is at the core of transdisciplinarity (cf. Moss, 2018), which extends beyond scientific models to those in social sciences, and to other extra-disciplinary communities and sectors (e.g., government, business, medicine) (Lawrence, 2010).

Messick (1998) reinforced "the superordinate role of construct validity ... as the unifying force" (p. 39) in validation arguments. He noted that validation research should accumulate evidence of differing kinds. Such evidence might be complementary or not. In the end, all evidence would be weighed in arriving at a judgment of its adequacy in supporting an assessment practice. As Messick (1989) explained, arguments for validity are never absolute: "To validate an interpretive inference is to ascertain the degree to which multiple lines of evidence are consonant with the inferences, while establishing that alternative inferences are less well supported" (Messick, 1989, p. 13).

As Cizek (2020) pointed out, his intended, general audience is disciplinary: the *assessment-centred community*, as he defined it, "psychometricians, psychologists, survey methodologists, graduate students or other testing [professionals]" (p. xv); and specifically, hands-on validation practitioners, who view "consequences as merely a tangential aspect" (p. xiv) of validation practice. Over the years, many in the assessment community (e.g., Borsboom, et al., 2004; Popham, 1997) have been frustrated by Messick's theory and its implications for traditional (disciplinary) psychometric and measurement practices. Cizek proposes an *integrated approach* in the validation of test score meaning and use (see Chapter 5 in Cizek, 2020, pp. 108–143), but expresses concern that "accepted standards for relevant evidence bearing on justification are lacking" (p. 166).

Kane (2012) indirectly addressed these frustrations in a paper discussing the *intersection of three perspectives* on validity in high-stakes bar examinations (i.e., an examination a lawyer must pass in order to practice law within a particular jurisdiction). Kane identified the three perspectives as the measurement perspective, the decision-making perspective, and the test candidate perspective. He pointed out that each perspective offered differing but useful information. As Cizek (2020) argued, and Kane (2012) agreed, "the measurement perspective is especially useful in designing testing programs that will yield reliable and valid information about candidate competence, and it can also be helpful in designing the decision procedures" (p. 14). However, following Messick (1989), Kane (2012) advised that dropping consequences in considerations of validity evidence is not the answer. Addressing the consequences of testing in contexts requires engagement with others (e.g., multiple stakeholders, beyond disciplinary communities, beyond the university, and beyond insiders within the testing industry). It "requires a broader and more pragmatic perspective" (Kane, 2012, p. 14): a transdisciplinary perspective. Arguably, transdisciplinary approaches are in keeping with Messick's central advice to apply multiple inquiry systems (worldviews, conceptual stances, methodologies) in validation. Assessment-centred communities are central in this endeavour. Their transdisciplinary engagement with other stakeholders, who share their interest in validity and validation or have a *stake* in the outcomes of assessment practices, is opening up promising new directions in validation research. Retrenching and reverting to former, narrow disciplinary practices within assessment-centred communities is not a useful way forward.

Advancing a transdisciplinary agenda: fulfilling the promise of Messick's theory

Over time and in different ways, Moss (1994, 1998, 2016, 2018) has pushed the *validity debate* forward. Recently, she argued for a "more complex theory of validity that can shift focus as needed from the intended interpretations and uses of test scores ... to local capacity to support the actual interpretations, decisions and actions that serve the local users' purposes" (Moss, 2016, p. 236). Moss (2016) called for "transdisciplinary" (p. 249) programs of research which would draw evidence in support of more "comprehensive" (p. 247) validity arguments. Such arguments would incorporate evidence drawn from local, situated, contexts of assessment use, in order to "locate the boundaries within which [generalization] holds" (Cronbach, 1988, p. 14).

Following Moss, Chapelle's (2021) elegantly detailed analysis of IUA validation methods highlighted the most recent definition of validity in the *Standards* (AERA et al., 2014). This definition emphasized test use as central to validation inquiry (cf. Chapelle, 2021; Kane, 2012, 2013b).

The *rhetorical art* (Messick, 1988) of validation relates to the quality and persuasiveness of the argumentative evidence that is brought to bear in support of the inferences drawn from an assessment. The *meaningfulness*, *usefulness*, *appropriateness*, and *relevance* (Messick, 1989) of an assessment practice depend upon the reciprocal and relational interplay of multiple, differing contextual perspectives with regard to purpose and use (e.g., from the local and situated to the global and generalizable). Validity evidence is inevitably unconvincing and circumscribed without this recognition. Pragmatic approaches (Morgan, 2007) to validation inquiry, characterized by engagement with methodological pluralism (Moss & Haertel, 2016) and enacted through transdisciplinary programs of research, are creating new possibilities for more *robust* (Moss, 2016) and convincing validity arguments.

Moss has not been alone in calling for and engaging in TR in validation practices (e.g., Addey et al., 2020; Maddox, 2015; Maddox & Zumbo, 2017; Tardy, 2017). For example, Addey et al. (2020) demonstrated the potential of transdisciplinarity in their richly theorized case study of international large-scale assessments in education (ILSAs). They argue for *assembled validity*, which is "negotiated and transformed" by engaging multiple actors [stakeholders] in validation processes, and drawing on their "legitimate arguments, evidence and perspectives" (p. 601) in considerations of validity.

The researchers Addey, Maddox, and Zumbo have diverse disciplinary backgrounds (e.g., sociology, education, anthropology, measurement, and psychometrics). They draw on both a prominent social theory, that is, Actor Network Theory (ANT) (e.g., Callon, 1986; Latour, 1987), and validity theory (e.g., Kane, 2013b, 2016; Messick, 1989) in a case study of argument-based validation practices at play in diverse ILSA contexts. They are critical of the currently dominant validation practices (e.g., Kane, 2013b, 2016), which have traditionally called for increased precision, coherence, and consensus (cf. Newton, 2012; Kane, 2016). They document the ways in which such practices tend to *blur* rather than elucidate substantive validation evidence arising from the multiple, diverse, socially situated contexts where ILSAs are administered.

Drawing on Callon (1986), Latour (1987, 2005) and Law (1991), Addey et al. (2020) argue for the ANT notion of *assemblage* as "the way that unstable networks of human actors and material artefacts align temporarily to achieve shared goals" (p. 590) within the diverse and variable systems/contexts of ILSA use and interpretation. They illustrate the need and *obligation* (Cronbach, 1988) for validators to recognize, understand, and endorse the legitimacy of evidence from the diverse and variable networks of actors that are engaged in assessment and validation practices. Arguably, this seminal contribution provides evidence of the transformative and illuminating potential of TR. This is the way forward.

Concluding comments

This chapter has provided a selective, historical overview of the contribution of assessment-centred communities to the evolving conceptions of validity and validation research practices. Although this history was likely to have been familiar to assessment-centred readers, it was arguably less familiar to language-centred ones. In keeping with a transdisciplinary approach, it was important at the outset to offer all readers a shared foundational base of information and background in order to support transdisciplinary dialogue, interaction, and reflection.

In Chapter 3, we turn our attention to the contributions of language-centred communities in defining the evolving *construct* of language itself (i.e., changing conceptions of what it is, and what we intend to assess, in language assessment). Examination of evolving conceptions of language leads naturally into a discussion of the critical role of theory as the explicit or implicit force that shapes and propels construct definition, research, and assessment practices.

As discussed in this chapter, we have moved beyond the purist notions that social theories and qualitative methods would undermine the potential generalizability of assessment practices (cf. Fulcher, 2013, 2015) to a more pragmatic stance. Following Lave (1996), such an open and flexible stance acknowledges "the value of the differences among our theoretical positions" (p. 28) and will support renewed insights regarding complex issues, such as the role of context in language assessment validation research.

Notes

1 Cronbach (1988) singles out McGuire's approach as a "best strategy" (p. 14) in validation research. In our view, McGuire made foundational contributions to *social* psychology through his meta-analytic approach. He argued that in spite of coherence across interrelated concepts and shared principles and insights, there had been a rise in terminology and labels which interfered with understanding by introducing a multiplicity of distinctions (e.g., interactionism, transactionism, constructionism, constructivism). McGuire was aware of the irony of introducing yet another label (*contextualism*) but felt the differing emphases of these different conceptualizations obscured the central focus on how theory develops through interaction with empirical observation; that one constructs a theory (rather than testing it), that theories hold in some contexts but not in others. He argued that theory emerges over time and one explanation for the rising number of labels was their partial and developmental state. McGuire discussed implications regarding the process of development of psychological theories, and he argued for openness and the usefulness of variety of theoretical perspectives in research.

2 Singer, E. A. Jr. (1873–1954) was an American philosopher whose most famous book, *Experience and reflection*, was published after his death in a volume edited by Churchman in 1959 and republished in 2015 by the University of Pennsylvania Press to mark the 125th anniversary of the Penn Press Collection. Messick (1989) cites Singer's book as a source for his *Philosophical Conceits*, the progressive matrix, and recursive and reflexive approaches to validation inquiry. Singer extended notions of pragmatism, drawing on William James, Charles Sanders Pierce, and John Dewey.

3 *Positivism* held to the "worldview" (Creswell & Plano Clark, 2011, pp. 38–39) that the study of human behaviour and social phenomena could and should be studied in the same way that phenomena were studied by natural scientists (e.g., as botanists study plants; as chemists study solids, liquids, and gases) through the application of the scientific method. As such, hypotheses were stated and then tested by narrowing human actions to variables of relevance in order to explore cause and effect relationships, which either confirmed or refuted the hypotheses. Results were quantified and assumed to be *objectively* derived. Whereas positivists argued that their endeavours were value-free (and therefore objective), *post-positivists* accepted (as an outcome of the paradigm wars) that all research is value-laden (a view held by Messick, 1989). Post-positivists in the social sciences continue to work on the basis of hypothesis testing aligned with quantitative approaches to research. For example, clinical research tests hypotheses based on clearly defined variables in controlled settings; experimental research tests hypotheses across experimental and control groups which vary on the basis of a carefully defined feature or intervention (variable). Both look for cause and effect relationships and argue on the basis of sampling strategies that it is possible to meaningfully generalize from a *robust* sample to the population it represents. Results are quantified though statistical and or other psychometric means. The post-positivist worldview continues to dominate research in psychology, which favours theories of cognition that view language as an underlying attribute or trait residing in the thinking of an individual, and methodologies that are quantitative.

An *interpretivist or constructivist worldview*, on the other hand, is associated with methodologies that are qualitative (e.g., Charmaz, 2006). Researchers informed by this worldview have as their purpose to better understand, describe, and explain actions and phenomena-in-context. They hold that it is impossible to exclude the values and interests of the individuals who act, interact, and otherwise engage in a context from investigation of a phenomenon. Thus, phenomena cannot be reduced to single measurable variables, because they are *constructed* collaboratively and embedded in context – as it is construed by the unique participants therein.

4 There are many different accounts of *pragmatism*. For example, Stone and Zumbo (2016) draw a distinction between the *folk meaning* of *being pragmatic* and a (capitalized) *Pragmatic Approach*, which draws explicitly on principles from the philosophy articulated by James (1907), Dewey (1938, 1941), or Rorty (1982). The folk notion of a pragmatic approach is akin to – *do whatever needs doing*, or *anything goes*. This is a far cry from the defining principles of Pragmatism as a philosophy, initially elaborated by William James, who had a very different view. James (1907) argued against the dominance of any one worldview or methodological approach pointing out that all were partial and limited because they were inevitably human. As such they were value-laden

and limited by personal experience, beliefs, knowledge, etc., and none could claim superiority because all were essentially differences in practices. Stone and Zumbo (2016) explain: "Pragmatism holds that understanding emerges through action in the world and that all our understandings ... are distinctions in how we act". It follows then, they explain, that "Pragmatism is not, in itself, a theory of scientific knowledge"; rather, it accounts "for how people make sense of the world through action in the world" (p. 557). The pragmatic worldview considers all research to be imbued with the interests, experience. and agendas of the researchers who design, collect data, analyze, and report findings – no research is value-free. Morgan (2007) proposed a "pragmatic framework" for social science research, which opposed the traditional dualistic distinctions of qualitative and quantitative research, and placed methodology at the centre of inquiry. He argued that pragmatism offered "a range of new opportunities for thinking about classic methodological issues in the social sciences" (p. 72). Pragmatism, pragmatic approaches, and pragmatic researcher stances have engendered extensive discussion with regard to mixed methods research (cf. Biesta, 2010; Niglas, 2010; Tashakkori & Teddlie, 2010) and are characteristic of transdisciplinary approaches.

5 In some research methods textbooks, *context sensitivity* may be paradigmatically attributed as it is in McMillan and Schumacher (2010), who explain it as an approach "In qualitative research, integrating aspects of the context in conducting the study and interpreting the results" (p. 486).

3 Unpacking the conundrum of context in language assessment

Why do social theories matter?

Janna Fox and Natasha Artemeva

Having examined the contributions of assessment-centred communities to considerations of validity in Chapter 2, in this chapter we highlight the contributions of language-centred communities to our changing conceptions of language itself (i.e., the construct of interest in language assessment). Changes in theoretical conceptions of what it means to know and use a language are traced in relation to their evolution in such language-centred communities as linguistics, language teaching, discourse studies, and writing studies. Throughout we emphasize the critical importance of theory, explain why it matters, and briefly discuss three prominent philosophical schools of thought as antecedents for selective descriptions of some of the many social theories that have been particularly useful in research regarding assessment as a social practice. To date, the additive benefits of social theories are not well understood, acknowledged, or incorporated by many in assessment-centred communities, and this has created what Lawrence (2010) referred to as an "applicability gap" (p. 125). Arguably, transdisciplinary research agendas, which engage researchers from different communities with different perspectives, who nonetheless share a common interest in assessment, may best address complex issues such as the conundrum of context in language assessment.

> *Theories … become instruments – not answers to enigmas.*
>
> (James, 1907/1996, p. 32)

> *[Teaching] methods are not neutral. Language teaching and learning do not occur in a vacuum. These two statements reflect the importance of context and the fact that where we do what we do is at least as important as how we do it.*
>
> (Curtis, 2017, p. 10)

DOI: 10.4324/9781351184571-5

> *Arguably the greatest challenge facing language testing is the issue of the context in which language testing is carried out, both at the micro and the macro level.*
>
> (McNamara, 2007, p. 131)

As discussed in Chapter 2, assessment-centred communities have focused on and contributed to evolving conceptions of validity theory and validation research practices. In this chapter, the focus shifts to language-centred communities, their contributions to evolving conceptions of language itself (the construct of interest in language assessment), and the role that theory has played in considerations of context in assessment practices. Whereas assessment-centred communities have largely been informed by cognitive theories which locate language within the heads of individuals as an underlying attribute, trait, ability, or capacity, language-centred communities have increasingly been informed by those social theories which locate language "in the relations between persons acting and the social world" (Lave, 1996, p. 5).

Within the field of language assessment, context has long been acknowledged as a concern (Bachman, 2007; Chalhoub-Deville, 2003, 2016; McNamara, 2007, 2008), particularly, but not exclusively, when assessments are used to rank, categorize, or label in order to license, award, select, or deny access. For example, high-stakes language testing in large-scale settings faces the following *conundrum*. On the one hand, the use of such language tests rests on the dual notions of meaningful interpretability and generalizability of inferences drawn from test scores, which are elicited across contexts of relevance through systematic test administrations. On the other hand, although such contexts may share common features, they also vary in meaningful ways: at macro levels (e.g., country, first language(s), economic opportunities; educational cultures; gender equality); and, at micro levels (e.g., school resources; local cultural settings; test taker characteristics). From an assessment perspective, there is a concern with regard to how context impacts the intended measurement of the construct, namely "factors irrelevant to the test itself" (Fulcher & Davidson, 2007, p. 25), such as noise, poor equipment, or high room temperatures during administration. However, other concerns regarding the appropriateness, meaningfulness, and usefulness (Messick, 1989) of such tests have also been raised. For example, within the local context of a language classroom, questions have been raised about how well the construct is actually represented by such tests (Macqueen et al., 2019). Chalhoub-Deville and Tarone (1996) argued against the use of externally developed (large-scale/industrial) proficiency measures in assessing language needs, achievement, or skills in local and unique classroom contexts. They explained that "the nature of the language proficiency construct is not constant; different linguistic, functional, and creative proficiency components emerge when we investigate the proficiency construct in different contexts" (p. 5).

Within assessment-centred communities, as noted in Chapter 2, Messick's (1989) requirement that validation evidence must support "the functional worth of scores in terms of social consequences of their use" (p. 13) has prompted considerable discussion, debate, resistance, and concern. For some within assessment-centred communities (e.g., Borsboom et al., 2004; Cizek, 2012, 2020; Popham, 1997), Messick's requirement was misguided. Part of the problem has been the scope and expertise that meeting this requirement demanded. Traditionally, focus has been on the technical quality of tests (i.e., *truth*). The consequences, actions, and decisions that result from their use were, such critics have argued, well-beyond appropriate disciplinary limits as they have traditionally been drawn. This viewpoint has led in part to a lack of familiarity regarding the scholarship that has accumulated over many decades outside assessment-centred disciplinary communities, scholarship which could inform and illuminate the consequences, actions, and decisions that result from assessment use.

For example, Cizek (2020) finds it *regrettable*, *perplexing*, and "troublesome" that the most recent *Standards* (2014) have "perpetuated confusion between validation and justification and conflated meaning and use" (p. 170). He takes particular issue with the following statement in the *Standards*: "It is important to note that the validity of test score interpretations depends not only on the uses of the test scores but specifically on the claims that underlie the *theory of action* [emphasis added] for these uses" (pp. 19–20; see also *Standard* 1.6). There is a vast amount of scholarship, accumulated over many decades with regard to theories of action (e.g., Burke, 1935; Husserl, 1989; Schutz, 1966, 1967; Weber, 2019) – *social theories* – but Cizek does not acknowledge them.

Further, while recognizing the need to broaden assessment concerns in the *Standards*, and noting "they were written primarily – or exclusively – to apply to large-scale testing", Cizek identifies the "few authors" who have provided guidance related to "the validity of classroom assessments" and praises this "modest work" (p. 167). However, the long tradition of research within language-centred communities concerned with classroom assessment (see Chapter 4) does not support his appraisal. It does suggest, however, borrowing from Lortie (1975), there is a critical need to *abandon the egg crate approach* to research, which confines research and researchers to disciplinary perspectives, and compartmentalizes and impedes scholarly exchange, dialogue, reflection, and learning. Throughout this book we have argued that moving beyond these disciplinary divisions and moving forward with transdisciplinary programs of research will increase dialogue beyond disciplines, the sharing of expertise, knowledge, information. Such dialogue will encourage reflection, self-awareness, new recognitions, and new directions for research. This chapter may be of greatest interest to those in assessment-centred communities – particularly those who are involved in the testing of languages – who have less familiarity with socio-theoretical perspectives on language.

It will also be of interest to those within language-centred communities (including those in the language assessment community itself) who have less familiarity with the social theories we have highlighted in this book. Given the book's emphasis on future directions for research in testing and other modes of assessment practice, of particular importance are students within these and other communities who share an interest in assessment and will shape the directions of research in future.

We set the stage for the examination of the "persistent problem" (Bachman, 2007, p. 41) of context in language assessment by discussing *why theories matter*. Evolving theoretical conceptions within language-centred communities – of what it means to know and use a language – have directly influenced how language has been researched, taught, and assessed. This evolution is selectively examined as it has played out in linguistics, applied linguistics, language teaching, discourse, and writing studies. It is followed by a brief discussion of what social theories share and how they differ, and highlights a few of the many social perspectives that have proved particularly useful in informing, framing, and interpreting findings in language assessment research.

Why do theories matter?

Theoretical understandings (whether tacit or explicit) govern how we make meaning, what we focus on, and how we interpret what we see. Burke (1935) provided a simple and meaningful response as to why theories matter: "A way of seeing is also a way of not seeing – a focus on A involves a neglect of object B" (p. 49). Although there are many different conceptualizations of *theory*, in this book we have applied what Bryman and Teevan (2005) suggest is "its most common meaning", namely "*an explanation of observed regularities or patterns*" (p. 3). Charmaz (2014), from a qualitative perspective, extends this definition to encompass either (or both) explanation and understanding, and McMillan and Schumacher (2010), from a quantitative perspective, add that theory is "prediction … of natural phenomena" (p. 491).

As Lemke (1995) pointed out, theories (whether articulated explicitly or not) allow us to make meaning from experience – "are themselves just ways of talking and doing", and inevitably they are "partial and incomplete" (p. 157). On the other hand, the relationship between a theoretical perspective and empirical research is reciprocal; theory shapes and is shaped in turn by data. Or, as James (1907/1996) put it, "theories become instruments" (p. 32) – shaping meaning (whether we are fully cognizant of them or not):

> We need a theory because we always already have one. If we don't formulate explicitly our ways of making meaning in particular contexts, the meanings we make will be governed automatically, by default, by

> the limiting meaning systems of our narrow communities, even when we are not aware of this.
>
> (Lemke, 1995, p. 157)

As researchers we situate the inquiry system we choose in relation to theory (tacitly or explicitly), relevant methodological approaches, and the empirical literature we value. Markus (1998) explained: "The inquiry system used is part of our perceptual process" (p. 15). The process is dynamic. Consequently, "the data flesh out and specify the theory, modifying, elaborating, and necessarily reshaping it in the context of what is observed – whether the modification is made explicitly by the researchers or not" (Freedman, 2006, p. 102).

However, this complex, reciprocal relationship also inevitably narrows the potential range of consideration, particularly when research is dominated by only one theoretical perspective which is reified and routinized within an academic discipline. The domination of one theoretical perspective or another is evidence of what Lemke (1995) referred to as "the trap of theory" (p. 156). When we fail to recognize, acknowledge, reflect on, and question our theoretical understandings and assumptions, which guide, inform, and support our interpretations, we fall into Lemke's *theory trap*. If we disregard, deny, or forget this, we may fall into another *trap* – the trap of *dualism* (Kramsch, 1993; Lemke, 1995; Niglas, 2010). Dualistic perspectives assume incompatible and incommensurate dichotomies, that is, one theoretical view opposes or negates the other; for example, one subscribes to either social or cognitive theory.

> A *transdisciplinary research agenda* rejects the *dualism trap* in favour of an expanding array of theoretical possibilities. Valuing and learning from differences in perspectives increases the potential for new awareness, new recognitions, creativity, and innovation. The goal of the present volume is to raise conscious awareness and understanding of social theories and socio-theoretical perspectives, because they are not well understood and are underutilized in validation research (see meta-review, Chapter 4). Following Messick (1998) the goal is not a synthesis, nor, as Lemke (1995) observed, to develop a "meta-theory" (p. 156). The goal is "to develop a *praxis*, a critical way of analyzing, doing, creating" (p. 157), which is "self-reflective and self-critical" (Lemke, 1995, p. 158; cf. Poehner & Inbar-Lourie, 2020b).

As Freedman (2006) explained:

> Theories help us to organize and understand data. When we discover a useful conceptual framework, so much more of what we

> have observed "makes sense". The metaphors commonly used for this phenomenon are revealing: theories "illuminate", "things fall into place". These metaphors suggest the degree to which theory can clarify the connections among data and make salient patterns that seemed to be there all along.
>
> (p. 101)

Lave (1996) and Lemke (1995) have pointed out that recognizing and critically reflecting on our own theoretical perspective with full regard for alternative theoretical perspectives that differentially account for and respectfully challenge what we see and how we make sense of it, allows us "to build more robust programs of research" (Moss & Haertel, 2016, p. 127). Arguably, Lemke's (1995) dualism trap may in part account for the challenges posed by context in language assessment validation research. This is discussed in the following section.

How have dualisms contributed to the problem of context in language assessment?

What can we learn from changing conceptions of language and context?

Within language assessment communities, some (e.g., McNamara & Roever, 2006) have pointed out that context has, at times, simply been backgrounded, disregarded, or dismissed in language assessment validation research. The location of language assessment at the disciplinary boundaries of language-centred and assessment-centred communities predisposed it for challenges in reconciling evolving conceptualizations of language constructs and their operational definitions in assessment.

There was a time, roughly from the 1930s through the 1960s, when prevailing psychological, linguistic, and educational theory neatly overlapped. Previously, English language teaching had largely comprised learning *about* languages.[1] This *classical humanist* tradition (Cheng & Fox, 2017; White, 1988) primarily utilized grammar/translation methods to read, translate, and memorize literary texts, applying techniques drawn from the study of *dead languages* (i.e., Latin, Ancient Greek, Middle English) to the study of living ones (e.g., Italian, Spanish, French). From the early 1930s, however, language teaching began to shift from knowledge about language to language use, and from the primacy of written texts to oral proficiency. Behaviourist psychology (e.g., Skinner, 1957) was a powerful motivator for this shift, as it was the dominant theoretical source for both conceptualizations of language in linguistics, and language teaching and learning in education. Learning was viewed as observable changes in behaviour (including linguistic behaviours) as a result of *operant conditioning*, that is, as the outcome of repeated stimulus and response, practice, repetition, and positive or negative reinforcement/feedback. In other words, learning was rooted in cause and effect relationships "in which external factors lead to a response, and over time, this response becomes a learnt behavior" (Duchesne, McMaugh, Bochner, & Krause, 2013, p. 160). Thus, in language teaching, repetition and practice of language structures and patterns would over time trigger *contiguity* – a voluntary, automatic response, whereby the learner would associate one pattern with another automatically. The focus was on form (i.e., grammatical accuracy). Rule-governed patterns were easy to teach and easy to assess with discrete point tests. In the classroom, however, teachers found applying this method of teaching could be monotonous. Language teachers often described what evolved as the audio-lingual approach (Lado, 1964) as the *drill and kill* method. Prominent educational theorists (e.g., Stenhouse, 1975) argued that education was much more than "the mastery of behaviours" (White, 1988, p. 32). Rather, learning was a matter of using knowledge to think with; a matter of reflection, speculation, and meaning making; a matter of ideas.

In the same year that Skinner (1957) published his definitive work, *Verbal behaviour*, Chomsky (1957) published *Syntactic structures*. This seminal publication in linguistics highlighted the individual learner's "own innate language learning capacities" (White, 1988, p. 22) and hypothesized the *ideal speaker-listener*, whose *competence* was distinguished from performance. Whereas Skinner's theory of language had structural/descriptive linguists physically *out in the field*, observing, describing, documenting, and classifying structures of language in taxonomies (e.g., of phonemes, morphemes, vocabulary), Chomsky's (1957) theory of language had transformational-generative linguists *at their desks* producing models of language as a mental phenomenon; documenting and diagraming relationships between hypothesized rules; explaining in abstract terms how these rules governed systems of grammars to generate language (e.g., how rules were combined to generate a sentence in language). Chomsky considered "a *language* to be a set (finite or infinite) of sentences, each finite in length and constructed out of a finite set of elements" (p. 13) (e.g., phrases, clauses). The sentence or its elements could be considered units of analysis, where a unit of analysis is the component of the phenomenon under consideration, or *what* a researcher focuses on or analyzes in a study, at the most basic or fundamental level. Selection of a unit of analysis is informed by theory, research purposes, methodological choices, etc.

Several points are of importance in this brief, historic overview of these changing conceptions of language:

1 language was considered a property of an individual's thinking;
2 the *cognitive revolution* within psychology, which was beginning to challenge behaviourism, intensified the focus on individual cognition as mental processing, meaning making, and problem solving (e.g., Bruner, Goodnow, & Austin, 1956); and

3 there was an increasing disconnect between developmental trends in linguistics and psychology, and language teaching, learning, and assessment practices.

Within this landscape, there lurked an underlying and unresolved *seismic fault* (cf. Klein, 2007), namely, the meaningful use of language and the persistent and largely unresolved problem of its social and contextual nature – particularly as it was operationalized and interpreted in language assessment (cf. Hughes, 1989; McNamara & Roever, 2006; van Lier, 1989). These seismic fault lines were evident in the research trends in second language acquisition (SLA) and language learning as well. Researchers in these fields were largely informed by cognitive perspectives of language learning development and progression, which "generally assumed that social factors do not directly influence the process of L2 [second language] acquisition", and thus "would probably have an indirect rather than a direct effect on L2 learning" (Ellis, 1994, p. 14).

Such cognitive perspectives did not accord with language teachers' experiences in their language classrooms. The new conceptions of language offered by Chomskyan linguistics were decidedly unhelpful in language teaching and learning. Chomsky's idealized, abstract model of language competence as a mental phenomenon of an *ideal speaker-listener* within a purely *homogeneous speech community* had no relevance in the language classroom. Teachers argued that this view of language failed to affirm or account for the importance of meaningful language use by diverse language speakers in a myriad of varying social and cultural contexts. Recognitions arising in language classrooms were addressed in a 1966 lecture by Hymes, who has been variously described as a linguistic anthropologist (Coste, de Pietro, & Moore, 2012) or sociolinguist (White, 1988). Hymes introduced the concept of *communicative competence*. He argued that "social life ... affected not merely outward performance but inner competence itself" (Hymes, 1972, p. 274). Hymes thus shifted attention to "the ability of a speaker to use language appropriately according to setting, social relationships and communicative purpose" (White, 1988, p. 16). He argued that competence was "dependent upon both (tacit) knowledge and (ability for) use" (Hymes, 1972, p. 282). The meaningful use of language required knowledge of "rules of use without which the rules of grammar would be useless" (p. 278). He asserted that communicative competence was "differential" as it arose within "heterogenous" speech communities, and both competence and community were "undoubtedly shaped" (p. 274) by the social and cultural contexts within which communication occurs.

The arguments put forth by Hymes prompted the *communicative turn* in conceptualizing language (Hymes, 1972; Savignon, 1991) and highlighted the role of meaningful communication and use. Concurrently, it accentuated the inadequacy of earlier linguistic models operationalized as language constructs for assessment purposes. As Savignon (1991) explained:

> A tradition of abstraction in linguistic inquiry [had] contributed to the neglect of [the] social context ... When language use is viewed as social behavior, learner identity and motivation are seen to interact with language status, use, and contexts ... The description and explanation of the differential competence that invariably results must include an account of this interaction.
>
> (p. 273)

The communicative turn heralded the advent of *communicative language teaching*. It was at this point that teaching and learning languages became increasingly distanced from mainstream linguistic theories accounting for language. As Widdowson (2003) noted, "there is a good deal of distrust of theory among English language teachers. They tend to see it as remote from their actual experience, an attempt to mystify common-sense practices by unnecessary abstraction" (p. 1).

The *distrust* that Widdowson's (2003) elegant review of language teaching practices accounts for was evidence of a dualism trap (Lemke,1995) as language teachers privileged what worked in practice – in their classrooms with their individual learners – and increasingly saw practice divorced from how it was accounted for in theory. Such *common-sense* practices, however, were deeply rooted in implicit theoretical understandings, arising from situated classroom experiences, which Woods (1996) argued informed, sustained, and reified unacknowledged tacit beliefs, assumptions, and knowledge inherent in teacher action and decision making (see Cheng & Fox, 2017, pp. 17–27, for a discussion of the relationship between implicit theories of teaching and learning and classroom practices).

The idiosyncratic, common-sense practices of language teaching, which Widdowson (2003) described and Woods (1996) investigated, tended to define much of the communicative language teaching era and continue to a certain extent today. As Curtis (2017) acknowledged, "some language teachers may be offended (and if so, my apologies!), by the notion that, methodologically speaking, sometimes 'we don't know what we're talking about'" (p. 45). The *communicative turn* gave rise to considerable eclecticism in language classrooms. Such eclecticism was further motivated by the large-scale export of native speakers of English who were hired to teach English as a foreign language simply because they spoke the language – not because they had any specialized education or professional experience in teaching English as an additional language.

By the late 1970s, there was growing dissatisfaction with Chomskyan views of language within a number of social science disciplines that viewed context and language as integral to, embedded within, and inseparable from social practices (e.g., anthropology, sociology). Within linguistics itself, Halliday (e.g., 1973, 1978, 1994) was advancing notions of language as social action integral to the sociocultural context of use. This led to what has been described as the *social turn* in applied linguistics (cf. Leung and Valdés, 2019). Halliday (1973) argued "language is as it is because of its function in the social structure" (p. 65). He explained, "words ... get their meaning from activities in which they are embedded, which again are social activities with social agencies and goals" (Halliday & Hasan, 1989, p. 5). Within language teaching, Hallidayan notions of language functions were appropriated by applied linguists in response to the unstructured classroom activity that often characterized the communicative language teaching of the day (Samuda, 2001). Given that functions carried intentions and purposes for use and could be described and classified (see *Systemic Functional Grammar*), they became an organizing principle for content in language syllabus design and in language teaching as well. However, as White (1988) noted, content initially consisted of *checklists* of functions and topics, and was not systematically sequenced or graded for difficulty. Further, there were from the outset problems in relating formal features of language to functions. However, over time, lists of language functions were contextualized and made more meaningful through the application of such *selection and grading criteria* as: *learner needs* (which resulted in the increasing use of needs analysis); *usefulness* (both immediate and long term); *coverage* or generalizability; personal *interest* (which increased the use of learner's interest inventories, checklists, self-assessment); and perceived *complexity* (see White, 1988, p. 48).

In discourse studies, Bhatia, Flowerdew, and Jones (2008) have identified a *discursive turn* around the 1970s, "influenced" in part by Halliday and others, "who at around the same time were becoming more and more concerned with the relationship of language to social actions and to the socio-cultural worlds of those who use it" (p. 2). Fairclough (2003) identified Halliday's linguistic theory and the textual analysis associated with it (i.e., *Systemic Functional Linguistics*) as his "main point of reference" (p. 5) in elaborating a framework which integrated descriptions of language with descriptions of context. As Ivanič (1998) explained:

> Fairclough shows how a text (written or spoken) is inextricable from the processes of production and interpretation which create it, and that these processes are in turn inextricable from the various local, institutional and socio-historical conditions within which the participants are situated.
>
> (p. 43)

Such ongoing retheorization of language embedded in context drew on Malinowski's (1923, 1935) notions of the *context of situation* and the *context of culture* (cf. Halliday & Hasan, 1989). The *context of situation* (Malinowski, 1923, 1935) was considered the physical, material setting, the social purposes, and social relationships of humans communicating (in speech or writing); and the *context of culture* (Malinowski, 1935) was considered the more abstract, but more powerful, competing influences of society on communication (e.g., norms, conventions, institutions, culture). Halliday (1999) explained this distinction in relation to teaching and learning:

> The principle that language is understood in relation to its environment is nowhere more evident than in the activities of language education. This principle was explicitly recognized when scholars first began observing spoken language, since it was impossible to interpret spoken text in isolation from its context; but it is equally true of all text, spoken or written. It is true also of the linguistic system that lies behind the text; but whereas the environment for language as text is the context of situation, the environment for language as system is the context of culture.
>
> (p. 1)

It is important to highlight the centrality of *text* (i.e., spoken and written language) or *monomodality* (Kress & Van Leeuwen, 2001) as the focus of linguistic theory and research at this time. Only later would the influence of Kress and Van Leeuwen's (2001) conceptualizations of multimodality contribute to a *visual turn* in language teaching and learning (cf. Kalaja and Pitkänen-Huhta, 2018). Kress and Van Leeuwen (2001) argued that so-called *paralinguistic* features (i.e., features accompanying communication outside of spoken and written texts) were fundamental resources in meaning making. Such resources were often dismissed in linguistic research (which continued to investigate spoken or written words, phrases, clauses, or sentences), but other modes, tactile and visual (e.g., gestures, images, facial expressions, movement, figures, media), were typically vital in making meaning *evident* (Kress, 2012).

However, such recognitions were not often built into the criteria for selection and grading of language functions (White, 1988). Inspired by Hallidayan linguistics, language functions continue to be used in language program design today, most often in relation to *task-based language teaching* (TBLT). Although variously defined, TBLT has arguably become the dominant language teaching approach over the past decades, in quite the same way that communicative language teaching had previously dominated practices. However, current tasks used in teaching and learning typically incorporate "the notion of context" (Kramsch, 1993, p. 67). In her landmark book, *Context and culture in language teaching*, Kramsch (1993) claimed that spoken and written text alone was incapable of accounting for all that language is and does. Informed by Bakhtin (1986) (discussed below), Kramsch (1993) asserted that "the notion of context is a relational one" (p. 67). She argued that "text and context cannot exist outside the individual voices that create them" (p. 14), and she introduced the notion of *third places* that are shaped by learners of additional languages engaging in the intercultural and multilingual spaces that typically characterize such language learning.

Curtis (2017) points out, although there remains some confusion and debate over what constitutes a task, in general task-based approaches to language teaching "highlight interactions", and collaborative engagement in a "connected series of activities", in order to complete tasks in relation to pre-defined "language-oriented [learning] outcome(s)" (p. 47). Such "language-oriented" outcomes are often derived from proficiency criteria and criterion-referenced benchmarks of language development (e.g., the Common European Framework of Reference [CEFR], or the Canadian Language Benchmarks [CLB]) and define what learners should know, be able to do, and/or value at the end of a course. (See also *outcomes-based assessment* in Biggs & Tang, 2011; and *backward design*, from learning outcomes to assessment tasks to classroom activities, in Wiggins & McTighe, 2005 and Cheng & Fox, 2017).

However, to this day there remains considerable confusion in language teaching over specific methods (Curtis, 2017), and studies suggest teachers report that they are using communicative or task-based methods without fully or deeply understanding the main principles of these methods (e.g., East, 2012). Some (e.g., Mellow, 2002) suggest that much language teaching is essentially eclectic. It seems that teachers continue to focus on day-to-day practices and what works in their classrooms, and do not spend or are not afforded sufficient time to reflect on or articulate *why*. They have tended to remain distrustful and dismissive of theory, which they see as divorced from their classroom practice and largely irrelevant (cf. Poehner & Inbar-Lourie, 2020a).

It should be noted that although they are not specifically language-centred, education disciplines and fields have played an ongoing and exceedingly important role in language teaching, learning, and assessment. In Chapter 4, we highlight some of these contributions in our discussion of the retheorization of classroom-based assessment. By the 1990s and early 2000s, in theoretical and empirical literature alike, there was mounting and well-articulated "recognition of the social and political significance of language teaching [which] ... led to a greater awareness of learners as social actors in specific relationships with the language they [were] learning" (Byram & Grundy, 2002, p. 193). Retheorization of language in/as context raised thoughtful and critical awareness of social, cultural, and political influences (cf. Canagarajah, 1999, 2011; Holliday, 2005; Phillipson, 1992). The *critical edge in the social turn* has been evolving into what some have referred to as a *multilingual turn* (Leung & Valdés, 2019; May, 2014; Ortega, 2013, 2014).

This renewed and vigorous reconceptualization of what it means to know and use a language has attacked the ideological dominance of *native speakerism* (cf. Curtis, 2017; Davies, 1991) and native-speaker norms in language teaching (Arias & Schissel, 2021; Fox, 2021; Schissel & Arias,

2021), and popularized the notion of *translanguaging*. Canagarajah (2011) defined translanguaging as "the ability of multilingual speakers to shuttle between languages, treating the diverse languages that form their repertoire as an integrated system" (p. 401). Curtis (2017) traces the rise of native-speaker myths in English language teaching to *the dark side* of the communicative language teaching era, which privileged speaking and idealized the varieties of English spoken in so-called inner circle (cf. Kachru, 1992), countries with long histories of English-dominant monolingualism (e.g., Britain, the United States). Curtis (2017) dismisses, however, any immediate impact of translanguaging in teaching and learning languages.

There are many other *turns* that have elaborated and are elaborating changes in theoretical accounts of language and communication. Kalaja and Pitkänen-Huhta (2018) provided a particularly thoughtful review of these, identifying not only the social turn and multilingual turn, but also the narrative turn and the affective turn. However, they highlighted the *visual turn* in their review, which has drawn increasing attention of researchers concerned with the *multimodality* of meaning making in communication (e.g., Camiciottoli & Fortanet-Gómez, 2015; Doody & Artemeva, 2022; Fogarty-Bourget, Artemeva, & Fox, 2019; Gray, 2021). These researchers are drawing attention to many other semiotic resources (cf. Kress & Van Leeuwen, 2001) at play and integral to meaning (e.g., diagrams, photographs, illustrations; equations, graphs; gestures, gaze, other embodied movements), which simultaneously occur at a particular moment and for a particular purpose in communication. These differing resources or modes propose differing units of analysis beyond the purely linguistic mode of text.

What have social theories contributed to conceptions of language?

What is important to emphasize in the previous accounts of the *turns* in conceptualizations of language over the past three decades is the role that social theories and socio-theoretical perspectives have played in the evolution of considerations of context and language as a social practice. Below we take a closer look at social theories in general, and then highlight a selective number of social theorists, theories, perspectives, and concepts. These have proved to be particularly helpful in informing research that addresses context in language assessment.

What general persuasions do social theories share?

Schwandt (1994) began his discussion of social theories by offering "sensitising concepts that steer researchers toward a particular outlook" (p. 118) and summarized the overarching "persuasions" that characterize socio-theoretical worldviews (in the quote below, we have identified antecedent theorists that Schwandt has drawn on):

> Proponents of these persuasions share the goal of understanding the complex world of lived experience from the point of view of those who live it. This goal is variously spoken of as an abiding concern for the life world [Husserl], for the emic point of view, for understanding meaning, for grasping the actor's definition of a situation, for Verstehen [Weber][2]. The world of lived reality and situation-specific meanings that constitute the general object of investigation is thought to be constructed by social actors.
>
> (p. 118)

The general persuasions of the selected social theories considered in this book share the following perspective: they account for, inform, and illuminate descriptions and explanations of situated (contextual) actions or states (e.g., of people, texts, discourse). As Lave (1996) explained, researchers informed by these social perspectives "typically focus on the activities of persons acting … [and] there is agreement that such phenomena cannot be analyzed in isolation from the socially material world of that activity" (p. 5). These are theories of social practices; these are theories of action (e.g., Burke, 1935; Husserl, 1989; Schutz, 1966, 1967; Weber, 2019) (compare with discussions in assessment, Bennett, 2010; or language assessment, Chalhoub-Deville, 2016). Following Lave (1996), these social theories are also inevitably theories of context, although each of the many different social theories views context in a different light. In general, none of the social theories considered here conceptualizes persons, actions, or activities as somehow separate from the situated context(s) in which they are acting and interacting. Put another way, "context is viewed as a social world constituted in relation with persons acting" (p. 5). Whereas assessment-centred communities informed by cognitive theories have *backgrounded*, contained, disregarded, or dismissed context in validation research (cf. McNamara & Roever, 2006), language-centred communities informed by social theories have typically *foregrounded* it as integral to "doing and knowing", which are viewed as "open-ended processes of improvisation with the social, material, and experiential resources at hand" (Lave, 1996, p. 13).

It is important to stress, however, that although there is a shared general *persuasion* in this regard, the conceptualization of context differs considerably across a wide array of social theories that offer very different accounts of "the relations that constitute the contexts, or more precisely the contextualization, of activity" (Lave, 1996, p. 17). As we and others have stressed, context is relational (cf. Kramsch, 1993; Lave, 1996); it is defined by the theoretical lens that bounds our perceptions of it and the character of the situatedness we choose to apply (cf. Artemeva, 2006; Fox, Haggerty, & Artemeva, 2016).

According to Willis et al. (2007), social theories address "the social context of human actions, arguing that the ways in which we act and our beliefs are generated partly by social structure but also in communication between individuals and in social groups" (p. 439). In this book, we have argued that, by drawing on a number of alternative social theories, language assessment researchers can uncover new knowledge and better account for the role of context in assessment practices. As noted earlier, there is a vast array of social theories that would be useful in language assessment research.

What about cognitive persuasions and their contributions?

It should be noted that throughout this book we have characterized cognitive theories solely on the basis of the *persuasions* that they share. Given the purpose and scope of this book, we have not discussed the many different cognitive theories which have frequently informed assessment, test development, and validation research. For example, in education, since the early work on *situated cognition* (e.g., Brown, Collins, & Duguid, 1989; Kirshner & Whitson, 1997) and classic transdisciplinary efforts to "better reflect the fundamentally social nature of learning and cognition", there have been ongoing attempts to "reorient education" through the consideration of alternatives to the dominant "tradition of individual psychology" (Kirshner & Whitson, 1997, p. 1). (See Chapter 4 for additional details.) Further, more recent cognitively informed theories have increasingly incorporated social and contextual recognitions. For example, Bandura's *Social Cognitive/Learning Theory* (1977; 1986), Dörnyei's *Theory of Motivation* (2000, 2009) or Weir's (2005) *Socio-Cognitive Framework*, along with other cognitive theories and frameworks, are widely applied in language assessment and validation research. However, social theories are not (see Chapter 4).

As discussed in Chapter 1, the *naming* of entities, groups, things are often particularly challenging given the *in-between* spaces created by transdisciplinary interactions. In keeping with the overall purpose of this book, we have named the selected theories considered here in terms of their cognitive or social *persuasions*. This is of course risky, as it could suggest another dualism trap, which would run counter to the main thrust of this book, namely, to encourage transdisciplinary dialogue across disciplines, theoretical perspectives, and empirical traditions. Given the purpose of this book, the section which follows below provides details solely on a selective array of social theories, but this is not intended to underestimate the significant and valuable contributions of the many cognitive theories that inform assessment research in general, and language assessment research in particular. This simply reflects the view (Lazaraton & Taylor, 2007; McNamara, 2007; Swales, 1993; van Lier, 1989) that assessment researchers tend to be less familiar with social theories, which are not generally well understood, and are therefore underutilized in assessment research – in spite of their value in considerations of context.

Selected social theories: prominence and usefulness in considerations of context

Many social theories have developed in relation to a number of different philosophical antecedents conceptualized by such prominent thinkers as Buber, Cassirer, Freud, Hegel, Husserl, Piaget, Weber, and others. A number of the theories, including the ones reviewed below, developed from these philosophical antecedents. Our choice of the selected social philosophical schools of thought was informed by both their prominence in research literatures within language-centred communities and/or their usefulness in the descriptions of transdisciplinary empirical research projects presented in Parts II and III of this book. The summaries are necessarily abbreviated; however, each one includes references to texts which can extend and deepen understanding of the theories. Further, the ideas and terminology in the summaries below are very complex. It is hoped that their definitions and the illustrative examples of their use in forthcoming chapters will provide initial exposure to socio-theoretical perspectives, and ignite curiosity and application to considerations of context in assessment research.

A selective account of some antecedent social theorists and theories

Bakhtin and language as communication

Michail Bakhtin (1986), in his discussion of the study of language versus the study of human communication, argued that language acquires meaning through the *utterance* rather than through words, phrases, clauses, sentences, etc. Bakhtin proposed the *utterance* as the unit of analysis of *communication*, where the boundaries of the utterance are defined by the change of speaking subjects. Moreover, Bakhtin defined somewhat stable and recurrent forms of utterances as *genres*.

According to Bakhtin (1986), in a particular sphere of human communication, one's oral or written production is situated within the speech of others. The utterance possesses the qualities of *responsiveness* and *addressivity* in that it is always directed towards a respondent in a communicative situation, or *the other.* Miller (1994a) notes that addressivity allows an "individual communicative action and social system ... [to] interact with each other" (p. 71). More specifically, "without an addressee to whom an utterance is directed, ... it turns into a separate statement belonging to nobody" (Artemeva, 2004, p. 10). Any utterance responds to previous utterances and anticipates future responsive utterances produced by others, thus forming a *chain of communication.* In other words, Bakhtin advocated the *dialogic* nature of human communication. According to Hynes (2014),

> The self is dialogic and always in relation to the other. We can only perceive things from the perspective of something else, through contrast that is always set against a time and space. Meanings are always generated through interaction between self and other, whether or not the other is real or imaginary. Since meanings are shaped by the anticipated audience (real or imaginary), they are imbued with meanings of the other. Meanings are generated from the relation between self and other rather than by self alone. Life is thus expressed as a continuum of networks of statements and responses.
>
> (p. 73)

The dialogic nature of speech, the necessity for a change of speaking subjects and respondents, and the process of utterance exchange all reveal the communicative sense of oral language; "much the same thing is said to happen in writing" (Flower, 1994, p. 60).

Bakhtin's contributions to the *philosophy of dialogue* were original and influential, even though Western scholars such as Buber, Hegel, Husserl, Kant (see Brandist, 1997; Mendes-Flohr, 2015; Pape, 2016), "the Marburg School of neo-Kantianism and its central figures – Hermann Cohen, Paul Natorp" (Sandler, 2015, p. 166), and, especially, Cassirer (see Brandist, 1997; Poole, 1998) significantly influenced Bakhtin's thinking. As Brandist (1997) observed, "while Bakhtin's own terminology differs significantly from that of Hegel and Cassirer, the structural features common to their works are too pervasive to be passed off as one influence among many" (p. 1).

Vygotsky and the sociocultural turn in psychology

Lev Vygotsky's (1896–1934) work in developmental psychology has been foundational in conceptions of the sociocultural historical theory of human development (e.g., Kirschner & Martin, 2010). Vygotsky's (2012b) *contextualist* (Stetsenko & Arievitch, 2010) perspective on human learning and communication emphasized the sociohistorical development of human higher psychological functions and the mediating role of cultural means, symbols, and signs in the relationship between humans and their environment. In other words, as Stetsenko and Arievitch (2004) noted, from Vygotsky's perspective, psychological processes "are conceptualized as emerging ... from the *collective practical involvements* of humans with the world around them and as subordinate to the purposes and goals of these practical involvements" (pp. 483–484). That is, Vygotsky and his school saw human development as a collaborative work leading to the transformation of the world. Further, according to Rogoff (1990), Vygotsky argued that "individual intellectual development of higher mental processes cannot be understood without reference to the social milieu in which the individual is embedded" and without consideration of "the social roots of ... the tools for thinking".

According to Bruner (1987), "Vygotský was not only a psychologist but a cultural theorist, a scholar deeply committed to understanding" humans as "an expression of human culture", and his theory of "development was also a theory of education" (p. 1). The understanding of the role of tools, signs, and symbols in the process of learning informed Vygotsky's theory of interaction between learning and development: "The path from object to child and from child to object passes through another person" (1978, p. 30). In other words, tools, signs, and symbols mediate (i.e., serve as mediational artifacts or means) in and for the processes of learning and doing. As Rogoff (1990) added, "with Vygotsky, the cognitive process is shared between people" (p. 192).

By investigating how schoolchildren solve problems in isolation and collaborating with more advanced peers, Vygotsky noticed that children were more successful in solving problems with assistance than on their own. Consequently, he suggested that instead of using the level of the child's *actual development* as a determinant of their mental development, one should use the *level of their potential development*, manifested by a child's ability to solve a problem in collaboration with an adult or a more capable peer who already knows how to solve the problem. This "difference between the mental age, or the level of the actual development determined by the problems that can be solved independently, and the level reached by the child through the solution of problems accomplished ... in collaboration" (Vygotsky, 1978, p. 85; cf. 2003a, p. 379, 2003b, p. 905), Vygotsky named "zona blizhayshego razvitiia" (Vygotsky, 2003b, pp. 894, 905) (*the zone of the nearest development*), which became known in the West as the *zone of proximal development* (Vygotsky, 1978, p. 85). From this perspective, individual cognitive change is seen as engendered by the social, and "the only 'good learning'" is defined as that "which is in advance of development" (1978, p. 80).

Matusov (2007) explains that Vygotsky's unit of analysis is "shaped by the purpose of the researcher" (p. 308) and the nature of the study itself. In other words, the unit of analysis depends on the phenomenon that is the focus of the research: or, as Vygotsky (1987) stated, the unit of analysis is "a unit that possesses the characteristics inherent to the integral phenomenon" (p. 47) of interest. (See *dynamic assessment*, Chapter 4.)

The social construction of reality: Schutz, Berger, and Luckmann

An important social perspective on reality and human knowledge, known as *social constructionism*, was developed by Berger and Luckmann (1967), who drew heavily on the work of Schutz. Wagner (1970) in his introduction to an edited collection of Schutz's work stated that Schutz was dedicated to creating "the foundations for a complete and self-sufficient system of sociological thought and procedure" (p. 2). For Schutz and, later, for Berger and Luckmann, society was seen as created by humans and human interaction. In their discussion of the socially constructed beliefs of how to be in the world, Schutz (1966, 1967) and Berger and Luckmann (1967) developed such core concepts as *typification* and *habitualization*. Schutz, whose thinking was inspired by Husserl and Weber, understood typification as a social phenomenon derived from human knowledge of actions based in situations which are perceived as having previously occurred. In his attempts to understand how humans communicate with each other, Schutz (1967) arrived at the conclusion that typification plays a key role in the process of making sense of lived experiences in society.

Bazerman (2003) further explained that typification is the process of moving to standardized forms of recognizable and easily understood communicative action (p. 462) based on the "socially defined and shared recognitions of similarities" (Bawarshi & Reiff, 2010, p. 219). That is, individuals understand, recognize, and therefore infer meaning from previous direct experiences, and thus can act appropriately according to social norms and expectations. This process is maintained, in part, through habitualization (i.e., the formation of habits), to which all human activity is subject (Berger & Luckmann, 1967, p. 70), whereby a habit is viewed as a behaviour that occurs automatically in response to specific associated conditions or contextual cues.

Essentially, when an action is repeated frequently in the situations that are recognized as similar, a pattern is formed, and the meanings involved in performing the action become part of routine (Berger & Luckmann, 1967). The process of habitualization helps individuals to identify and respond appropriately to recurrent and recognizable social situations "with the same economical effort" (Berger & Luckmann, 1967, p. 71; cf. Kim & Berard, 2009). For example, when writing a multiple-choice quiz in class, the student who has written similar tests recognizes what to do (typification) and draws on previously formed habits (habitualization), for example, looking for a correct answer amongst item distractors, observing time limits, relating effort to point values.

A selective review of some socio-theoretical perspectives

Rhetorical Genre Studies

Rhetorical Genre Studies (RGS)[3] is a sociocultural theoretical approach to the study of typified patterns in human communication, or genres. RGS originated in the work of Miller (1984) and Bakhtin (1986) considers *genre* as a typified (Schutz, 1967) utterance (Bakhtin, 1986), or as a "socially situated" way "of communicating" (Tardy, 2012, p. 165). The term *rhetorical* in RGS refers to "the use of language to accomplish something" (Swales, 1990, p. 6). This perception of genre departs from the traditional literary view of genre as a stable textual form of literary composition (cf. Frow, 2005), and, rather than focusing on "form or function", it focuses on "the action" that genre "is used to accomplish" (Miller, 1984, p. 151).

In response to the Bakhtinian notion of addressivity and the Vygotskian notion of mediation, Bawarshi (2000) observes that "the speaker's very conception of the addressee is mediated by genre, because each genre embodies its own typical conception of the addressee" (p. 348). Therefore, from the RGS perspective, genre is seen as a typified pragmatic response to a recurrent social situation, the response, which mediates "between private intentions (purpose) and socially objectified needs (exigence)", and accomplishes a "social action, which creates meaning" (Miller, 2015, para 2). In other words, RGS sees genres as being produced in response to the participants' interpretations (or construals) of recurrent social situations (Miller, 1984; Miller & Devitt, 2019).

One of the central premises of Bakhtin's theory of genre is that "human consciousness ... comes into contact with reality only through the mediation of ideology ... and every genre has its own value-laden orientation" (Hanks, 1987, p. 671). This "value-laden" quality of genre does not allow it to be viewed as a finished product; genres "remain partial and transitional" (p. 681). Genres involve both form and content, which are inseparable (Giltrow, 2002). As Freedman and Medway (1994) state, "particularly significant for" RGS "has been Bakhtin's insistence that ... generic forms 'are much more flexible, plastic and free' [1986, p. 79] than grammatical or other linguistic patterns" (p. 6). Far from being rigid templates, genres can be modified according to rhetorical circumstances (e.g., Berkenkotter & Huckin, 1995).

According to Miller (1984), genres develop, change, and decay. Within the RGS framework, genres are viewed as situational expectations. A complete description of a genre from the RGS perspective "requires attention to how the form is rhetorical, to how it embodies the type of recurring situation that evokes it, and how it provides a strategic response to that situation" (Coe et. al., 2002, p. 6). In other words, genre is a concept that accounts for the social roles assigned to various discourses, and for "the mode of being of those who participate in the discourse" (Bawarshi, 2000, p. 339). In other words, genres are seen as types of discourse originating from "the interplay between systems of social value, linguistic convention, and the world portrayed. They derive their practical reality from their relation to particular linguistic acts, of which they are both the products and the primary resources" (Hanks, 1987, p. 671). Rhetors learn genres while being immersed in the situational context (Miller, 1992). Genres, thus, can be "expertly used by speakers [and writers] even though they may be unaware of generic parameters" (Hanks, 1987, p. 681).

Situated Learning

Situated Learning (e.g., Lave & Wenger, 1991; Rogoff, 1990) is a socio-theoretical approach to learning and knowing, which views them as occurring when humans co-participate in contextually bound social activities (Brown et al., 1989; Lave & Wenger, 1991). Theories of situated learning originated with Vygotsky's (2012b) explanation of individual higher mental functions as internalized social activities (cf. Artemeva, 2006). Two analytical viewpoints on situated learning, guided participation (GP) and legitimate peripheral participation (LPP), were developed in the late 1980s by Rogoff (1990) and Lave and Wenger (1991), respectively (cf. Freedman & Adam, 1996).

GP focuses on learning and learners and identifies its unit of analysis as a dyad that includes a teacher/instructor/parent/caregiver and student(s)/learners. It sees both the guidance provided by the instructor and the active participation of the students as key to the learning process. GP is characterized by tasks and activities that instructors design intentionally to facilitate students' learning and is typically observed in classroom settings.

In contrast, LPP focuses on social practice that has as its purpose material or symbolic production, and identifies its unit of analysis as a *community of practice* (CoP), or a group of people "who share a concern or a passion for something they do and learn how to do it better as they interact regularly" (Wenger-Trayner & Wenger-Trayner, 2015, What are communities of practice? section, para. 1).

Learning in LPP occurs incidentally as a by-product of participation in the practice of the CoP. LPP can be observed in the workplace, in a situation wherein a CoP is invested in integrating novices in the practices of the community and assists them with their initially peripheral but legitimate tasks, which contribute to the shared practice of the community (Artemeva et al., 2017).

Communities of practice

It is important to remember that the discussion of CoPs significantly predates both Lave and Wenger's (1991) and Wenger's (1998) books and dates back to the early conceptualizations of learning as cognitive apprenticeship or situated cognition (e.g., Brown et al., 1989; Lave, 1977, 1988). Unlike the concept of *discourse community* developed by Swales in the late 1980s (1988, 1990, 2016), which is based on the oral and written discourse its members share, a CoP "has an identity defined by a shared domain of interest" (Wenger-Trayner & para. 1, What are communities of practice? section, para. 2) and "is formed by people who engage in a process of collective learning in a shared domain of human endeavour" (para. 1). It is a group of "peers in the execution of real work. What holds them together is a common sense of purpose and a real need to know what each other knows" (Brown, as cited in Allee, 2000). Wenger (1998) named three main elements of a CoP: a) the domain of knowledge, which brings people together and which people who form a CoP organize around in a "joint enterprise" (p. 77); b) the community, as a social entity (Wenger-Trayner & Wenger-Trayner, 2015), which binds people together through *mutual engagement*, "because they sustain dense relations of mutual engagement organized around what they are there to do" (Wenger, 1998, p. 74); and c) the practice, which allows CoP members (practitioners) to share a *repertoire* of stories and resources that embody the accumulated knowledge of the community put into play in accomplishing its collective outcome or product. The combination of these elements, according to Wenger (1998), constitutes a CoP (cf. Wenger-Trayner & Wenger-Trayer, 2015; see also Chapter 8).

Gee (2004), as noted earlier in Chapter One, took issue with the labelling of groups as *communities of practice,* particularly with regard to students' learning in schools, because of the "vexatious" issues of "participation, membership, and boundaries that are problematic" (p. 78) with the notion of community itself (e.g., deciding who is a member and who is not; how much participation is required; what is the shared goal in the face of individual differences). He was particularly interested in the processes of *situated learning* outside of formal learning in schools (e.g., in computer and video gaming) and the implications for learning in traditional classroom contexts. He preferred the notion of "semiotic social spaces" (p. 79), rather than groupings of individuals as communities, and suggested the alternative idea of "affinity spaces" (pp. 77–89), wherein learners were motivated to engage, interact, and act in relation to technology and others, while demonstrating complex literacy, innovative strategies, and resourcefulness.

Cultural-Historical Activity Theory (CHAT)

Cultural-Historical Activity Theory (CHAT) (e.g., Engeström, 1987; Leont'ev, 1981; Stetsenko & Arievitch, 2004, 2010) is another social theory which shares its origins with the Vygotskian view of the development of human higher psychological functions in sociocultural contexts (Vygotsky, 2012b). CHAT has focused on *long-term, stabilized human activity* (Spinuzzi & Guile, 2019) in such areas as health, law, or education. The theory is currently seen as having developed through four generations (Spinuzzi & Guile, 2019). The focus of what is now considered the first generation of CHAT, developed by Vygotsky (2012b) (please note that Vygotsky never used the term *activity theory*), was on the individual "object-oriented action" (Engeström & Miettinen, 1999, p. 4) mediated through cultural material or symbolic artifacts, with language being one of them. The unit of analysis in this Vygotskian version of CHAT was word meaning.

The second generation of the theory, developed by Vygotsky's student Leont'ev (1981), distinguished between an individual action and collective activity mediated by material or symbolic artifacts. The unit of analysis in this version of AT was activity that includes both the individual and the individual's culturally defined environment (cf. Cole & Wertsch, 1996). The mediated collective human activity in this generation was viewed as a triad – "often depicted as a triangle" (Artemeva & Freedman, 2001, p. 167) – consisting of the collective subject, the object towards which the activity is directed, and the material or symbolic artifact that mediated the activity (Leont'ev, 1981). Engeström (1999) and others criticized Leont'ev's theory for the use of the object-oriented activity both as an explanatory principle of the theory and as the object of the study. In an attempt to resolve the contradiction caused by collective and individual units of analysis, Engeström (1987) introduced a new unit of analysis, an activity system (AS), which included "the object-oriented productive aspect and the person-oriented communicative aspect of the human conduct" (Engeström, 1996, p. 67). AS has often been depicted as an expanded Leont'ev's triangle, with the bottom part of the triangle representing the collective aspect of activity (i.e., the community, its rules, and division of labour).

The first and second generations of AT considered a single activity. The goal of the third generation of the theory was to consider interactions between at least two stable and well-bound ASs with a clear object (Engeström & Miettinen, 1999). According to Spinuzzi & Guile (2019), however, the applications of the third generation of AT to complex configurations of more than one AS have revealed its limitations, especially in the cases of not-yet-stabilized activities directed towards fractional and emergent objects. In 2009, Engeström issued a call for the development of the next, fourth generation of AT, which would account for the interactions among multiple, not necessarily stable ASs with not always well-defined objects toward which the activity is directed. While some research has been dedicated to the new version of AT, it has not been fully developed yet (Spinuzzi & Guile, 2019).

Distributed cognition (Hutchins, 1995a, 1995b)

Edwin Hutchins (1995a) argued that "human cognition is always situated in a complex sociocultural world and cannot be unaffected by it" (p. xiii). In his early work, he provided an ethnographic description of his experiences on board a large, naval ship. His intent was to demonstrate, through an example of a complex human activity in the everyday world, that is, "in the wild", that "the performance of cognitive tasks that exceed individual abilities is always shaped by a social organization of distributed cognition" (p. 262). Hutchins argues that operating complex systems requires a team effort, as no single individual is capable of building a coherent interpretation of a given problem, nor entirely accountable for its outcomes. As examples of such contexts – "where context is not a fixed set of surrounding conditions but a wider dynamical process of which the cognition of an individual is only a part" (Hutchins, 1995a, p. xiii) – he cites the operators at a nuclear power plant, an aircraft flight crew, and the bridge team on a large ship, all of which demand "a distributed interpretation formation" (p. 241).

Hutchins (1995a) reflected on what his theory was intended to do, namely,

> [to] put cognition back into the social and cultural world ... to show that human cognition is not just influenced by culture and society, but that it is in a very fundamental sense a cultural and social process. To do this I will move the boundaries of the cognitive unit of analysis out beyond the skin of the individual person and treat the navigation team as a cognitive and computational system.
>
> (p. xiv)

In a similar way, Hutchins (1995b) and Hutchins and Klausen (1996) investigated the cockpit of a commercial airliner, which requires a dynamic interplay between two or more pilots and their interaction with a range of artifacts and technological and mediating tools to accomplish safe flights. First, Hutchins (1995b) highlighted the importance of shifting the view from the individual mind to the expanded socio-technical system, as a way to direct "our attention beyond the cognitive properties of individuals to the properties of external representations and to the interactions between internal and external representations" (p. 287). Later, Hutchins and Klausen (1996) stated that the analysis of a flight crew performing in a flight simulator revealed "a pattern of cooperation and coordination of actions among the crew which on one level can be seen as a structure for propagating and processing information and on another level appears as a system of activity in which shared cognition emerges as a system level property" (p. 15).

Distributed cognition was also considered as a theoretical framework in the study of other complex systems. For example, Fields, Wright, Marti, and Palmonari (1998) focused their study of the system of air traffic control (ATC) on the "representations present in the ATC cognitive system, how they are used, and how they are distributed across multiple artifacts and agents" (p. 85). Ultimately, their goal was to, through the analysis of representations, "reflect critically on the part that new technologies and new representational systems might play in future in this complex work domain" (p. 90). Another example is the work of Hollan, Hutchins, and Kirsh (2000), who applied distributed cognition as a foundation to advance the field of human–computer interaction, aiming to "better understand the emerging dynamic of interaction in which the focus task is no longer confined to the desktop but reaches into a complex networked world of information and computer-mediated interactions" (p. 192).

English as a lingua franca (ELF)

In a globalized world characterized by multilingual and multicultural interactions, sociocultural theories help us to achieve a broader understanding of context and to define what characterizes a proficient communicator. English as a lingua franca (ELF) is one of those theories, which explains the changing communicative needs that require the ability to "shuttle between different varieties of English and different speech communities" (Canagarajah, 2006, p. 233).

Despite the fact that ELF research is a relatively recent activity, "both ELF itself and other lingua francas (contact languages used among people who do not share a first language) have existed for many centuries" (Jenkins, Cogo, & Dewey, 2011, p. 281), for example, as a trade language or as a means of colonization. But it was not until the publication of the first seminal works in ELF communication (Jenkins, 2000; Seidlhofer, 2001) that the phenomenon began to attract interest. It has since become a prevalent focus of research in applied linguistics and sociolinguistics (Cogo, 2015). Nonetheless, scholars have noted that defining what ELF means has not been without controversy. Jenkins (2006) states that "in its purest form, ELF is defined as a contact language used only among non-mother tongue speakers" (p. 160), while the majority of ELF researchers currently adopt a more comprehensive view of the concept, one that also includes first language (L1) speakers of English as users of ELF for intercultural communication (e.g., Seidlhofer, 2004, 2011; Jenkins, 2007; Mauranen, 2012). This reflects the reality that "English is spoken in situations with widely varying combinations of participants, including first-language speakers of different varieties" (Mauranen, 2017, p. 8) and also confirms that "English is no one's native language in ELF communication since all participants will need to adapt and adjust their language and other communicative practices to ensure successful communication" (Baker, 2015, p. 11).

Jenkins, Cogo, and Dewey (2011) provide a detailed account of ELF research and early studies conducted at a range of linguistic levels: i) phonology (e.g., Jenkins, 2000, 2002); ii) lexis/lexicogrammar (e.g., Cogo & Dewey, 2006, 2012; Seidlhofer, 2004); and iii) pragmatics (e.g., Cogo, 2009; Kaur, 2009; Mauranen, 2009; Pitzl, 2005; Seidlhofer, 2009). However, over time, research orientation has shifted from the "observed regularity in forms" to a greater interest "in the underlying processes that motivate the use of one or another form at any given moment in an interaction" (Jenkins et al., 2011, p. 296). As Cogo (2015) explains, this "places more importance on speakers' creative practices in their use of plurilingual resources to flexibly co-construct their common repertoire in accordance with the needs of their community and the circumstances of the interaction" (p. 3), and aligns research agendas with a view of language as a social practice (Baker, 2015; Canagarajah, 2006).

It follows that, regardless of their language backgrounds, interlocutors who engage in ELF communication acquire a range of strategies such as accommodation, negotiation, clarification, cooperation, adaptability, and openness to difference (e.g., Baker, 2012; Harding, 2015; Harding & McNamara, 2017; Jenkins et al., 2011). However, this brings challenges to language testing and assessment (Harding & McNamara, 2017). The existing privilege of L1 speakers' norms in testing policies, coupled with their exemption from being formally assessed as ready to cope with real-world communicative demands (Elder, McNamara, Kim, Pill, & Sato, 2017), reveals the conservative values embedded in some contexts of assessment (Harding & McNamara, 2017), which can have negative consequences for stakeholders.

Theories of intercultural communication

In her account of what *intercultural communication* consists of as a field of study, Zhu (2016) points out that it is engaged with "how people from different 'cultural' backgrounds interact with each other and negotiate 'cultural' or linguistic differences perceived or made relevant through interactions, as well as the impact such interactions have on group relations and on individuals' identities, attitudes and behaviors" (p. xxii). She adds that this field of inquiry has a multi-disciplinary background, informed by a number of theoretical perspectives, including: i) interactional sociolinguistics, pragmatics, cross-cultural/intercultural pragmatics (e.g., Kecskes, 2014), discourse studies, translation studies, ELF, and bi-/multilingualism studies; ii) intercultural education, language learning, and teaching; iii) cultural and linguistic anthropology, ethnicity studies, and gender studies; iv) communication studies and interpersonal communication; v) cross-cultural psychology; vi) critical discourse studies and critical cultural studies; and vii) sociocultural theory of learning in SLA (p. xxiii).

Some of the theories and concepts that help us understand intercultural communication are summarized below:

- *Face-negotiation theory*. Ting-Toomey's (2005) theory explains that any conflict is a "face-threatening phenomenon" (p. 72), where face is related to "identity respect and other-identity consideration issues within and beyond the actual encounter episode" (p. 73). In order to manage conflictual situations, participants will enact *facework*, that is, "the specific verbal and nonverbal behaviors that we engage in to maintain or restore face loss and to uphold and honor face again" (p. 73), based on individual, relational, and situational factors.
- *Conversational constraints theory*. The theory that focuses on understanding "the cultural underpinnings of choices of communication strategies among people of different cultural backgrounds" (Kim, 2005, p. 94), in terms of five conversational constraints: concern for clarity, concern for minimizing imposition, concern for avoiding hurting the hearer's feelings, concern for avoiding negative evaluation by the hearer, and concern for effectiveness.
- *Expectancy violation theory*. Burgoon and Hubbard (2005) argue that "every culture has guidelines for human conduct that carry associated anticipations for how others will behave" (p. 149). These expectancies involve "a predictive and a prescriptive component"

(p. 151), that is, reflecting both what is common and regular in terms of communication within a given culture and also what is envisaged as standards of conduct.

- *Communication accommodation theory*. This theory assumes that accommodation is "the process through which interactants regulate their communication (adopting a particular linguistic code or accent, increasing or decreasing their speech rate, avoiding or increasing eye contact, etc.) in order to appear more like (accommodation) or distinct from each other (non-accommodation)" (Gallois, Ogay, & Giles, 2005, p. 137).
- *Anxiety/uncertainty management theory*. Gudykunst (2005b) states that everyone we meet is a potential stranger, as "we do not share all of our group memberships with anyone" (p. 285). Therefore, dealing with the ambiguity of new situations requires managing uncertainty and anxiety, "because we do not want to appear prejudiced or [to be] perceived as incompetent communicators" (p. 287).
- *Face and politeness perspectives*. Brown and Levinson (1987) associate "face with notions of being embarrassed or humiliated, or 'losing face' " (p. 63). They highlight the emotional investment of interacting interlocutors, the possibility that face "can be lost, maintained, or enhanced, and must be constantly attended to in interaction" (p. 63), and the role of politeness strategies, which allow for communication amongst "potentially aggressive parties" (p. 1).
- *Impoliteness theory*. Culpeper's (1996) impoliteness framework is oriented towards attacking face and includes strategies that seek to cause social disruption, through hostile communication or confrontational discourse, such as being unsympathetic, seeking disagreement, making the other feel uncomfortable, and associating the other with a negative aspect.

Especially in multilingual and multicultural contexts, in which English is used as a lingua franca (ELF), effective intercultural communication requires more than cultural awareness (Baker, 2011), a component typically included in prominent intercultural communicative competence (ICC) frameworks (e.g., Byram, 1997; Deardorff, 2006; Fantini, 2000). It also requires increasing levels of *Intercultural Awareness* (ICA), defined as "a conscious understanding of the role culturally based forms, practices and frames of reference can have in intercultural communication, and an ability to put these conceptions into practice in a flexible and context specific manner in real time communications" (Baker, 2011, p. 202). This concept highlights the need to approach culture in a dialectical and dynamic way, considering what is fluid or emergent, but also what is fixed or defined *a priori* (Kecskes, 2014) as a result of our participation and/or membership in multiple discourse groups or discourse systems (Scollon & Scollon, 2001) and our individual expectations.

Theory of interactional competence

Interactional competence (IC) is another social theory that emphasizes the interactional nature of spoken ability, broadening its construct to include "a more social view where communicative language ability and the resulting interactional performance reside within a social and jointly constructed context" (Galaczi & Taylor, 2018, p. 220). Based on the notions that "communication is not one-way ... but a two-way negotiative effort" (Kramsch, 1986, p. 368) and that our involvement in interactive practices can be described as "a movement between the two, a dialogue" (Hall, 1999, p. 143), the theory of IC has been discussed by a number of scholars in the field of second language learning, teaching, and testing (e.g., Galaczi & Taylor, 2018; Hall, 1993, 1995, 1999; He & Young, 1998; Kramsch, 1986; May, Nakatsuhara, Lam, & Galaczi, 2020; McNamara, 1997; Plough, Banerjee, & Iwashita, 2018; Roever & Kasper, 2018; Young, 2008, 2011).

The definition that Young (2011) adopted for IC includes "the pragmatic relationship between participants' employment of linguistic and interactional resources and the contexts in which they are employed ... [and] how those resources are employed mutually and reciprocally by all participants in a particular discursive practice" (p. 428). Although the concept of IC has been applied by distinct scholars in slightly different ways, it is worth highlighting some of its core features. Interactional competence (IC):

- has its foundation in the concept of co-construction (Jacoby & Ochs, 1995);
- is located within *interactive practices* (Hall, 1995) or *discursive practices* (Young, 2008, 2011), which Young (2011) defined as "recurring episodes of social interaction in context, episodes that are of social and cultural significance to a community of speakers" (p. 427);
- presupposes the use of generic (Hall, 1993), linguistic, and pragmatic resources (He & Young, 1998), or, as Young (2008) expanded, identity, linguistic, and interactional resources;
- is context-dependent and locally situated (Hall, 1993; Young, 2008, 2011); the context of practices, according to Young (2011), "includes the network of physical, spatial, temporal, social, interactional, institutional, political, and historical circumstances" (428) in which participants act; and
- requires the construction of intersubjectivity, a "shared internal context" (Kramsch, 1986, p. 367) between interactional partners, or the establishment of "a triangular relationship between the sender, the receiver, and the context of situation", as explained by Wells (1981), in which "the sender intends that, as a result of his communication, the receiver should come to attend to the same situation as himself and construe it in the same way" (p. 46).

Regarding the assessment of interactional competence, the co-constructed nature of IC has posed some challenges for language assessment (e.g., Brooks, 2009; Chalhoub-Deville & Deville, 2005; Fulcher, 2003; McNamara, 1997; McNamara & Roever, 2006; Young, 2011). Nonetheless, May et al. (2020) argue that over the last few decades IC has attracted a lot of attention in the field of speaking assessment research, and, therefore, the resulting body of research has provided "useful insights about the co-construction of interaction … paving the way for a comprehensive definition of the IC construct (e.g., Ducasse & Brown, 2009; Lam, 2018; Galaczi, 2008, 2014; May, 2011; Nakatsuhara, 2013; Plough et al., 2018; Roever & Kasper, 2018)" (p. 166). Yet, May et al. (2020), referring to the "rather fluid and complex construct of IC" (p. 186), and other scholars (e.g., Galaczi & Taylor, 2018; Plough et al., 2018; Youn, 2020), remind us of the need for continued research, pointing out areas that still need to be further investigated.

What evidence is there of the contributions of social theories to language-centred communities?

Within language-centred communities such as discourse studies (e.g., Fairclough, 2003; Gee, 1990; Lemke, 1995) and writing studies (e.g., Bawarshi, 2000; Bazerman, 1988, 1994a, 1994b; Dias et al., 1999; Freedman & Medway, 1994; Giltrow, 2002; Schryer, 1993), scholars have been actively engaged in richly retheorizing language by drawing extensively on differing socio-theoretically informed perspectives. For example, within discourse studies, following Bakhtin (1981a, 1986), language has been theorized as social action:

> Language is but a "piece of the action" – and a social action is constituted as a social practice with value and meaning only in and through the Discourse of which it is a part – just as an assortment of cards constitutes a hand only in and through the card game of which it is a part. The card analogy breaks down in one respect, though: when we are playing cards we usually know exactly what game we are playing. But when we play a piece of language within a specific social practice, what Discourse we are in is often a matter of negotiation, contestation, and hybridity (Bakhtin, 1981a, 1986). By hybridity I mean an integration or mixture – differently tight in different cases – of several historically distinct Discourses. Discourses "capture" people and use them to "speak" throughout history … people "capture" Discourses and use them to strategize and survive.
>
> (Gee, 1990, p. 149)

Within the stream of discourse studies with which Gee is associated, the capital letter in Discourse is meaningful in terms of what a *Discourse* is and does:

> A Discourse is a socially accepted association among ways of using language, other symbolic expressions, and 'artifacts', of thinking, feeling, believing, valuing, and acting that can be used to identify oneself as a member of a socially meaningful group or 'social network', or to signal (that one is playing) a socially meaningful 'role'.
>
> (Gee, 1990, p. 131)

Moving from the abstract definition to concrete examples, Gee explains through rich descriptive detail the discursive interactions in a biker bar, at a job interview, or in the first year of law school. Capital 'D' discourse is relevant to the disciplinary languages and cultures of academia – as Gee illustrates in his discussion of law school.

On the other hand, Fairclough (2003), drawing on the Hallidayan tradition in linguistics as discussed above, is associated with a different stream of discourse studies. He explains his approach in this way: "Discourse analysis ... was taken to entail detailed linguistic analysis of texts, which is not the case for much discourse analysis" (p. 215). Fairclough (2003) defined discourse "in the general sense for language (including visual images) as an element of social life" (p. 214). The point of interest in relation to this book as a whole is that both of these streams of discourse studies (and others not mentioned here) have extensively theorized the nature of language by drawing on social theories.

The influence of social theories is also evident in writing studies which actively moved away from writing as solely a textual product in which grammatical accuracy was the main focus of assessment. Writing was retheorized as process (e.g., Britton & Pradl, 1982; Elbow, 1983, 1998) and, later, as social action (Cooper & Holzman, 1989). Freedman (1994) described this shifting focus on process as the context for a "rhetorical turn" in writing theory and pedagogy which focused attention on the "demands of the *occasion*" (p. 4). Looking back at this history, Tardy (2009) defined rhetorical knowledge as knowledge of "the intended purposes and an awareness of the dynamics of persuasion within a sociotheorical context" (p. 21). (See *Rhetorical Genre Knowledge,* Chapter Six.)

Faigley (1995) considered some of the many possibilities afforded by "taking a social perspective" (p. 235) in writing research, alluding to a number of the theorists and theories, which are identified in some of the bracketed inserts below:

> Researchers taking a social perspective study how individual acts of communication define, organize, and maintain social groups [e.g., *situated learning/communities of practice*]. They view written texts not as detached objects possessing meaning on their own, but as links in communicative chains, with their meaning emerging from their relationships to previous texts and the present context [Bakhtin,

> 1981a, 1986] ... [and] to consider issues such as social roles, group purposes, communal organization, ideology and finally theories of culture.
>
> [*Activity Theory*/Vygotsky, 2012b] (pp. 235–236)

While the *social turn* in writing and discourse studies was underway, however, language assessment remained uneasily positioned and influenced by the dominant Discourses of the assessment-centred communities. There was only limited acknowledgement, knowledge of, or reflection on alternative, richly theorized perspectives on language as a social phenomenon. Shaped and informed by social theories and characterized by extensive accounts of context, language-centred communities such as discourse studies and writing studies tended to view language assessment as theoretically impoverished, misguided, threatening, and potentially undermining. Arguably, language assessment's location at the boundaries of language-centred and assessment communities created particular challenges with regard to context.

This section has provided a selective summary of prominent social philosophical schools of thought, discussed a number of the many social theories that have been useful in conceptualizing context in situated social practices (i.e., such as assessment), and examined the reconceptualization of language afforded by social theories within the language-centred communities of discourse studies and writing studies.

Lave (1996) noted, as we have, that although social theories share "commonalities" (i.e., *persuasions*), there are important differences between them. She identified two overall "viewpoints" which were evident in her transdisciplinary partners' socio-theoretical perspectives on activity and context:

> One argues that the central theoretical relation is historically constituted between persons engaged in socioculturally constructed activity and world with which they are engaged. Activity Theory is a representative of such theoretical traditions. The other focuses on the construction of the social in social interaction; this leads to the view that activity is its own context. Here the central theoretical relation is the intersubjective relation among co-participants in interaction. This derives from a tradition of phenomenological social theory. These two viewpoints do not exhaust the positions taken ... but cover the majority.
>
> (p. 17)

She reflected on these differing viewpoints, indicating that "it now seems more appropriate to sum them up, respectively, as explaining how it is that people live in *history*, and how it is that people *live* in history" (p. 21). Lave's (1996) discussion of these viewpoints on *context as situated activity* (see pp. 17–22) may be useful in illustrating the differing approaches to context afforded by the social theories summarized above. In Part II of this book, these theories and perspectives are illustrated in empirical examples of transdisciplinary language assessment research projects.

Having provided a selective overview of some prominent social theories and perspectives, below we discuss their additive benefits as alternative perspectives in assessment research. As an example, Kane's (1990) use of Toulmin's (1958, 1969) *model of argumentation* is examined in relation to Miller's (1984, 1994b) discussion of the same model. Kane (1990, 2006, 2013b), as we have previously noted, is a well-known contributor to considerations of validity and validation in assessment-centred communities. Miller (1994a, 1994b) is a prominent rhetorician whose conception of genre as social action is frequently drawn on by researchers in writing studies. Toulmin (1958, 1969, 1972, 1990) is considered a philosopher of rhetoric and argumentation.

What are the additive benefits of social theories in assessment research?

Over the past two decades, we have observed that theoretical frameworks and theorists who have been prominent in communities focused on *language* have begun to inform research within communities focused on *assessment*. For example, within mainstream assessment/measurement, Kane (e.g., 1990, 2006, 2013b) has explicitly drawn on the work of Toulmin (e.g., 1958) to frame his argument-based approach to validation (see also, Chapelle, Enright, & Jamieson, 2008; Chapelle, 2021).

Argumentation, as Van Eemeren, Grootendorst, and Kruiger (2019) define it,

> is a communicative and interactional act complex aimed at resolving a difference of opinion with the addressee by putting forward a constellation of propositions the arguer can be held accountable for to make the standpoint at issue acceptable to a rational judge who judges reasonably.
>
> (p. 7)

The history of the study of argumentation, or argumentation theory, is long and "goes back to Antiquity" (Van Eemeren, 1995; Van Eemeren et al., 2019). Argumentation theory allows researchers to develop methodological approaches that "provide adequate instruments for analyzing, evaluating, and producing argumentative discourse" (p. 12), and thus have a "practical value" (p. 146).

Different argumentation theories propose different views on argumentative discourse, different fundamental concepts, and different types of argumentation analysis. For example, if, according to Van Eemeren et al. (2019), "the traditional rhetorical approach is based on Aristotle's view"

(p. 18), approaches proposed in the twentieth century by, for example, Toulmin in 1958 (Toulmin's model of argumentation), Perelman and Olbrechts-Tyteca (1958, 1969) (the New Rhetoric), Schiffrin (1990) (narrative discourse and discourse analysis), and many others have their roots in a variety of traditions. In this book we focus on Toulmin's model of argumentation because it was discussed by Messick (1989), elaborated by Kane (e.g., 1990, 2006, 2013b), applied by Chapelle et al. (2008) and Chapelle (2021), and is the focus of ongoing discussion (cf. Addey, Maddox, & Zumbo, 2020), as the dominant approach to the collection of assessment evidence in support of a validity argument.

Kane applied variations of the six interrelated components of Toulmin's (1958) model of argumentation, that is, claims, grounds, warrants, backing, qualifier(s), and rebuttal(s), in order to define a logical, systematic, evidence-driven procedure for validation research. The approach was intended for validation during the design and development of new assessment practices (e.g., tests, inventories, checklists), as well as the validation of currently-in-use/ongoing ones. Kane (1990) viewed the approach as part of a "strong program" (Cronbach, 1988, p. 162) of validation research, "with a definite place to begin and criteria for choosing what to do next at each stage in the inquiry" (p. 34).

Kane (1990) saw the process as iterative and "open-ended" (p. 34). He stressed that it was "not intended as a checklist or a cookbook to be used in conducting validation studies" (p. 34). In building an argument for the validity of inferences drawn from assessment practices, Kane sought to outline steps in validation, "without getting into specific examples" (p. 34). He argued that validation was "the chain of evidence" (Kane, Crooks, & Cohen, 1999, p. 6) required to support the "sequence or network of inferences and assumptions involved in getting from ... observed [assessment] performances to the conclusions and decisions to be based on these performances" (Kane, 2013c, p. 448). Kane's purpose was clear, and explicit: to provide a practical, systematic approach to validation which nonetheless honoured the breadth and depth of conceptualizations of validity (e.g., Messick, 1989; the *Standards*, 2014); to provide a pathway for validation, marked by steps in concrete, workable terms.

Given this purpose, Kane may have intentionally underplayed Toulmin's emphasis on *context* (cf. Addey et al., 2020). Arguably, in his original conceptualization, Kane applied the Toulmin model as a "field-invariant" or as a "self-contained ... logical formula" (Lunsford, 2002, p. 111), whereas Toulmin (1958) stressed the importance of context, asserting that "utterances are made at particular times and in particular situations, and they have to be understood and assessed with one eye on this context" (p. 182). A similar point is made by Addey et al. (2020), who also remark on Toulmin's "strong emphasis on a pluralistic approach to argument, context and diversity" (p. 589) (cf. Toulmin, 1972, 1990).

Miller (1994b) explained why Toulmin emphasized *context*, which he viewed as the enabling requirement for "interpretation [or meaning]"

(p. 32). Rather than a chain of evidence and inference (which suggests linear, static, and stable links), Toulmin proposed a hierarchy of relationships between utterance (linguistic proposition), illocutionary force (the actions that utterance performs), and context (which makes meaning possible). Thus, Kane's original application of Toulmin's model of argumentation was attenuated to a degree by not fully acknowledging the role of context in the meaning-making, evidence-driven cycle of the validation process.

Rather, context is largely reduced to a field-invariant *domain definition* (cf. Chapelle, 2021) by drawing on cognitively informed concepts and terminology from measurement, psychology, and psychometrics (i.e., target domain, assessment/test domain, and construct domain).[4] Kane's argument-based model of validation is most fully explained in Chapelle's (2021) exquisitely detailed, experience-laden account of its application in practice. Although she encourages multiple (e.g., qualitative, mixed methods) approaches in the accumulation of validation evidence, acknowledges Messick's (1989) incorporation of sociocultural concepts, and recognizes the potential of alternative theoretical perspectives, the role of *context* remains undertheorized and largely uninterrogated because, implicitly or explicitly, the approach is informed by cognitive theory, and the Toulmin model cannot be fully applied without the benefit of the alternative perspectives afforded by social theories.

Well before its application in validation research, Toulmin's (1958, 1969) model of argumentation was the focus of prominent socio-theoretically informed scholars in rhetoric (e.g., Miller, 1984), sociocultural theory (Cole, 1995; Wertsch, 1993), and writing studies (e.g., Coe, 1990, 1994; Freedman & Medway, 1994; Paré & Smart, 1994; Prior, 1991). Arguably, extending Kane's argument-based validation approach by drawing on the perspectives afforded by social theories would allow for Toulmin's full model of argumentation to be incorporated in validation practices and address the issue of context. An example of the use of social theories to extend Kane's validation approach is the recent paper by Addey, Maddox, and Zumbo (2020), who demonstrated the benefits derived from transdisciplinary research partnerships. This 2020 paper was the result of the collaboration of a sociologist (Addey), an educational anthropologist (Maddox), and a measurement/psychometric specialist (Zumbo) who shared a common interest in validation research in the context of large-scale, high-stakes standardized testing. They addressed the omission of context in Kane's (1990, 2006, 2013b) application of Toulmin's (1958, 1972) model in validation practices, applying Actor Network Theory (ANT) (Latour, 2005) (a systems-based social theory; see Chapter 7 for additional background on ANT) to expand current validation approaches and take into account the diversity of actors and contexts in assessment validation practices.

Further, although it is rarely acknowledged and certainly underappreciated, research partners drawn from outside traditional research communities can provide extraordinary insights on complex problems. For example, while we were researching the use of Toulmin's model in writing studies, an article by Lunsford (2002) stood out. She was a classroom teacher at the time her research was published in the prominent journal *Written Communication*. Lunsford provided a particularly useful commentary on "contextualizing" (p. 109) Toulmin's model of argument. She was critical of researchers who discounted or ignored Toulmin's emphasis on context, and whose formulaic, decontextualized applications of the model privileged a "single viewpoint" with a "static lens" (p. 115). Applying Toulmin's (1958, 1969) model of argumentation in her writing classroom, she documented its use in a case study. Her findings indicated that it acted both as a heuristic and an analytic tool which engendered *context* through the dynamic, mutable, reflexive and recursive processes of co-construction arising from "layered negotiations", "complex interactions" (p. 159), tensions, contradictions, and, ultimately, richer, thicker, deeper, and more meaningful understanding.

Lunsford's (2002) account of the application of Toulmin's model as an ultimately rewarding but "complex, entangled process" (p. 161) is similar to the accounts of those in the assessment-centred community who have applied it. For example, Chapelle (2021) acknowledged that "fortitude is required" (p. xviii). She pointed out that guidance from the literature has been limited and confusing. It is often riddled with terminology, and typically assumes "background knowledge of technical concepts and socially situated issues in the field" (Chapelle, 2021, xviii). Lunsford (2002) had the benefit of social theories to account for her application of Toulmin's model in her classroom. As Toulmin (1958) emphasized, Miller (1984/1994b) explained, and Lunsford (2002) illustrated, the model's potential is only realized through the *context* it engenders in practice by participants who engage in the recursive, reflective, dynamic, situated, and mutable process it entails. This is the process of validation which is consistent with Messick's (1989) view that "validity is an evolving property ... validation is a continuing process" (p. 13), and a *rhetorical art*. Fully realizing the promise of Messick's conceptualization of validity (cf. Moss, 2018) and the potential of Kane's argument-based approach to validation will require an expanded understanding and application of social theories to account for context, and concomitant methodological pluralism (Moss, 2013, 2016; Moss & Haertel, 2016).

Conclusion

While Swales (1998) identified the problem of context in applied linguistics research, it has been particularly evident in the language assessment community, and most evident in validation research (e.g., Chalhoub-Deville, 2001, 2003; McNamara, 2007). Because validation has been a central concern of assessment-centred communities (e.g., educational and psychological measurement, psychology), in general there has been almost exclusive reliance on cognitive theories. At the same time, there has also been general recognition that assessment and validation are social practices (Addey et al., 2020; Markus, 1998; McNamara & Roever, 2006; Messick, 1998). Context in a complex social practice such as *language* assessment continues to be an issue, because it is "simply too complex to be adequately understood from a single [theoretical or] methodological perspective" (Moss & Haertel, 2016, p. 130). Further, seeking *alternative rival* explanations (as Cronbach, 1988 and others have advised us to do) offers a productive means of addressing this issue. Such an alternative is available in the richly elaborated landscape of social theories and concomitant approaches to research.

In validation research, social theories can inform alternative perspectives consonant with alternative inquiry systems, and result in rich and thick alternative descriptive and explanatory detail. Such detail would clarify the limitations of inferences drawn from tests and other assessment practices in *context* (however we choose to bound it). When there are questions of context (and one may ask when there wouldn't be), social theories may inform our perspective on and evoke the methodologies and methods that are best suited to the validation questions we are asking. The problem is that social theories have not traditionally been widely studied or understood in language assessment research (McNamara, 2007; McNamara & Roever, 2006), and when they have been used, they have tended to be only "thinly accounted for" (Swales, 1998, p. 110).

Over 50 years after the beginning of the *communicative turn* in conceptualizing language and language-in-use, the disconnect between how language is defined in language-centred communities and how it is operationalized and measured by assessment-centred communities continues to alienate and discourage the active engagement of those who have language as the focus of their interest and expertise (e.g., in language teaching, discourse studies, writing and composition studies). It is our impression that many who are involved in such language-intensive fields continue to distrust and reject research on language assessment, because they variously see it as misguided, atheoretical, or beyond their reach. In our view, such deeply entrenched disciplinary views have created an impasse. As Young (2006) noted: "Language is rooted in social life and nowhere is this more apparent than in the ways in which … language is assessed" (p. xiv). After 50 years, it should be clear that the problem of context in assessment practices cannot be adequately addressed by one theoretical perspective endemic to the disciplinary practices of assessment-centred communities alone (e.g., psychology, measurement, psychometrics).

In keeping with the transdisciplinary research agenda of the present book, and given our goal of motivating research collaboration across research communities, our primary concern has been to create conditions for *praxis* – "self-reflective, self-critical, *unstable,* creative meta-practices"

(Lemke, 1995, p. 158) of an enlarged transdisciplinary research community which shares concerns about assessment practices (e.g., Poehner & Inbar-Lourie, 2020a re researcher–teacher praxis). Lemke explained that *unstable* conditions create "the dynamics of the social system of practices, its way of generating its own future by acting on itself and transacting with its environment" (p. 158). Such a praxis requires a foundation of shared knowledge, mutual respect, and the valuing of what different perspectives offer. It does not require synthesis. Rather, as Lave (1996) pointed out, it offers new possibilities for learning from what others know, do, and understand.

In Chapter 2 we examined the contributions of assessment-centred communities to our understanding of validity and validation practices. In this chapter we traced the contributions of language-centred communities to evolving conceptualizations of language itself, afforded by social theories and sociocultural perspectives. In Chapter 4 we will examine the contributions of the language assessment community. While acknowledging research contributions aligned with dominant, assessment-centred perspectives in language assessment, we highlight the emergence, development, and current state of a social thread. Chapter 4 completes Part I of this book, which aims to develop a foundation of knowledge and understanding across readers as a modest step toward collective and collaborative programs of transdisciplinary research. Arguably, such programs are essential if complex issues such as the conundrum of context in language assessment are to be addressed. Part I serves as a prelude to Part II of this book, which describes several transdisciplinary language assessment research projects that were informed by a range of alternative social theories.

Notes

1 In the classic European tradition, people who had access to education learned both dead and living/current languages and graduated being fluent in a variety of European languages, German and French being a must in the nineteenth and twentieth centuries. Arguably, this was less the case in English traditions. White (1988) provides an account of the divergence in traditions of language teaching (geographically, between American and British traditions; and those in continental Europe), and between modern language teaching (e.g., French, Spanish, Italian) and English language teaching as a second or foreign language.

2 Husserl (1989/1936) defines *Lebenswelt* (lifeworld, life-world, life world) as the world that is shaped within the immediate experience of each person. For Weber, the concept of *Verstehen* (understanding, empathic understanding, interpretive understanding) serves as "a methodological tool to explain not all behavior, but behavior which is of a social nature" (Tucker, 1965, p. 158, emphasis in original). Methodologically, the concept is applied through, for example, participant observation.

3 Also known as North American genre theory and New Rhetoric genre theory.

4 Following Chapelle (2021), a target domain is "an area of knowledge, content, theory, practice, or interest that is demarcated" (p. 90) in relation to an assessment purpose and mandate. The test/assessment domain describes in detail the items or tasks that could appear on a test and their value, weight, and organization (i.e., the test blueprint or specifications). Performance on a test is seen as a representation (or sample) of performance in the target domain. But, in this case, performance involves action, interaction, and construction *in situ* within social and cultural situations, which are often only weakly theorized. (We have argued that social theories provide the richest accounts of performance.) Finally the construct domain is systematically detailed when the purpose of an assessment is the measurement of underlying traits (e.g., motivation, test anxiety, empathy). A construct map is generated on the basis of theoretical and empirical evidence of its primary characteristics.

4 The contributions of language assessment research

Evolving considerations of context, constructs, and validity

Janna Fox with Ana Lúcia Tavares Monteiro and Natasha Artemeva

Chapter 4 concludes Part I by offering a selective overview of the contributions of the language assessment community to validation research – particularly with regard to context in assessment use. Throughout we have argued that selected social theories provide a useful, but currently underutilized alternative for validation research. This claim is substantiated in this chapter by a meta-review of publications in four prominent assessment journals over 17 years, from 2004–2020. Research in language assessment has largely been informed by individualist, cognitive perspectives and methodological practices of assessment-centred communities; however, reliance on these perspectives and practices has not resolved long-standing concerns over the "persistent problem" (Bachman, 2007, p. 41) of context in testing and other modes of assessment. In this chapter, these concerns are discussed along with increasing evidence of a social thread in language assessment research, which is consistent with many of the social perspectives and methodological practices of language-centred communities. The chapter underscores the potential and importance of drawing researchers from assessment-centred and language-centred communities together, to mutually engage in shared transdisciplinary programs of research in addressing complex problems.

Any discussion of trait constructs must take into account the question of situational specificity.

(Anastasi, 1986, p. 8)

When selecting or developing tests and when interpreting scores, consider context.

(Chalhoub-Deville, 2001, p. 227)

DOI: 10.4324/9781351184571-6

> *... investigators have become accustomed to the notion that no theory is absolutely a transcript of reality, but that any one of them may from some point of view be useful.*
>
> (James, 1907/1996, p. 33)

> *... there is no single prescription for "doing" praxis but rather a willingness to engage in and with practice and practitioners as an integral part of research. This engagement is defined by mutual trust and by an interest in critically examining what is as part of determining what might be.*
>
> (Poehner & Inbar-Lourie, 2020b, p. 19)

This final chapter of Part I completes what we view as background in building a shared foundation of knowledge and understanding between *assessment*-centred and *language*-centred communities, at the site where their interests meet – in *language assessment*. Shared background can serve as a modest first step toward increasing transdisciplinary partnerships in language assessment validation research.

Chapters 1 and 2, respectively, developed background on transdisciplinary approaches to research and provided a selective, historical overview of validity – the dominant concern of assessment-centred communities. These communities (e.g., measurement, psychology, psychometrics) have largely been informed by cognitive theories which view language as a stable underlying ability, attribute, or trait of an individual. From this perspective, language resides in an individual's thinking, conceptual processing, and meaning making. Therefore, when context is not controlled as a variable of interest, it is backgrounded, diminished, dismissed, or disregarded.

This cognitive perspective has traditionally dominated validation research in the field of language assessment as well (Bachman, 2007). However, as Chapter 2 explained, Messick (1989) argued that validation necessarily required evaluation of both the *plausible truth* (i.e., technical quality) of an assessment practice, as well as its *actual worth in contexts of use* (i.e., the consequences, decisions, and actions that result from inferences based on assessment interpretations and uses). Given the dominance of cognitive perspectives, Messick's (1989) focus on assessment use cast an entirely different and problematic light on *context*. This remains an unresolved problem or source of debate within assessment-centred communities today (as we have discussed in previous chapters), and one that has been confronted in language assessment validation research as well:

> The individualist and cognitive bias of psychometrics and the linguistics that most neatly fitted it has meant that 40 years after the advent of the communicative movement the [language assessment] field still encounters difficulties in conceptualizing and operationalizing the measurement of the social dimension of language use; a problem that

> was recognized more or less from the outset of the testing of practical communicative skill.
>
> (McNamara & Roever, 2006, pp. 4–5)

Chapter 3 reinforced the importance of theory (whether tacit or explicit) in shaping research practices and examined the contributions of language-centred communities (e.g., discourse studies, writing studies, language teaching, linguistics), in reconceptualizing language itself through lenses afforded by social theories. In this regard, the communicative movement or *turn*, followed by the *social turn*, and currently the *visual* and *multilingual turns* were highlighted in relation to evolving conceptions of language (cf. Kalaja & Pitkänen-Huhta, 2018; Leung & Valdés, 2019). At the end of Chapter 3 we provided an introductory overview of social theories – what they share in general (i.e., their *persuasions*), and their potential additive benefits – if language-centred and assessment-centred dialogues were an integral part of researchers' validation practices in language assessment. We also selected some more prominent social theories from the wealth of possible theories and discussed the differing, alternative perspectives they offer. Our selection was motivated in part by the theories that informed, shaped, and accounted for the findings in the transdisciplinary empirical research projects described in Part II of this book, but also because they have proved to be very useful in understanding context (e.g., Addey, Maddox, & Zumbo, 2020; Artemeva & Fox, 2010; Fox, Haggerty, & Artemeva, 2016).

The selective introduction to social theories was intended for those assessment-centred readers who may be unaware of the many social theories that could usefully inform considerations of context in assessment validation research. We also envisioned this as useful for readers with backgrounds in language assessment who routinely encounter *thinly* theorized research in applied linguistics (Swales, cited in Freedman, 2006, p. 107; cf. Swales, 1990, 1993) and who may wish to anchor their understanding of social theories in definitions and examples drawn from the literature. As well, readers who engage in research on second language education or classroom-based assessment and/or who teach languages may also find this overview of social theories useful in informing and encouraging new research partnerships (cf. Poehner & Inbar-Lourie, 2020a).

In this chapter, we begin by discussing the awkward disciplinary position of the language assessment community, situated as it is at the interface of other disciplinary communities, and their dominant Discourses and cultures (cf. Gee, 1996; Widdowson, 2003). In particular, assessment-centred communities and language-centred communities have been characterized by alternative theoretical perspectives, histories of inquiry, and predispositions toward assessment research and language itself. Such differing worldviews, conceptual stances, and methodological preferences have contributed to an *applicability gap*

(Lawrence, 2010), as a result of "the compartmentalization of scientific and professional knowledge" (p. 123). This *trap* (Lemke, 1995) has undermined "effective collaboration" (Lawrence, 2010, p. 123) and impeded the dialogic exchange of and reflection on "disciplinary and other kinds of knowledge" (p. 129).

We then investigate a claim we have made throughout this book that social theories have been underrepresented in language assessment validation research. Evidence in support of this claim is reported in a summary of a meta-review of the literature published in four prominent assessment journals over a 17-year period. A summary of the meta-review is followed by a selective discussion of seminal contributions of language assessment researchers. Although we acknowledge the contributions of research aligned with the worldviews and inquiry approaches of assessment-centred communities in an effort to achieve more balance and in keeping with the overall motivation for this book, we highlight the social thread of research in language assessment. This research, informed by selected social theories, has made considerable contributions to considerations of context and consequences in language assessment. As trends in the meta-review attest, there is growing awareness and use of social theories in such considerations which suggest promising new directions for assessment validation research.

Having looked ahead to the future, we begin below by examining how and why the disciplinary position of language assessment was *precarious* (vis-à-vis other sub-fields, fields, and disciplines) and, how this position contributed to an *applicability gap* (Lawrence, 2010) in language assessment validation research. Arguably, one consequence of this gap was the inability to adequately address 'the problem of context' in assessment validation research, which has remained an issue for decades.

Why and how has the challenging disciplinary position of language assessment impeded progress in addressing the complex issue of context?

While language assessment has most frequently been located as a subfield (e.g., Davies, 1990) within the "discipline of Applied Linguistics" (p. 2) and viewed as "central" (p. 1) to language teaching, learning, and research, it has also been variously described as an awkward child of an awkward discipline, which, Davies (2007) observed, "does not lend itself to an easy definition" (p. 2). Although there is general agreement that applied linguistics is interdisciplinary (Liddicoat, 2010), disciplinary influences vary, often in relation to where applied linguistics is housed within a university's physical/disciplinary structure. In some cases it is part of a larger language studies unit which includes both linguistics and applied linguistics (among other language-related fields such as discourse studies, writing studies, teaching and learning languges). In other cases it is located within a linguistics department; or in English, education, teaching and learning English as a foreign/second language (TEFL/TESOL); or media or communication studies. Where it is situated is telling in terms of the size of its faculty, range of its focus, and degree of its influence.

From the perspective of TEFL/TESOL, Widdowson (2003) elegantly discussed the awkward position of applied linguistics in relation to the disciplinary interests of linguistics and linguistic theory, which he argued was largely considered either unreasonably abstract or of little practical use by most language teachers, who were working day by day to support the language development of their diverse students in diverse classroom settings. Nor were the everyday practices of teaching and learning of interest to the theoretical linguists of the day.

He pointed out that "Applied Linguistics is often said to be concerned with the investigation of real-world problems in which language is implicated". However, he noted, such problems are identified by and explained "in culturally marked ways" (p. 12). In other words, Widdowson considered applied linguistics research to be uncomfortably situated between the theoretical conceptualizations of language, offered by the discipline of linguistics, and the dynamic realizations of language, evident in the processes and practices of teaching and learning in the language classroom. He considered a defining issue of applied linguistics was that it was caught between two distinct cultures that shared neither the same motivations nor purposes (cf. Turner, 2012). Applied linguistics research, he argued, "brings together two discourses or versions of reality and this requires an adjustment of it whereby an area of convergence is created, compounded of elements of both discourses, but belonging exclusively to neither" (p. 12). Widdowson (2003) described such an "anomalous position" as a "no-man's land" wherein applied linguists were "not unfrequently under fire from both sides" (p. 12).

This *dualism trap* was evident in empirical accounts of language teaching and learning within applied linguistics research, which typically backgrounded theory and foregrounded practice (i.e., method). In other words, the emphasis was on *how*, and *why* was left underacknowledged, underexamined, and underarticulated. As previously noted, Swales (1993) lamented the lack of attention paid to theory by applied linguistics researchers, which he viewed as particularly evident in their treatment of context. Such research, he argued, often left "contextualization as undifferentiated background" (Swales cited in Freedman, 2006, p. 107). Following Widdowson (2003), the origins of this *lack of attention* to context may be traced to applied linguistics' challenging disciplinary position. What has this meant for language assessment as a sub-field of applied linguistics?

It should not be surprising, given the ambiguous disciplinary position of applied linguistics, that prominent researchers have variously described the position of language assessment as "marginal" (Davies, 1990, Preface); "isolated" (McNamara & Roever, 2006, p. 254); and "vulnerable"

(McNamara, 2007, p. 136). As a sub-field of applied linguistics, language assessment was even more precariously situtated – between language-centred and assessment-centred communities. As previously discussed, assessment-centred communities were largely informed by an array of *cognitive theories* which accounted for language as a stable mental phenomenon by which individuals perceive, understand, remember, and/or act in the world. From this theoretical perspective, language constructs were ubiquitously conceptualized as abilities, attributes, and traits, and operationally defined for purposes of assessment in approaches that specified their component parts.

The dominance of a cognitive perspective is evident in Bachman's (2007) historical overview of approaches to *construct definition* from 1960 to 2007' (Figure 3.1, pp. 44–45) – all of which are represented in relation to *ability/trait*. See, for example, the *skills and elements approach* (Carroll, 1961, 1968; Lado, 1961), or Bachman's 1990 model of *communicative language ability* operationalized in his *interaction-ability approach*. Although these approaches were 30 years apart, they are both informed by cognitive perspectives of language. To be fair to Bachman, he provided this overview in order to illustrate the "persistent problem" (p. 41) of context in language assessment. This 'problem' gave rise to much distrust of assessment in general, and of language assessment in particular. As Hughes (1989) acknowledged at the beginning of his early book on testing for language teachers:

> Many language teachers harbour a deep mistrust of [assessment] … this mistrust is frequently well-founded … Too often language tests have a harmful effect on teaching and learning; and too often they fail to measure accurately whatever it is they are intended to measure. (p. 1)

This "mistrust" continues to the present day, as the edited collection of Poehner and Inbar-Lourie (2020a) attests. Informed by social theories and rooted in clasroom-based experiences of language teaching, their edited collection is an appeal to revitalize collaborative and cooperative partnerships between language assessment researchers and teachers, who share a mutual interest in second language education, teaching, and learning. The table of contents alone suggests the primary issue the book is addressing. For example, sections defined by the editors call for "Resisting researcher–teacher hierarchies" and "challenging assessment culture"; chapters from contributors call for "Bringing the teacher back in" (Michell & Davison, 2020) and advocate for "teacher–researcher partnership(s)" (Harding & Brunfaut, 2020).

Classroom-based assessment (cf. Fox et al., 2022) has long been a source of socially informed perspectives on assessment practices. However, as Turner (personal communication, 2021) pointed out, "it's in the classroom where language testers have been so uncomfortable due to the complexity of ongoing human behavior and action (e.g., teacher processes in assessment, decision making; the dynamic nature of learning and the impact of context)". Turner's perspicacious comment reflects the dominance of cognitive theories in assessment-centred communities – particularly those in language testing. Their concomitant definitions of language constructs as stable underlying abilities and traits of individuals are far removed from assessment as practiced by teachers and their lived experience of language constructs as dynamic, fluid, developmental, and situated.

To this point in the book, we have asserted throughout that social theories are underutilized and underrepresented in language assessment research, and supported this claim by citing others (e.g., Chalhoub-Deville, 2001, 2003; McNamara, 2007; McNamara & Roever, 2006), who have made similar claims. In the section below, we report on a meta-review of the assessment literature from 2004 to 2020 which substantiates this claim. This is followed by a selective discussion of the contributions of language assessment researchers to considerations of validity and context, informed by socio-theoretical perspectives.

What role have social theories played in the assessment research literature? A meta-review of four prominent assessment-focused research journals (2004–2020)

As background to the present volume, we undertook a review of the assessment literature published over 17 years (2004–2020) for the purpose of identifying trends in the frequency with which researchers acknowledged *context* and their use of *social theories*. Articles, editorials, and book reviews were examined in four major journals: *Language Testing* (LT), *Language Assessment Quarterly* (LAQ), *International Journal of Testing* (IJT), and *Educational Measurement: Issues and Practice* (EM:IP). (Due to space limitations of the book, the selectively annotated list of publications identified during the meta-review is not included here, but it is available at APPENDIX – CHAPTER FOUR, https://carleton.ca/slals/people/fox-janna/).

Two of these journals are currently of central importance to language assessment researchers (i.e., LT and LAQ). They are most likely to publish research of interest to this community and to be read by members of it. The other two journals are of interest to measurement and psychometric communities, particularly those working in testing and evaluation. EM:IP reflects and represents the interests of the National Council on Measurement in Education (NCME); IJT is associated with the International Test Commission. Although research on language assessment appears in all four journals, it is the central focus of LT and LAQ. It is also an important concern of researchers and readers of EM:IP and IJT – but these journals represent many different types of tests/assessment practices which do not specifically focus on language. In order to triangulate, clarify, and extend findings, two other journals which publish assessment research were reviewed but were not included in the summary tables and figures included in this chapter.

In order to conduct the review, three research assistants were recruited and trained in review procedures by the lead researcher.[1] All of the research assistants were doctoral students at the time of the study, with backgrounds in social theories and assessment. It was agreed that each member of the Search Team would review one of the four journals under consideration, beginning with publications in the year 2004. Details of the review process are provided below.

Inclusion/exclusion criteria and the meta-review process

The meta-review Search Team used a keyword search of articles, book reviews, and editorials, identifying such terms as "context", "social", "culture", and "sociocultural" (see Table 4.1 for a list of lexical items used in the search). Synonyms such as locale, situation, or setting, and description beyond a single reference were also counted as evidence of context recognition. Such descriptions typically contained specific mention of assessment contexts (e.g., "In such a high stakes testing context within Bengali, grade 12 classrooms" or "Testing situations with larger class sizes (>40) that take place at the post-secondary versus elementary school levels"). On the other hand, publications with a passing or implicit mention of context at a general level, which did not reoccur in the interpretation of the findings, were excluded (e.g., "The study took place in a mid-sized American university").

Segments of text (surrounding sentences or paragraphs) in which the keywords appeared were assessed to ensure that the keywords related to social recognitions or awareness of socio-theoretical perspectives. For example, "in such a testing context" was included, because additional information extended this reference in the preceding paragraph,

Table 4.1 Keywords and word roots used in the keyword search

Context		*Social theory*	
Keyword	*Root*	*Key term*	*Root*
Conditions	Condition	Cultural	Cult
Context/s/ual	Context	Culture	
Circumstan/tial/ce/ces	Circ	Social	Soci
Environment/s/al	Envi	Socio	
Setting/s	Set	Sociocultural	
Situation/s	Situ		
Situated(ness)			

whereas "in the context of this article" was excluded (see Maxwell & Miller (2008) for additional details on the procedures followed by the meta-review Search Team).[2] In addition, reference lists were reviewed for the identification of any social theories or theorists that had been selected by the author(s) to inform their work. All publications which contained reference to social theorists *and* included mention of specific social context(s), and/or were supported by social theories, were counted as including *both* context and social theory.

At two-week intervals over a three-month period, the Search Team met to validate procedures, and compare and confirm frequency counts, by recoding randomly selected texts across issues of the journals and verifying totals. The meetings offered an opportunity to resolve issues and share recognitions. The period from 2014–2020 was of greatest interest in the review, as there was an expectation that this period would show an increased recognition of social context and social theories. This expectation was confirmed by initial work undertaken by the Search Team.

As a result, the review of publications during the 2014–2020 period refined classification procedures to allow for a more precise distinction between the explicit *use* of social theories to frame, account for, and illuminate research, as opposed to implicit or suggested *awareness* of social or contextual features. For example, some publications *mentioned* socio-theoretical concepts (e.g., "Given the situated nature of the responses in the rural schools"), but did not apply or draw on social theories or theorists to expand, explain, clarify, or illuminate such comments. In publications from 2014–2020, the Search Team noted an emergent trend toward what they referred to as "socio-theoretical contextual awareness", wherein authors mentioned the use of a socio-theoretical perspective and demonstrated some awareness of the importance of local, ecological, or contextual features in their research, but failed to explain or extend this awareness (e.g., by applying actual social theories; interpreting their findings through the lenses afforded by social theorists; or explaining why a particular socio-theoretical perspective was chosen to inform their work). All publications with such references were counted as showing *socio-theoretical contextual awareness*. As a result, publications from 2014–2020 were reviewed systematically, with the distinction between *awareness* (SCA) versus *use* (C/ST) clearly identified. In presenting the results of the review, additional figures are provided for this period to disaggregate awareness from use. The summary figures representing trends for the full period of the meta-review, from the beginning of 2004 to the end of 2020, do not take this finer distinction into account.

Applying the inclusion/exclusion criteria, the final keyword counts were tabulated to provide an overview by year and journal as evidence of social theories and context (a bibliographical list by year and journal of publications identified through the meta-review search criteria is available

Table 4.2 Publications categorized by the inclusion/exclusion criteria

2018 Language Testing	
Total articles (including editorial and book reviews)	30
Include context	23
Do not include context	07
Include both context and social theory (C/ST)	03
Include context and socio-theoretical contextual awareness (SCA)	04

at APPENDIX – CHAPTER FOUR, https://carleton.ca/slals/people/fox-janna/). As an example of the tabulation approach, Table 4.2 illustrates the findings for one year, 2018, from the journal LT.

Once the Search Team had concluded its review and reported on its findings, all data and findings were independently reviewed and verified by a fourth research associate. Subsequently, data were entered into an Excel spreadsheet and the percentages of total publications that met the inclusion/exclusion criteria were calculated. A selective overview of key findings is presented in the next section.

An overview of the key findings of the meta-review

Two interesting trends were identified as a result of the meta-review of the four journals from the beginning of 2004 to the end of 2020 (i.e., 17 years inclusive) (Figure 4.1 and Table 4.3). There was evidence of:

1. increasing awareness of social theories, and detail regarding context, although awareness, as noted above, was not generally accompanied by application, explanation, or development; and
2. increasing use of social theories and/or discussion of the work of social theorists in relation to considerations of context.

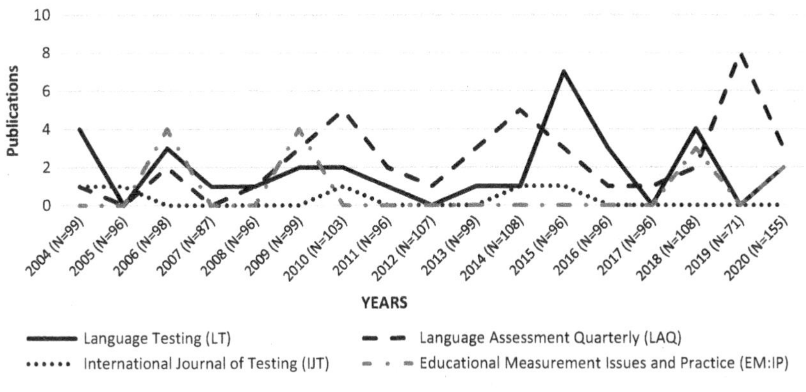

Figure 4.1 Publications that included both context and social theory (C/ST) by journal (2004–2020).

Table 4.3 Overview: considerations of context through socio-theoretical (C/ST) perspectives across four assessment journals (2004–2020)

	Language Testing			*Language Assessment Quarterly*			*International Journal of Testing*			*Educational Measurement*			*Overall (across four journals)*		
	# Total public.	*# [C/ST]*	*% [C/ST]*	*# Total public.*	*# [C/ST]*	*% [C/ST]*	*# Total public.*	*# [C/ST]*	*% [C/ST]*	*# Total public.*	*# [C/ST]*	*% [C/ST]*	*# Total public.*	*# [C/ST]*	*% [C/ST]*
2004	32	4	**12.5%***	24	1	4.17%	25	1	4.00%	18	0	0.00%	99	6	6.06%
2005	25	0	0.0%	24	0	0.00%	26	1	3.85%	21	0	0.00%	96	1	1.04%
2006	24	3	**12.5%**	21	2	9.52%	24	0	0.00%	29	4	**13.79%**	98	9	9.18%
2007	24	1	4.17%	19	0	0.00%	21	0	0.00%	23	0	0.00%	87	1	1.15%
2008	27	1	3.70%	22	1	4.55%	26	0	0.00%	21	0	0.00%	96	2	2.08%
2009	29	2	6.90%	23	3	3.04%	23	0	0.00%	24	4	**16.67%**	99	9	9.09%
2010	36	2	5.56%	26	5	**19.23%**	21	1	4.76%	20	0	0.00%	103	8	7.77%
2011	33	1	3.03%	26	2	7.69%	19	0	0.00%	18	0	0.00%	96	3	3.13%
2012	36	0	0.00%	22	1	4.55%	22	0	0.00%	27	0	0.00%	107	1	0.93%
2013	31	1	3.23%	26	3	**11.54%**	21	0	0.00%	21	0	0.00%	99	4	4.04%
2014	33	1	3.03%	26	5	9.23%	18	1	5.56%	31	0	0.00%	108	7	6.48%
2015	32	7	**21.88%**	21	3	**14.29%**	19	1	5.26%	24	0	0.00%	96	11	**11.46%**
2016	34	3	8.82%	24	1	4.17%	18	0	0.00%	20	0	0.00%	96	4	4.17%
2017	29	0	0.00%	28	1	3.57%	18	0	0.00%	21	0	0.00%	96	1	1.04%
2018	30	4	**13.33%**	32	2	6.25%	16	0	0.00%	30	3	**10.00%**	108	9	8.33%
2019	25	0	0.00%	15	8	**53.33%**	10	0	0.00%	21	0	0.00%	71	8	**11.27%**
2020	36	2	5.56%	28	3	**10.71%**	14	0	0.00%	77	2	2.60%	155	7	4.52%

Note: **Bold** typeface denotes 10% or more.

Overall, across the span of the 17-year period examined for the meta-review (Figure 4.1), there was an uneven but fairly steady increase in the number of journal publications that acknowledged context and were informed by social theories. However, the overall number of such publications across the four journals remained very low (Table 4.3), barely exceeding 10% of total publications in only two years, namely, 2015 (11/96 or 11.46%) and 2019 (8/71 or 11.27%). Fluctuations by year were often the result of the topics of special issues. Some of these topics were related to specific contexts (e.g., the special issue on *Trends in language assessment in Canada* [Fox, 2015]), whereas others were not (e.g., the special issue on *Corpus linguistics in language testing research* [Cushing, 2017]). Across the four journals, IJT was the least likely to include any publications with recognitions of context and the use of social theories. The two language-focused journals (LAQ and LT) were much more likely to include publications informed by social theories and considerations of context (C/ST). Two years stood out. In 2015, seven of 32 (i.e., 21.9%) publications in LT included socio-theoretically informed considerations of context. This was exceeded by LAQ in 2019, with eight of 15 (i.e., 53%) publications including such considerations.

Given EM:IP's focus on *practice*, it was surprising to find such limited evidence of the use of social theories to inform considerations of practices and/or contexts. Further, although there was an increasing acknowledgement of context in the journals, and a similar trend was evident with regard to increasing awareness of social theories or socio-theoretical concepts (e.g., *situatedness*, *zone of proximal development*, see Chapter 3), many publications that provided information about context did not draw on social theories or theorists, or suggest awareness of social theories.

Although, as noted above, there was only limited use of social theories in considerations of context across publications in the four journals, the Search Team emphasized that in the most recent years of their review there was increasing evidence of socio-theoretical awareness. Therefore, from 2014 to 2020, as noted above, a distinction was drawn between evidence of awareness of social theories (SCA) in considerations of context and their explicit use (C/ST). This distinction painted a different picture of the role of socio-theoretical perspectives in considerations of context (Figure 4.2). All four journals demonstrated an uneven but upward trend in this regard.

Figure 4.3 provides additional detail on the trends from 2014 to 2020, illustrating the distinction between general awareness of social theories, social concepts, or so-called social perspectives (SCA) and actual use of social theories and/or reference to the work of social theorists (C/ST).

In 2014 and in 2019 the use of social theories exceeded awareness, and in 2015 there was evidence that awareness was equal to the use of social theories across the four journals.

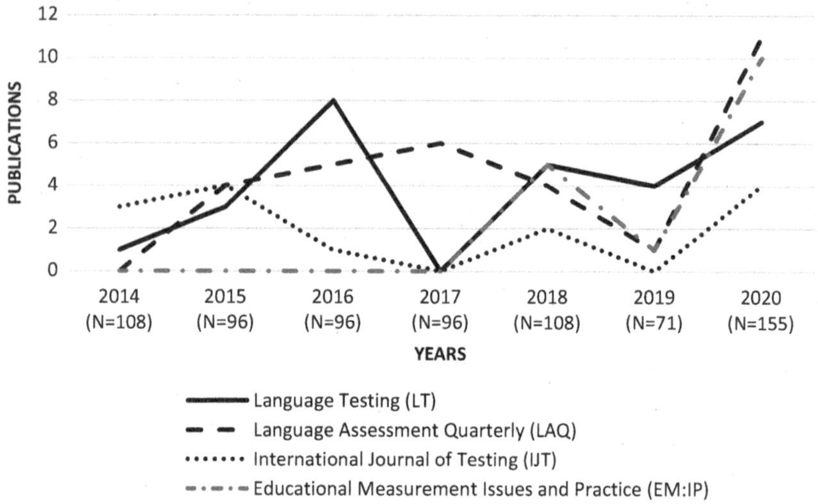

Figure 4.2 Publications that included both context and socio-theoretical contextual awareness (SCA) by journal (2014–2020).

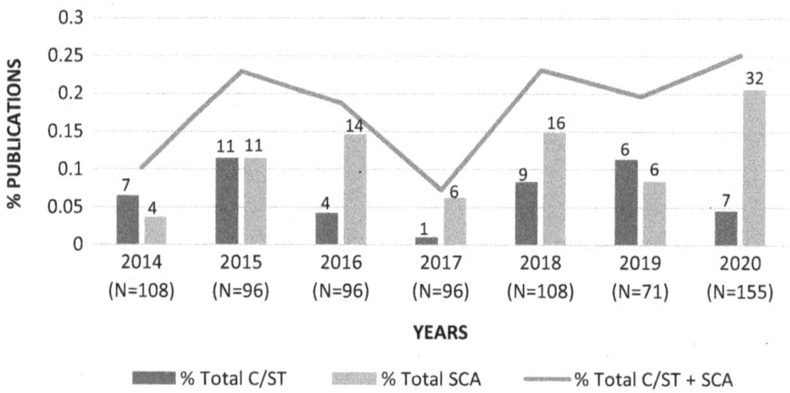

Figure 4.3 Context and social theory (C/ST) versus socio-theoretical contextual awareness (SCA); and (C/ST + SCA) trends across the four journals (2014–2020).

While publications that used actual social theories were more prominent in 2014, 2015, and 2019, overall, there were many more publications produced during this period that did **not** apply social theories.

In sum, although the meta-review suggested both increased acknowledgement of context and increased awareness and use of social theories, the trends were uneven across the four journals (Figure 4.2). As anticipated, the lowest levels were evident in IJT and in *EM: IP*. Both of these journals tend to represent the interests and practices of large-scale, high-stakes testing measurement and psychometric communities. The two journals which focused on language as the construct of interest, LT and LAQ, were far more likely to consider context and either apply or demonstrate awareness of social theories. However, the meta-review provided evidence that social perspectives and context remain underconsidered and undertheorized in the research literature regarding assessment, as McNamara (2007), McNamara and Roever (2006), and Deville and Chalhoub-Deville (2006) have observed.

It is important to acknowledge some of the limitations of the meta-review:

1 The Search Team did not itemize specific references to individualist, cognitive theories as part of their review. Rather, such perspectives were generally inferred on the basis of a publication's treatment of context and methodological choices.
2 Although the lists of *socio-theoretically informed* publications were checked independently, both within the Search Team and later by another independent reviewer, it is likely that some socio-theoretically informed publications were missed.
3 It is also possible that the selection of the four journals skewed the results of the review.

In order to validate findings, publications in two other journals were reviewed by the Search Team, namely, *Assessment in Education: Principles, Policy and Practice* (AiE) and the *Journal of English for Academic Purposes* (JEAP). Both of these journals publish articles on educational/language assessment. According to the publishers' descriptions, AiE "publishes international research from a wide range of assessment systems and seeks to compare different policies and practices" (retrieved June 1, 2021, www.tandfonline.com/toc/caie20/currentonline.com). It is assessment-focused, within education, whereas, JEAP publishes "a wide range of linguistic, applied linguistic and educational topics ... treated from the perspective of English for academic purposes [including] ... assessment of language, needs analysis; materials development and evaluation" (retrieved June 1, 2021, www.journals.elsevier.com/journal-of-english-for-academic-purposes). Assessment is only one of a number of topics that are published by JEAP.

It was not possible to review these journals for the entire 17-year period covered in the main meta-review. Years for review by journal were randomly drawn: AiE was reviewed for socially informed publications from 2004–2006; JEAP from 2004–2008 and 2014–2016 (Table 4.4). The percentage of publications that included both context and social theories was highest in JEAP (i.e., 18%), whereas AiE's assessment-focused

Table 4.4 Summary of review of additional journals for validation/comparison

2004–2008 Journal of English for Academic Purposes	*Count*	*Percent*
Total articles (including editorial and book reviews)	143	100%
Include context	80	56%
Do not include context	63	44%
Include both context and social theory [C/ST]	26	18%

2014–2016 ***Journal of English for Academic Purposes***	*Count*	*Percent*
Total articles (including editorial and book reviews)	124	100%
Include context	98	79%
Do not include context	26	21%
Include both context and social theory [C/ST]	17	14%
Include context and social awareness [SCA]	29	23%

2004–2006 ***Assessment in Education***	*Count*	*Percent*
Total articles (including editorial and book reviews)	65	100%
Include context	21	32%
Do not include context	44	68%
Include both context and social theory [C/ST]	5	8%

publications averaged around 8% during the period reviewed (which was roughly comparable to the four assessment journals in the meta-review). On the other hand, the review of JEAP's publications from 2014–2016 indicated that, in keeping with the journal's focus on second language education, teaching, and learning, approximately 80% of its publications either demonstrated socio-theoretical awareness (23%) or explicitly applied social theories (14%) in framing, accounting for, or interpreting outcomes (i.e., 37% in total). This is evidence that publications in language teaching and learning are becoming more *thickly* theorized, which should please critics like Swales. Further, although the overall trend toward more recognition of context, socio-theoretical awareness, and the use of social theories is modest, it appears to be increasing in assessment-centred journals as well.

The meta-review findings supported the contention that language assessment in particular and assessment in general have underapplied social theories in journal publications. There is additional evidence as well of an applicability gap between considerations of context in publications related to language teaching and learning and its consideration in publications related to language assessment. Arguably, considerations of assessment practices from the alternative perspectives social theories afford (as in second language teaching and learning) would benefit research in assessment.

The social theories we have selected for discussion in this book have conceptualized language in relation to and inseparable from contexts of use, although these conceptualizations differ from theory to theory. Socio-theoretical perspectives foreground context. Across disciplinary communities there is general agreement that assessment (including testing) is a social practice. However, the meta-review confirmed the limited number of socio-theoretically informed publications in four prominent assessment journals and provided evidence that context continues to be largely backgrounded in these publications. This is particularly ironic, given the long history of concern over context in the language assessment community. Lave (1996) viewed context in social practices as a "theoretical problematic" of "traditional cognitive theory" (p. 11). She reviewed the "silences and paradoxes" that individualist, cognitive perspectives generate: "questions that cannot be asked and issues for which no principled resolution is possible" (pp. 11–12). Arguably, long-standing concerns about context in language assessment are most likely to be addressed by social theories. We briefly examine the history of concerns about context in language assessment in the next section.

Confronting the problem of context in language assessment: what is the construct? what is the role of context?

In Bachman's 1990 model of communicative language ability, value was placed on measuring the components of a model, which were elaborated in terms of *relatively independent competencies*. As Bachman (1990) explained, knowledge of language or language competence "comprises, essentially, a set of specific knowledge components that are utilized in communication via language" (p. 84.). Grammatical competence is one of these components, which was viewed as measurable in terms of such variables as a student's or test taker's knowledge of, for example, vocabulary, morphology, or syntax. Further, a causal relationship was assumed between components of the model and communicative language ability in communicative language use: "Communicative language ability (CLA) can be described as consisting of both knowledge, or competence, and the capacity for implementing, or executing that competence in appropriate, contextualized communicative language use" (Bachman, 1990, p. 84).

What is of importance in cognitive models of language is the emphasis on an individual's *knowledge of* and *capacity for* language. In other words, language is measured as a property that resides in the individual – separable from contexts of use. *Capacity for use* in "appropriate, contextualized communicative" ways was often operationalized in usage sections of high-stakes tests wherein multiple-choice items could test for recognition of appropriate registers, word choices, etc., given a brief description of a situation or scenario. However, context was typically *backgrounded* in the measurement of an individual's underlying traits or abilities. Cognitive theories conceptualized the measurement of *language* (through a test or other assessment practice) as evidence of an individual's essentially *stable* or *static* underlying traits or attributes, *at a distance* from the fluctuating and dynamic contexts in which language is used.

Conversely, social theories have conceptualized language in relation to and inseparable from contexts of use. Context is foregrounded, because the assessment of language (in a test or other assessment practice) draws evidence in relation to (and inseparable from) the circumstance or situation that prompted it, the activity that it motivates, the network or systems of relationships within which takes place, or the social actions it performs.

As previously noted, the theoretical foundations of language assessment were historically rooted within psychology, measurement, and psychometric traditions, which "obscured, perhaps deliberately, its social dimension", and tended to ignore or underestimate it as a "social practice" (McNamara & Roever, 2006, p. 1). Thus, recognitions of the *social* and *contextual* in the language assessment literature have continued to be "grafted (somewhat uneasily ...) onto the tradition of the psychological dimensions of measurement" (p. 12).

Because measurement- and other assessment-centred communities have drawn almost exclusively on "individualist, cognitive" (McNamara & Roever, 2006, p. 2) theories to inform validation research, context has typically been regarded as a potential threat to validity as a source of what Messick (1989) identified as *construct irrelevant variance*. Therefore, context is said to be *controlled* by reducing it to key variables of interest (e.g., age, educational background, nationality), or well-defined tasks, treatments or interventions, to contrast experimental and control groups. The definition of key variables simultaneously defined and constrained the inferences and interpretations that could reasonably be drawn from research on assessment outcomes. This reductive containment of context was increasingly unsupported by language-centred communities and disconnected from evolving theoretical conceptualizations of language. Contributors to language assessment found incorporating the social and contextual a particularly challenging issue to address, and arguably their increasing awareness of the problem dates back to the *social turn* (Chapter 3) and the retheorizing of language within language-centred communities.

As previously discussed, the dominant Discourses (Gee, 1996) within measurement and assessment have been and continue to be anchored in trait-based, cognitive perspectives. Therefore, language constructs (e.g., abilities, attributes, skills, knowledge) as properties of an individual (i.e., in the head) are separable from the situations or settings in which they are manifested in assessment performances. In general, context continues to be defined by variables of interest to a study, or *backgrounded*. A colleague who was editing a journal's special issue on multilingualism reported that an extensive search of the assessment literature revealed "very little on *context*". When context was mentioned, he noted it was typically in reference to "the study took place in the Netherlands, or Canada – but little more than that". At times, there might be a description of the research site. Generally, however, in keeping with traditional quantitative research designs, when details regarding context were important they were operationalized as *variables* of interest. Context was controlled in order to allow for generalizability across test sites and administrations. Control was ensured through *systems* (e.g., in development, production, administration, rating).

Downing and Haladyna (2006) included the following in a summary of key requirements for such systems:

- test administrators must be trained and monitored to ensure systematic test administration procedures with regard to time limits, physical arrangements of rooms, space, accoustics, heat, light etc.;
- raters must be systematically trained and monitored for consistency and accuracy; and
- test scores, performances, outcomes must be systematically researched to investigate and provide evidence of their reliability and consistency.

However, as Skehan (1998) noted, in spite of these systematic efforts to control for variability due to context, there was a growing recognition of the "dilemma" posed by "the abilities/performance/context conflict" (p. 155). Evidence of growing recognition of the context problem in assessment is found in the increasing number of articles and chapters appearing before and after 2000, which focused on concerns about *context*. Such recognitions were particularly evident in research examining the relationship between motivation and second language acquisition (SLA), as in the research of Gardner and Lambert (1972), who noted a connection between motivation and aptitude. This connection evolved into the development of a *socio-educational model* (Gardner, 1988) in language acquisition, which considered the social and cultural sphere in which learning occurs to be an important factor influencing motivation (Ellis, 2015).

Skehan's concerns regarding the interaction of tasks, teaching, learning, and assessment in classroom contexts were similarly raised by Chalhoub-Deville (2001) in language testing. Drawing on Omaggio Hadley (1993), she discussed *contextualization* (cf. *contextualism* in Cronbach, 1988, p. 14) in language assessment, pointing out that "language use occurs in contexts 'where any given utterance is embedded in ongoing discourse as well as some particular circumstance or situation' " (Omaggio Hadley, cited in Chalhoub-Deville, 2001, p. 215). She identified two important features of contextualization which she argued were critically important in both test development and validation – *ongoing discourse* and *situational embeddedness*.

Ongoing discourse was defined as the connected and coherent use of language for meaningful expression, communication, or interaction – features which characterize typicial, recurring language use outside that which is elicited by or produced in response to a test. Situational embeddedness related to Brown, Collins, and Duguid's (1989) consideration of *situated cognition*, namely, that "knowledge is situated, being in part a product of the activity, context, and culture in which it is developed and used" (p. 32). Motivated in general by a concern for learning and education, *theories of situated cognition* (see Kirshner & Whitson, 1997) attracted a large number of researchers from diverse disciplines (e.g., psychology. anthropology, education) who were dissatisfied with traditional individualist, in-the-head cognitive perspectives. Collectively they viewed "knowledge and learning as fundamentally social and cultural" (p. viii) and drew from a broad range of social theories and analytical approaches to investigate learning (Brown et al., 1989; Collins, Brown, & Newman, 1989; Kirshner & Whitson, 1997).[3] Contributors to this "family" shared the view "that thinking is connected to, and changes across actual situations and is not usually a process of applying abstract generalizations, definitions, or rules" (Gee, 2004, p. 49).

In keeping with the *family* of pespectives associated with situated cognition, Chalhoub-Deville (2001) examined three task-based tests of oral language proficiency with regard to the degree of ongoing discourse the tests elicited and the situational embeddedness of the tasks: 1) the oral proficiency interview (OPI)/simulated oral proficiency interview (SOPI); 2) the contextualized speaking assessment (CoSA); and 3) the video/oral communication instrument (VOCI). Her findings suggest that each of the three tests had a method-effect, and that the methods used were to a degree "mask[ing] the knowledge and skills that underlie the performance ratings", with the result that "appropriate interpretation and use of test scores" (p. 225) was *undermined*. She concluded with a plea, following Anastasi (1986), to consider context, one that she later expanded by calling for a *theory of context* (see Chalhoub-Deville, 2003), arguing that such a theory was essential if we were to draw valid inferences from language tests (cf. Chalhoub-Deville, 2016).

Over the years, many language assessment researchers have identified a similar need (e.g., Deville & Chalhoub-Deville, 2006; McNamara & Roever, 2006; Norton, 2013). Some (e.g., McNamara & Roever, 2006) have favoured a so-called moderate interpretation of context which arguably is more aligned with psychometric traditions in the validity literature. For example, in their seminal discussion of the *social dimension of language testing*, McNamara and Roever (2006) argue for a "more adequate theorization of the social context of testing" (p. 198), while acknowledging that "understanding the social function of tests can be seen by many authors as introducing an unmanageable aspect into language testing research, opening a Pandora's box of issues with no chance of practical resolution" (pp. 40–41). They discuss the resistance "to going further in examining the social implications of test use" (p. 41) and remark that this is the position taken by "influential" (p. 41) members of the larger assessment community. (See also McNamara, 1995, 1997.)

Concern over the social consequences of tests in use is evident in Fulcher's (2015) discussion of the relationship between context and inference in testing. In reference to McNamara's allusion to Pandora's box, he remarks that social theories of context may seem to pose serious challenges to the testing enterprise (i.e., threats to interpretability and generalizability), because such theories generally consider that inferences from scores are "constructed from much more than individual ability ... allowing all the plagues of the real world to infect the purity of the link between a score and the mind of the person from whom it was derived" (p. 227). The issue here, of course, is whether the link between score and mind was ever *pure*.

Fulcher acknowledges that the notion of the link between individual score and individual mind is an assumption which characterizes the purist tradition of radical, ideologically driven positivists and post-positivists. As discussed in Chapter 2, such purists have tended to rely solely on cognitive (underlying trait-based) theory and quantitative/statistical approaches in validation as the only meaningful or trustworthy source of empirical data in support of inferences drawn from test scores. Fulcher argues that there are ideologically driven purists within the "more radical" constructivist treatments of context in language testing" (Fulcher, 2015, p. 227) as well. In the end, however, Fulcher suggests avoidance of "extreme responses to the complexity of context" (p. 235): neither to ignore it, nor to be overwhelmed by it. The more productive approach, he argues, is to move away from ideologically driven views to more pragmatic views of validation – in much the same way as the ideological battle lines that were drawn regarding methodology during the so-called *paradigm wars* (see Chapter 2) ultimately moved toward the pragmatic (Morgan, 2007; Turner, 2014).

Following Messick (1989, 1998), we argue that rather than undermining the *testing enterprise*, the application of multiple inquiry systems, informed by alternative theoretical perspectives and pluralistic methodological approaches, will enrich and deepen our understanding of the inferences we draw from test scores and other assessment practices. Contextualizing inferences, delimiting the boundaries within which our generalizable inferences hold, calls for social theories which provide differing and alternative theoretical perspectives on assessment *action-in-context* (cf. Bennett, 2010; Chalhoub-Deville, 2016) and thereby improve the quality of inferences drawn from assessment practices.

However, as evidenced by the meta-review and the observations of numerous researchers in the field of language assessment itself, contributions to validation have been dominated by research aligned with the mainstream, traditional worldviews, conceptual stances, and methodologies of assessment-centred communities. The calls for more *balance* and *diversity of perspectives* and *approaches* have a long history in the language assessment literature (e.g., Hamp-Lyons, 1991, 2000; Inbar-Lourie, 2008; Taylor, 2005; van Lier, 1989). As Lazaraton and Taylor (2007) noted years ago, "it has become increasingly apparent that the established psychometric methods of test validation are effective, but limited, and other methods are required for us to gain a fuller understanding of the language tests we use" (p. 126).

In keeping with the overall purpose of this book, we too have argued for more balance, multiple perspectives, and alternative approaches in validation research. Although we are focusing on context, and individualist, cognitively informed psychometric approaches to test development and validation research have largely *backgrounded* context (cf. Hongwen, 2020), we do not intend to suggest a dualistic, "either-or" opposition of cognitive versus social perspectives. Rather, we emphasize that these are *alternative perspectives.* Drawing on alternative perspectives offers additive potential. Therefore, in summarizing the contributions of language assessment research to validity, validation, and considerations of context, a selective overview of research that is informed by cognitive perspectives and aligned with assessment-centred communities is provided. Three topics were chosen for this selective overview:

1 *fairness;*
2 *bias;* and
3 *localization.*

This overview is followed by a more extensive discussion of the social thread of research in language assessment.

Contributions of the language assessment community

Examples of research aligned with assessment-centred, individualist, cognitive perspectives

Fairness

As McNamara, Knoch, and Fan (2019) have pointed out, fairness is "the aspect of test score validation, internal to the test itself" (p. 21). When researchers within assessment-centred communities state that the primary purpose of their validation research is to address *fairness*, their focus has typically been directed at improving the technical quality of *tests* (rather than other modes of assessment). Such validation evidence tends to be presented numerically as *scientific fact*, and overall concern is for *truth* (albeit partial and progressive) (e.g., Borsboom et. al., 2004; Borsboom & Markus, 2013; Cronbach, 1988).[4] In this regard, the use of the psychometric techniques of Rasch measurement have been promoted by the language assessment community, which has found them particularly useful (cf. McNamara et al., 2019). This family of techniques is further discussed below in relation to bias.

Bias

Messick (1989) advised test researchers to attend in particular to the *unintended negative consequences and side effects* of tests in use. In large-scale testing much research attention has focused on detecting and addressing *bias* – as an unintended consequence. Bias occurs when measurement of a construct of interest (e.g., achievement, proficiency, ability) is systematically undermined for one group of test takers (or systematically favoured for another), based on characteristics outside the bounds of, or irrelevant to, the construct being measured. Bias analysis has taken many forms.

Within language assessment, Rasch models have provided a sophisticated collection of psychometric techniques for the detection of bias. Although in past decades they have been controversial, and there have been numerous "debates" over their use (McNamara et al., 2019, p. 173), in recent years they have emerged as mainstream techniques in language assessment practices (particularly those involving tests). Rasch models vary in relation to research purpose, data type, scoring or response formats, analysis, and software choices (see, McNamara et. al, 2019). Basic Rasch analysis is applied to dichotomous data arising, for example, from true/false or multiple-choice items (treated as dichotomous), whereas the many-facets Rasch model (MFRM) is applied to polytomous data (see *facets* in MFRM analysis). In an assessment context, MFRM models are typically used to investigate three facets: *person* (test taker ability as measured by a test), *criterion* (e.g., item, task, scale), and *rater* (judge).

As noted above, these and other psychometric techniques for detecting bias are most often used in large-scale testing and are *top-down* in that the analysis focuses on known or pre-determined groups. Further technical discussion of these and other analytical approaches to bias detection (e.g., Differential Item Function or DIF; generalizability theory) is beyond the scope of the present volume; however, McNamara and Roever (2006) provide an extensive discussion of differing psychometric approaches to bias detection, their history, relative strengths, and use in language assessment research (e.g., Elder, 1996; Elder, McNamara, & Congdon, 2003; Kim, 2001; Kunnan, 1990; Takala & Kaftandjieva, 2000).

McNamara and Roever (2006) and McNamara et al. (2019) clearly favour MFRM approaches to detecting bias in interactions based on undisputed, clearly identifiable groups (i.e., raters, tasks/items, test takers): "Multifaceted analysis is more useful for detecting specific instances of differential task or rater functioning" (McNamara & Roever, 2006, p. 121).

Another important contribution of language assessment researchers aligned with assessment-centred (e.g., psychometric, measurement) perspectives relates specifically to the role of context in high-stakes standardized language testing, and the role of local development and use of such tests, or localization.

Localization

We see evidence of growing attention being paid to context in language test development and validation in research that is aligned with the cognitive perspectives of assessment-centred communities (e.g., O'Sullivan, 2016; Su, Weir, & Wu, 2019). For example, the use of socio-cognitive theoretical models (e.g., Weir, 1993, 2005, 2019) which incorporate the social and cultural needs of local contexts of use has become increasingly prevalent in the language assessment literature. O'Sullivan (2014, 2016) drew attention to this trend in his consideration of what he referred to as the need for *localization* to better address issues related to the consequences of test use by increasing the quality of meaningful communication with and the involvement of local stakeholders.

Context has tended to be foregrounded where there has been accelerated growth in TEFL accompanied by parallel growth in the demand for high-stakes proficiency testing. Su et al. (2019) drew on examples of six locally developed tests in specific Asian contexts to examine both the limitations of external, high-stakes proficiency tests such as the TOEFL iBT and IELTS in addressing local needs, and provide evidence of the meaningful and useful role that such high-quality local tests are playing. Taken together, the examples in this edited collection demonstrate ways in which these local tests are better suited to meet the needs of the social and cultural contexts within which they are used.

Weir (2019) offered a particularly thoughtful contribution as the final chapter in the Su et al. (2019) collection by elaborating *glocal* approaches which would *blend* the advantanges of global standardized testing with the needs of local test users. He argued that such a blend increased the relevance, interpretability, and usefulness of assessment outcomes by recognizing context. His account is consistent with the socio-cognitive theoretical model he had earlier proposed in 2005. He maintained that "both operations and performance conditions should match target situation use as closely as possible" and suggested "they should demonstrate context validity". His socio-cognitive theoretical model was "required", he observed, in order to "identify the elements of both context and processing and the relationships between them" (p. 19).

Within the larger assessment-centred community (e.g., Kane, 2008, 2013b), renewed emphasis has been placed on the need to consider context and consequence (Messick, 1989) in the validation of the interpretations and uses of assessment:

> Historically, validity has covered evaluations of interpretations (e.g., see Cronbach & Meehl, 1955) and uses (e.g., see Cronbach & Gleser, 1965). Interpretations involve claims about test takers or other units of analysis (e.g., teachers, schools), and score uses involve decisions about these units of analysis. Interpretations and the uses of the test scores tend to be entwined in practice; tests tend to be developed with some interpretation and some use or uses in mind, and arguments for the appropriateness of a score use typically lean heavily on the relevance of score interpretations.
>
> (Kane, 2013b, p. 2)

In keeping with the perspectives of assessment-centred communities, informed by theories and research traditions in measurement, psychometrics, and statistics, Kane identified potential units of analysis as variables of interest in validation research. As such, individuals (test takers), groups (e.g., teachers), or organizations (e.g., schools) are identified as potential contextual variables or units to be analyzed in validating test interpretations and uses. An implicit theoretical framework consistent with the traditional approaches of assessment-centred communities informs Kane's proposed unit(s) of analysis. Social theories (see Chapter 3) would motivate different units of analysis (e.g., practice, activity, event, discourse). For example, informed by Actor Network Theory (ANT; e.g., Callon, 1986; Latour, 1987, 2005; Law, 1991), Addey et al. (2020) take the "unstable networks of human actors and artefacts [which] align temporarily to achieve shared goals" (p. 590) as their unit of analysis. It is the interdependence or relationship that is of interest: "the unit of analysis in network analysis is not the individual, but an entity consisting of a network of individuals and the linkages among them" (Wasserman & Faust, 1997, p. 5). Such alternative perspectives allow for different evidence and support different inferences with regard to the interpretations and uses of tests and other modes of assessment.

Having briefly acknowledged some of the seminal contributions of language assessment research aligned with the individualist, cognitive perspectives that have traditionally informed such research in assessment-centred communities, below we highlight the social thread in language assessment research. Four topics were chosen for discussion of research contributions aligned with socio-theoretical perspectives that to a large extent have informed research in language-centred communities, namely:

1 fairness and bias (reconsidered from the alternative perspectives of social theories);
2 the discursive construction of test takers, tests, and testing;
3 washback and impact; and
4 critical language testing.

Examples of research aligned with language-centred, socio-theoretical perspectives: the social thread

Fairness and bias

For many years there have been alternative research approaches published in the assessment literature which were informed by social theories and which investigated technical quality and/or bias as part of test development and use. Although, as the meta-review suggests, this social thread of research is quite modest in comparison with the mainstream, assessment-centred approaches described above, it has ably illustrated how technical quality can be undermined and how bias can arise at local levels for groups of test takers, whose lived experience, knowledge of the world, and representations of it systematically changes their understanding of and engagement with assessment. Such changes can alter what is being assessed and undermine the validity of the inferences drawn from performance.

One alternative approach to improved technical quality and bias research is Fox's (2003) study of groups that formed dynamically during a trial administration of a new version of a high-stakes language proficiency test. Trialling occurs in a test development process when a prototype is administered to groups of test takers in order to assess the usefulness of new items, tasks, or test versions. Fox's (2003) study drew on Bronfenbrenner's (1979, 1994) *ecological theory* and applied his unit of analysis (person + process + context + time), or the unit of *proximal process*, in exploring the relationship of raters (n = 12) and test takers (n = 423) that formed during the trialling of a writing task as part of the development of a new science version of the existing test. The test was *fully integrated* (e.g., Lewkowicz, 1997), with all tasks "thematically linked" by lectures, readings, diagrams, etc. which provided "input that ... [formed] the basis for the response(s)to be generated by test takers" (p. 121).

Applying qualitative methods to probe test taker and rater accounts of the new writing task allowed for detection of rater bias, which disadvantaged a small group of test takers who happened to take a particular position in their writing and espouse a particular view. Writer stance or viewpoint did not figure in other, validated *anchor* (i.e., established) versions of the test, nor was it a criterion in the rating scale. On the new science version, however, and particularly when raters had difficulty evaluating the writing in relation to a critical cut-off on the rating scale, they tended to use the test taker's position regarding the topic of the task in arriving at a final score. This introduced bias, which favoured some test takers and disadvantaged others on the basis of a feature of the writing that was irrelevant to the construct operationalized by the task (see Messick, 1989, re *construct irrelevant variance* as a threat to the validity of inferences drawn from a test).

Fox (2003) argued that when testing occurs it creates an *ecological niche* (Cole, 1985), which "locates interacting individuals (e.g., test developers, raters, test takers) within the context of the proximal and layered relationships that shape the activity in which they engage" (p. 24). The dynamic outcome of that interactive relationship may at times lead to bias, which systematically disadvantages test takers in groups that form as a result of the process of testing itself. Quantitative approaches are unable to detect such subtle but consequential forms of bias.

Another example of socially informed research on bias that was detected during test development is Maddox's (2014) ethnographic study of literacy assessment in Mongolia, which demonstrated "how apparently standardised 'assessment events' display unruly and idosyncratic characteristics" (p. 486) with regard to the local, situated interpretations of test takers. His study examined how items on a globally administered "psychometric literacy assessment" (p. 474) undermined measurement of the intended construct as it was developed and understood by external testers. Maddox underscores "the challenge of maintaining cross-cultural validity" (p. 482) in external, large-scale comparative assessments – a concern that Messick (1989) directly acknowledged in noting the role of "cultural context" (p. 57) in test takers' responses to tests. In this regard, he referred to a "dictum" in Cole's work, namely, that "cultural differences reside more in the differences in the situations to which different cultural groups apply their skills than in differences in the skills possessed by the groups in question" (Cole, cited in Messick, 1989, p. 57; cf. Hamp-Lyons, 2000). When test takers interpret the meaning of a test question and the response or action that is called for, interpretation and action are rooted in the test taker's understanding, experience, beliefs, and assumptions, what Schutz (1946) referred to as their *stock of knowledge*. As Schutz noted, "there is a stock of knowledge theoretically available to everyone, built up by practical experience, science, and technology as warranted insights" (p. 463). Test takers' social, cultural, political, and historical understandings are inevitably brought to bear on their responses to items, tasks, and tests (see Schutz, Chapter 3). *Cross-cultural validity* studies, like that of Maddox (2014), have provided evidence that representations of meaning are neither neutral nor shared. Rather, they are shaped by and arise in situation and in culture, and can contribute to bias.

Maddox's (2014) study problematized the notion of global assessment approaches because of the inherent disadvantages they can create for some locally situated groups of test takers. Further, he highlighted the complexities of external, *outsider* attempts to recontextualize such global standardized assessment, for example, by introducing content (i.e., camels, in the literacy test that is the focus of his study) in an attempt to increase the relevance of the test for test takers in Mongolia. His example illustrated how external test developers who do not share test takers' *stock of knowledge* can *get it wrong*.

A similar point is evident in the research reported by Norton and Stein (1998). At the time of their study, they described themselves as two "White" (p. 233) university educators engaged in the development of a reading test to be used in the context of university admission for "Black students" (p. 232) in post-aparthied South Africa. The test was part of an initiative to "identify students of color who [had] ... the potential to succeed academically and professionally, despite the debilitating effects of an apartheid legacy" (p. 232).

Norton and Stein (1998) explained how a passage about monkeys on the test, which they trialled as part of the "routine" (p. 232) process of test development, triggered an unanticipated response from test takers. The monkeys passage was read by many of the students in relation to their lived experience, historical and political, as a marginalized and oppressed group in society. The white instructors/test developers had a completely different representation of the meaning of the text.

Norton and Stein pointed out that "the social meaning of a text is not fixed, but is a product of the social occasion in which it is read" (1998, p. 244). Further, they contrasted the responses of the students across two phases of the trial of a new reading comprehension test: 1) in the *test administration phase*, "where they [the students] understood that they were expected to comply with the dictates of the genre, and to reproduce the test-makers' reading of the text" (p. 243); and 2) in the *discussion phase* which followed. During the test administration, the students "appeared isolated, silent and unenthusiastic" (p. 244). After the administration, when the students were invited to discuss the test and the meaning of the reading text, the students were animated and engaged as they cricially interpreted the text through the lens of their own lived experience and understanding.

The discussion phase, as Norton and Stein demonstrated, has important implications for test developers and teachers. Contrary to the multiple-choice meanings offered in the test, which were in keeping with the worldviews of the white test developers, the students' complex, critical, and independent interpretations were framed by South Africa's violent, contested history of unequal power and opportunity. The complex level of critical reflective reading the students demonstrated in discussion was clearly underrepresented on the test. Ironically, their critical, reflective interpretations of the passage were far more indicative of their readiness to engage with reading in university-level disciplines. The multiple-choice, pre-packaged responses to reading on the test clearly underrepresented the construct of interest.

Given the small number of students/test takers who participated in the trialling of the test, Norton and Stein explained that they could not evaluate the role of bias in test performance. Arguably, however, the potential for bias was great. In this situation, students were forced as test takers to choose meanings for texts that were pre-packaged externally. The test in this high-stakes context was an extension of the power of a white (i.e., historically dominant race) university (i.e., privileged class) which would allow or deny educational access to students of colour on the basis of their test responses. The students were positioned to accept the received interpretations of the external white test developers. Those who chose the multiple-choice distractors that corresponded with the received representations/worldviews would be more likely to gain acceptance to the university. Those who did not would be more likely to be denied access.

Hamp-Lyons (2000) pointed out the important role of alternative research approaches in test development and validation in order to ensure the technical quality or fairness of a test. She noted "the contingent nature of knowledge" and recognized that "different stakeholder groups will have competing goals and values" (p. 581). Like Cronbach (1988), she singled out the *obligation* of test developers to fully investigate alternative explanations of test performance as part of ethical testing practices.

The discursive construction of testing, tests, and test takers

In 2006, Huhta, Kalaja, and Pitkänen-Huhta published a landmark paper in the journal *Language Testing*, entitled "Discursive construction of a high-stakes test: the many faces of a test-taker". They noted "in contrast to many previous studies on test-taking our aim is not to examine learners' cognitive processes and strategies, but the meanings they give test-taking" (p. 328). They acknowledged that at the time of publication the use of qualitative methodologies and "non-psychometric approaches" to research in language testing was a "recent development", which was "slowly gaining ground" (p. 328). Theirs was one of the first studies to use discourse analytic techiques (cf. Brown, 2003; Fox, 2001; Jacoby & McNamara, 1999) to investigate stakeholder accounts (e.g., test takers', teachers', raters') of testing as a dynamic, situated, emergent, and constructed process of meaning making. Drawing on social theories of situated learning (Lave & Wenger, 1991) and the concept of communities of practice (cf. Brown, Collins, & Duguid, 1989; Wenger, 1998; see Chapter 3), Huhta et al. contributed to our understanding of the "underlying values and social consequences of testing" (2016, p. 330), evidenced in the voices of test takers themselves, which were captured over time in oral and written diaries. Using Potter and Wetherell's (1987) basic unit of analysis, *interpretive repertoires*, Huhta et al. collected and analyzed how test takers "come to talk or write about a test in attempts to make sense of taking it or rating it, and at the same time evaluating aspects related to it, including actions, thoughts and feelings" (p. 331). Similar to Norton and Stein (1998), Huhta et al. (2006) illustrate the important ways in which test takers construct their identities (cf. McNamara, 2007) and the identities of other stakeholders (e.g., raters) in coming to terms with what testing means and how to make sense of it as a powerful influence on their lives (Norton, 2000). Shohamy (2001, 2007), Flores and Schissel (2014), Norton and Stein (1998), McNamara (2007), and others have ably demonstrated through their research the ways in which powerful tests shape the identities of test takers.

Washback and impact

At a recent international conference, a well-known psychometrician responded to a question from a language teacher who described the negative, undermining effects of external high-stakes tests on her students' confidence and motivation to learn. In responding, he spoke of the important contributions of researchers in language assessment, singling out research on *washback* (i.e., the influence of such testing on teaching and learning at classroom/local levels) and *impact* (i.e., the influence of testing on societies as a whole, both nationally and internationally). He highlighted the seminal work of Alderson and Wall (1993), who drew attention to issues of washback and impact, and observed that the ongoing focus on these issues within language assessment research was making a significant contribution.

In their early, foundational research, Alderson and Wall (1993) challenged taken-for-granted assumptions regarding tests, testing, and other assessment practices, by shattering unreflective and underresearched views on the influence of tests on classroom teaching and learning. Since the publication of their seminal article, which asked, "Does washback exist?", multiple, expansive lines of inquiry have investigated both washback of assessment practices (particularly tests) on teaching and learning (e.g., Cheng, 1997; Cheng, Watanabe, & Curtis, 2004; Green, 2007) and the impact of assessment on society as a whole (e.g., Kempf, 2016; Schissel, 2019; Shohamy, 2007, 2011).

In responding to the teacher's question, the psychometrician acknowledged that more needed to be done in addressing issues regarding the unintended negative consequences of assessment on both the micro/classroom and macro/societal levels. We agree. However, research investigating washback and impact is often undertheorized or theorized on the basis of measurement or psychometric theoretical traditions. Arguably, when social theories have framed such research (e.g., Fox, 2003; Fox & Cheng, 2007; Maddox, 2014; Norton & Stein, 1998), the results have been more informative, textured, and richly detailed as to how and why washback or impact occurs. The application of social theories creates the potential for expanded, alternative insights and deeper interpretations and understanding.

Critical Language Testing

Norton and Stein's research resonates with the concerns of *critical language testing* (Shohamy, 1998, 2001, 2007), which has become an important focus in language assessment research. Through Shohamy's theoretical and empirical examination of the roles and uses of tests, she has highlighted their *power* in shaping, defining, and (often) narrowing opportunity for some test takers. The past two decades have been characterized by a dramatic increase in policy and curricular reform initiatives (e.g., *No Child Left Behind Act*, 2002; *Common Core State Standards Initiative*, n.d.) motivated by accountability and concerns for the attainment of educational standards (e.g., in language, mathematics, literacy, numeracy). Such reform agendas have typically been implemented by standardized tests. Often standards-driven tests, which operationalize what it means to know and use a language at a particular level of development or grade, have been "informed by *monoglossic language ideologies*" (p. 454), with "monolingualism as the norm" (Flores & Schissel, 2014, p. 455). The failure of such tests to recognize that a monolingual norm is inappropriate as a standard for the dynamic language development of emergent bilingual/multilingual language learners prompted many language assessment researchers (e.g., Leung, 2005; Schissel, 2019; Shohamy, 2007, 2011) to question this *one-size-fits-all* approach because it systematically underrepresented *language* for this group.

Shohamy (1998, 2001, 2007, 2016) has inspired research and reflection on the role of tests – particularly language tests – in "creating *de facto* language policies, often operating covertly and implicitly, yet with strong ramifications, in terms of academic, personal, and human rights" (p. 152). Spolsky (e.g., 1967, 1981, 1984) was one of the first to highlight issues related to the ethics and social consequences of high-stakes, standardized testing practices. As he noted, "from the beginning public tests and examinations were instruments of policy" (2009, vii). Following Shohamy, increasingly researchers have investigated the overt and covert *power* of language tests and other assessment practices (e.g., Abedi, 2004; McNamara, 2007; Schissel, 2019; Solano-Flores & Trumbull, 2003). This research has been framed and interpreted through the lenses of such social philosophers and theorists as Butler (1997), Bourdieu (1991), and Foucault (1980, 1982, 1976/1990, 1997). The focus has often been directed at issues of justice (or *injustice*), that is, the evidence that justifies (or disavows) the use of tests or other modes of assessment, "the defensibility of the policies and values implicit in their use" (McNamara et al., 2019, p. 8), and the ethics and responsibilities of those who develop, interpret, and use assessment outcomes.

For example, Shohamy's research (e.g., 2001, 2006, 2007) has been informed by the social theories of Foucault (e.g., 1975/1977), who examined, explained, and reflected upon the power of institutions and systems in exercising, maintaining, and perpetuating social control. Foucauldian perspectives have informed much of the empirical research within *critical language testing*, including McNamara and Roever's (2006) review of the role of language tests in the discursive contruction of identities. For example, they apply Foucault's theoretical perspective to their discussion of Bessette's (2005) study of tests of bilingual proficiency and the Canadian government's *Second Language Evaluation* (SLE) test battery, administered in English to French-dominant test takers, and in French to English-dominant test takers (see also Chapter 8). McNamara and Roever note that both applicants for government positions and employees of the Canadian federal government are required to provide proof of their level of bilinguism by taking the SLE in order to compete for or keep a bilingually designated position. They draw on Foucault's (1975/1977) analysis of the test as a ritualized "technique by which power ... holds (its subjects) in a mechanism of objectification" (Foucault, cited in McNamara & Roever, 2006, p. 193), and the SLE test battery as "the point of insertion of power (the policy) in the lives of those to whom it is directed" (p. 193).

Fulcher (2013) applauded Shohamy's (2001, 2006, 2007), and McNamara's (2007) research because it has revealed hidden policy agendas and provided an alternative perspective on the actions and consequences of test use (Messick, 1989). However, he also warned that one of the issues with Foucault's theory is its deeply pessismistic view: "for Foucault there is no escape from despair, and tests will forever be instruments of oppression" (Fulcher, 2013, p. 13). He advocated for social theories in assessment research that were not so "ideologically driven" (p. 12). Indeed, as the chapters in this book attest, there is a vast array of underutilized social theories to inform alternative approaches to assessment validation research.

Fulcher's concerns are of interest in relation to Elder's (2021) review of the role of language testers as they have been described in the research literature over the past 30 years. She reported that testers have been "viewed primarily as enacting policy (for better or worse) rather than as potentially informing policy formation and review". She argued that the tester's role is more complex and potentially far more positive than the literature would suggest. The most important role of testers is far less often reported in the literature, namely, to influence ethical and informed " 'policy responsible' language assessment" (p. 34) (cf. Moss, 2016; see Chapters 5 and 8).

The role of social theories: alternative considerations of the consequences of test interpretation and use

As Fox (2003), Huhta et al. (2006), Maddox (2014), and Norton and Stein (1998) have illustrated, socio-theoretically informed qualitative approaches to trialling new items, tasks, or tests in relevant contexts with representative stakeholder groups can detect significant forms of bias that at-a-distance quantitative approaches may miss. Evidence of bias is used by test developers to revise new test versions accordingly. However, Flores and Schissel (2014) and Shohamy (1997, 2007, 2011) have demonstrated that bias may go undetected in large-scale standardized assessments if constructs are underrepresented (Messick, 1989) for some groups of test takers. Further, when only *at-a-distance* psychometric approaches are used, wherein groups are defined in advance, small numbers of test takers are affected, and modest or low amounts of bias are at play, significant bias may be missed. Qualitative approaches informed by social theories, however, are useful in detecting bias for small numbers of test takers in local contexts of test use. Stakeholders' responses are an important source of data in this regard. The most recent version of the *Standards* (AERA, APA, & NCME, 2014) identified response processes as one of five key sources of validation evidence; however, as Zumbo and Hubley (2017) point out, response processes are not well understood and are underutilized in validation research. They are also typically defined in relation to mental processing – from cognitive theoretical perspectives. The studies considered above underscore the usefulness of socially informed investigations of response processes defined with the alternative benefits of social theories. McNamara and Roever (2006) reinforced this point: "researchers need to go beyond the test booklet to understand fairness and bias in its social context" (p. 128).

Social theories in teaching and learning languages: classroom-based assessment

Fulcher (2013) acknowledged the useful role that social theories have played in unpacking co-constructed interactions in oral proficiency assessment (e.g., Brooks, 2009), and he highlighted the potential of *dynamic assessment* (e.g., Lantolf & Poehner, 2011; Swain, Kinnear, & Steinman, 2010). Lantolf and Poehner's (2011) research on dynamic assessment in language teaching and learning is explicitly informed by their understanding of Vygotskian theory (see Chapter 3). Although there are different approaches to dynamic assessment, all involve *mediation* in social interactions between an assessor/teacher/interlocutor/collaborator and a test taker/student/learner, who engages in completing one or more tasks. Mediating support may consist of advice, materials, prompts, or strategies of a greater or lesser kind; offered to a greater or lesser degree in supporting the student's engagement and task completion. Tasks might include classifying objects, describing how a problem was solved, predicting what might happen next based on a series of pictures, etc. Dynamic assessment approaches help diagnose learning difficulties and accomplishments by focusing on the processes engaged by an individual student, alone and in collaboration, in meeting the demands of a task.

Lantolf and Poehner (2011) identified two different types of mediation used in dynamic assessment, namely, *interventionist* and *interactionist.* The interventionist approach works on the basis of scripted, predetermined interventions to support task completion, whereas the interactionist approach allows mediating support to freely arise as part of the performance itself. These alternative approaches have been increasingly used by teachers to better understand the needs of their students and to tailor classroom activity to support learning.

Dynamic assessment, like many of the assessment practices informed by social theories, has primarily arisen as a result of research in second language education (e.g., Lantolf, 2000; Lantolf & Appel, 1994; Poehner & Inbar-Lourie, 2020a; van Lier, 1989), and most often in the context of the language classroom (e.g., Kramsch, 1993; Swain, 2000; Swain et al., 2010). In this regard, of particular interest is Lantolf's (2000) edited book, *Sociocultural theory and second language learning*. The first chapter, entitled "Introducing sociocultural theory", provides an overview of social theories of relevance to language learning and teaching. The emphasis on *introducing* social theories is important, as it is evidence that in 2000 this book explicitly acknowledged that language teachers were only marginally familiar with social theories – if at all. A similar view is articulated in 2020 by Poehner and Inbar-Lourie, who argue for a new "epistemology of action for understanding and change in L2 classroom assessment". They explain that "conceptual frameworks for appraising specific assessment practices and determining how they may be developed ... [have] remained elusive" (2020b, p. 1).

The chapters in Lantolf's (2000) book provide a particularly discerning window on the envisioned role of social theories in informing research on language learning, teaching, and assessment. In the final chapter, van Lier (2000) draws on Gibson's (1979) *ecological theory*, which traces learning and learning development to "the reciprocal relationship between an organism and a particular feature of its environment" (p. 252). van Lier discusses the implications of Gibson's *ecological* perspective for language learning, arguing that "if the language learner is active and engaged, she will perceive linguistic affordances and use them for linguistic action" (p. 252). He highlights the "centrality of interaction in the concept of affordances" (p. 253) in Gibson's theory, and defines such affordances as "opportunities in the environment" (e.g., language, objects, individuals, space), which collectively provide an "active, participating learner" (p. 253) with mediating resources to support learning. He argues that the unit of analysis for a socially and/or ecologically informed researcher is "not the perceived object or linguistic *input*, but the active learner or the activity itself" (p. 253). Drawing on Bakhtin (1981b, 1986) (see Chapter 3), van Lier emphasizes the need for research on language learning to move away from narrow, decontexualized analysis of linguistic elements – "words that are transmitted through the air, on paper, or along wires from a sender to receiver", and to avoid "seeing learning as something that happens exclusively inside a person's head" (p. 258). van Lier directly addresses the implications for construct definition in language assessment, connecting his discussion to a socially and/or ecologically informed approach in testing, and arguing against "assessment practices that attempt to locate success in the solitary performance of a learner" (p. 259).

An ecological view, like that described by van Lier, might at first suggest, as Fulcher (2013) feared, an ideological stance which would preclude the possibility of testing an individual test taker and generalizing from the test taker's test performance to a target domain of use. But, we argue, a social perspective and reconsideration of *opportunities in the environment* (van Lier, 2000) help us to better understand testing activity, and can enrich and clarify the meaning and interpretability of test performances, just as van Lier argued an ecological perspective helps to better understand learning in a classroom. We have highlighted the work of van Lier (2000) above, because in Part II of this book we provide examples of socio-theoretically informed, transdisciplinary research (TR) which applied a number of the social theories and concepts he discussed (e.g., affordances, situated learning, interactional competence).

At approximately the same time that van Lier was advancing an ecological view of classroom-based learning, teaching, and assessment, both within the language assessment community (e.g., Hamp-Lyons & Condon, 2000; Leung, 2004; Leung & Mohan, 2004; Rea-Dickins, 2006; Rea-Dickins & Gardner, 2000) and external to it, in education (e.g., Assessment Reform Group, 2002; Black & Wiliam, 1998), writing studies (e.g., Elbow & Belanoff, 1986), and other disciplines, classroom-based assessment was being retheorized and reconceptualized as a "pedagogically desirable approach to assessment, which is capable of supporting learning" (Leung & Mohan, 2004, p. 335). Working with teachers and students, Rea-Dickins (2006) highlighted the important role of formative assessment in teaching and learning, the role of assessment evidence in the classroom, and its usefulness as an alternative and essential source of evidence, alongside external tests, in clarifying decisions and actions by policy/decision makers. Two decades later there remain tensions in the utilization of this important source of evidence in relation to the dominant role of external testing. There is evidence instead of considerable misalignment between external tests and classroom-based learning and the negative consequences that have accrued as a result (cf. Fox et al., 2022; Kempf, 2016; Macqueen et al., 2019). However, it is within classroom-based assessment that we have seen the most dramatic growth in the application of social theories and qualitative research. Fox et al. (2022) view this as affirmation of "the value of local, variable, unique [assessment] evidence ... which arises in and from the day-to-day interaction between teachers and students in the classroom" and recognition of the contribution such evidence makes to validation, because it enhances "our understanding of how much, of what kind, and for whom language learning is taking place" (p. 128). As Messick (1989) argued, there is a need for different kinds of evidence for different types of inference. The *rhetorical art* of a validity argument lies in achieving a meaningful and credible balance between different types of evidence. However, at the present time such a balance between evidence from classroom-based assessment and that derived from external standardized tests has not been achieved (e.g., Addey et al., 2020; Kempf, 2016; Macqueen et al., 2019).

In 2007, McNamara added weight to other calls in the literature (cf. Chalhoub-Deville, 2001, 2003; Swales, 1998; cited in Freedman, 2006; van Lier, 2000) for more thoughtful, and richly theorized considerations of *context* through the lenses of social theories. Above, we have selectively summarized some of the research that addressed McNamara's call. He has also consistently highlighted the need for more alternative approaches to assessment validation research (cf. McNamara, 2007; McNamara et al., 2019), which are better suited to investigate the impact of external assessment practices on the individuals who, within education, are most affected by them – learners and teachers in diverse classroom settings. As Cizek (2020) rightly points out, there is little attention paid to classroom-based assessment in the *Standards* (e.g., 2014, pp. 166–167). The assessment-centred communities (such as those which produce the *Standards*), remain focused on external tests and validation practices, which are not best suited to the exploration, examination, or clarification of the interactions between students and teachers in the rich and varied settings of learning and teaching. This terrain is best accounted for by social theories and best investigated by an array of alternative research practices. There is a pressing need to acknowledge, value, and validate the evidence that is collected day to day within classrooms which, when combined with evidence generated by external tests, would serve to clarify, extend, and validate inferences drawn from assessment (e.g., Kempf, 2016; Rea-Dickins, 2006; Turner, 2014).

As evidenced by the meta-review of journal publications reported at the beginning of this chapter, the presence of the social thread in language assessment research pales in comparison with research that is aligned with the worldviews and conceptual stances of assessment-centred communities. However, social theories have informed a vital and increasing number of publications, which have addressed context, constructs, and validity. This social thread was and is evident in the list of contributions below, which is necessarily restricted given limitations of space. See, for example,

- ongoing investigations of *washback* and *impact* (e.g., Chalhoub-Deville, 2016; Cheng, 2014; Cheng et al., 2004; Macqueen et al., 2019);
- research on fairness, bias, and justice (e.g., Macqueen et al., 2019; McNamara et al., 2019);
- advances in theory and the elaboration of new research framewords, such as *Framework of Learning-Oriented Assessment (LOA)*

(Turner & Purpura, 2016; Purpura & Turner, forthcoming), which provides an overarching and unifying framework for classroom-based assessment research by conceptualizing the "synergies among assessment, teaching, and learning" and addressing "how information from assessment can be used to close learning gaps" (Fox et al., 2022, p. 125) (see also Chapter 7);

- elaboration and implementation of Language for Specific Purposes (LSP) assessment (Douglas, 2000) in contexts of language use (e.g., *target domains,* such as academic classrooms, aeronautical workplaces) (see also Chapter 5);
- expansion of LSP assessment to Language Assessment for Professional Purposes (LAPP) (Knoch & Macqueen, 2020), by "identifying layers of context embedded in operationalized constructs" (p. 53), which are situated within relevant domains (see also Chapter 5);
- extension of LSP conceptualizations to include disciplinary, workplace, and other discourses (e.g., Fox & Artemeva, 2017) (see also Chapter 6);
- efforts to increase understanding and use of social theories in assessment, teaching, and learning practices, through accessible textbooks, which introduce social theories to researchers, teachers, and students who may be unfamiliar with them (e.g., Swain et al., 2010);
- application of social theories in critical language testing (Lynch, 2001; Shohamy, 2001, 2007, 2017);
- explicit, fully articulated explanations of social theories in framing and interpreting empirical research (e.g., Addey et al., 2020; Artemeva & Fox, 2010; Fox, Haggerty, & Artemeva, 2016) (see Parts II and III);
- development of innovative assessment practices framed within socio-theoretical perspectives, such as dynamic assessment (e.g., Poehner, 2008; Lantolf & Poehner, 2011); or paired, oral interaction proficiency testing, which addresses "the need to account for the joint construction of performance in a speaking test in both construct definitions and rating scales" (Brooks, 2009, p. 341);
- contributions to our understanding of *response processes* through the application of qualitative approaches in research, particularly research involving key stakeholders (e.g., test takers/students; raters/teachers) (e.g., Doe, 2015; Fox & Cheng, 2007; Fulcher, 1996; Huhta et al., 2006; Turner, 2000; Turner & Upshur, 2002);
- clarification of constructs through the alternative lenses provided by social theories (e.g., Kim & Elder, 2009; Monteiro, 2019) (see also Chapter 5);
- use of discourse approaches to communication which are richly framed by social theories (e.g., Brooks, 2009, Brooks & Swain, 2014; Huhta et al., 2006; van Lier, 1989; Young & He, 1998);
- promotion of methodological pluralism (Moeller, Creswell, & Saville, 2016; Turner, 2014) within new research partnerships (e.g.,

Deygers & Malone, 2019; Poehner & Inbar-Lourie, 2020a) and transdisciplinary programs of research (Moss, 2016);
- emphasis, following Messick, on assessment as ultimately a "rhetorical art" (Messick, 1988, p. 43), which is discursively constructed; and
- increasing recognition that all assessment practices involve actions in context and social theories are urgently needed (Inbar-Lourie, 2008; McNamara, 2007) in order to account for the validity of the inferences we draw from such practices.

The above list is only a selective sample of research. (A more comprehensive list, including some annotated references, is available at APPENDIX – CHAPTER FOUR, https://carleton.ca/slals/people/fox-janna/). McNamara concluded in 2007 that "theories of the social context of language testing should be the site of urgent exploration" (2007, p. 137). The language assessment community has responded to a degree, but as the meta-review of the assessment literature above suggests, there is so much more to do.

In the early 1990s concern over fairness, washback, impact, justice, and ethics in assessment practices – particularly those associated with large-scale, high-stakes testing – resulted in the formation of an association of language assessment professionals from around the world, the International Language Testing Association (ILTA). ILTA developed and adopted a *Code of Ethics* in 2000 (available at www.iltaonline.com/general/custom.asp?page=CodeofEthics) and *Guidelines for Practice* in 2007 (www.iltaonline.com/page/ILTAGuidelinesforPractice), both of which are regularly reviewed and affirmed. The annual meeting of ILTA typically coincides with the Language Testing Research Colloquium (LTRC). See Douglas (2015) for a history of LTRC and ILTA. Further information about ILTA can be found at: www.iltaonline.com/.

Socially informed considerations of justice, power, and policy in assessment

Over the years, increasing concern for impact and washback has found voice in publications within educational measurement (cf. Chatterji, 2013; Flores & Schissel, 2014; Kempf, 2016; Madaus & Kellaghan, 1992; Moss, 2013; Solano-Flores & Trumbull, 2003; Zumbo, 2014) and continues as a prominent stream of research in language assessment (e.g., Abdulhamid & Fox, 2020; Cheng et al., 2004; Macqueen et al., 2019). The rise in accountability and reform agendas implemented by powerful tests external to the classroom has increased attention and concern over the consequences and side effects of such tests. However, any assessment practice which changes teaching and learning could be considered to have washback, for example, curricular changes requiring that specific learning outcomes be measured by teachers at the end of a term of study (see Stoller, 2015), or portfolio-based language assessment enacted across classrooms as part of a reform agenda (Abdulhamid & Fox, 2020; Fox, 2014; Shohamy, 2001). Unfortunately, there is evidence of a continuing applicability gap in considerations of fairness and ethics, as assessment-centred communities continue to be influenced by dualistic perspectives (cf. Cizek, 2020; Walters, 2022), and many in language-centred communities continue to distrust, disregard, and reject external testing and other modes of assessment as remote, distorting, and undermining influences (cf. Poehner & Inbar-Lourie, 2020a, 2020b). Bridging such an applicability gap will require new transdisciplinary approaches to research (Moss, 2016, 2018), methodological pluralism (Moss & Haertel, 2016), and new relationships with collaborating research partners (e.g., teachers, decision makers).

The social thread in language assessment: requirements for transdisciplinary practices

Recognizing and addressing applicability gaps

As noted throughout, we have identified communities as language-centred or assessment-centred as a rhetorical strategy that served the purposes of the book. Although, arguably, these communities have most highly influenced the language assessment community itself, clearly, other disciplinary communities, such as those that are learning- and/or teaching-centred (i.e., in education, educational linguistics), or culture-centred (i.e., in anthropology), or centred on the study of society and patterns of interactions and relationships (i.e., in sociology) have also influenced language assessment validation research and practice. Along with the language-centred communities considered here, these other disciplinary communities have extensively theorized language from social perspectives. Such socially informed perspectives are more in keeping with the practices and processes of teaching and learning and/or education within diverse classroom contexts. More recent theoretical accounts of learning, teaching, and assessment practices (e.g., Eynon & Gambino, 2017, 2018; Little, 2020; Tynjälä & Gijbels, 2012) are emerging as important resources for language assessment research.

We have described the disciplinary position of the sub-field of language assessment as precarious. In 1991, Alderson described language testing as the *ugly* member of the applied linguistics family. However, by 1993 he appeared more positive, observing that "language testing used to be the Ugly Duckling of applied linguistics, much reviled, often ignored" (1993, p. 2), implicitly suggesting the potential for a swan-like transformation. The transformation has remained incomplete. A decade later, McNamara (2007) remarked that the "isolation of language testers is ... one of the most vulnerable aspects of our field" (p. 136). Yet another decade would pass, and McNamara et al. (2019) would again reaffirm the vulnerable position of language assessment: "language testing is little understood by people outside the charmed circle of its practitioners, and even those inside the circle typically aren't equipped by their training to understand the social and policy roles that language tests play" (p. 1). However, the ongoing investigation of the influence (impact and washback) of assessement "on individuals, policies or practices, within the classroom, the school, the educational system or society as a whole" (Wall, 1997, p. 291) has played an important role and encouraged a more positive view of language assessment. This has been enhanced by the self-critical views advanced within the stream of critical language testing (e.g., Shohamy, 2001, 2007, 2018).

Although there remains a dualistic tendency in the research literature to separate testing from assessment – "with assessment more often than not, referring to anything *but* tests" (Fox et al., 2022, p.119) – as noted in the introduction and reinforced throughout this book, we have viewed assessment as an overarching term, encompassing many different modes and methods (tests, portfolios, presentations, interviews, posters, etc.). Further, applicability gaps continue to exist between language assessment researchers and other key stakeholders. For example, much as Hughes (1989) and Widdowson (2003) did decades ago, Poehner and Inbar-Lourie (2020b) discuss the tensions in the relationships between teachers and researchers:

> the epistemological foundations of much assessment scholarship to date ... have led, on the one hand, to prescribing assessment practices to teachers (a unidirectional relationship between theory/research and practice), or, on the [other] hand, to documenting existing classroom assessment practices without any attempt to consider them in a broader context or to improve upon them.
>
> (p. 1)

Recognizing and developing theoretical understanding

Unlike critical streams of research or research in writing and discourse studies, journal publications in language assessment have tended to prioritize *what*, *how*, and *so what*. They have rarely devoted much space to the discussion of *why*, explicating the theories that informed a research study, motivated its implementation, and supported its interpretation. As the meta-review attests, language assessment publications are far less likely to be informed by social theories, and conversely more likely to be informed by individualist cognitive theories, which are often assumed to be understood by those who read such publications. Such theories are rarely fully explained or developed in the opening pages of research articles. They are more often alluded to with the apparent assumption that there is a commonly shared and widespread understanding of them, or ascribed to validity theory with citations and/or a reference or two. As previously noted, editors of assessment journals will often ask authors to cut explanations of the theoretical framework informing a study – particularly when the research is explicitly informed by social theories, which require a good deal more explanation than cognitive theories because concepts and terminology may be less familiar and less shared background can be assumed. Further, social theories typically inform qualitative approaches, which also require more space in order to provide credible amounts of textual evidence in support of interpretations.

Poehner and Inbar-Lourie (2020a, 2020b) urge a change in researcher–teacher partnerships, which is bi-directional and rooted in mutual respect and recognitions, and they reinforce the need for increased understanding of social theories and sociocultural perspectives in defining a new *praxis* as,

> a unity of theory/research and practice wherein these inform one another and change together. Specifically, theory offers principles and concepts that teachers may draw upon to construct practices in a reasoned manner that is responsive to but that goes beyond firsthand experience. Practice, for its part, serves to identify ways in which theory may need to be revised and expanded. Understood as praxis, general conceptual frameworks of classroom assessment and the ways in which it is practiced in particular contexts must be developed in tandem.
>
> (p. 1)

While Poehner and Inbar-Lourie focus on the pressing need for a new praxis informed by socio-theoretical perspectives, which would build the mutual engagement of teachers and researchers in assessment scholarship, we have focused on the potential of extending partnerships to a broader array of stakeholders through a larger TR agenda. Such transdisciplinary approaches involving multiple stakeholder groups, which use assessment to make policy decisions and/or are affected by the impact and consequences of assessment practices, are increasingly prevalent in the research literature (e.g., Cheng, Andrews, & Yu, 2011; Moeini, 2020; Monteiro, 2019; Turner, 2009). Addressing complex problems, such as the role of context in language assessment validation, requires recognition of current applicability gaps and the development of a new validation research praxis (Lemke, 1995; cf. Poehner & Inbar-Lourie, 2020a) (see Chapter 3) that engages research partners beyond academia and the testing industry in assessment research (Moss, 2016), draws on the strengths of all relevant communities, dismisses none, and thus moves the research agenda forward.

Looking ahead to Part II

Part I of this book has aimed at building an initial foundation of shared knowledge, understanding, and recognitions across communities and stakeholders concerned with the assessment of language. Taking a pragmatic stance (Morgan, 2007), drawing on multiple perspectives, and negotiating the "tension" (Messick, 1998, p. 37) that may arise will open the door to new insights, reflections, experience, knowledge, and learning. We argue that such learning may best be achieved within transdisciplinary programs of research which involve multiple research partnerships with stakeholders that have varying disciplinary, professional, and other expertise (e.g., Herndl, 2004; Herndl et al., 2011) who share a common interest in addressing a complex issue and have developed alternative worldviews, practices, ways of seeing, being, and doing as part of their lived experience. The point is, a disciplinary researcher does not have to *go it alone* or continually engage in research practices of their known and bounded research community. So much more is possible when scholarship is shared with others who bring alternative, rival worldviews and perspectives, engage in mutually respectful exchange and dialogue, and acknowledge and come to understand differences in addressing complex issues and challenges of shared interest.

Increasing collective understanding of alternative theoretical perspectives, and broadening the methodological range of approaches to investigate complex problems, will provide "valuable insights into how we can enrich the ways in which we conceptualize what we assess and how we go about assessing it" (Fox, 2004, p. 70). This does not disallow the contribution of traditional psychometric/cognitive perspectives, rather it eschews reliance on any one perspective to the exclusion of others because arguably such reliance has limited assessment researchers' potential to see, understand, and improve the quality of assessment practices and the validity of inferences we draw from them. In Part II we connect the discussion in Part I to examples of TR partnerships in empirical research projects that were informed by social theories. They offer practical evidence of the benefits of illuminating assessment practices from *alternative* viewpoints (Cronbach, 1988; Messick, 1988, 1989, 1998).

Notes

1 The meta-review was funded by an internal grant of Carleton University to Janna Fox, Director of the Language Assessment and Testing Research Unit within the School of Linguistics and Language Studies. Members of the Search Team included Research Assistants Tina Beynen, Chloe Grace Fogarty-Bourget, Claire Reynolds, and Research Associate Ana Lúcia Tavares Monteiro. Chloe Grace Fogarty-Bourget prepared the initial report. Ana Lúcia Tavares Monteiro reviewed and verified results and prepared the final version of the bibliographical list of publications with selected annotations by journal (available at https://carleton.ca/slals/people/fox-janna/).

2 Maxwell and Miller's (2008) seminal chapter on the qualitative analysis of discourse served as a detailed guide to the procedures followed by the meta-review Search Team. Maxwell and Miller distinguished between two types of analysis based on: 1) similarity (categorization); and 2) contiguity (connections), which

they viewed as "two fundamentally different kinds of relationships between things, neither of which can be assimilated to the other" (p. 462). In the meta-review, the Search Team applied the conditions for *similarity* through a process of comparison that identified shared or similar features across texts with regard to context and social theories. These were labeled and categorized. Contiguity was identified in relation to the connective relationships within texts (i.e., in sequences). The meta-review reported in this chapter applied both similarity/categorizing and contiguity/connecting strategies in arriving at the classifications used for the reported frequency counts. Maxwell and Miller (2008) traced this as a distinction that has been drawn by researchers in the qualitative analysis of discourse in numerous disciplines (e.g., linguistics, sociology, psychology).

3 The book entitled *Situated cognition: Social, semiotic, and psychological perspectives*, edited by Kirshner and Whitson (1997), is a laudable example of a transdisciplinary approach, which drew on a broad range of scholars who shared an interest in situated cognition. Their views differed. The editors did not attempt to integrate or synthesize the diverse contributions included in this edited collection. Rather, they highlight its "intertextuality" (p. ix) as "from its inception to the last submission, each author has developed [their] ... contribution in response to the existing chapters" (p. viii). However, some tension is evident, as the editors accuse certain perspectives on situated cognition of *co-opting* or *misusing* the theory and thereby revealing "certain insufficiences in the anthropological and sociocultural traditions that currently underpin situated cognition theory" (p. viii). The tension appears to relate to apprenticeship models of education, which abandoned all or most forms of traditional or formal schooling. Later, other tensions became evident with regard to the storing of experience "in the mind/brain" as "perceptions" (or "perceptual simulations"), and the degree to which such perceptions supported comprehension and action (Gee, 2004, p. 49).

4 Walters (2022) takes a traditional psychometric approach to fairness/ethics, arguably falling into a *dualism trap* by characterizing alternative perspectives informed by socio-theoretical conceptual stances and worldviews (e.g., Hamp-Lyons, 2000; Inbar-Lourie, 2008) as "philosophical extremes" that are "near the 'subjective' end of the spectrum" and positioned in opposition to "absolutist" or "objective" perspectives at the other end (p. 564). He argues for a "middle ground" (p. 564). Ironically, so much more is to be gained by reconsidering these divergent approaches as alternatives; as *additive* sources of differing kinds of evidence in arguments for validity, rather than as dichotomous and incommensurate extremes.

Part II

Transdisciplinary research (TR) in practice

Building connections

5 Clarifying the testing of aural/oral proficiency in an aviation workplace context

Social theories and transdisciplinary partnerships in test development and validation

Ana Lúcia Tavares Monteiro and Janna Fox

In this chapter, we address the problem of context in the field of specific purposes language testing. The chapter provides a descriptive example of assessment practices which are situated within the occupational domain of international aviation with multicultural and multilingual actors. The chapter describes a transdisciplinary research (TR) approach to high-stakes test development (i.e., construct specification and validation), informed by selected social theories (English as a lingua franca, intercultural awareness, interactional competence, and distributed cognition). We highlight the role of these social theories and the engagement of transdisciplinary stakeholders from different disciplinary and professional communities who share a collective interest in the complex issue of testing the English aural/oral language proficiency of pilots and air traffic controllers, to illustrate the value of a transdisciplinary approach in high-stakes test development within specialized professional contexts.

As a passenger travelling by airplane to a destination for work or for pleasure, it may never occur to you that much of your safety, when taking off, during the flight, and when landing, depends on the communications taking place in the cockpit and on the ground between pilots and air traffic controllers. In most international and many national contexts these communications are primarily in English and often involve multilingual and multicultural interactions. This specialized use of language is referred to technically as *aeronautical radiotelephony (RT) communication*. It involves listening without visual cues (e.g., no facial expressions, no gestures) as in listening to a radio; speaking as if on a telephone; and simultaneously monitoring and controlling instruments (e.g., dials,

DOI: 10.4324/9781351184571-8

levers, gauges) which provide a constant stream of data and information. Further, the sound quality is not always perfect – there may be ambient noise, interference, or echoes; and the situation is fluid and may suddenly change without warning, leaving very little time to adjust or respond under pressure. In order to ensure passenger safety, it is critical to assess the aural/oral proficiency in English (i.e., the listening and speaking capabilities/skills) of pilots and air traffic controllers through high-stakes testing. Such tests are mandated by the International Civil Aviation Organization (ICAO), a United Nations specialized agency, which is responsible for the Standards and Recommended Practices (SARPs) for aviation. ICAO (2010) defines RT communications as "a specialized subcategory of aviation language corresponding to a limited portion of the language uses of only two aviation professions – controllers and flight crews. It includes ICAO standardized phraseology and the use of plain language" (p. 3–2).

After a series of accidents and incidents in which language and communication played a contributing role, ICAO set international regulations which strengthened the language proficiency requirements of aviation professionals involved in international operations, defined a testing policy, and specified the minimum level of aural/oral language proficiency (hereafter language proficiency) for safe radiotelephony communications across the globe.

As widely reported in the assessment research literature (e.g., Douglas, 2000; Harding & McNamara, 2017; Kim & Elder, 2009; Knoch & Macqueen, 2020; Monteiro, 2019), this specialized use of aviation or aeronautical English in international, multilingual, and multicultural aviation workplaces has been of central interest in language testing. Researchers (e.g., Kim, 2012; Monteiro, 2019) have observed that what needs to be measured in the testing of pilots' and air traffic controllers' (ATCOs) use of English (i.e., *the construct*) has been ill defined. In other words, they have identified a *lack of fit* between what is tested and the actual communicative needs of speakers and listeners. The danger is clear. An unintended consequence of failing to test what needs to be tested could be pilots flying internationally without the minimum language skills required for safe communications, or ATCOs instructing pilots to take off or land without being able to clearly, efficiently, comprehensively, flexibly, and intelligibly explain *what, when, where*, and *how* in English.

Although aeronautical English can be considered a more specialized sub-language of Aviation English (c.f. Tosqui-Lucks & Silva, 2020), both of these terms have been used in this specialized domain to refer to pilot–controller radiotelephony communications (e.g., Estival, Farris, & Molesworth, 2016; Garcia & Fox, 2020). In this chapter, we use Aviation English to refer specifically to such communications. Aviation English[1] is generally considered to encompass both the English-based standardized phraseology, prescribed by ICAO, and plain English used for the specific purpose of aeronautical communications (see, e.g., Douglas, 2014;

Estival et al., 2016; Kim & Elder, 2009; Knoch & Macqueen, 2020; Moder, 2013).

Among the general features of RT communications, we highlight: a) the use of speaking and listening skills in receptive, productive, interactive, and mediating activities; b) the reliance on specific technical knowledge; c) the absence of visual cues; d) the separation of speakers in space; e) the transmission of one speaker at a time; f) the poor acoustic conditions, background noise, and speakers' imperfect microphone techniques; and g) the divergence of purpose and standpoint (ICAO, 2010) (simply put, the difference between being on the ground and in the air). The example below shows a standard communication between a pilot and an ATCO. It illustrates the concise language that is used and the need to repeat or *read back* crucial information to avoid misunderstandings:

> ATCO: *Fastair 345, climb straight ahead until 2 500 feet before turning right. Runway 24, cleared for take-off.*
> PILOT: *Straight ahead 2 500 feet, right turn. Cleared for take-off runway 24, Fastair 345.*
>
> (ICAO, 2007a, p. 4–8)

There is clearly a great deal at stake for those involved in RT communications and for all who are directly or indirectly affected by the decisions made on the basis of test scores. Therefore, the ultimate purpose of this chapter is to describe a transdisciplinary research (TR) approach to construct specification and validation of the discursive, co-constructed practices and processes of radiotelephony communication between pilots and ATCOs in the multilingual and multicultural context of Aviation English (AE). We have highlighted the role of a number of social theories and transdisciplinary stakeholder partnerships. We argue that test development and construct specification are strengthened when they are informed not only by theory and empirical research, but also by transdisciplinary stakeholders (e.g., pilots, ATCOs, test developers, trainers) whose expertise is rooted in varying lived experience of the construct as it plays out in actual practice. Improved construct specification leads to tests that are more aligned with the communicative needs of test takers and, as a result, have fewer unintended consequences.

An overview of this chapter's organization and purpose by section: some 'heads-up' advice

In keeping with the overall purpose of this book, namely, to build shared knowledge and mutual understanding across differing disciplinary, professional, and other communities, we begin in the first section by providing background on test development and focusing on important considerations that inform the development of tests in language for specific purposes (LSP) contexts. The process of test development is described by spelling out how we move from a context of language use to an actual test: the design of a test's overall *architecture* (Fulcher & Davidson, 2007, 2009). The primary concern in testing is discussed, namely, the definition of the *construct* (Messick, 1989) being assessed and its centrality in arguments for the validity of inferences drawn from test scores or other assessment outcomes (see Chapter 2). We highlight the importance of context and construct definition in complex LSP testing, especially in high-stakes, multicultural workplace contexts, and the role of selected social theories and sociocultural perspectives in this regard.

The background on test development provided in the first section will be familiar to those who are already working in test development, and those within assessment-centred communities. However, there may be less familiarity with the test development process as it is carried out within LSP contexts and the role of alternative social theories in this regard. The first section may be useful for readers from language-centred communities (e.g., in discourse or writing studies, or in language teaching within applied linguistics) who are not familiar with formal, high-stakes test development and/or the role of selected social theories in construct definition. Readers are advised to read and review the first section in relation to what they feel they need to know.

The second section describes construct specification and validation in the occupational context of aeronautical RT communications, informed by policy, selected social theories, empirical research, and stakeholders' engagement. We begin by addressing the issue of overlapping contexts in language testing practices and describing the wider social and policy context within which the testing of pilots' and ATCOs' language proficiency is embedded, focusing on the policy mandated by ICAO and its implementation worldwide. Also, we highlight the usefulness of social theories and sociocultural perspectives in informing and extending construct specification through the lenses afforded by: 1) distributed cognition (Hutchins, 1995a, 1995b; Hutchins & Klausen, 1996); 2) English as a lingua franca (ELF) (Baker, 2015; Canagarajah, 2006; Jenkins, 2000, 2006; Jenkins, Cogo, & Dewey, 2011; Mauranen, 2012, 2017; Seidlhofer, 2001, 2004, 2009); 3) intercultural communication (ICC) (Gudykunst, 2005a; Kecskes, 2014; Scollon & Scollon, 2001; Zhu, 2016)/intercultural awareness (ICA) (Baker, 2011, 2017); and 4) theories of interactional competence (IC) (e.g., Galaczi & Taylor, 2018; Hall, 1995, 1999; He & Young, 1998; Kramsch, 1986; May, Nakatsuhara, Lam, & Galaczi, 2020; Roever & Kasper, 2018; Young, 2011). Further, we emphasize the value of working in a TR space with stakeholder partners and participants who contribute their workplace experience and expertise to the test development process.

Background on LSP test development

In reference to the process of language test development, Fulcher and Davidson (2009) use architecture as a metaphor to discuss layers of *architectural documentation* – a set of documents that articulate design decisions in the process of designing a test. The authors define three main layers or levels of design, which move from the general to the specific, in terms of test purposes and contexts of test use: i) *theoretical models* – "a theoretical overview of what we understand by what it means to know and use a language" (p. 127); ii) *assessment frameworks* – a document that "states test purpose for a particular context of score use ... [and] lays out the constructs to be tested, selected from models" (p. 127); and iii) *test specifications* – "also referred to as 'blueprints' ... they are literally architectural drawings for test construction" (p. 128).

However, all of the development process is situated within a context and subject to the mandate and purpose which guides it. McNamara and Roever (2006) point out that test developers must "consider the context in which tests are commissioned ... [and] problematize the determination of test constructs as a function of their role in the social and policy environment" (p. 24). The mandate, which triggers the entire test development process (Cheng & Fox, 2017), sets out the rationale for and purpose of a test, its scope, use, and the allowances accorded to test developers in designing the test.

The relevance of relying on *test architecture* is that it provides a clear route to follow in test development and supports design decisions along the way. Above all, Fulcher and Davidson (2009) clarify that in a test, "the claim we wish to make is about knowledge, skill or ability of a test taker on a construct of relevance, as selected from a model and articulated in a framework" (p. 131). Therefore, it is important that we first build such a model (derived from our theory of language use and supported by empirical research), and then proceed to the selection of constructs to be tested, which should be "*relevant* to the specific context in question, and *useful* in the decisions that need to be made" (p. 127). This is why theory is so important. Our theoretical understanding of what it is we need to test (i.e., the construct) influences the entire design of the test itself.

The importance of a clear definition of the construct to be measured in assessment contexts is highlighted by Messick (1996), as it is of critical importance to the technical quality of a test. Technical quality is the extent to which a test 1) maps key constructs of interest in a context of language use onto operational tasks and items, and 2) provides a score which is a useful indicator of a test taker's proficiency, ability, etc. Messick explained that the "specification of the boundaries of the construct ... to be assessed – that is, determining the knowledge, skills, and other attributes to be revealed by the assessment" (p. 10) is key in arguing for the validity of the inferences to be drawn from a test (see Chapter 2 for a detailed discussion of Messick's view of validity). The critical access points for ensuring the technical quality of a test are when it is initially under development and later, when validation evidence arising from its use informs revisions to items, tasks, etc. Increasing the technical quality of a test increases its fairness (McNamara et al., 2019).

Construct and context in language for specific purposes (LSP) testing

As noted above, constructs in language assessment are defined by drawing on theoretical and empirical literature and by examining language use in situated social practices. From the theoretical perspectives afforded by a number of social theories, the focus is on both context and activity: "of persons acting and interacting and their activities … [wherein] context is viewed as a social world constituted in relation with persons acting" (Lave, 1996, p. 5). Within LSP testing, test performances are relevant only insofar as they allow for meaningful, useful, and appropriate inferences to be drawn from a score or other outcome (Messick, 1989), based on a test taker's language use in a context, which is defined by specific purposes, processes, and practices.

In test development circles, context is often referred to as the *domain of interest*. Chapelle (2021) defines a domain as "an area of knowledge, content, theory, practice or interest that is demarcated because of its social significance or utility" (p. 90). She further identifies two types of domains which are central to specific purposes language test development. On the one hand, the *target domain* is defined by developers on the basis of their knowledge and/or description of tasks, discourse, actions, performances, understandings, etc. that characterize practices in non-test, lived experience within the specific purposes context. On the other hand, the *test domain* is intended to be a representative sample, systematically drawn from the definition of practices that characterize activity within the target domain. The test sample identifies "all of the types of tasks that could appear on the test and the rules for organizing them … [it] is also referred to as the 'universe of generalization'" (Chapelle, 2021, p. 90), because it delimits the boundaries of inferences that can be drawn on the basis of test performances (cf. Messick, 1996, re *construct domain*).

The target domain *or target language use domain (TLU)* is generally defined by proficiency testers in *construct* definition, namely, in identifying what it is we select to measure from the immensely complex array of skills, knowledge, attitudes, strategies, procedures, and other behaviours that characterize language use. Subsequently, test developers *specify* or define what is selected for the test domain. These *test specifications* set out all the requirements (e.g., number of tasks/items, types of tasks/items, formats, time allowed, point values) for each version of a test. Within specific purposes language testing, the TLU domain or *context* is paramount in construct definition and test specification.

As suggested above (see also Chapters 2 and 3), in order to define a construct for any language proficiency test, we typically draw on theories and/or empirical research to inform test development. When a test of language proficiency is situated within a specific workplace setting, however, it is essential to thoroughly theorize the domain of use in order to ensure that the key characteristics of the context are operationalized by the test tasks. Knoch and Macqueen (2020) corroborate this view when they state that in language assessments for professional purposes (LAPP), "theoretical constructs must encompass domain-specific content, as well as domain-specific ways of mobilizing it in discourse if they are to fully represent their stated uses" (p. 46).

Research on domain-specific/workplace practice has focused on activities, tasks, and individuals who engage through language and other resources in doing work. As noted by Knoch and Macqueen (2020) in the testing of domain-specific language activity, there is agreement that language/discourse is not separate from, but rather situated within and responsive to "the socially material world of that activity" (Lave, 1996, p. 5). However, as Lave (1996) has argued,

> less attention has been given to the difficult task of conceptualizing *relations* between persons acting and the social world. Nor has there been sufficient attention to rethinking the "social world of activity" in relational terms. Together, these constitute the problem of context. (p. 5)

Twenty-five years after Lave recorded her concern, there continues to be a lack of research examining such relations within language assessment (although notable exceptions include Brooks, 2009; He & Young, 1998; van Lier, 1989). However, in the intervening years there has been considerable growth in theoretical and empirical research related to *lingua franca*, *intercultural competence*, and *interactional competence* in language use within specific contexts – but these constructs are not clearly specified or operationalized in RT proficiency testing. Further, since Douglas' (2000) seminal text on the testing of LSP, the relationship of the TLU domain to discursive practices (i.e., persons acting through language and other mediational means, within a material social world) has attracted increased attention. This is evident most recently in Knoch and Macqueen's (2020) exploration of testing practices in LSP/professional settings, such as health, education, engineering, law, and aviation. Douglas (2020) explains that Knoch and Macqueen's goal is "to extend the sphere of responsibility in the specific-purpose assessment field and its underlying principles ... tak[ing] the field of language assessment in professional contexts many steps forward in the important areas of fairness and risk management" (p. 43). Having made a case for the embedded, domain-specific nature of discursive practices in Language Assessment for Professional Purposes, Knoch and Macqueen (2020) argue that test fairness is increased in relation to improved test quality (see also McNamara et al., 2019). Increasing the technical quality of a test means language is assessed more accurately in relation to the uses it performs within the domain, and this in turn reduces risk to stakeholders (e.g., patients, passengers, clients). A critical step in test development, which ultimately impacts the technical quality of a test, is construct specification.

LSP test development: a transdisciplinary approach informed by policy, selected social theories, empirical research, and stakeholders' engagement

In order to engage in a test development project within an LSP context, the contributions of policy, practices, selected social theories, empirical research, and multiple stakeholders are typically essential in the test development process. In other words, LSP testing naturally evokes a TR space, because it draws together professional or workplace experiences and expertise and testing experience and expertise in representing, defining, and operationalizing constructs of interest which are often bounded by policy, practices, rules, and regulations. LSP contexts (like all contexts) are relational. Here the relations are constituted between persons acting in received/ritualized ways through language and other mediating tools in the co-construction of meaning. Meaning is purpose- and context-specific; one is contingent upon the other (Lave, 1996).

An example of a transdisciplinary approach to construct specification and construct validation undertaken within the LSP context of the proficiency testing of aeronautical RT communications is provided in this section (see Monteiro, 2019 for complete details). Monteiro's (2019) study described the process of test development in this occupational context, focusing on the movement from *Models* to *Frameworks* to *Test Specifications*, based on the layers of design in the test architecture discussed in the first section. Within the scope of this chapter, however, only Phase Two of her study will be presented, which focused on the development of theoretical models of language use that account for the communicative needs of pilots and ATCOs in order to inform the specification and validation of the construct within this specific occupational domain. Table 5.1 provides a summary of the steps followed in this qualitative study, including research questions, participants, instruments, procedures, analysis, and results.

In order to build theoretical models of language use, it is necessary that we first answer the question: *What is the context?* Below, we address this question in relation to Monteiro's (2019) study, through an elaboration of the macro and micro contexts of the language proficiency testing in RT communications. First, we introduce the macro or policy context in relation to empirical research, that is, we discuss policy, mandate, and purpose along with selected empirical research studies that have addressed some of the issues related to the social and policy context in which the testing of pilots' and ATCOs' language proficiency is located. Then, we examine communication in this complex workplace through the lenses afforded by alternative social theories in relation to empirical research.

Table 5.1 Steps in construct specification and validation

	Research question	*Participants*	*Instruments*	*Procedures*	*Analysis*	*Results*
Step 1: Models of language use	What theoretical models of language use would account for the communicative needs of pilots' and ATCOs' occupational domain?	No interaction with human participants	Literature review (theoretical, empirical, and practical studies)	Selection of relevant features of each domain (AE, ELF, ICA and IC) that apply to intercultural RT communications, and/or that could impact their outcomes, according to their suitability to build different representations of the context	Three models proposed, from the general to the specific Criteria that guided the design of the models: ✓ comprehensiveness ✓ interpretability ✓ usefulness to inform test development	1) Model of the discursive space of RT communications 2) Model of RT communications in intercultural contexts 3) Model of ESP in RT communications = AE, ELF, ICA, and IC overlap

(*continued*)

Table 5.1 Cont.

	Research question	*Participants*	*Instruments*	*Procedures*	*Analysis*	*Results*
Step 2: Matrix development	How can this construct be articulated and specified from the models to a framework which informs test development?	No interaction with human participants	Literature review (theoretical, empirical, and practical studies)	Definition of the structure of the matrix (four theoretical perspectives and four dimensions – awareness, knowledge, skills, and attitudes), informed by the proposed models A synthetic organization of recurring themes and patterns emerging from the studies	Categorization of components of the construct, i.e., relevant features of the RT context that pilots and ATCOs should be aware of, know, use appropriately, and display as attitude for successful interactions Organization of the components according to their best fit to each cell of the matrix	Preliminary matrix: first attempt to specify the construct Confirmation of overlap of construct components across theoretical perspectives and dimensions

Step 3: Matrix validation	What components of the construct are validated by key aviation stakeholders?	128 aviation stakeholders (20 L1 and 108 L2 English speakers): 22 pilots, 21 ATCOs, 36 AE teachers, 36 AE examiners, six AE researchers, six regulators, one AE curriculum developer	Transcript of six scenarios of authentic international RT communication (one per group) and a set of six questions to guide participants' discussions	26 focus group discussions, triggered by scenarios of RT communications and a set of questions (audio-recorded); Inter-group discussions (four to seven groups at a time), moderated by the researcher, to present participants' perspectives on the scenario analyzed (audio-recorded)	Audio files transcribed and imported to NVivo version 12 Files classified as "monolingual" or "multilingual" First and second cycles coding: Provisional Coding (Saldaña, 2009) Components of the construct from the preliminary matrix used as nodes, sub-, and sub-sub-nodes.	Confirmation of most components of the construct from the preliminary matrix Components that emerged during participants' discussions (highlighted in bold, see Table 5.2) Identification of the four most cited components of each cell, based on the number of coding references, to define the final matrix

Note. AE = Aviation English; ATCO = Air Traffic Control Officer; ELF = English as a Lingua Franca; ICA = intercultural awareness; IC = interactional competence; RT = radiotelephony.
(based on Monteiro, 2019)

What is the context?

There is no test that can be said to be situated outside a context. Contexts imbue or permeate testing and other discursive practices in a variety of ways. In other words, such practices are *nested* (Artemeva & Fox, 2011; Maguire, 1994); they are simultaneously "situated within cultural, institutional, national, linguistic, social" (p. 346), and, in the case of AE, political, governmental, and other macro contexts.[2] Discursive/testing practices are "communicated and instantiated, negotiated and contested, reproduced and transformed" (Garrett & Baquedano-López, 2002, p. 339) in relation to the multitude of overlapping nested contexts – including those specific to individuals in workplaces at micro levels. However, when elaborating language testing policies and mandates, which define and may codify what needs to be measured (i.e., the construct), institutional and/or government bodies/stakeholders do not typically share the same purposes, knowledge, or expertise as test developers. The role of policy and/or decision makers is very different from that of test developers in workplace settings. Policy/decision makers may not fully understand the importance and impact of all these nested contexts on the stakeholders involved. LSP testing is a fertile ground for transdisciplinary collaboration; however, it is prone to many misunderstandings rooted in taken-for-granted assumptions, miscommunications, or communications breakdowns (see Chapter 8), particularly when the stakes are high. As a result, open and flexible mutual understanding of stakeholders is a critical first step in navigating what can be a challenging operational terrain.

Cheng and Fox (2017) explain that mandates can arise internally, for example, within a language program where test development may be mandated as a positive means of addressing needs for program changes or refining group placements, etc. In such cases, they may generate collaborative interaction and professional development amongst stakeholders within the program. However, external mandates for testing which are not informed by the specific and unique character of the programs they impact may not have similar, positive outcomes (e.g., Kempf, 2016; Macqueen, Knoch, Wigglesworth, Nordlinger, Singer, McNamara, & Brickle, 2019).

Further, external mandates for tests and testing practices have rarely been the focus of discussion in language testing, even though they play a critical role in the entire test development process (Davidson & Lynch, 2002). As Cheng and Fox (2017) state, "the mandate ... shapes in fundamental ways how the test will be designed", and in addition "provides parameters for the definition of useful constructs in the test" (p. 110). Ultimately, arguments for the validity of inferences drawn from test performances are structured in relation to the mandate and the purpose for the test. External mandates for test development and implementation may also arise as a result of government policies on language use, legal definitions inscribed in law, or as the outcome of the lobbying of powerful stakeholder groups, who may shape both mandate formation and interpretation (p. 110). In this respect, McNamara (2014) asserts that the lack of discussion about context (and the mandates that inform test development within them) is "symptomatic of a wider failure in language testing to engage with the policy and administrative context in which language tests are located" (p. 231). In addition, he further explains that

> engagement with the theory of the social context represents a response to one of the requirements of test validation as expressed by Messick (1989), that the values implicit in test constructs be investigated and articulated. These values can be understood in social and policy-related terms and can be revealed by considering the discourses within which language tests are located and have their meaning.
>
> (McNamara, 2007, p. 137)

In reference to Messick's argument for the social dimension in considerations of validity, McNamara and Roever (2006) also remind us that test developers should be concerned with the fact that "our conceptions of what it is that we are measuring and the things we prioritize in measurement, will reflect values, which we can assume will be social and cultural in origin, and that tests have real effects in the educational and social contexts in which they are used" (p. 12). The authors criticize models of test development that do not adequately consider the social and policy environments within which tests are designed and used. When mandates and policy fail to align with domain representation, for example, the validity of inferences drawn from tests may be undermined by construct underrepresentation (Messick, 1989). Construct underrepresentation has a negative impact on the relevance, appropriateness, and adequacy of the interpretation of test scores.

Further, given the powerful role of tests in society, Shohamy (2017) points out that "there is an expectation that those who construct tests will follow updated and current theories and definitions of language knowledge as these change over time, based on ongoing research about the construct" (p. 585). However, this is not always the case. As discussed above, there has been a growing theoretical understanding of language use as a discursive practice, "constantly affected by our common participation in the available social stock of knowledge" (Berger & Luckmann, 1966, p. 56) (see Chapter 3). In addition, there has been increased attention paid to theories of, and empirical research relating to, the use of ELF in a multicultural and globalized world (e.g., Baker, 2017; Harding and McNamara, 2017; Jenkins, 2000). However, many language proficiency tests are not informed by these current or updated theoretical understandings of language use. For example, in their discussion of proficiency testing in the aviation workplace, Douglas (2014) and Kim (2012, 2018) point out the inadequacy of the proficiency construct being measured in the licensing of pilots and ATCOs. Moder and Halleck

(2009) also argue that "the aviation language testing situation has been driven more by politics and expediency than by best practices in language test design and validation procedures" (p. 25.3). In addition, Kim and Elder (2015) discuss the *lack of fit* between policy mandates and language proficiency testing in the context of RT communication. Arguably, a TR agenda can better address this issue, but in general most research remains within the sphere of disciplinary research (see Chapter 1) and is failing to reach policy decision makers as a result.

To better understand this lack of fit, below we examine the ICAO policy, which is operationalized in the *ICAO Language Proficiency Requirements* (LPRs) for international RT communication and in the accompanying rating scales. The first nested context of importance to test development in this specific context is that of the ICAO policy, standards, and requirements.

What is the construct (in the context of ICAO policy, standards, and requirements)? The role of mandate and purpose in LSP test development

In 2003, in response to a number of aeronautical accidents and incidents arising from miscommunication attributed to inadequate English proficiency, ICAO introduced language proficiency requirements for pilots, ATCOs, and aeronautical station operators involved in international communications (ICAO, 2010). Since that time, research (e.g., Friginal, Mathews, & Roberts, 2020; Monteiro, 2019; Monteiro & Bullock, 2020) has shown that more than language proficiency is required for safe and efficient radiotelephony communications: "limitations in intercultural awareness of pilots and air traffic controllers" (Friginal et al., 2020, p. ix) are also a "potential threat" (Monteiro, 2019, p. 177) to safety. The ICAO language-related SARPs stipulate the use of ICAO standard phraseology, clarify that both *phraseology* and *plain language* proficiency are required, and strengthen the requirements that English shall be made available when pilots are unable to use the language of the station on the ground (ICAO, 2010, p. 4–2). Standard phraseology can be understood as a type of formally prescribed formulaic speech for pilots and ATCOs involved in aeronautical RT communications. It is a "restricted or coded use of language comprising fixed standard phrases or lexical and syntactical routines ... formally prescribed for special or professional purposes" (ICAO, 2010, p. ix). Plain language, on the other hand, is defined as "the spontaneous, creative and non-coded use of a given natural language" (p. 3–5), to be used when standard phraseology is not enough to achieve a communicative purpose or when there is no standard expression available for a particular situation. However, its use is subject to the "specific safety-critical requirements for intelligibility, directness, appropriacy, non-ambiguity and concision" (p. 3–5) required in aeronautical RT communications. The excerpt below illustrates a dialogue between an

Airbus 319 pilot and an ATCO in Bristol, UK during a rejected take-off situation,[3] in which plain language was necessary. Bullock (2015)[4] used this example to highlight instances of standard phraseology (in bold), domain-specific non-coded language (underlined) added to expressions used for more general purposes (in italics) to support the discourse:

> ATC: **EZY64LW surface wind 28015 knots, runway 27 cleared for take-off.**
> PILOT: **Runway 27 cleared for take-off, EZY64LW.**
> PILOT: **Tower, EZY64LW stopping.**
> ATC: **EZY64LW roger,** *are you able* to taxi *or do you need to stay there for a moment or two?*
> PILOT: *We'd like* to taxi to the end and vacate, **EZY64LW.**
> ATC: **EZY64LW roger, taxi and vacate at the end of the runway and taxi holding point G4.**
> PILOT: **Roger, taxi to the end and vacate and taxi holding point G4, EZY64LW.**
> ATC: **EZY64LW** *just for* planning purposes *are you planning on* returning to stand *or* taxiing round for departure?
> PILOT: *You'll have* to stand by on that, *we're going to need to do some drills when we* clear the runway *and then it will become clear whether we need* to go back to stand.
> ATC: **EZY64LW roger,** *and* do you require any assistance *or do you need me to make any phone calls to* people on the ground?
> PILOT: *At the moment no, we are fine as we are.*
> ATCO: *Ok no problem.*
>
> (Bullock, 2015, presentation slide 12)

More specifically, the regulations in ICAO Annex 1 to the *Convention on International Civil Aviation* (i.e., the testing policy) stipulate that pilots, ATCOs, and aeronautical station operators "shall demonstrate the ability to speak and understand **the language used for radiotelephony communications** [emphasis added] to the level specified in the language proficiency requirements in Appendix 1" (ICAO, 2010, p. 4–4).[5] In order to meet these requirements, it is necessary to demonstrate, in a manner acceptable to the licensing authority, compliance with the holistic descriptors and with the ICAO Operational Level (Level 4) of the *ICAO Language Proficiency Rating Scale*. The ICAO Rating Scale defines six levels of language proficiency ranging from Pre-elementary (Level 1) to Expert (Level 6) across six skill areas of linguistic performance: pronunciation, structure, vocabulary, fluency, comprehension, and interactions (See ICAO Doc 9835, 2010 for a detailed explanation of the five holistic descriptors as well as the descriptors included in the rating scale).

However, the testing policy, through ICAO SARPs, exempts L1 or expert speakers of English from being formally assessed (ICAO, 2010).

In this respect, Alderson (2011) comments that no expertise in language assessment is required to identify "Expert" or Level 6 proficiency, as the "regulations allow for a simple conversation to be held with putative native speakers, by staff who are not qualified in language assessment, in order to certify native speakers as being at Level 6 (which affords lifetime certification) without formal testing" (p. 396). Consequently, despite the specificity of the aeronautical RT context, "native speakers of English are automatically regarded as English proficient for the purposes of aviation" (p. 396). The exemption of L1 speakers of English from formal assessment reveals the values espoused by ICAO, which are political, cultural, and governmental, having a direct impact in the wider social context of test development and use – values which may potentially pose a threat to safety.

In order to implement the ICAO LPRs, each ICAO Contracting State, that is, a State or country that has adhered to the Chicago Convention on International Civil Aviation, developed its own implementation plan and decided on ways to comply with the assessment criteria designated by ICAO. Although guidelines have been published to assist Contracting States in this endeavour, that is, *ICAO Doc 9835 – Manual on the Implementation of ICAO Language Proficiency Requirements* (ICAO, 2010), test developers were left with a challenging task, especially with regard to a clear definition of the construct to be measured (e.g., Emery, 2014; Farris, 2016; Garcia, 2015; Garcia & Fox, 2020; Monteiro, 2019). In that manual, ICAO (2010) states that there is no presupposition that L1 speakers of English necessarily conform to the language proficiency requirements (p. 4–8), adding that they are equally accountable for successful RT communications. This led to the inclusion of a number of recommendations for L1 and expert speakers of English in the guidance material, based on ELF interactions, comprising a range of accommodation strategies and a clear call for the development of linguistic and cultural awareness. However, only a few of these recommendations were included in the testing policy, and as McNamara (2011) highlighted, the reference to an ELF construct is not explicit (p. 46). For the Expert Level (Level 6), Farris (2016) explains that "despite ICAO's endorsement of what could be considered accommodation strategies in ELF interactions, such strategies are not reflected in the assessment criteria outlined in the rating scales for Expert Level 6" (p. 82). Instead, the descriptors include behaviours that could negatively affect the outcomes of pilot–ATCO interactions using AE as a lingua franca, such as varying speech flow for stylistic effect or using vocabulary that is idiomatic and nuanced. In this context, such behaviour may run counter to the demands for clarity, conciseness, and correctness. This illustrates the contradictory nature of the language proficiency requirements (Douglas, 2014; Farris, 2016) by creating "leeway and room for interpretation for stakeholders such as civil aviation authorities, test developers and test service providers" (Farris, 2016, p. 74).

In relation to the social consequences of the current ICAO testing policy, Read and Knoch (2009) emphasize that "they place the onus on L2 speakers to improve their proficiency and by implication give native-speaking aviation personnel no incentive to develop their communicative competence in ELF terms" (p. 21.7). As explained by John Read in a recent interview (Hirch, 2020), "problems with international communication in aviation come from the fact that native-English speaking pilots don't know how to modify the way that they speak in order to communicate with nonnative speaking air traffic controllers or to other pilots" (p. 210). Along these lines, Kim's (2012) findings based on Korean aviation experts' perspectives also suggest that the "policy unfairly targeted NNESs [non-native English speakers] and overlooked the fact that NES [native English speakers] members of the aeronautical community often do not adhere to the requirement to use prescribed phraseology and 'plain' English in routine and abnormal situations" (p. 221). When commenting on Kim's (2012) research results, McNamara et al. (2019) argue that "the policy itself was the problem, not the tests used to implement it", as the test construct "represents the values and privileges of native speakers at the expense of non-native speakers" (p. 19). Harding and McNamara (2017) add that the fact that L1 English speakers are often exempted from demonstrating ELF communication skills "provides evidence of an institutionalized conservatism ... around the place of the native speaker in language assessment policy" (p. 579), concluding that native speakers will not "relinquish their privilege easily" (p. 575).

ICAO also states in Doc 9835 (ICAO, 2010) that the purpose of testing is to assess only plain language proficiency in an operational aviation context. This creates tension between testing policy and real-world communication and raises the question: Is it possible to separate language proficiency within this specialized context from background knowledge, social and professional competence? This issue has been identified and addressed in a number of research studies and publications (Douglas, 2000; Emery, 2014; Garcia & Fox, 2020; Kim, 2018; Knoch, 2014; Knoch & Macqueen, 2016; McNamara, 2011; Monteiro, 2019; Monteiro & Bullock, 2020), which arrived at the consensus that elements of technical/operational knowledge and professional behaviour/attitudes should also be part of the construct.

In sum, considering the multicultural context of international RT communications and its multifarious communicative needs, we argue that the operational definition of the construct in response to the ICAO testing policy may be inadequate. Among specific characteristics of the AE domain, features of ELF, intercultural awareness (ICA), and interactional strategies are not accounted for.

Below, we examine features of the complex communications between pilots and ATCOs through the lenses afforded by the socio-theoretical perspectives of distributed cognition (Hutchins, 1995a), ELF, ICA, and IC. All of these perspectives informed the development of models in

Monteiro's study (2019), have figured in empirical research, and provide an enriched reconceptualization of *construct* and *context*.

What is the construct (in the context of radiotelephony communication)? The affordances of alternative social theories and empirical research in LSP test development

First and foremost, it is important to underscore that in the complex, highly technical and dynamic multicultural workplace context of RT communications, pilots and ATCOs interact over the radio without the benefit of visual cues or other face-to-face features of communication. They perform their roles, which rely on specific technical knowledge and "clear, concise and unambiguous" speech (ICAO, 2010, p. 3–6), in busy airports and airspaces that demand rapid and efficient communications. Moreover, poor acoustic conditions, background noise, and clipped messages make RT communications even more challenging for interlocutors, who may well have different levels of language proficiency (ICAO, 2010).

Distributed cognition

The complexity of tasks performed by pilots and ATCOs requires a joint cooperative effort, including distribution of knowledge and high levels of communication and coordination with artifacts (e.g., microphones, radar screens), technology, and other mediating tools. Hutchins (1995a) viewed such joint, interactive, and mediated efforts as *distributed cognition*. In the context of naval vessels, the author studied the work of the navigation team and explored "the computational and cognitive properties of systems that are larger than an individual ... how these larger systems operate and how their cognitive properties are produced by interactions among their parts" (p. xv). Hutchins (1995b) also investigated the performance of tasks in the cockpit of a commercial airliner, presenting "a theoretical framework that takes a distributed, socio-technical system rather than an individual mind as its primary unit of analysis" (p. 286) as a way to provide "a bridge between information processing properties of individuals and the information processing properties of a larger system, such as an airplane cockpit" (p. 287). Similarly, Hutchins and Klausen (1996) analyzed audio and video recordings of flight crews, which revealed not only coordination of actions and cooperation, but also the crucial role of 'intersubjectivity' as a support for efficient communication and the functioning of the system, emphasizing that "the construction of intersubjectively shared understandings depends on a very special distribution of knowledge in the pilot community" (p. 23). Distributed cognition also applies to the air traffic control system. Fields, Wright, Marti, and Palmonari (1998) conducted a distributed cognition analysis of "the representations present in air traffic control, and their distribution, manipulation, and propagation through the ATC system" (p. 85). As a result, Monteiro (2019) concluded that pilot–ATCO interactions are, thus, considered even more challenging because "while interacting with ATCOs, who are operating within their complex system, pilots are also engaged in their activities within their own system, which has interfaces with the environment, hardware and software" (p. 15). These two complex systems overlap (are nested) in ATCO–pilot communications, generate yet another even more complex system, and in relation shape the context of RT communications.

Based on the contextual features highlighted above, which represent only some of the challenges pilots and ATCOs face in their communications over the radio, it follows that the *co-constructed* (Jacoby & Ochs, 1995; see also Chapter 3) and *intersubjective* (Hutchins & Klausen, 1996) dynamic, discursive nature of their interactions should be taken into consideration when defining constructs in contexts for assessment purposes.

Regarding construct specification, Bachman (2007) presents a historical overview of approaches to defining the construct in language assessment, including the 'ability-focused', 'task-focused', and the more contemporary 'interaction-focused' approach. The latter, he explains, "views the construct we assess not as an attribute of either the individual language users or of the context, but as jointly co-constructed and residing in the interactions that constitute language use" (p. 42). In this sense, the social interactional perspective provides useful insights into how we conceptualize constructs and contexts in language assessment. McNamara and Roever (2006) also mention the existence of other emerging research areas that take the social dimension of assessment into consideration, from which we highlight the testing of ELF coupled with the challenges to native-speaker norms (cf. Leung & Valdés, 2019). Not surprisingly, McNamara and Roever recognize that this topic "raises complex sociolinguistic, policy, cultural, and political issues" (p. 252), as we discussed in the previous section.

English as a lingua franca (ELF)

There are many definitions and perspectives on a lingua franca. In this chapter we apply the definition provided by Jenkins et al. (2011), who defined it as "an additionally acquired language system which serves as a common means of communication for speakers of different first languages" (p. 283). According to the authors, a key feature of the definition of ELF is that "it does not exclude native speakers of English (henceforth NSEs), since ELF is not the same as English as a Native Language (ENL) and must therefore be 'additionally acquired' by NSEs too" (p. 283) (see also Chapter 3). Actually, many L1 speakers of English are not good ELF communicators (cf. McNamara, 2012; Harding & McNamara, 2017). They may not have acquired the skills of accommodation or negotiation; they are not always able to adjust and adapt to the communicative needs at hand, or to pre-empt misunderstandings and to deploy strategies to solve communication breakdowns. Therefore, in contexts of professional communication in multicultural workplaces, such as international RT communications, where pilots and ATCOs use AE as a lingua franca, speakers of English as a L1 also need to acquire AE as an additional language system (Bieswanger, 2016; Estival, 2016; Intemann, 2008). Bieswanger (2016) argues that both the "specialized registers" of standard phraseology and plain English specific to aeronautical radiotelephony are not "among the many registers native speakers acquire 'automatically' without any extra effort" (p. 83). In other words, the language used for RT communications has no native speakers, and as such it should be equally learned by, mastered, and demonstrated through testing by those who speak English as a first and as an additional language.

Researchers in the field of international aeronautical communications have addressed the crucial role of ELF competencies for successful interactions in this occupational domain and the need for L1 speakers of English to share the responsibility for successful communication with speakers of English as L2 (e.g., Douglas, 2014; Estival et al., 2016; Garcia, 2015; Kim, 2012, 2013; Kim & Elder, 2009, 2015; Monteiro, 2019; Monteiro & Bullock, 2020; Read & Knoch, 2009). Harding and McNamara (2017) also emphasize the value of an ELF approach in LSP assessment contexts, such as aviation communications. The authors describe what competencies an ELF construct would comprise, including accommodation, negotiation, clarification, cooperation, adaptability, and openness to different varieties of English (p. 577). Regardless of those efforts, the ICAO testing policy still exempts native and expert speakers of English from demonstrating their abilities to communicate in intercultural contexts through ELF, which can result in negative consequences.

The rise of ELF has contributed directly to the *multilingual turn* (see Leung & Valdés, 2019; Chapter 3). Effective intercultural communication through the use of ELF also requires increasing levels of ICA. The next section will explore the role of theories of intercultural communication in expanding our understanding of the contexts in which ELF is used and the skills required to participate successfully in those sociocultural contexts, with a specific focus on the role of intercultural competence/awareness in international RT communications.

Intercultural communication and intercultural awareness (ICA)

Baker (2017) argues that ELF "is deeply intercultural both as a means of communication and as a research field"[6] with regard to "viewing communication from a post-structuralist perspective where categories of language, identity, community and culture are seen as constructed, negotiable and contested" (p. 25). The author emphasizes that "intercultural communication needs to be viewed as a *sociocultural process* [emphasis added] in which the cultural dimension is crucial" (Baker, 2011, p. 200).

In this respect, Kecskes (2014) takes a pragmatic stance by defining interculturality as "a phenomenon that is not only interactionally and socially constructed in the course of communication but also relies on relatively definable cultural models and norms that represent the speech communities to which the interlocutors belong" (p. 14). He explains that culture is "neither relatively static nor ever-changing, but both" (p. 4), arguing that culture has *a priori* elements (ethnic or cultural marking in communicative behaviour) and emergent features (co-constructed in the moment of interaction), which should be combined to approach culture in a "dialectical and dynamic" (p. 5) way. This is the view of culture that is used in this chapter.

The notion of intercultural communication as a discourse approach (Scollon & Scollon, 2001) adds to this view, as it considers individuals as members of a range of different discourse systems or groups, such as an occupation, an organization, a generation, or a region. For example, we could have on one end of the radio a 59-year-old airline transport pilot flying for British Airways, based in London, UK, and on the other end a 27-year-old military ATCO working as a Tower Controller at Guarulhos International Airport in Brazil. The authors explain that "virtually all professional communication is communication across some lines which divide us into different discourse groups or systems of discourse" (p. 3). These distinct group identities shape participants' expectations in a conversation, which in turn have a direct effect on their interpretation of meaning. Scollon and Scollon (2001) explain that problems arise in intercultural encounters because interlocutors may have distinct assumptions as a result of belonging to different groups or may even be exacerbated "when communication is across more than one group boundary" (p. 83).

As a consequence, considering that all communication is a form of cultural practice (Baker, 2017), it follows that even in the context of aeronautical radiotelephony communication, which is highly technical and governed by a set of established procedures, rules, and standard expressions, cultural interferences will be present in one way or another. This can be explained by the fact that "communication is always embedded in and constitutive of social situations and involves speakers with purposes and positions, none of which are neutral" (Baker, 2011, p. 199).

In the aviation context, several studies investigated the impact of culture on professional interactions and communication, informed by distinct philosophical worldviews (see Chapter 3). A number of studies have applied Hofstede's (1991) cultural dimensions – individualism vs. collectivism, high vs. low power distance, masculinity vs. femininity, high vs. low uncertainty avoidance. Some of these studies investigated pilots' behaviour inside the cockpit, and others included the impact of culture on aircraft incidents and accidents (e.g., Hazrati, 2015; Helmreich, 1994; Helmreich & Merritt, 1998; Merritt, 2000; Merritt & Helmreich, 1996; Ragan, 2004).

Monteiro (2016), informed by Hofstede's cultural dimensions added to theories of intercultural communication (Gudykunst, 2005a), analyzed two communication practices involving international pilots and ATCOs, using a Cultural Discourse Analysis approach (Carbaugh, 2007) and its five modes of inquiry: theoretical, descriptive, interpretive, comparative, and critical. Her findings highlighted specific features of air–ground communications that are affected by cultural differences and suggested that, in order to cope with all pilots' and ATCOs' communicative needs, a more comprehensive notion of communicative competence is necessary. In addition, in another study, drawing on a pragmatic view of culture (i.e., fluid and fixed, having *a priori* and emergent features), Monteiro (2019) explored culturally influenced factors that may bring additional challenges to pilot–ATCO interactions, based on the analysis of authentic scenarios of RT communication between participants from different cultural backgrounds. The Bakhtinian utterance was identified as the unit of analysis, as a link in the chain of speech communication, in relation to previous utterances and to subsequent ones, giving rise to "responsive reactions and dialogic reverberations" (Bakhtin, 1986, p. 94) (see Chapter 3 for details regarding the Bakhtinian utterance). Thus, an understanding of the dialogic and negotiated nature of this type of intercultural discourse was made possible. Monteiro's (2019) study was informed by several theories of intercultural communication and related concepts, which provided a particular perspective on, and were relevant to, an understanding of intercultural communication in aeronautical radiotelephony. They include: *face-negotiation theory* (Ting-Toomey, 2005); *conversational constraints theory* (Kim, 2005); *expectancy violation theory* (Burgoon & Hubbard, 2005); *communication accommodation theory* (Gallois, Ogay, & Giles, 2005); *anxiety/uncertainty management theory* (Gudykunst, 2005b); the notion of *face* and *politeness strategies* (Brown & Levinson, 1987); and the *theory of impoliteness* (Culpeper, 1996) (refer to Monteiro, 2019 and Chapter 3 for a brief description of each theory and concomitant concepts).

There is some evidence of the application of these theories in the language assessment research literature (e.g., Harding & McNamara, 2017), but the direct application of this rich theoretical framework is underrepresented in language assessment research (cf. McNamara & Roever, 2006).

In order to incorporate the intercultural dimension to the traditional models of communicative competence, scholars in the field of intercultural communication have proposed models of intercultural communicative competence (ICC) (e.g., Byram, 1997; Deardorff, 2006; Fantini, 2000). According to Byram (1997), someone with ICC is able to "interact with people from another country or culture in a foreign language ... negotiate a mode of communication and interaction which is satisfactory to themselves and the other ... act as mediator between people of different cultural origins" (p. 71). What these models have in common is the inclusion of the dimensions of attitude, knowledge, skills, and awareness to describe what is required for effective communication in intercultural situations. However, despite the value of ICC in developing awareness of cultural differences, Baker (2011) acknowledges that ICC has some limitations, especially in global lingua franca contexts, as it is still associated with pre-defined target communities or cultures. He argues for an expanded and more dynamic framework for intercultural competence, which he called intercultural awareness (ICA), defined as "a conscious understanding of the role culturally based forms, practices and frames of reference can have in intercultural communication, and an ability to put these conceptions into practice in a flexible and context-specific manner in real time communications" (p. 202). Baker's definition is consistent with Bakhtin's notion of utterance as the "link between language and life" (Bakhtin, 1986, p. 83) within "spheres of human activity" (Freedman, 2006, p. 105). Baker (2012) summarizes the "speech flow" (Bakhtin, 1986, p. 83) of interlocutors within sociocultural contexts of intercultural/multilingual communication, including

> accommodation in adapting language to be closer to that of one's interlocutor in order to aid understanding and solidarity. Negotiation and mediation skills are also key, particularly between different culturally based frames of reference, which have the potential to cause misunderstanding or miscommunication. Such skills result in the ability of interlocutors to adjust and align themselves to different communicative systems and cooperate in communication.
>
> (p. 63)

The concepts of accommodation, negotiation, mediation, and cooperation highlight the connections between ELF, intercultural communication, and the use of interactional strategies. In the next section, we will continue our considerations of alternative social theories to better understand the contexts and constructs embedded in multilingual encounters, focusing on IC.

Interactional competence (IC)

Young (2011) argues that IC "is not to be described in the knowledge and actions of an individual participant in an interaction; instead, IC is the construction of a shared mental context through the collaboration of all interactional partners" (p. 428). As Kramsch (1986) details, successful interactions require not only "a shared knowledge of the world, the reference to a common external context of communication, but also the construction of a shared internal context or 'sphere of inter-subjectivity' that is built through the collaborative efforts of the interactional partners" (p. 367). Kramsch's (1986) view of IC advances the notion of language proficiency, as, according to the author, it also enables learners to recognize the "personal intentions" and "cultural assumptions" behind the words, through "a critical and explicit reflection of the discourse parameters of language in use" (p. 369).

Along these lines, Hall (1999) explains that "all of our [interactive] practices are sociocultural constructions, developed, maintained, and modified by the members of the groups to which we belong as we together engage in these practices" (p. 139). It follows that the responsibility for successful communication is shared between interactional participants, as interactional competence "is not what a person *knows*, it is what a person *does* together with others" (Young, 2011, p. 430).

These notions of intersubjectivity, collaborative efforts, sociocultural construction, and shared responsibility already appeared in our discussion of the interaction of complex systems in aviation through distributed cognition (Hutchins, 1995a, 1995b), which are in line with Young's (2011) view that "IC is distributed across participants and varies in different interactional practices" (p. 430). These concepts are directly applicable to the interactive practices of pilots and ATCOs who use AE as a lingua franca. However, in the context of international radiotelephony, communication breakdowns are too often attributed to professionals who speak English as an L2 (Estival et al., 2016). Yet, Cogo and Dewey (2012) remind us that understanding is "an active (not passive) ability, collaboratively achieved by the speakers in the interaction. Therefore, speakers and listeners (as opposed to merely listeners) are both responsible for the construction of understanding in conversation" (p. 115). Despite the fact that ICAO (2010) acknowledges the fundamental role of L1 speakers of English in increasing communication safety through the use of skills of accommodation and a range of interactional strategies, the ICAO testing policy exempts L1 or expert speakers of English from being formally assessed on these same strategies, as explained in previous sections. As a result, a number of studies have called attention towards the development of IC for effective communication in aviation, including the need for L1 speakers of English to share the responsibility for lack of success while communicating with less proficient speakers (e.g., Douglas, 2014; Estival et al., 2016; Garcia, 2015; Kim, 2012, 2018; Kim & Elder, 2009, 2015; Monteiro, 2017, 2019). In this respect, Harding and McNamara (2017) argue that what previous studies "have revealed of the role of native-speaker behavior in communicative failure in ELF, particularly in high-stakes contexts such as aviation and medicine" (p. 570) reinforces the idea that the current testing policy should be called into question.

The concept of communication as "a two-way negotiative effort" (Kramsch, 1986, p. 368) emphasizes the role both participants have in achieving mutual understanding. Interlocutors are "both pro-active and re-active at the same time, simultaneously deconstructing messages as listeners and constructing their own message as speakers" (Galaczi & Taylor, 2018, p. 219), in a purposeful and meaningful way. However, in contexts where a lot of shared background knowledge is necessary for effective interactions, as is the case of the specific professional context of aviation interactions, Kim (2018) argues that "the demonstration of interactional competence is systematically embedded in the procedural conventions in radiotelephony communications" (p. 406). Therefore, she argues for "an expanded construct of oral communication incorporating elements of professional knowledge and behaviour with a focus on interactional competence specific to this context" (p. 403).

Taking a sociolinguistic-interactional perspective in conceptualizing a speaking construct, Roever and Kasper (2018) also focus on situational and social aspects of language use, explaining that

> in any activity, at any moment, participants calibrate interactional methods and resources to the interactional goals and circumstances at hand. Their IC allows them to deploy these methods for local, context sensitive and practice specific use (Young & Miller, 2004) and the achievement of mutual understanding. Participants' IC is their repertoire of methods and their ability to adapt them to the interactional context at hand.
>
> (p. 334)

Of special relevance to the discussion in the present chapter is Roever and Kasper's (2018) view of the importance of the assessment of interactional abilities, as they "support inferences as to test takers' ability to engage in interactive talk with others, which is an ability that is currently not explicitly assessed but commonly and incorrectly assumed by users to be inferable from scores" (p. 348).

Based on the discussions presented in this section related to the contribution of social theories considered here to understanding contexts and specifying constructs, a reconsideration of what is required of pilots and ATCOs, both speakers of English as L1 and L2, for successful RT communications is of the utmost importance.

Building theoretical models

As explained above, Monteiro (2019) drew on policy, social theories, and empirical research to build theoretical models of language use that address the communicative demands of intercultural RT communications in aviation. They were developed, as she explains, "from the general, i.e., a broader theoretical view of language use in intercultural communications, to a more specific model for the occupational purpose of international RT communications" (p. 191).

As Table 5.1 shows, the outcomes of Step 1 include three models, which represent this occupational context in different ways. The first model,

Model of the discursive space of RT communications, is represented by a radar screen and incorporated "the intercultural dimension within the more traditional communicative competence framework" (Monteiro, 2019, p. 201), not aiming to move into "a post-communicative framework ... but into one enhanced by a major focus on intercultural communication" (Sussex & Curtis, 2018, p. 4). The second model, *Model of RT communications in intercultural contexts,* conceptualized the notion of ICA (Baker, 2011) within the RT communication context. It is a model that accounted for

> each individual's – pilot or ATCO – own set of expectations, assumptions, values, perceptions and interpretations, according to the various cultural groups they are inserted in, ... which also includes a more dialogic, dynamic and emergent interaction of culture, language and communication.
>
> (Monteiro, 2019, p. 205)

In other words, in the RT context of AE, communications arise intersubjectively; meaning is co-constructed (see also Chapter 3) in relation to the context, which is bounded by time, space, mediating artifacts, individual interlocutors, and so forth. As McDermott (cited in Lave, 1996) argued, "context is not so much something into which someone is put, but an order of behavior of which one is a part" (p. 19).

Monteiro (2019) further explains that the third model, *Model of ESP in RT communications,* where ESP stands for English for Specific Purposes, "illustrates clearly each one of the critical constructs that interact in this intercultural workplace context [AE, ELF, ICA, and IC], how and where they overlap" (p. 206); or in other words, "where exactly the test should be situated" (p. 207) – at the centre of the overlapping constructs, which is the ESP context. She concludes that "all three proposed models convey, in different ways, the message that background knowledge is relevant for performance in the aeronautical RT occupational context" (p. 208), which corroborates findings from previous studies (e.g., Douglas, 2000; Emery, 2014; Garcia & Fox, 2020; Kim, 2018; Knoch, 2014; Knoch & Macqueen, 2016; McNamara, 2011). For a more detailed explanation of the three models and their graphic representation, see Monteiro (2019, pp. 202–208).

Construct specification

In Step 2, the constructs of interest were mapped from the *Models* to a *Framework,* or a matrix of construct specification, drawing from the same set of conceptual (theoretical), empirical (study-based), and practical (policy-driven/experiential) publications used in Step 1. The objective was to better inform test development, as a bridge between the models and test specifications. Table 5.2 is a 4 × 4 matrix which considers language use in the occupational domain of aeronautical radiotelephony from four theoretical perspectives (i.e., AE, ELF, ICA, and IC) across four dimensions (i.e., awareness, knowledge, skills, attitudes). The table was populated with the construct components, that is, key and recurring features of the context representing the communicative needs of pilots and ATCOs involved in intercultural RT communication, based on empirical evidence of *best fit* to each cell (see Monteiro, 2019 for additional details). This approach to construct specification is consistent with Cronbach and Meehl's (1955) notion of a "nomological network" (p. 290), as it relies on explicit theoretical and empirical foundations with which to base both the development of a test and the interpretation of test scores.

The preliminary matrix, that is, the outcome of Step 2 and the first attempt to map the construct of RT communications, still required validation by different groups of aviation stakeholders. The goal was to give voice to their perspectives in relation to the awareness, knowledge, skills, and attitudes required for effective communication in this particular context.

The following section will address this topic by emphasizing the role of transdisciplinary perspectives, through the engagement of domain stakeholders.

The contributions of stakeholders in transdisciplinary test development spaces: validation

In the context of specific-purpose language assessments, defining constructs and assessment criteria should rely on the analysis of specific-purpose language use situations and take into account the expert knowledge of domain specialists (Douglas, 2000, 2001; Elder, McNamara, Kim, Pill, & Sato, 2017). These *indigenous* assessment criteria (Jacoby & McNamara, 1999) represent "an insider's view", which is essential in identifying and addressing "the complex issues involved in communicating competently" (p. 214) in a TLU domain. A number of scholars in different fields of research have articulated the construct of professional communicative competence based on *indigenous* assessment criteria (e.g., Douglas & Myers, 2000; Elder & McNamara, 2016; Elder et al., 2017; Fox & Artemeva, 2017; Jacoby & McNamara, 1999; Pill, 2016; for a review see Knoch & Macqueen, 2016). Regarding the assessment of professionals involved in international aeronautical communications, Douglas (2004) emphasizes the value of test developers learning more about "the indigenous criteria experienced pilots and ATCOs use when evaluating the performance of their colleagues, so that these criteria can inform aviation English performance assessment" (p. 10) (see also Chapter 6). This approach has been adopted by some researchers investigating the context of RT communications (e.g., Aragão, 2018; Kim, 2012, 2018; Kim & Elder, 2015; Knoch, 2014; Monteiro, 2019; Monteiro &

Bullock, 2020). Although with different methodologies, these studies addressed the perspectives of domain stakeholders in identifying what matters for effective communication between pilots and ATCOs. Most of these studies had L2 speakers of English as participants, with the exception of Monteiro (2019), in which around 20% of participants were L1 speakers of English, and Knoch (2014), which relied solely on L1 speakers of English. Findings from these studies include, but are not limited to, the role of background knowledge and professional behaviour; adherence to prescribed rules and RT conventions; sensitivity to each other's roles and tasks; shared responsibility for communication failure; and the ability to accommodate and adjust to the communicative demands of the context.

Relevant to the present discussion are some of the implications Elder et al. (2017) mention in relation to adopting this approach – indigenous criteria – to judge communicative effectiveness, which corroborate some of the issues considered in this chapter. First, the need to broaden our understanding of communicative competence to include other abilities that participants deploy in actual contexts of language use. Second, a reduction in the already "tenuous distinction" (p. 19) between L1 and L2 speakers, as what promotes successful communication in occupational contexts will be the same, regardless of participants' language background. Third, the need to reconsider "the relevance of the native-speaker norm ... and the justification for specific tests for L2 speakers, when assessing readiness to manage the complex communicative demands of real-world encounters" (p. 19).

However, stakeholder involvement extends beyond the collaborating members of the target domain community (in this case, pilots and ATCOs). In addition to test developers, researchers, and raters, there is a need for policy makers, regulators, test takers, and others who are affected by or *have a stake* in the outcomes of the test to engage in these discussions.

Matrix validation

In order to confirm the construct components specified in the preliminary matrix and have a sense of their importance, Step 3 involved multiple stakeholders as collaborating partners in this TR space. With the same common interest but each one bringing his/her own worldview, pilots, ATCOs, AE teachers, AE examiners/test developers, AE researchers, AE curriculum developers, and civil aviation authorities engaged in focus group discussions, triggered by authentic scenarios of pilot–ATCO radiotelephony communication (Monteiro, 2019). The goal was to provide a space for the sharing of knowledge, experience, and perceptions of what is required for effective communications in aviation, in terms of awareness, knowledge, skills, and attitudes. Their comments were coded and the number of coding references for each component was used to define the final matrix. Results from the matrix validation are displayed in Table 5.2, which include: i) the four components with the highest number of coding references (in parentheses) for each cell; ii) components of the construct confirmed by aviation stakeholders; and iii) components not previously included in the preliminary matrix, but which emerged during the focus group discussions (highlighted in bold).

According to Monteiro (2019), these findings indicate that:

> intercultural communications in aviation require a broader view of communicative competence, including specific-purpose language ability and background knowledge (AE), the need to speak English as a lingua franca and to adjust to the communicative needs at hand (ELF), to accommodate and negotiate sociocultural differences (ICA), and to solve misunderstandings between members of different cultures, while at the same time sharing responsibility for successful communication (IC).
>
> (p. 241)

These features appeared in our discussion of the selected social theories considered throughout this chapter and, therefore, confirm their useful role in informing construct definition in testing practices, which are situated within specific and intercultural contexts of language use. Not only was a wider range of competencies disclosed in Monteiro's (2019) study, but the high number of coding references for some components in the domain of AE revealed how critical they are as part of the construct.

In order to have another perspective on the importance of each construct component, Monteiro listed each of them in relation to the number of focus groups in which they were mentioned by domain experts (p. 222). Not surprisingly, *background knowledge* was mentioned in all 26 focus groups, followed by *professional tone and attitude*, and *compliance with prescribed rules and procedures (e.g., use of phraseology, readback/hear back)*, both mentioned by 25 groups. On one side, these results corroborate what other researchers have found in their studies (e.g., Douglas, 2014; Estival, 2018; Kim, 2012, 2018; Knoch, 2014), and on the other, they strengthen the argument that the ICAO testing policy underrepresents the construct of international aeronautical communications, leading to questions regarding the validity of inferences drawn from current testing practices. Table 5.2 indicates that much more than just linguistic competence is required for effective RT communications in multicultural contexts, which may have direct (consequential) implications for safety if L1 speakers of English continue to be exempted from being assessed. As Elder et al. (2017) mentioned, the distinction between L1 and L2 speakers in occupational contexts should not prevail, as both groups need to acquire and deploy a range of knowledge, skills and attitudes that go beyond linguistic competence alone.

Table 5.2 Final matrix of construct specification

Construct definition within the aviation radiotelephony domain				
	Awareness	*Knowledge*	*Skills*	*Attitudes*
Aviation English (AE)	- **situational awareness** (67) - **group identities and authority gradients in aviation** (50) - rules of use that characterize the domain (27) - threats presented by cross-cultural communications (19)	- background knowledge (rules and procedures) (78) - standard phraseology (36) - plain English for the specific purpose of aeronautical RT communications (26) - **communication as a Human Factor** (6)	- **Crew Resource Management (CRM)** (55) - **language proficiency (ability to use the language)** (45) - communicate effectively in routine and in highly unpredictable situations (39) - **conflict management** (12)	- professional tone and attitude (195) - compliance with prescribed rules and procedures (e.g., use of phraseology, read back/hear back) (193) - assertiveness (87) - clarity, conciseness, and correctness (37)
English as a lingua franca (ELF)	- challenges faced by speakers of EFL and interlocutors' possible linguistic difficulties (34) - difficulty presented by the use of jargon, idioms, slang, and colloquialisms (17) - the need to speak English as a lingua franca (17) - different varieties of English and speech communities (9)	- **nuances of the language** (5) - language as a social practice (4) - one's own communicative style and the problems it could pose to ELF interactions (3) - characteristics of one's L1 phonology that may influence English pronunciation (2)	- adjust and align to different communicative systems (new patterns of phonology, syntax, discourse styles) (23) - eliminate ambiguous expressions and sentence patterns (21) - adapt linguistic forms to the communicative needs at hand (20) - self-repair, rephrase, paraphrase, and clarify (13)	- patience (68) - collaborative behaviour (45) - avoidance of any kind of superiority of one variety over another (39) - tolerance (12) - openness and humility to negotiate differences (12)

Intercultural awareness/ competence (ICA)	- how the cultural background of participants can impact the complex and dialogic nature of their communications (58) - **power distance** (27) - **gender expectations** (17) - **face concern** (12)	- what is involved in intercultural interaction (11) - potential threats posed by intercultural communications (11) - different cultural frames of reference (communication style, conflict management, facework strategies, etc.) (10) - how social groups and identities function (3)	- move beyond cultural stereotypes and generalizations (11) - engage with and negotiate sociocultural differences (5) - engage with politeness conventions (5) - accommodate to difference and to multilingual aspects of intercultural communication (4)	- politeness (90) - willingness to cooperate (25) - respect (20) - readiness to suspend disbelief about other cultures and belief about one's own (9) - willingness to relativize one's own values, beliefs, behaviours (9)
Interactional Competence (IC)	- shared responsibility for successful communication (5) - discourse as co-constructed among participants (3) - communication as 'a two-way negotiative effort' (1)	- register specific to the practice (10) - an appropriate participation framework (3) - the processes we go through to solve communication issues (1)	- deal adequately with apparent misunderstandings, by checking, confirming, and clarifying (44) - **use of communicative/ interactional skills** (36) - accommodate to the constraints of the context and perceived ability of the hearer (20) - **declare non-understanding** (9)	- **avoidance of intimidation and threatening behaviour** (10) - cooperation (9) - tolerance (6) - flexibility (4)

Note: In **bold**, additional components of the construct suggested by aviation stakeholders during focus group discussions.
In (parentheses), the number of coding references for each component of the construct.
(Monteiro, 2019)

Conclusion

The present chapter began with a discussion of the need to prioritize *context* not only in considerations of language for specific-purpose assessment within domains of use, but also within the wider social and policy contexts in which such assessments are situated. We argued that in multicultural professional contexts in which participants use ELF alongside workplace-specific terminology, such as international radiotelephony communications in aviation, the testing policy should be aligned with current theories of language use and test *contexts* and *constructs* should be defined based on characteristics of the TLU domain anchored in the perspectives and accounts of domain stakeholders. In this regard, alternative social theories offer perspectives on language-in-use-in-context that can enrich our understanding of what we need to represent and thus improve the test's technical quality. Applying Fulcher and Davidson's (2007, 2009) test development framework in elaborating the architectural design of a test, explicitly referencing the theoretical and empirical space within which the test is to act (cf. Cronbach & Meehl's nomological network, 1955), and empirically populating that space with evidence drawn from the domain of interest as part of test development, leads to a deeper and more meaningful elaboration of the constructs of interest in a test. It also provides a blueprint for ongoing test validation, and the revision of tasks and items in relation to the use of the test and the consequences of the decisions that lead from the inferences drawn from test scores.

In the example provided in this chapter (cf. Monteiro, 2019), however, the reality of the ICAO policy and its implementation revealed values still rooted in outdated and limited conceptions of language proficiency, with a clear prioritization of L1 speakers' norms and the notion that these expert speakers do not need to be assessed on the skills required for effective communication in this occupational context. However, the utterances of L1 speakers of English are links in a dialogic communication chain (Bakhtin, 1986). These utterances construct meaning and understanding in relation to the utterances of other interlocutors and therefore, we argue, L1 speakers of English should not be exempted from being tested. It cannot be assumed that they are automatically competent to communicate in such a high-stakes professional context. In the world of postmodern globalization where English is used as a lingua franca, "it is not what we know as much as it is the versatility with which we do things with English that defines proficiency" (Canagarajah, 2006, p. 234). This understanding of proficiency requires a shift of emphases "from language as a system to language as social practice, from grammar to pragmatics, from competence to performance" (p. 234). It follows that globalized uses of English entail more than just linguistic ability for successful intercultural communication. There is also the need "to understand the sociocultural contexts of English as a global lingua franca" (Baker, 2012, p. 64). Concerning the wider social context of ELF, McNamara (2011) maintained that globalization has had a profound impact on the role of English, in the sense that "the emergence of English as a lingua franca as a key feature of a globalized world presents a powerful challenge to assumptions about the authority of the native speaker, an authority which is enshrined in test constructs" (p. 49). This means that L1 speakers of English continue to be used as models for test development, even in situations where alternative definitions of proficiency would be more appropriate. Further the *idealized notion of an L1 native-speaker norm* is belied by the enormous variety of L1 speakers' linguistic and cultural diversity. Despite the discussion among scholars related to the arguments for and implications of the assessment of ELF (for a detailed discussion see Harding & McNamara, 2017; Monteiro, 2019), there is still resistance to change, and we have seen the prevalence of conservative values embedded in many assessment constructs.

Monteiro's (2019) study and this chapter illustrate the problem with ICAO's policy and its narrow, monolinguistic definition of proficiency (Leung & Valdés, 2019) in the context of co-constructed communication in the aeronautical workplace. The decision not to test L1 speakers creates potential for unintended negative consequences. Following Messick (1988), we have "draw[n] attention to vulnerabilities in ... proposed test interpretation and use", because of the underrepresentation of proficiency construct and the tests that operationalize it, largely ignore the complex and situated co-construction of communication in this workplace. Probing the use of language in this context exposed the "tacit value assumptions" at play in the policy and highlighted the need for further "examination and debate" (Messick, 1988, p. 80).

This chapter also demonstrated the benefits of examining language-in-use-in-context through the lens of selected social theories, that is, distributed cognition, ELF, ICA, and IC. The theories help illuminate what stakeholders understand but do not articulate, unpack, or reflect on, allowing for an enriched reconceptualization of *construct* and *context* in the specific-purpose language testing of pilots' and ATCOs' communication. Following Cronbach (1988) and Messick (1988, 1989), the chapter clarified the value of *alternative socio-theoretical perspectives* (see Chapters 2 and 3) in informing construct specification, test development, and test validation. Furthermore, the matrix of construct specification validated by groups of stakeholders (Monteiro, 2019) provided an example of their important contribution to construct specification through transdisciplinary partnerships. Such an approach could be usefully adapted to other LSP contexts. It would be necessary to replace the first row of the matrix (Table 5.2), which is specific to the AE professional domain, with what stakeholders from another TLU domain identify as required in terms of awareness, knowledge, skills, and attitudes for successful communication in that domain. As most of our communications nowadays occur in multicultural contexts and all of them are socially constructed, components of the construct related to ELF, ICA, and IC would also be applicable to and useful in specifying the construct.

Finally, we argue that social theories are under-utilized in informing language test development, in spite of the fact that they are very useful resources and essential to domain-specific testing. As Canagarajah (2006) argues in relation to the changing communicative needs in the globalized world, assessment objectives need to be revised and "we have to move from the 'either-or' orientation in the testing debate to a 'both and more' perspective" (p. 233). Arguably, drawing more *appropriate, meaningful, and useful* inferences (Messick, 1989) from tests and other assessment outcomes necessitates: 1) the adoption of a *pragmatic stance* (see also Chapter 2) in considerations of constructs in contexts; 2) the increasing application of social theories to inform and interpret results; and 3) the involvement of diverse stakeholder partners within transdisciplinary programs of validation research.

There is evidence of increasing awareness and involvement of multiple stakeholders who have a "shared collective interest" in the factors beyond language proficiency that impact the outcomes of aeronautical communications. For example, a recent webinar promoted by the International Civil Aviation English Association (ICAEA) entitled *Factors affecting real-world pilot and ATC communication – Part 2*, took place on April 8, 2021, and attracted 208 participants from all over the world.[7] Pilots, controllers, linguists, language instructors, Human Factors in Aviation trainers, and test developers were invited to register and had the chance to follow a panel discussion with experienced pilots, ATCOs, and linguists analyzing a non-routine radiotelephony communication scenario. Participants were able to interact and ask questions via the webinar chat box, which gave voice to many different perspectives, including positive feedback from the *aviation industry* in terms of a transdisciplinary approach being a step in the right direction. Not surprisingly, many comments addressed the need for more training and ICAO testing of L1/native speakers of English. Participants reported that English native speakers often failed to accommodate and adjust their language for clarity and interpretability, nor did they consistently adhere to standard phraseology when communicating. As we mentioned earlier in the chapter and as was acknowledged by one of the panellists, the testing of English native speakers should be mandated by policy makers at a national or international level.

Fortunately, it appears that the industry is starting to move in that direction as evidenced by its growing awareness of the *multilingual turn* in conceptualizing language use. May (2014) and Leung and Valdés (2019) argue that just as conceptualizations of language underwent a *communicative turn*, and a *social turn*, this is the era of a *multilingual turn* (see Chapter 3), which "has increasingly challenged bounded, unitary, and reified conceptions of languages and related notions of 'native speaker' and 'mother tongue'" (May, 2014, p. 1). We conclude that a broader range of stakeholder participation, the incorporation of differing worldviews, and increased opportunities for dialogue, reflection, and engagement in transdisciplinary programs of validation research promise to support this trend in future.

Notes

1 Estival (2016) provides a more detailed description of Aviation English from a linguistic perspective, both in terms of standard phraseology and plain English, including examples of the dialogic, syntactic, lexical, and phonological levels, and drawing from naturally occurring RT exchanges (for more information, see ICAO Annex 10 – Vol. 2, ICAO, 2014; ICAO Doc 4444 – Chapter 12, ICAO, 2007b; and ICAO Doc 9432, ICAO, 2007a).

2 As previously noted, assessment-centred communities make very limited references to context. Their intent, as quantitative researchers, is typically to decontextualize so that results can be generalized (McMillan & Schumacher, 2010) and avoid what they view as the "context bound" (p. 13) limitations of qualitative research. Vogt (2007) has only one indexed reference to context in his very popular book *Quantitative research methods for professionals*. We draw attention to this reference on p. 216 because it deals with nested contexts from the alternative assessment-centred perspective, informed by individualist, cognitive theories. For example, Vogt explains that differences in achievement might be influenced by other "nested variables" such as other students, classes, programs, and institutions, and proposes the statistical technique of multilevel modelling "to sort out" their relative influence at different levels. Vogt's consideration of nested contexts differs dramatically from the one considered in this chapter, through the lenses afforded by selected social theories. A key issue in most research is that the same terminology is applied to very different meanings. Meaning is indeed a matter of context.

3 Available at www.youtube.com/watch?v=55BLAtAvcRE.

4 Due to publication requirements, we were not able to use the original color-coding in Bullock's (2015) presentation. We have used instead bold, underline, and italics in adapting his original presentation slide for this chapter.

5 Amendment 164 to Annex 1 – Personnel Licensing – introduced strengthened language proficiency requirements for flight crew members and air traffic controllers. They became applicable on November 27, 2003. For more information, please refer to Annex 1, Chapter 1, paragraph 1.2.9 (ICAO, 2020, which is now in its 13th edition).

6 For more details on points of contact between ELF and intercultural communication research, see also Baker (2012, 2015, 2016).

7 The full recording of this and previous ICAEA webinars is available to ICAEA members at www.icaea.aero/webinars/webinars-2021/. Anyone can join ICAEA for a fee.

6 Validation of a rating scale in a post-admission diagnostic assessment

A Rhetorical Genre Studies perspective

Janna Fox and Natasha Artemeva

Chapter 6 provides an example of a particular event in a 10-year transdisciplinary research (TR) project. The project had resulted in the development, implementation, and ongoing validation of a post-admission, engineering-specific diagnostic assessment, administered in the initial weeks of an undergraduate engineering program. The mandate for and purpose of the diagnostic assessment were to identify entering first-year students in need of additional academic support, and tailor that support to their individual needs early in the program in order to prevent failure and attrition. The diagnostic assessment was directly linked to course content and an Engineering Academic Support Centre staffed by collaborating partners from applied linguistics (e.g., writing studies, teaching and learning second languages) and engineering, who acted as raters during the initial assessment and subsequently as Support Centre instructors in follow-up academic support. The chapter focuses on the benefits afforded by the alternative socio-theoretical perspective of Rhetorical Genre Studies (RGS) (introduced in Chapter 3). Reconsidering the students' responses to one of the writing tasks from the RGS perspective deepened the raters' interpretive consistency and understanding of the analytic rating scale and supported their meaningful transdisciplinary dialogue and collaboration as instructors in the Academic Support Centre.

Introduction

Chapter 6 provides an example of a particular event in a 10-year transdisciplinary research (TR) project, which resulted in an engineering-specific diagnostic assessment, administered to entering first-year undergraduate students during the initial weeks of their engineering program. This event was one of many we might have chosen to highlight in this

DOI: 10.4324/9781351184571-9

book, as we have engaged as TR partners in many such projects over the past 25 years. However, both the extraordinary potential of socio-theoretical perspectives in assessment validation research and the benefits of the alternative experience, knowledge, and expertise of collaborating research partners are well illustrated by the event, which involved the validation of an analytic rating scale used for a writing task in the diagnostic assessment.

As we have argued throughout this volume, validation is an ongoing process which continuously elicits differing kinds of evidence of, for example, construct representation, specifications, items, tasks, and rating scales, in order to argue for the validity of inferences drawn from test performances (Cronbach, 1988; Messick, 1989). In keeping with the purpose of this volume, and as explained in Part I, herein we have repurposed Tardy's (2017) call to tap into "the untapped potential of a truly transdisciplinary approach to language" (p. 187), in pursuing a *transdisciplinary* validation research agenda (Moss, 2016; Moss & Haertel, 2016). This research agenda has drawn on the collaborative, collective response of differing disciplinary and other research partners, who have shared an interest in undergraduate student retention and academic success.

The *research event* that is considered here involved refining a rating scale used for diagnostic purposes in the post-admission assessment of entering undergraduate engineering students' writing. The diagnostic assessment had been informed through the transdisciplinary collaboration of disciplinary experts in engineering education, assessment, and writing studies, along with teachers, students, community professionals, and other research partners, who shared their unique expertise and understanding of the first-year experience in undergraduate engineering (e.g., Artemeva & Fox, 2010; Fox & Artemeva, 2017; Fox, Haggerty, & Artemeva, 2016). As a group, research partners addressed the common problem of diagnosing first-year engineering students who were in need of additional academic support at the beginning of their university program.

In general, the main purpose of diagnostic assessment in educational contexts is to link the diagnosis to an *intervention,* which involves some form of additional academic support (Read, 2016). In the case of entering engineering students, the assessment's purpose was to provide specific pedagogical support, which was individually *tailored* to meet a student's specific needs. In order to tailor the support to an individual student's needs, the analysis must be *fine grain* (cf. Fox & Hartwick, 2011) – the finer the grain, the more effective the pedagogical support. In the diagnostic assessment of writing considered here, the analytic rating scale was the principal means for interpreting performance and translating it into specific pedagogical support. Therefore, refinement of the analytic rating scale was an ongoing focus of validation research (Chapelle, Cotos, & Lee, 2015).

The analytic rating scale was primarily developed by assessment experts who had disciplinary backgrounds in writing assessment, diagnostic assessment, and the assessment of logical argument (see Fox, von Randow, & Volkov, 2016). An effective means of refining an analytic rating scale as part of ongoing validation is to apply an alternative theoretical perspective to the analysis of test takers' responses (cf. Cronbach, 1988; Messick, 1998). In our work, we have used Rhetorical Genre Studies (RGS), which, as a theoretical perspective, has shed new light on the students' written responses in the diagnostic assessment (Artemeva & Fox, 2010). To echo Moss (1998), "the importance of an outside perspective [is] to illuminate what is taken for granted (as natural, normal, the 'way things are done') and thereby to provoke critical self-reflection" (p. 62). This chapter provides an example of how reconsidering test taker performances from an alternative, socio-theoretical perspective (i.e., RGS) can enrich a diagnosis by increasing the quality and interpretability of an analytic rating scale, and thereby improving the usefulness of the pedagogical inferences drawn from the assessment. Before presenting the empirical study and situating it within the literature on diagnostic assessment, we further discuss background on RGS (see also Chapter 3).

Background

Rhetorical Genre Studies

As introduced in Chapter 3, RGS is largely based on the concepts of *typification* and *habitualization* (Berger and Luckmann, 1966; Schutz, 1966), grounded in "Husserl's description of typification processes" (da Costa, 2016, p. 85). Typification and habitualization are the processes whereby recognizable and easily understood activities (patterns) become standardized (cf. Bazerman, 2003, p. 462) based on the "socially defined and shared recognitions of similarities" (Bawarshi & Reiff, 2010, p. 219). In other words, the process of habitualization helps individuals to identify and respond promptly and appropriately to recurrent social situations (cf. Miller, 1984), which are characterized by recognizable patterns. When people find themselves in recognizable and familiar situations, they rely on their previous experiences and act habitually to respond to such situations appropriately. As noted in Chapter 3, habitualization cannot be considered separately from the context in which it occurs. The context of the diagnostic assessment procedure encompasses (at one level) the undergraduate university engineering program that mandated it. The assessment is situated in this context, which is "simultaneously *improvised* locally, and *mediated* by prefabricated, historically provided tools and practices" (Prior et al., 2007, p. 17). For example, when students *improvise* a response to a writing task on an assessment, they use both physical tools and objects (e.g., prompts, pen and paper, a computer), and draw on a repertoire of semiotic resources and practices (e.g., language, conventions, previous test taking experiences) (see Chapter 3 for a discussion of Vygotsky's mediational artifacts). All resources and practices are configured by the institutionally structured environment, or context, of the diagnostic assessment itself. In other words, students responding to the diagnostic assessment draw on their cumulative prior experience in academic literacies.

From the RGS perspective, and as Bakhtin (1986) observed, while each utterance is individual, each social sphere develops its own habitualized, temporarily stabilized (Schryer, 1993) *types* of utterances, or *discourse genres* (cf. Miller & Kelly, 2017). A discourse genre is described as a "macro speech act", a pragmatic "typified rhetorical response" to "a recurrent rhetorical situation" (Miller, 1984, p. 57). This response mediates "between private intentions (purpose) and socially objectified needs (exigence)" (p. 57).

In study of first-year engineering students enrolled in a communications course, Artemeva and Fox (2010) asked students to write a *report* as a *task* on a diagnostic assessment. The purpose of the assessment was to identify the needs of individual engineering students in order to assist instructors in tailoring their teaching to the students' needs. Artemeva and Fox observed that students, asked to write a report on the failure of the Challenger spacecraft, tended to inappropriately draw on antecedent (Jamieson, 1975) academic genres frequently used in high school (e.g., essay, narrative), unless they had some engineering workplace writing experience. That is, by the time students entered university they had "accumulated over time from lived experiences, interactive discourse and from simply navigating the social world" (Elster, 2017, p. 275), what Schutz (1982) referred to as *a stock of knowledge* (cf. Durkheim, 1952), or the *sedimentation* of previous experiences (p. 146). This study finding reflects Miller's (1994b) observation that "our stock of knowledge is useful only insofar as it can be brought to bear upon new experience" (p. 29) in an appropriate way.

In an academic classroom, assessment can be viewed as a typified and habitual activity that is familiar to the participants – teachers and students. In this chapter, we argue that this understanding of assessment practices, rooted in social theories, can contribute to deepening our understanding of the *rhetorical expectations*, defined as "the expectations of how to use language to achieve a ... purpose" (St. Amant, 2013, p. 35), which are related to assessment activities engaged in by students in classrooms, and by teachers or test developers who are responsible for the tasks and the inferences they draw from them. In their responses to a new experience, students draw on the "previous experiences which appear to have some sort of similarity" (Goettlich, 2011, p. 497). For a student, new experiences evoke previous tacit and, at times, explicit *types* (cf. Schutz, 1966) of understandings, recognitions, expectations (including rhetorical ones), and actions, which may or may not be appropriate to a new situation.

For example, when new undergraduate engineering students encounter an initial classroom task or activity (i.e., a writing task on a diagnostic assessment), they typically draw on their familiarity with previous recurring assessment practices (e.g., tests, essays), the associated distribution of roles (e.g., teachers, students), recognition of what is expected by the audience, and the discourses/genres that have defined the students' participation in previous academic classrooms, wherever they may have been located (cf. Artemeva & Fox, 2010). In other words, by drawing on previous experiences, students shape their uptake *rhetorically*, where by uptake (Freadman, 1994) we understand "the taking up or contextualized performance of genres in moments of interaction" (Bawarshi, 2015, p. 189). That is, they manipulate and strategically form texts, organize their ideas, choose words, and so on, in what they sense may best meet the demands of the task.

From the assessment perspective (e.g., of teachers, raters), the construct of rhetorical expectations is represented by the criteria in rating scales, which reflect what the assessors value for a specific purpose in a particular assessment context. These are the criteria that are used to draw meaningful inferences regarding qualities of students' performances. Where there is a match between the assessors' and students' rhetorical expectations, the inferences are positive. Where there is a mismatch, the inferences are not.

In this chapter we apply the RGS lens (see Chapter 3) to the consideration of a diagnostic assessment in the classroom context of an undergraduate first-year engineering program. As mentioned above, we consider classroom-based assessment to be a typified and recurrent social practice.

It is important to note that most of the entering first-year students considered in this chapter had not had any academic or workplace experience related to engineering prior to beginning their university program. Although the majority of these students complete their first-year courses successfully, a number do not. The Engineering Faculty that identified a need for the diagnostic assessment (e.g., Fox & Artemeva, 2017) was concerned about entering students who were unsuccessful, as they either withdrew from the program after one or two terms of study, or persisted, in spite of failing the same courses repeatedly. The aim of the diagnostic assessment was to provide early identification of those undergraduates who were entering the university without "communicative 'savvy'" (Dannels & Martin, 2008, p. 154; see also Schryer, Lingard, & Spafford, 2005) and/or without essential threshold concepts (e.g., Meyer & Land, 2003, 2005, 2006; Meyer, Land, & Baille, 2010) (e.g., in language, mathematics, chemistry). In other words, in the diagnostic assessment, rhetorical expectations were operationalized by the two constructs of communicative savvy and disciplinary (i.e., engineering-relevant) threshold concepts (and troublesome knowledge).

Communicative savvy was defined as a kind of "rhetorical flexibility" (Dannels & Martin, 2008, p. 154), realized through "an openness" which allows students to adjust to the demands of "particular circumstances"

(Schryer et al., 2005, p. 256) and act "in situations of uncertainty" where they must "improvise and manage" (p. 256) communication in order to meet the demands arising. Schryer and Spoel (2005) refer to this process as "improvisation" (p. 414).

The constructs of *threshold concepts* and *troublesome knowledge* drew on the original conceptualizations of Meyer and Land (e.g., 2003, 2005, 2006), who provided a particularly insightful metaphorical description of a threshold concept as a "portal" or "transformative waypoint" in learning, that opens "new and previously inaccessible ways of thinking ... without which the learner cannot progress" (Meyer & Land, 2006, p. 3). Individual students vary in timing and types of transformative waypoints, and these portals or waypoints are distinctly disciplinary. Such transformative experiences may occur suddenly or prove to be "troublesome" (p. 3) if they take place over an extended period of time. Unfortunately, given the demanding nature of engineering programs, if such concepts become "troublesome", and if students' "communicative savvy" does not allow them to act, adjust, "improvise" or "manage" (Schryer et al., 2005, p. 256) issues arising in their courses, they are likely to fall behind and ultimately to fail. The diagnostic assessment was developed to identify such troublesome, disciplinary "stuck places" (Meyer, 2010, p. 216) early enough in an individual student's program to provide essential academic support to prevent failure and to help the student succeed.

Evidence that some entering undergraduate students did not have an understanding of threshold concepts/disciplinary knowledge and/or communicative savvy indicated that they might encounter difficulty with the rhetorical expectations of engineering faculty.[1] Further, research (e.g., Fox, 2005b; Tinto, 1993) suggests that if early academic support is not provided to such students, they are more likely to drop out or fail. In response to recognitions arising from the chalk face and from the literature on student success in transition, the Engineering Faculty funded the development of a diagnostic assessment to identify entering students in need of additional academic support (cf. Read, 2016). Following Russell's (2013) call "to interrogate the context" (p. 166), we begin below with a review of principles that inform the development of diagnostic assessment. We then reconsider the diagnostic assessment in engineering from the alternative, socio-theoretical perspective of RGS and provide an example of RGS-informed, evidence-driven validation of a diagnostic rating scale.

Background on the development of a diagnostic assessment

Within educational settings, the general purpose of a diagnostic assessment procedure has been to identify an individual learner's specific strengths and weaknesses and the "successful translations" (Harding, Alderson, & Brunfaut, 2015, p. 333) of the diagnosis into academic support. Alderson,

Brunfaut, and Harding (2014) introduced a set of five principles to guide such diagnostic procedures within a classroom teaching and learning context. We summarize these principles, following Harding et al. (2015):

Principle 1: *Who should diagnose?* A "skilled 'diagnostician'" (p. 318), namely, a well-trained and highly experienced classroom teacher or other language teaching expert/professional, who understands that "it is not the test which diagnoses, it is the user of the test" (p. 318).

Principle 2: *Which assessment practices or tools should be used?* Although many different types of assessment practices or tools may be used, they should all be designed with specific, targeted, diagnostic purposes, as a means of generating "rich and detailed feedback" (p. 318) for both teachers and students alike.

Principle 3: *Who should contribute to the process?* All relevant stakeholders, including teachers, students, and other language teaching/testing professionals, whose varying experiences and accounts will enrich and inform the process.

Principle 4: *How should a diagnosis take place?* Four key stages are identified by Alderson et al. (2014) and Harding et al. (2015):

- 4.1 preliminary but systematic data collection (e.g., teacher observations, teacher–student conferences; student self-assessments);
- 4.2 identification of potential areas of difficulty for an individual student;
- 4.3 initial collection of specific evidence to verify individual needs for support by "drilling down" (Fox & Hartwick, 2011, p. 50) in order to target the sources of difficulty and/or enhance areas of strength; and
- 4.4 targeted intervention, follow-up, and monitoring, that is, the identification of specific support in relation to the feedback from the assessment (e.g., human and material resources).

Principle 5: *What are the desired outcomes?* If the diagnosis is clear, it results in a learning plan, which provides specific, timely pedagogical support (e.g., targeted feedback, resources), and ongoing monitoring and review of learning progress/development. Outcomes include interactional dialogue (between the teacher and student and/or between students), reflection, goal setting, etc. as part of the process of learning.

Harding et al. (2015) emphasize "the need for a symbiotic relationship between curriculum, diagnostic assessment" (p. 333), classroom teaching and learning, and pedagogical support. In the assessment that is the focus of the present chapter, curricular outcomes (e.g., understanding of threshold concepts in mathematics, physics, chemistry), the assessment itself, and the individual interventions worked symbiotically in support of individual students' engagement in engineering at the outset of their first year of study. The diagnostic assessment operationalized a set of constructs, which, taken together, provided an indication of academic readiness for engineering.

The design of the diagnostic assessment was based on Fox's (2005b) and Meyer and Land's (2003) observation that disciplinary literacies (Lea & Street, 1998) and academic resources are key issues in student retention and program completion. As noted elsewhere (e.g., Fox, Haggerty, & Artemeva, 2016), engineering literacies are often challenging for entering students. Acquiring new disciplinary "literacy in the mother tongue" may be likened "to learning a foreign language as it involves immersion in a new [disciplinary] culture" (Nocetti et al., 2017, p. 1). As such, we may view the assessment as representing a Language for Specific Purposes (LSP) construct (Douglas, 2000; Fox & Artemeva, 2017) because the assessment evaluated a student's "threshold readiness for specific disciplinary purposes" (Fox, Abdulhamid, & Turner, 2022). The symbiotic relationship which Harding et al. (2015) define as central to diagnostic assessment is evidenced in the relationship between the course content and demands of the first-year engineering program; the information arising from the diagnostic assessment of entering first-year undergraduates in that program; and the resulting pedagogical support provided to individual students.

Further, the diagnostic assessment exemplified the five principles described above (cf. Alderson et al., 2014). In agreement with Alderson et al. (2014), drawing on our previous research in diagnostic assessment (Fox, 2009; Fox & Hartwick, 2011) and writing-in-the-disciplines (e.g., Artemeva & Fox, 2010), we began the development of the assessment by articulating a socio-theoretical framework that informed it. First, we conducted empirical research to identify indicators of academic risk for entering undergraduate engineering students (e.g., McLeod, 2012; Fox & Artemeva, 2017). From the collected empirical data, we elaborated the constructs of interest; that is, the constructs that represented the domain of academic work in first-year undergraduate engineering. Working in collaboration with engineering stakeholders (e.g., faculty members, teaching assistants, students), an experienced test developer designed diagnostic tasks to operationalize these constructs. Students' responses to the tasks were then evaluated by trained raters, using analytic rating scales with *indigenously drawn* (Jacoby & McNamara, 1999), engineering-specific criteria (Fox, Haggerty, & Artemeva, 2016; Fox, von Randow & Volkov, 2016). Jacoby and McNamara (1999) pointed out that distinctively different disciplinary and professional communication arises naturally "for members of some specific culture [in a specific context]" (Jacoby & McNamara, 1999, p. 224). The most useful source of information about the features of that communication is the communicative interactions of the disciplinary members themselves (e.g., professors/teaching assistants/administrators interacting with students; student to student interactions) – from which assessment criteria were drawn for the analytic rating scale used in the engineering diagnostic assessment.

Detailed feedback on student performance was communicated to each student in the form of a *learning profile* (Fox, Haggerty, & Artemeva, 2016). The learning profile included the identification of specific resources that could be used to support the students' work, and an invitation to make an appointment at an Academic Support Centre for first-year engineering students. Feedback from the learning profiles was used by tutors in the Centre (upper-year or graduate students with applied linguistics or engineering backgrounds) as the initial step in guiding targeted individual support. Pedagogical support was linked directly to activities and assignments originating in the students' courses.

Having provided background on the diagnostic assessment, in the sections that follow, we reconsider it from the RGS perspective (e.g., Bakhtin, 1986; Freedman, 2006; Miller, 1984), a social theory we found particularly useful in illuminating the practices and processes engaged by the engineering diagnostic assessment.

Unpacking a diagnostic assessment writing task through the RGS lens

The diagnostic assessment was designed to be administered during the first week of a new academic year, when entering undergraduate students first engaged with their engineering program (Fox & Artemeva, 2017; Fox, Haggerty, & Artemeva, 2016; Fox, von Randow, & Volkov, 2016). The two overarching constructs of threshold concepts (understanding of disciplinary knowledge) and communicative savvy (disciplinary genre competence) were assessed by a range of five tasks (see Fox & Artemeva, 2017; Fox, Haggerty, & Artemeva, 2016). Two of these were writing tasks. The first writing task (see Fox & Artemeva, 2017) tested listening, reading, and writing and was embedded in a classroom lecture sequence. The second task involved writing an email within a simulated workplace context. This simulated workplace writing task (i.e., the email task) and the analytic rubric or rating scale used to evaluate the task are the focus of the present chapter.

Defining and reinforcing key RGS notions: the diagnostic writing task and analytic rating scale

Although *task* has been defined in many different ways by different authors (e.g., Bygate, Skehan, & Swain, 2001; Curtis, 2017; Skehan, 2001; van den Branden, 2006), in this chapter we view a test task as a means of eliciting response or performance from students who need to comprehend the task and manipulate it, so that their response/performance presents their competence, proficiency, and ability in their best possible light. As noted above, the development of the diagnostic assessment is well conceptualized within the framework of LSP testing (Douglas, 2000; Fox & Artemeva, 2017), which operationalizes constructs within target language use (TLU) domains, or a specific *context* of use; however, RGS highlights the heavily contextualized performance of the test taker at a "moment of interaction" (Bawarshi, 2015, p. 189), by exploring the test taker's uptake. RGS throws new light on the task as the test taker acts within the layered contexts of the task, its instructions, time limits, resources, and so on, all in the larger contexts of the classroom, program, institution, etc.

Thus, the assessment as a social practice is *nested* (Maguire, 1994, 1997) within the network of relationships and practices that connect stakeholders (e.g., test takers/students, raters/teachers, test developers, test users) through the assessment within these layered contexts. This practice may be viewed as "a single encompassing theoretical entity" (Lave, 1996, p. 7). In other words, from the RGS point of view, we cannot separate the domain of language use from the language performance that is elicited by an assessment operating within that domain (cf. Artemeva & Fox, 2010). It is a "dynamic interaction between the situation, the language user and the discourse" (Bachman, 1990, p. 4), or, in other words, an interaction amongst an assessment/assessment task, a student/test taker, and the set of circumstances, which are relevant to the completion of the assessment task.

The writing task considered here through the lens of RGS asked students to write an email in the context of a simulated work placement, which reflected the type of workplace-learning experiences integrated into the engineering program (also known as a cooperative program or *co-op*). The task was situated within multiple *nested contexts* (Maguire, 1994, 1997): prior experiences of the students, simulated work placement, writing task, diagnostic assessment, classroom, program, discipline, faculty, educational institution, higher education, learning culture – to name but a few. The task itself required the test taker to assume the role of a co-op student who was working at an engineering firm, and write a formal email to clients (on behalf of their co-op supervisor), who wanted to know if they could use iron roofing for their house near the ocean:

Writing Task Two: Email Diagnostic Assessment © Fox 2017

Context

You are working in an engineering firm on a co-op assignment. You have been asked to respond to two clients, Mr. and Mrs. Smith (jlsmith@tracker.com), who have consulted your supervisor (Gina

M. Rieke, P. Eng.) about building a home near the ocean. They are interested in using iron roofing but would like some advice since they do not know much about roofing products.

Task

Write a short email on behalf of your supervisor to the clients, explaining why they should not use iron roofing near the ocean. At the end of the email, ask the clients if they are available for a meeting on September 27, 2018 at 10:00 a.m. to discuss other roofing options.

Note: The email should be approximately 1–2 paragraphs in length and should be written in a professional style, following proper formatting and grammar conventions. Keep the audience in mind; the clients are intelligent but may be unfamiliar with iron roofing or chemistry terms. You will show this handwritten draft to your supervisor before sending it to the clients.

The task included information on one of the threshold concepts, a redox reaction (see definition on p. 210) related to the process of rusting, identified as *troublesome* for first-year engineering students by chemistry professors, engineering professors, instructors, and students. A definition of the redox reaction, adapted from a first-year undergraduate chemistry textbook and reduced in complexity, was provided in the task. The email was to be written on behalf of a work placement supervisor. The test taker was asked to explain why the iron roofing option was problematic, schedule a meeting with clients, and suggest that other possible roofing options should be discussed at the meeting. The email was to be drafted for the supervisor and for her signature.

For various reasons, this task, which simulates an actual TLU domain, is exceptionally complex. The task is nested within the context of the actual assessment but evokes two types of audiences: 1) the audience of the teacher/assessor and 2) the audiences within the simulated context of the task (i.e., clients of the engineering firm to whom the email is addressed and the student's supervisor on whose behalf the email is written). Thus, it is important to note that the test taker's uptake on the task is only meaningful and appropriate within the simulated context of the task; however, test takers/students situate this uptake within the actual context of the classroom assessment.

The writing task requires, among other things, reading and following complex instructions in a test booklet, filling in an email template, and monitoring time limits and point values. First and foremost, the task is part of a test – whether diagnostic or not, students in academic classrooms understand this as a recurrent, recognizable (often anxiety-producing) classroom practice. Further, the task is demanding. The students/test takers need to understand and explain a scientific concept to a lay audience (i.e., the clients), follow workplace email conventions, and write on behalf of a superior. In order to perform the task meaningfully and appropriately in meeting the rhetorical expectations of the task (Figure 6.1), the students/test takers need to draw on their threshold knowledge of the redox reaction (*Disciplinary Knowledge*) and demonstrate their communicative savvy by drawing on their knowledge, if any, of email communication in a professional setting (*Antecedent Genre Knowledge*), and their understanding, if any, of how engineers communicate (*Disciplinary Genre Competence*). For our purposes, we have treated these "as distinct" while recognizing that "in practice ... they are deeply intertwined" (Yates & Orlikowski, 2007, p. 70).

To reinforce how the RGS lens informed consideration of the email task, the complex notions of RGS are defined in APPENDIX – CHAPTER SIX (see https://carleton.ca/slals/people/fox-janna/) and briefly discussed in relation to the engineering diagnostic assessment. Due to space limitations of this book, this supplementary information was provided for readers unfamiliar with RGS; however, these notions were introduced and explained in Chapter 3.

In the section below, informed by the RGS perspective, we discuss an empirical example drawn from an ongoing validation research related to the diagnostic rating scale that was developed for the email writing task. The example illustrates how the investigation of student responses, viewed through the RGS lens, contributes to the validity of the inferences we can draw from students' written performance.

An example of RGS-informed, evidence-driven validation of a diagnostic rating scale

After all the responses of a cohort of entering engineering students to the diagnostic assessment were evaluated (N = 1,500), we selected two sets of student responses to the writing task considered here (see above) for further analysis: ten responses from a group of students who had been identified as *in need of academic support*, and ten from a group who were

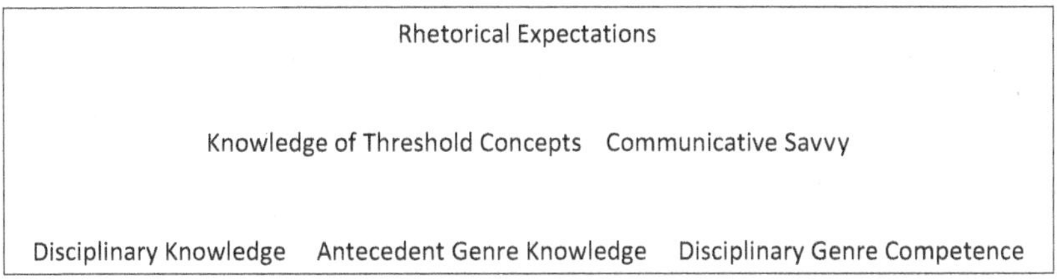

Figure 6.1 A concept map of rhetorical expectations: the email task.

not identified as such by their overall assessment results. We were guided by the following questions:

1 How does RGS contribute to deepening our understanding of the match (or mismatch) of rhetorical expectations of raters/engineering faculty and test takers/students in their management of the email task?
2 What are the implications for the rating scale?
3 What are the implications for the provision of pedagogical support for students diagnosed as needing additional academic support?

As previously discussed, in diagnostic assessment the criteria that comprise the rating scale are critical in determining the subsequent intervention/provision of academic support.

In the email writing task above, understanding Disciplinary Knowledge was represented by a student's management of the following information on rust (*redox reaction*) presented in the task instructions for their writing:

> *Rust*
>
> A common example of a redox reaction is the process of rusting. When iron and iron alloys are exposed to water and air moisture for long periods of time, a redox reaction occurs and rust appears. Rust is a flaky-brown substance that forms, most frequently, on iron and iron alloys.
>
> (Writing Booklet, p. 4)

Antecedent Genre Knowledge was identified through a student's ability to handle the assessment task scenario (or context) of workplace email communication (see Context on pp. 207–208).

Disciplinary Genre Competence pertained to a student's ability to follow instructions (a critical feature of engineering practice, as was repeatedly asserted by our engineering partners), demonstrate audience awareness, and write a meaningful and appropriate text that would be deemed as suitable by engineering faculty/raters. For example, at the beginning of the Writing Booklet (part 3 of the assessment), students were advised that there were two tasks that required a written response. They were also advised that the time allowed for completion of both tasks was 30 minutes. The instructions for the first task (a graph interpretation task discussed in Fox & Artemeva, 2017) included, in boldface all caps, "**DO THIS TASK FIRST, before going on to the next task**" (Writing Booklet, p. 1). This instruction was intended to frame the students' uptake of how to proceed with their responses to the assessment of writing in the Writing Booklet, across the two tasks. In other words, students who followed the instructions in the test might have reviewed both tasks but would begin by responding to the first task. Further, the instructions for the second (email) task began with the following instructions: "**If you have completed the first writing task, read the following passage on rust. Then read the Context and write a short email on page five**" (Writing Booklet, p. 4). These instructions were intended to reinforce the importance of completing the first task before writing a response to the second task.

However, on closer examination, it is important to note that there were actually two sets of instructions for the second task, with one set nested within the other. Not only was the task framed by the overall instructions, reviewed above, information essential for response to the task was nested within the context description, namely, the simulated co-op workplace scenario. The scenario described in the task was followed by these instructions:

> a Your supervisor asks you to write a short email on her behalf to the clients, explaining why they should not use iron roofing near the ocean (use the form on page 5).
>
> b At the end of the email, ask the clients if they are available for a meeting on September 27 at 10 a.m. to discuss other roofing options.
>
> (Writing Booklet, p. 4)

These nested email task instructions were intended to shape the precise nature of the communication the student drafts. All of the following were requirements the students needed to address:

- complete their response to task one before beginning task two, under pressure of time;
- read the task instructions carefully, including the definition of rust, the Context, and the detailed scenario instructions;
- fill in the provided email form or template on p. 5 of the Writing Booklet with appropriate information drawn from the scenario;
- write on behalf of another person (i.e., their supervisor);
- address the clients' concerns;
- explain a rusting process to the clients, without assuming any prior knowledge on their part;
- invite the clients to a meeting to discuss other roofing options on a particular date, at a particular time; and
- leave the signature line open for the review and signature of the supervisor.

In the following section, we present three examples of student responses to this task along with our comments on the evidence of the students' management of rhetorical expectations, as operationalized by their understanding of Disciplinary Knowledge (DK), Antecedent Genre Knowledge (AGK), and Disciplinary Genre Competence (DGC) (cf. Artemeva & Fox, 2010; Beaufort, 2004; Berkenkotter & Huckin, 1993; Devitt, 2015, Tardy,

2009). Before discussion of the actual examples, we provide a brief explanation of our approach to coding, which draws on Saldaña's (2009) top-down (deductive) *protocol* (pp. 130–133) approach, namely, "the coding of qualitative data according to a pre-established … system" (p. 130), based on the three concepts informed by the RGS theoretical perspective, namely: 1) Disciplinary Knowledge; 2) Antecedent Genre Knowledge; and 3) Disciplinary Genre Competence. In the examples below, boundaries of coded chunks of text are indicated by backslashes (/). These codes serve as evidence that a test taker has resources for managing academic expectations in engineering. It is important to stress, however, that the coding in the examples below highlights one type of evidence in each instance for purposes of illustration. At times, however, more than one code could arguably apply. In some cases, a chunk of text is underlined. The underlined chunks of text suggest gaps in the writer's management of the task. When the gaps are numerous, and they are not outweighed by other evidence (arising from performance on the task or on the other tasks in the assessment), the diagnosis would be: *in need of additional academic support*. We identify evidence in the examples *only* to illustrate how RGS informs inferences drawn from a student's performance (see **boldface text** for our commentary). Analysis of the students' responses supports enriched construct definition as represented by the analytic rating scale in that it provides empirical evidence of how students manage the task and is part of an ongoing process of validation.

Example 1
From: test taker's first and last name
To: Mr. and Mrs. Smith (/jlsmith@tracker.com/)[AGK]
CC: Gina M. Rieke
Subject: Iron Roofing/

/Dear Mr. and Mrs. Smith/[AGK]

/Iron roofing is not recommended for your home/[DGC]. /The issue with Iron is that when it is exposed to water and air moisture over a long duration of time, rust appears. Because your home is to be located so close to the ocean, water exposure is greater and your roof would be more at risk of rusting/ [DK]. /Our firm would recommend other roofing options/[DGC].

/To discuss these options, our firm/[AGK] /can meet with you/ on September 27th at 10 a.m/[AGK].

Let us know
Student's signature

Summary of analysis:

- Disciplinary Knowledge (DK) is expressed in sentences two and three:
    - /The issue with Iron is that when it is exposed to water and air moisture over a long duration of time, rust appears. Because your home is to be located so close to the ocean, water exposure is greater and your roof would be more at risk of rusting/.
        - The presentation of the meaning of the redox reaction is accurate.
- Antecedent Genre Knowledge (AGK) is evident in how the test taker manages communication ("communicative savvy"):
- /Dear Mr. and Mrs. Smith/; /jlsmith@tracker.com/; /To discuss these options, our firm/; /on September 27th at 10 a.m./
- Disciplinary Genre Competence (DGC) is evident in sentences one and four:
    - /Iron roofing is not recommended for your home/ is evidence of the test taker's ability to draw on disciplinary knowledge to communicate information pertaining to the client's case; it is consistent with the engineering rhetorical expectation to present a concise summary of an issue at the outset of a communication (Fox, von Randow, & Volkov, 2016) (in the analytic rubric this is defined as a framing statement).
    - /Our firm would recommend other roofing options/
        - Evidence of disciplinary/professional quality communication.
- Gaps in the test taker's mastery of this writing task are underlined:
    - From: /test taker's first and last name/
    - CC: /Gina M. Rieke/ Evidence that the instructions were not followed correctly. The email was to be written on behalf of Gina M. Rieke.
    - /Iron roofing is not recommended for your home./ Evidence of a gap in the test taker's AGK as a) there is no opening statement referring to the preceding email communication (e.g., "Further to your email of …" or "In response to your question regarding …") and b) this statement reflects insufficient audience awareness: the sentence is too direct to serve effectively as a first sentence in the email addressed to a client.
    - … /can meet with you on/ … / Let us know/ This is evidence of a gap in the test taker's AGK: the formality of the language in a workplace communication, which is reflected in the earlier parts of the message, contrasts with the informal and colloquial tone (change in register).
    - /Student's signature/ Evidence that the instructions were not followed correctly, as the email was to be written on behalf of Gina M. Rieke.

Diagnosis

The main inference that was drawn regarding *Rhetorical Expectations* (one of three dimensions considered by raters on the analytic rating scale, as discussed above; see also Fox, von Randow, & Volkov, 2016) was that the test taker demonstrated an acceptable degree of DK, AGK, and DGC for an entering first-year undergraduate at the outset of their engineering program. Gaps in the test taker's understanding would be addressed through regular courses. In other words, from the RGS analysis of the test taker's written response, there was no need for additional, immediate academic support. The RGS analysis and resulting diagnosis was consistent with inferences drawn from the other tasks on the diagnostic assessment.

Example 2
From: My work email
To: jlsmith@tracker.com
CC: my Supervisor/
Subject: /Issue with Iron Roofing/[DGC]

/Dear Mr. and Mrs.Smith,/[AGK]

/My name is Gina M. Rieke, and I am the head engineer for the project of your future home in Virginia Beach/. /After assessing your request to use iron roofing for your house/[AGK], /I am writing to you in order to inform you about the issue of using such material for houses located near water.

The ocean, being a constant source of humidity, and therefore, particles of water in the air, has /a very/ dangerous impact on iron, since after a certain time, rust forms. Rust weakens the material, making iron unsafe for roofing. /In other words, it is unfortunately impossible for us to follow your request to use iron roofing in our plans, due to safety hazards/[DK].

Nonetheless, you should not be disappointed, since /there are plenty alternative solutions/[DK] that I would love to present to you. /Would you be able to meet with me on September 27th at 10:00 AM?/[AGK]

Please RSVP
Gina M. Rieke's Signature

Summary of analysis

- **Disciplinary Genre Competence (DGC) is evident in the following unit:**
  - Subject: /Issue with Iron Roofing/
    - **The subject line accurately and succinctly represents the main idea of the email, which is consistent with the expectation in workplace email communication.**
- **Antecedent Genre Knowledge (AGK) is evident in the following units:**
  - Subject: /Issue with Iron Roofing/
  - /Dear Mr. and Mrs. Smith,/
  - /After assessing your request to use iron roofing for your house/
  - /Would you be able to meet with me on September 27th at 10:00 AM?/
    - **Evidence that the test taker has an appropriate understanding of the rhetorical structure of the workplace email communication.**
- **Disciplinary Knowledge (DK) is evident in the following units:**
  - /I am writing to you in order to inform you about the issue of using such material for houses located near water./
  - The ocean, being a constant source of humidity, and therefore, particles of water in the air, has /a very/ dangerous impact on iron, since after a certain time, rust forms. Rust weakens the material, making iron unsafe for roofing. /In other words, it is unfortunately impossible for us to follow your request /to use iron roofing in our plans, due to safety hazards/.
  - /there are <u>plenty alternative</u> solutions/
    - **Evidence of the test taker's understanding of the redox reaction and availability of other roofing options. This unit may also be interpreted as evidence of DGC because the test taker makes an attempt to address a lay audience while communicating disciplinary knowledge.**
- **Gaps in the test taker's mastery of this writing task are underlined:**
  From: /<u>My work email</u>
  To: <u>jlsmith@tracker.com</u>
  CC: <u>my Supervisor/</u>
  <u>/My name is Gina M. Rieke, and I am the head engineer for the project of your future home in Virginia Beach/</u>
  <u>/Gina M. Rieke's Signature/</u>
  - **Evidence of the test taker's inability to read the task closely and follow the instructions. What makes the email addresses in the From, To, and CC fields inappropriate is the first sentence of the email. The first sentence presupposes that the email is sent directly from Gina M. Rieke's address; however, the test taker sets up the headings in this email template so that the communication appears to be sent from the co-op student's work email to the clients and is copied to Gina.**

Diagnosis

The main inference that was drawn regarding *Rhetorical Expectations* was that the test taker demonstrated an acceptable degree of DK, AGK, and DGC for an entering first-year undergraduate at the outset of their engineering program. Gaps in the test taker's understanding would be addressed through regular courses. In other words, from the RGS analysis of the test taker's written response, there was no need for additional, immediate academic support. The RGS analysis and resulting diagnosis was consistent with inferences drawn from the other tasks on the diagnostic assessment.

> Example 3
> From: /JohnDoe@xxxx.ca/[AGK]
> To: jlsmith@tracker.com
> CC: the material of roofing
> Subject:
>
> ---
>
> Hi, /Mr. and Mrs. Smith/[AGK], I am John, in charge of building your new house. /Picking the iron roofing is not a proper choice for your house/ [DGC]./ The iron material will provide the rust when the surrounding environment is wet/ [DK] /and cold, which can make your new house become cold and/ fragil/[DK]. /Maybe we can meet on September 27 at 10 am to talk about this/[AGK]. / I can provide more options for your roofing/ [DK].
> Best wishes

Summary of analysis:

- **Antecedent Genre Knowledge (AGK) is evident in the following units:**
  - From: /JohnDoe@xxxx.ca/
  - /Maybe we can meet on September 27 at 10 am to talk about this/
    - **Evidence that the test taker has limited understanding of the rhetorical structure of the workplace email communication.**
- **Disciplinary Knowledge (DK) is evident in the following units:**
  - /Picking the iron roofing is not a proper choice for your house. The iron material will provide the rust when the surrounding environment is wet/
  - .../fragil/ ...
  - /I can provide more options for your roofing/
    - **Evidence of the test taker's partial understanding of the redox reaction and availability of other roofing options.**

- Disciplinary Genre Competence (DGC) is not evident in the email. See example below:
    - Picking the iron roofing is not a proper choice for your house.
- Gaps in the test taker's understanding of this writing task are underlined below:
    - To: jlsmith@tracker.com
      CC: the material of roofing
      Subject:
      I am John, in charge of building your new house.
        - Evidence of the lack of understanding of the task, instructions, and context. The email was to have been written on behalf of the supervising engineer, Gina M. Rieke, and should not have been directed to the clients from the co-op student's email without being reviewed and approved by the supervisor. The email subject is provided in the CC line and the Subject field is left blank. The way the test taker presents himself and his role to the clients is inappropriate (I am John) and inaccurate (in charge of building your new house). First, a co-op student is not in charge of the project, and second, the engineering company is advising on material rather than building the house.
    - Hi,
      Picking the iron roofing
      provide
      Maybe
      Best wishes
        - Evidence of informal, imprecise, and inappropriate word choice and style.
    - and cold, which can make your new house become cold
        - Evidence of a possible misunderstanding of the redox reaction (cold is not a cause of rust, nor would the house become cold because of a rusting roof).

Diagnosis

The main inference that was drawn regarding *Rhetorical Expectations* was that the test taker demonstrated an insufficient degree of Disciplinary Knowledge (DK) and Antecedent Genre Knowledge (AGK), and a lack of Disciplinary Genre Competence (DGC). Gaps in this test taker's understanding of task requirements (including following directions, reading closely for details, and understanding threshold concepts) are significant. Example 3 suggests that the student may be in need of initial, immediate support in order to meet the demands of introductory engineering courses. Based on overall performance on this and the other tasks in the diagnostic assessment (e.g., academic vocabulary, graph interpretation, mathematics background), this student was identified for intensive feedback and additional academic support.

From RGS analysis to the rating scale, rater training, and pedagogical support

The RGS perspective led to empirically driven explanations of what to look for as evidence of academic readiness or potential academic risk in the engineering undergraduate students' written responses to the email task. Table 6.1 provides an example of how the three student responses to the email task, analyzed above, were used to support the uptake of the raters engaged for the marking of the test. Used as a training resource, Table 6.1 helped to expand the raters' understanding of the analytic criteria in the rating scale (see also Figure 6.2).

The alternative perspective afforded by RGS encouraged discussion amongst the raters as they viewed the analytic criteria on the rating scale from a different (RGS) perspective, and developed a language for systematically evaluating *rhetorical expectations* in terms of students' communicative savvy and understanding of threshold concepts, operationalized by Disciplinary Knowledge, Antecedent Genre Knowledge, and Disciplinary Genre Competence. The raters, who were drawn from graduate or upper-year undergraduate programs in Applied Linguistics (i.e., writing studies and/or Teaching English as a Second Language/TESL) and Engineering disciplines (e.g., civil, mechanical, aeronautical and space, computer systems, environment, biomedical), subsequently served as tutors in the Academic Support Centre that was established to provide pedagogical support. The discussion that emerged from the analysis of the students' responses to the email task had a number of positive outcomes, including: 1) validation

E-mail task analytic rating scale

Did the student respond to the email task? NO SOMEWHAT YES (Circle one)
→***If yes***, Was the first task (graph interpretation) addressed as instructed (i.e., prior to proceeding to the email task)? If this is the case, it is an initial indication that the student may not need additional academic support. Were one or both tasks incomplete? If this is the case, it is an initial indication that the student may need additional academic support.

□***If no***, this is an initial indication that the student may need additional academic support.

If the task was attempted, circle a number in response to each of the questions below. [The preponderance of yes or no responses should provide triangulation for the overall assessment regarding the need for additional academic support]. Please add up the numbers and enter the total in the space below the table along with comments.

Criterion	NO	SOMEWHAT	YES	No response/too brief to judge =
1. Was the content correct?	0 1 2 3	4 5 6	7 8 9	0
2. Was the language appropriate?	0 1 2 3	4 5 6	7 8 9	0
3. Are email conventions of professional communication observed	0 1 2 3	4 5 6	7 8 9	0
4. Did the test taker understand the task and follow directions?	0 1 2 3	4 5 6	7 8 9	0
5. Could this e-mail be sent to a client?	0 1 2 3	4 5 6	7 8 9	0

Comment: (Key evidence? Any pedagogical observations?)

Total score: ______

Figure 6.2 Email task analytic rating scale.

Table 6.1 Adapted rating scale for training raters/academic support centre staff: the email writing task

EMAIL TASK ANALYTIC RATING SCALE:

[Construct of interest – ***rhetorical expectations:*** *communicative savvy + threshold concepts]*

Did the student respond to the email task?

→ If yes, was the first task (graph interpretation) addressed as instructed (i.e., prior to proceeding to the email task)? If this is the case, it is an initial indication that the student may not need additional academic support. Were one or both of the tasks incomplete? If this is the case, it is an initial indication that the student may need additional academic support.

→ If no, this is an initial indication that the student may need additional academic support.

#	*Criterion #*	*Evidence of readiness*	*Evidence of potential need for academic support*	*Comments/explanations and academic support that is indicated by the assessment*
1	Was the content correct?	"The issue with Iron is that when it is exposed to water and air moisture over a long duration of time, rust appears. Because your home is to be located so close to the ocean, water exposure is greater and your roof would be more at risk of rusting" [Example 1]	"The iron material will provide the rust when the surrounding environment is wet and cold, which can make your new house become cold and fragil" [Example 3]	**[DK]** If disciplinary knowledge regarding a threshold concept is lacking, academic support may be needed. This should be provided directly by the engineering instructors in the Centre. Using the inventory of threshold concepts, engineering instructors should interview new students based on their knowledge of those concepts and provide support for those concepts as needed (see inventory of resources in the course management system).
2	Was the language appropriate?	"Dear Mr. Smith and Mrs. Smith" [Example 1]	"Hi, Mr. and Mrs. Smith" [Example 3].	**[AGK]** Although a very small example, students who do not have or are unable to draw on relevant antecedent genre knowledge do not adapt their language to the requirements of a situation. This may indicate that they need additional academic support, provided by applied linguistics instructors in the Centre. For example, instructors may ask the students to bring in copies of emails they have

(*continued*)

Table 6.1 Continued

#	*Criterion #*	*Evidence of readiness*	*Evidence of potential need for academic support*	*Comments/explanations and academic support that is indicated by the assessment*
				written (e.g., to professors, administrators, friends) and review these with the student in order to raise awareness of how expression changes in relation to audience and the levels of formality required.
3	Are email conventions of professional communication observed?	"Our firm would recommend other roofing options" [Example 1]	"CC: the material of roofing Subject: ________" "Picking the iron roofing is not a proper choice for your house." [Example 3]	**[DGC]** The lack of familiarity with conventions of professional communication is evident in Example 3. The student appears to misunderstand what CC calls for and leaves the Subject of the email, blank. Further, overall, the student attempts to communicate meaningful information; however, the expression is colloquial, lacks formality, and is inappropriate to professional communication. In order to address the needs of the student who lack readiness to meet the demands of engineering [Example 3], a collaborative meeting between the students and both applied linguistics and engineering instructors should be arranged early in the academic year to further assess needs and define specific approaches.
4	Did the test taker understand the task and follow directions?	"After assessing your request to use iron roofing for your house I am writing to you in order to inform you …" [Example 2]	"I am John, in charge of building your new house." [Example 3]	**[AGK]** Example 3 indicates the student requires additional academic support. A collaborative approach needs to be undertaken in order to address this student's needs. (see row 3 above)
5	Could this email be sent to a client?	Examples 1 and 2 could not be sent but demonstrate readiness which courses within the engineering program along with co-op work placements would address.	Example 3 could not be sent, and it demonstrates a lack of readiness which would require additional academic support.	**[DK]**, **[AGK]**, **[DGC]** Evidence from the email task response needs to be considered in relation to the other tasks on the assessment.

of the consistency of the raters' interpretations of the analytic criteria; 2) identification of follow-up pedagogical support that would be useful in addressing the needs of individual students; and 3) development of effective collaborative transdisciplinary partnerships. Over time, resources developed by the raters/tutors in the Academic Support Centre were collected and stored on a course management system, which became a rich repository of activities, exercises, videos, internet links, etc. to address specific needs of individual students. While special arrangements were in place for students in need of additional academic support, all first-year undergraduate engineering students were invited to use the Centre (see Fox & Artemeva, 2017 for additional details).

Conclusion and implications

In this chapter, we have described research which drew on an RGS perspective for ongoing analytic rating scale development, validation, and rater training in the context of an engineering-specific diagnostic assessment. The purpose of the diagnostic assessment was to identify students in need of additional academic support at the outset of their undergraduate engineering program. Re-examining students' responses to the email task on the diagnostic assessment through the alternative perspective afforded by RGS threw new light on the construct of rhetorical expectations, operationalized in the assessment as understanding of threshold concepts and communicative savvy (Figure 6.1), in the first-year engineering program.

The RGS-informed perspective on students' writing generated discussion amongst the raters, who practiced collaboratively in identifying evidence of a student's understanding of Disciplinary Knowledge, Antecedent Genre Knowledge, and Disciplinary Genre Competence (Figure 6.1; Table 6.1, APPENDIX – CHAPTER SIX at https://carleton.ca/slals/people/fox-janna/), in assessing samples of students' writing in response to the email task. Given the diagnostic purpose of the assessment, rater training also served as a professional learning opportunity, because the raters were also tutors in the Academic Support Centre, which was set up to meet the academic needs of the entering engineering students. Rater training was repeated at intervals throughout the academic year, as the diagnostic assessment was administered at the beginning of each academic term. In addition to examples of students' written responses to the assessment tasks, at times student assignments were examined when the raters/tutors wanted to share and discuss them. Ongoing interrogation of the relationship between test writing and first-year students' writing on engineering course assignments further anchored collective understanding of the assessment criteria in the lived experience of the academic classroom. Ultimately, this relationship resulted in more precise and meaningful inferences drawn from the diagnosis, and more appropriate and useful pedagogical support.

In sum, the RGS perspective, chosen as an alternative theoretical framework in this chapter, enriched and deepened understanding and increased the collective consistency of raters in assessing students' knowledge of threshold concepts and communicative savvy, deemed essential for meeting the demands of first-year undergraduate study in engineering. As an outcome, raters/tutors were better informed when drawing inferences regarding how students might meet the demands of the engineering program as evidenced by their written responses to the email assessment task. Raters' judgment was anchored in their ongoing experience with students as tutors in the Academic Support Centre. Their assessment was supported by collaborative discussion and borne out over time in relation to students' success over the first year of their program. The reciprocal relationship between the initial diagnosis and ongoing pedagogical support created an ideal context (cf. Alderson et al., 2014; Harding et al., 2015) for meaningful, useful, and appropriate (Messick, 1989) diagnostic assessment (cf. Fox & Artemeva, 2017).

A strong program of validation requires ongoing research which accumulates evidence of the validity of inferences drawn from an assessment over time, from an array of alternative perspectives, and with regard to its use (Cronbach, 1988; Messick, 1989; Moss, 2016). For example, RGS directed our attention to students' demonstrated understanding and management (Artemeva & Fox, 2010) of Disciplinary Knowledge, Antecedent Genre Knowledge, and Disciplinary Genre Competence which allowed us to consider texture and depth in their writing, which had not previously been evident. The examples provided in this chapter illustrate how useful it can be to engage in transdisciplinary validation research (Moss, 2016; Moss & Haertel, 2016), to leave the comforts of one's discipline, and to collaborate with researchers who bring with them alternative theoretical and methodological perspectives and practices.

Note

1 The engineering program includes a mandatory engineering communication course offered in the first and second years. The academic support, which results from the diagnostic assessment discussed in this chapter, is offered to first-year students at the very beginning of their program.

7 Social theories and transdisciplinarity

Reflections on the learning potential of three technologically mediated learning spaces

Peggy Hartwick and Janna Fox

Transdisciplinarity is often a natural response to complex problems that cannot be addressed with the typified and recurrent empirical approaches of a single disciplinary community. Engaging stakeholders with differing worldviews, knowledge, expertise, and experience to address such complex problems increases the potential quality and usefulness of research. In this chapter, we report on research initiatives that were undertaken in order to enhance the learning of adult, university-bound English for Academic Purposes (EAP) students. The initiatives involved multiple partnerships with other stakeholders (e.g., software engineers/developers, language teachers, educational technologists), and used technology to optimize learning opportunities beyond the temporal and physical constraints of the traditional classroom. In this chapter we describe research regarding the affordances of three technologically mediated online learning spaces: 3D Virtual Learning Environments, ePortfolios, and an HTML Content Creator. An affordance is defined as a "characteristic of an online space that facilitates or promotes learning" (Hartwick, 2018, p. 23). These spaces offer unique opportunities for learning-oriented assessment (LOA) *(cf. Turner & Purpura, 2016).*

> *... the notion of input can be replaced by the ecological notion of affordance, which refers to the relationship between properties of the environment and the active learner.*
>
> (van Lier, 2000, p. 257)

> *Ecological educators see language and learning as relationships among learners and between learners and the environment.*
>
> (van Lier, 2000, p. 258)

DOI: 10.4324/9781351184571-10

All observation is a view from somewhere.

(Kaptelinin & Nardi, 2006, p. 18)

This chapter highlights how language development was promoted through interaction in and with three online learning *spaces* within several university-level English for Academic Purposes (EAP) courses. Drawing on research reported by Hartwick (2018), an affordance is considered here as a distinctive "characteristic of an online space that facilitates or promotes learning" (p. 23). Technologically mediated spaces can offer an array of new types of learning, teaching, and assessment opportunities, but this depends upon the unique affordances of each. In this chapter, we highlight how social theories (cf. Chaiklin & Lave, 1996; van Lier, 2000) provided useful lenses to deepen our understanding of learning and assessment in such online learning spaces (Savin-Baden, 2008). Based on a clearer understanding of the concept of affordances, "critical insights … emerged" (Hartwick, 2018, p. 207). For example, we recognized that the affordances of each distinct online space and the digital tools available within that space needed to be considered in order for learning to take place. This is consistent with Turner and Purpura's (2016) *Framework of Learning-Oriented Assessment*, which "prioritizes learning when considering the interrelationships across instruction, assessment, and learning" (Turner & Purpura, 2016, p. 255). On reflection, we have recognized the critical importance of teacher flexibility in using such spaces. These reflections are reported at the end of the chapter in relation to the fully (i.e., 100%) online delivery necessitated by the COVID-19 pandemic of 2020.

The following questions have guided our discussion in this chapter:

- Within the concept of affordances, which social theories can help us to see *what's going on*, understand, interpret, and account for learning in an online learning space?
- How and what do we assess in these spaces, or as van Lier (2000) asked, "How does learning emerge" (p. 255)?
- What is different about assessment in each online learning space?
- What evidence should we collect? How do we document learning?
- How can transdisciplinary stakeholders support positive learning outcomes in online spaces? Which collaborating partners are essential in designing and understanding these learning spaces from a pedagogical perspective?

Putting space in context: defining terms and situating the discussion

We begin by defining key terms that are central to the discussion in this chapter. For our purposes, *space* is a term used to describe a physical or online space, like a learning management system (LMS)[1] or electronic portfolio[2] (hereafter, ePortfolio), but this book is about reconsidering context – what is the difference? In this chapter, whereas space is a reference to a material or concrete space (e.g., a classroom, workbook, ePortfolio), context is an all-encompassing reference to the pedagogical circumstance, setting, or situation. It includes, to name but a few, the teacher or facilitator, the learner, the task, the actions, the interactions, and the assessment practices. These features, taken together with affordances, dynamically generate the pedagogical contexts wherein teaching, learning, and assessment take place. Therefore, simply applying traditional assessment methods within such learning contexts may undermine their potential to support an expanded understanding of student development. As Savin-Baden (2008) pointed out, once the digital space has been located, we need to "confront the possibility of new types of visuality, literacy, pedagogy, representations of knowledge, communication and embodiment" (p. 81).

In this chapter, we apply the following definitions to distinguish digital tools, learning space, and pedagogical context:

Tools = a mediating digital resource within a learning space (e.g., online chat, forum, videos, digital flash cards) (see Chapter 3)

Space = a physical, material, or online space (e.g., a classroom, workbook, ePortfolio)

Context = an all-encompassing reference to the pedagogical circumstance, setting, or situation, including all features therein (e.g., teacher, learner, facilitator, affordances)

To comprehend the types of interactive activities observed in an online context, we drew on research (Hartwick & Savaskan Nowlan, 2018; van Lier, 2000) that views learning as social and assumes social interaction is necessary for language to develop (cf. Vygotsky, 1934/2012a). In this regard, we moved away from assessment of student language development based solely on the traditional emphasis on the mastery of language features (e.g., vocabulary, grammar) to include evidence of effective interaction and the development of so-called 21st Century Skills (Dede, 2010), such as collaboration, problem solving, and negotiation. In this chapter, we discuss how evidence of interaction as learning was assessed in technologically mediated EAP classroom contexts as outcomes of three online learning spaces, namely:

1 3-dimensional virtual learning environments (3DVLEs), defined as internet-hosted spaces wherein users can interact synchronously through voice, movement, or text; see, for example, ViRbela (www.virbela.com/why-virbela) and Second Life (https://secondlife.com);

2 ePortfolios ("electronically hosted space[s] used in education to showcase students' work and learning progress through digitally enhanced or created artifacts" (Hartwick, 2018, p. xv); see, for example, open-source software Mahara (https://mahara.org); and
3 open-source content creators (HTML applications used to create, build, and share interactive content that can easily be viewed on a web-browser or embedded into an LMS); see, for example, the HTML5 package, known as H5P (https://h5p.org).

Viewing learning spaces through lenses afforded by theory and empirical research

Many models and frameworks have specified what makes learning, teaching, and assessment effective. For example, the *How People Learn* framework (Bransford, Brown, & Cocking, 2000) identified four lenses in learning environment design: (1) learner-centred, (2) knowledge-centred, (3) assessment-centred, and (4) community-centred, to which Hartwick (2018) proposed a fifth lens, space-centred, to acknowledge the unique affordances of each online space. Similarly, in the field of computer-mediated communication (CMC), Garrison, Anderson, and Archer (2000) defined the *Community of Inquiry* (CoI) framework, which included three components as interconnected experiences: teaching presence, social presence, and cognitive presence. Although the CoI framework was originally designed for research purposes in computer-mediated contexts, Garrison et al. (2000) argued that the interconnectedness and interaction of these three *presences* were integral to learning in computer-mediated spaces (cf. Bransford et al., 2000).

While these frameworks mapped the various intersecting lenses, presences, or components onto the construct of *learning*, van Lier (2000), drawing on Bronfenbrenner and Ceci's (1994) model of learning development, argued for the conceptualization of learning as a socially constructed *proximal process* (see Bronfenbrenner's unit of analysis as person + process + context + time). Similar to Lave (1996), and consistent with Turner and Purpura's LOA framework (2016), van Lier (2000) and Bronfenbrenner and Ceci (1994) viewed learning and development as relational and dynamic, occurring within the interactions and activity of those acting. As Lave (1996) noted, "if context is viewed as a social world constituted in relation with persons acting, both context and activity seem inescapably flexible and changing" (p. 5). Learning is therefore found in relations between actors and resources (i.e., digital tools), and is "characterized [by] changing participation and understanding in practice" (p. 5). Like van Lier (2000), Turner and Purpura's framework values the *process* of learning in assessment, as opposed to simply measuring a result. These frameworks and models help us to make sense of online spaces as potentially effective, but different, learning contexts and to *reconsider* assessment practices within their ecological settings. Such ecological considerations (Bronfenbrenner & Ceci, 1994; Chaiklin & Lave, 1996; van Lier, 2000) assume that we need to understand "the whole to understand its parts" (Fuhrer, 1996, p. 189).

Many different disciplinary fields and sub-fields have defined what constitutes learning (cf. Chaiklin & Lave, 1996, for an overview of disciplinary distinctions). While we have consulted theories from second language acquisition (SLA), Computer Assisted Language Learning (CALL), and education, our perspective has been informed by our understanding of affordances through a socio-theoretical lens. A logical place to begin with to inform research related to language learning in technologically mediated spaces might have been SLA; however, SLA research has been dominated by individualist, cognitive perspectives (e.g., Gass & Selinker, 2008), which tend to define language development in terms of quantifiable, often discrete, linguistic changes in, for example, vocabulary, syntax, length of utterance. When the learning context is considered, it is controlled as a variable (e.g., in experimental or quasi-experimental designs). Further, participants tend to be grouped according to perceived homogeneous backgrounds (e.g., first-language speakers of Spanish or Chinese; primary or secondary students). Research tends to be focused on language acquisition at a single moment in time (or limited periods of time), and may be carried out in laboratories under quasi-experimental conditions; non-linguistic mediating factors are not considered. Such research is necessarily reductive. A participant's *lived, situated experience over time* (which is essential to and the core of development) is not generally taken into consideration.

While important, many cognitive theories tend to locate language as a stable property of an individual and do not generally consider context. Only recently have considerations of social perspectives in language teaching and learning begun to influence SLA perspectives (e.g., Leung & Valdés, 2019; May, 2014; Ortega, 2013). While we recognize the contribution of cognitive perspectives in research related to technologically mediated spaces, for the purposes of this chapter we reconsider learning from the alternative perspective afforded by social theories.

As van Lier (2000) argued in his critique of the traditional SLA view of language learning, "we learn language the same way an animal 'learns' the forest or a plant 'learns' the soil" (p. 259), and in technologically mediated learning contexts we need "to look at the active learner in her environment and study interaction in its totality in order to show the emergence of learning" (van Lier, 2000, cited in Ellis, 2008, p. 272). For this reason, there was little to draw on from traditional approaches to SLA research, which were informed by such cognitive 'in the head' theories. However, SLA theorists have begun to contextualize their findings more richly. For example, Swain's (2000) and Swain and Lapkin's (2013) work shifted towards a more sociocultural perspective to include the role of the interlocutor. Brooks (2009) and Brooks and Swain (2014) expanded the theoretical framework informing research on oral proficiency interviews and articulated in explicit terms the role of the co-construction of discourse in group-based oral interviews, as well as the tester/interlocutor in interactions arising within one-on-one interview-based assessments. Further, in recent years Swain et al. (2010) have published a textbook which draws explicitly on Vygotskian sociocultural theory and illustrates its key tenets and potential to inform teaching, learning, and assessment through short illustrative narratives of classroom experience.

Further, May (2014) and Ortega (2013) capture the relevance of transdisciplinarity in SLA in order to develop a reciprocal and critical awareness of the breadth of disciplines that might contribute to a shared knowledge of SLA. The 2019 *state-of-the-art* centennial review of Leung and Valdés (2019), mentioned in Part I of this book, furthers this point and reports on current trends in the field of SLA. Leung and Valdés note that "monolingualist perspectives have been problematized ... and the expansion and increasing epistemological diversity in the field of SLA has led to what some ... have referred to as the 'multilingual turn'" (p. 348). Leung and Valdés compare this trend to the dramatic shift in the 1980s from grammar-based teaching to meaningful communication (the so-called *communicative turn*). This new trend reflects growing dissatisfaction with narrow conceptualizations of language, recognition of the multilingual diversity of language learners, and trends toward translanguaging and transdisciplinary frameworks in language teaching (see Chapter 3).

As a comparatively new field, CALL has typically drawn on theories from multiple domains. Hubbard and Levy's (2016) article categorized CALL theories as borrowed, adapted, or constructed (as examples) and suggested that these "evolve as a result of being applied in an environment they were not originally conceived for" (p. 26). In an effort to make visible a theoretical landscape, Chapelle (2009) looked for relationships between SLA and CALL and pointed to the need to consider multiple theoretical perspectives in the examination of these online, digitally mediated spaces. Currently, CALL draws on social and integrative theoretical perspectives to account for technology that affords synchronous learning and sharing. Hartwick (2018) examined recurring theoretical elements from a *buffet of theories* (Hubbard & Levy, 2016) to help inform, frame, and interpret research and practice in online or technologically mediated spaces. Lantolf and Thorne (2007), following Vygotsky (see Chapter 3), suggested that language and objects mediate behaviour and are used "to mediate their connection to the world, to each other, and to themselves" (p. 205). This suggestion fits nicely with our own thoughts about how people learn in online contexts.

Social theories of learning: a focus on affordances

In this chapter we have applied social theories to our consideration of language learning in relation to an online learning space. From social perspectives, learning occurs as part of social processes that develop, are shared in interactions with others, and are often constructed through mediating artifacts (e.g., semiotic resources, texts, tasks) or affordances (Lantolf, 2000; van Lier, 2000). These social processes include notions of self-directed and self-regulated learning (Turner & Purpura, 2016), constructed learning (Brown, Collins, & Duguid, 1989), negotiated understanding (Lave & Wenger, 1991), Communities of Inquiry (Garrison et al., 2000), and experiential learning (Kolb, 1984). Importantly, social learning theories necessarily help practitioners *reconsider* practice, including assessment, in online and digitally enhanced learning contexts. Social practices are not restricted to human-to-human social interactions but include interactions that are mediated by the affordances of the technology, the space, the user, and/or the language – it is not purely a linguistic interaction.

As Lave (1996) pointed out, "doing and knowing are inventive ... They are open ended processes of improvisation with the social, material and experiential resources at hand" (p. 13). The concept of human and tool-mediated (e.g., language, pen, computer mouse, avatar – or a personalized representation of self) action and interaction is long-standing, consistent with other sociocultural theories, and fundamental to understanding affordances within digitally enhanced learning contexts. For example, the work of Hutchins (1995a, 1995b) on *distributed cognition* (see also, Chapters 3, 5, and 8) illustrated ways in which cognition and action are distributed across humans and their tools, whether in steering a large naval vessel at sea or landing an airplane on a runway. As Hutchins (1995b) noted: "The successful completion of a flight is produced by a system that typically includes two or more pilots interacting with each other and with a suite of technological devices" (1995b, p. 265). Like Hutchins (1995a, 1995b) or Lave (1996), we see human activity (whether landing a plane or writing a report for an engineering project) as distributed – "across, social, material, and experiential resources at hand" (p. 13).

Consequently, our perspective is most profoundly influenced by affordance theory. James Gibson (1979/2015), an ecological psychologist, first defined an affordance as something in the environment that had a perceptual quality – good or bad – and that offered an *action possibility*. He claimed, "an affordance is not bestowed upon an object by a need of an observer and his act of perceiving it. The object offers what it does because it is what it is" (p. 130). Accordingly, the affordance exists whether it is used or not. Although the term is widespread in many disciplines, such as Human–Computer Interaction (HCI) studies and CALL, Hartwick (2018) pointed out, the concept has not been consistently defined. This has led to some ambiguity, misunderstanding, and confusion. A clearer understanding of how an affordance mediates learning in online and computer-based contexts will help researchers and practitioners (teachers and designers) improve the usability of an online learning space and the quality of the experience for the learner (Blin, 2016).

What are the affordances of online contexts for assessment?

For our purposes we have defined an affordance as "a unique combination of technological, social, educational, and linguistic" factors (Blin, 2016, p. 55) and as "a characteristic of an online space that facilitates or promotes learning" (Hartwick, 2018, p. 23). van Lier (2000) explains how an affordance is more than a linguistic unit of analysis as it includes the degree to which the learner participates or interacts. van Lier (2000) also suggests that "the notion of input" (please note that SLA has viewed input as the primary resource for language learning) "can be replaced by the ecological notion of affordance, which refers to the relationship between properties of the environment and the active learner" (p. 257). Much like theories of distributed cognition (see Chapter 3), we want to look beyond the "skin or skull of an individual" (Hollan, Hutchins, & Kirsh, 2000, p. 176) and observe "interactions between people and structure in their environments" (p. 177).

As mentioned earlier in this chapter, in 2016, Turner and Purpura introduced the *Framework of Learning-Oriented Assessment*, an assessment framework comprised of seven dimensions – all of which support learning in the context of the language classroom. The LOA framework is intended to represent the multifacetedness of assessment practices (beyond testing) to include spontaneous feedback, student interaction, and so on. As Turner and Purpura noted, "the contextual dimension is a critical dimension of LOA in that it sets parameters for how instruction, learning, and assessment will transpire within the social, cultural, and political context of learning" (2016, p. 262). The contextual dimension includes factors like sociocultural norms and teacher choices pertaining to content, assessment, and feedback.

As teaching practices shift online, the impact that these new contexts have on learning processes, outcomes, and assessment practices cannot be ignored, but then what should be measured and how? How will we interpret the scores and how do these changing contexts impact our interpretations? How do we know if a student has learned? Designing the online teaching context needs to consider why we are assessing, what we are assessing, and whether it is relevant, necessary, and purposeful. We need to understand what students already know that will help further their learning experiences. Traditional assessment practices are both formative and summative – while the former focuses on assessment for learning, the latter focuses more on assessment of learning at the end of a unit or course (see Fox, Abdulhamid, & Turner, 2022). The move to online and digital contexts affords new opportunities to prioritize the learner and learning through an examination of the learning process. It is an opportunity to reconsider dynamic learning processes and relevant benchmarks of success in terms of changing outcomes which recognize and shift our assessment practices to take the affordances of technological learning spaces into account, including the learners' prior experiences, observable interactions, and increased demonstration of skill, and an understanding of how to observe and measure these. It is an ideal time to reconsider features like task, timing of feedback, and assessment processes in classroom assessment (Turner & Purpura, 2016).

Online and digitally enhanced delivery provide rich opportunities for frequent and timely feedback, which targets and develops skills and has the potential to better align with formative assessment practices as well as with summative assessment goals, and to inform teaching in order to prioritize learning. Following Turner and Purpura's (2016) LOA approach, the focus remains on the individual learner, and online learning spaces are particularly helpful because these contexts may afford greater opportunities for feedback (whether formal or informal) and for the accumulation of evidence of learning and progress toward learning outcomes.

Transdisciplinarity: a requirement for teaching in online learning spaces

One of the immediate recognitions that accompanies a shift from traditional, physical classroom-based language teaching to online language teaching is, *I need help to do what I would like to do and make this work*. Help comes in the form of other stakeholders, with other disciplinary or professional expertise, experience, and worldviews, who are mutually engaged by and interested in the learning potential of such online learning contexts. In each of the examples below, transdisciplinary research (TR) agendas, informed by social theories in general, and affordance theory, were carried out in collaboration with multiple partners. Collaborating research partners shared the common goal of ensuring quality language learning for EAP students in online language learning contexts, but differed in ideas, skills, knowledge, and expertise. Each of the examples below illustrates TR in practice within three language learning spaces: 1) a 3D Virtual Learning Environment; 2) an ePortfolio; and, 3) an open-source content creator/tool embedded in an LMS. Each example describes the transdisciplinary partnerships that were involved and illustrates the importance of systematically identifying and maximizing the affordances of each space and situating a task/activity within the LOA framework. In each case we highlight the learning process to demonstrate how assessment prioritizes learning.

The three examples below illustrate how an online space may afford learners the opportunity to actively engage in learning. However, in our view the affordances of online spaces depend on the teacher's and/or learner's awareness of the unique affordances of each space. For example, as explained by Hartwick (2018), a learner who does not know they can embed multimedia (i.e., affordance of adaptability) in their ePortfolio as evidence of making creative connections (a learning outcome) is not afforded the same opportunity as a learner who has this knowledge.

Further, it is essential that the teacher be able to choreograph how much or how little an online space is used in relation to ongoing in-person classroom activity.

Example 1: 3DVLE

The 3DVLE described in this chapter is technically classified as a low-immersion virtual environment (LiVR), because it lacks the high degree of immersion experienced in more spatially realistic environments or high-immersion virtual environments (HiVR) afforded by head-mounted devices, such as an Oculus Rift headset (Kaplan-Rakowski & Gruber, 2019). In HiVRs, the user has the sensation of being physically immersed, whereas in a LiVR or 3DVLE the users' sense of immersion is experienced in real-time voice and movement, but by extension of their avatar as opposed to a physical sense of immersion. Blake (2008) and Chapelle (2000) suggested that 3DVLEs are engaging contexts that promote social interactions. In our example, users experienced learning synchronously through their avatars. Often, the avatar becomes an extension of self and can interact in real-time through text, movement, and voice. These interactions are facilitated by specific *learning outcomes* (i.e., what we want our students to know and be able to do, and/or value as the result of a course). Learning outcomes are identified first, followed by *assessment tasks* (Cheng & Fox, 2017), which in the case of online learning spaces are designed to make use of the affordances of the unique space. The assessment task is aligned with the learning outcome through *backward design* (Wiggins & McTighe, 2005).

Transdisciplinary partnerships

This 3DVLE space was built under the supervision of a professor in the department of Systems and Computer Engineering and in collaboration with his graduate students. The space shifted to a teaching and learning context as these relationships extended to a professor in the department of history and a teacher in EAP (one of the co-authors of this chapter). The intention was to pilot the 3DVLE for immersive learning experiences across multiple disciplines. These shared experiences morphed into further collaboration with language teachers of Russian, Spanish, and French. In continued collaboration and sharing of expertise with the department of Systems and Computer Engineering, a 3D immersive environment developer from outside the university, and language instructors from multiple language backgrounds, the space took shape after many iterations. Up until the closure of this particular 3DVLE in the summer of 2020, stakeholders included language teachers in training from a university in the USA, language learners and instructors, and researchers and graduate students from the department of Systems and Computer Engineering. These stakeholders each had a role in optimizing the teaching and learning context through effective space design and a clearer understanding of suitable task and assessment practices in relation to the affordances of the space. This shared collaborative engagement of stakeholders is in keeping with the *new praxis* called for by Poehner and Inbar-Lourie (2020a), who argue that teachers' perspectives and voices need to be affirmed as key stakeholders and equal partners in research projects; it is also in keeping with the broader *transdisciplinary praxis* which is the focus of this book.

Detailed description of the 3DVLE

The 3DVLE was originally designed to replicate a university campus which included classrooms, desks and chairs, and auditorium-style lecture theatres. These initial design features were simple attempts at reproducing a traditional brick and mortar university instead of taking advantage of the affordances these novel immersive spaces could provide due to the expansiveness of the space; a space not constricted by physical boundaries. After several iterations and piloting the space with learners across many terms, the transdisciplinary design team added a residential area with furnished houses in various states of tidiness and décor, a downtown core, and outside classroom area with breakout rooms (see Hartwick, 2018, for a complete description). Eventually and after several iterations, task design and assessment practices evolved to tap into the affordances of the space rather than simply trying to recreate traditional classroom-based practices.

For example, upon recognizing the differences in students' abilities to navigate comfortably in the space and in keeping with the LOA framework, a *Navigation Maze* was designed to orient students to the novel technical and spatial learning context (Hartwick & Savaskan Nowlan, 2018). According to Efklides (2006), students' confidence increases when they can repeatedly practice a task. If practice reduces the difficulty of the task, students are better able to evaluate whether or not their responses are correct. The Navigation Maze allowed students to practice moving their avatars through a series of progressively more challenging tasks that required them to interact with instructions and the various functions that would enable them to move with ease through the space. This prepared students for the tasks ahead and helped eliminate any barriers presented by the technology and new learning context (for a more complete description, see Hartwick, 2018, Chapter 5).

The design team was motivated to design tasks that made use of the affordances of space, and incorporated assessment that moved beyond traditional assessment practices. For example, they collected and examined the type and frequency of user interactions, and the location and movement in the space. Consequently, after eight years of practice and several design iterations, the 3DVLE evolved to include game-based options, teleporting features, collaborative surfaces, and outdoor spaces, to name a few of the new design features. These *reconsidered* practices created a new social context for learning and assessment.

Affordances

In this chapter we highlight two affordances of 3DVLEs as identified by Hartwick (2018) – *fidelity of space* and *immersion*. Hartwick described fidelity of space as the ability of a 3DVLE to replicate authentic physical places, like a museum or a city, whereas she described the affordance of immersion as the quality or sensation of *being there* as in a physical space. Fidelity of space and immersion afford such learning benefits as experiential and mediated learning, real-time social interaction, and lower user anxiety (Table 7.1).

Reconsidered teaching practice

The Navigation Maze described above helped support the transdisciplinarity of the learning context and created a level playing field so that all learners could engage in the instructional activities on equal footing. As an example, this instructional activity (cf. Hartwick & Savaskan Nowlan, 2018) was designed in an advanced level EAP as part of a thematic unit on the concept of sustainable development (the thematic content through which the students were developing academic language and skills). This task had students actively explore (i.e., by experiencing, interacting, and collaborating in the 3DVLE) three houses, inside and out, and make recommendations to a hypothetical family as to how their houses could be more environmentally sustainable. Due to the fidelity of space, students were able to explore the houses, something not otherwise possible in a traditional, brick and mortar classroom. This active and social exploration afforded an opportunity for students to observe

Table 7.1 Affordances and associated learning benefits of 3DVLEs

Affordances of 3DVLEs	*Learning benefits*
Fidelity of space/visually rich	• Experiential learning mediated by others or object • Real-time social interaction that leads to construction of knowledge and problem solving (as examples)
Immersion and sense of presence created through gestures and customizability	• Extensions of self • Social interaction/community • Lower anxiety • Leads to experiential, negotiated, and collaborative learning (as examples)

(Adapted from Hartwick, 2018, p. 27)

through movement and interaction, while collaborating with peers and co-constructing knowledge and understanding. "This active exploration of the space, not an option in a physical classroom space, was intended to promote collaboration, experiential learning, and learning-by-doing" (Hartwick & Savaskan Nowlan, 2018, p. 126).

Reconsidered assessment practice

Our "conception of teaching" highlighted assessment. Like Bass (2012), we assumed that language develops socially and within a context that promotes engagement and leads to integrative learning, language development, and language use. The learning environment design framework by Bransford, Brown, and Cocking (2000) included an assessment-centred perspective, which assumed that learning contexts should be flexible enough to provide opportunities for various types of assessment. These explanations helped us to reconsider assessment, but how could we assess what was going on as learners interacted fluidly and naturally in such a new learning space? It was no longer enough to measure language complexity and accuracy as evidence of language learning.

As a result of an exploratory study aimed at evaluating the pedagogical potential of 3DVLEs, Hartwick (2018) devised an observation instrument (Figure 7.1) aimed at recording observed user interactions while completing an assessment task. The observation instrument was designed

Recorded time	**Task/Activity**	**Location in Space**	**Other Features of space**				**Teacher practice**							**Learner's interactional behaviour**									
			Use of writing pad	Use of web renderer	Use of text function	Use of collaboration surfaces	Teacher discourse			Task grouping				Interaction with teacher			Interaction with peer			Interaction with space or tools (including movement and gestures)			Other
							Informal	Task-based or instructional	Housekeeping/ technical support	individual	pairs	½ group +	whole group	Very low (0–2 instances)	Low (3–4 instances)	High (5+ instances)	Very low (0–2 instances)	Low (3–4 instances)	High (5+ instances)	Very low (0–2 instances)	Low (3–4 instances)	High (5+ instances)	

Figure 7.1 Observation matrix for 3DVLEs.

to record the frequency and type of interactions in these new contexts and helped to account for *what is going on* with each learner at a particular point in time and where.

The matrix in Figure 7.1 can be used by teachers unfamiliar with assessment practice in 3DVLEs as a sampling instrument. It can be used to document individual behaviours over short periods of time and in specific locations in the 3DVLE, for example, the frequency of interactions with peers and the teacher, and the frequency of interactions with the various features of the space, such as the various interactive surfaces (shared access to web screen) and text chat function. An observation matrix such as this can help teachers understand:

- if the frequency of interaction supports a student's learning;
- how a student engages with different features of space (e.g., with non-player avatars, signs, teleporting stations);
- how the student's interactions with specific features support the completion of tasks; and
- whether the student's interactions also increased understanding and confidence in using language.

Results derived from recorded segments can allow teachers to review and reflect on learning-in-action after the fact. Observing, recording, and reflecting on *learning-in-process* is a rich source of information for both teaching and assessment in support of learning. The collection of information from an observation matrix supports teachers' assessment decisions and actions and is an example of formative/evidence-driven teaching or LOA in practice (Turner & Purpura, 2016). Working together with researchers as equal partners, such data could support research clarifying how and why 3DVLEs facilitate language learning by generating evidence of learning as a social process and practice.

Another advantage of this learning space is the provision of timely and supportive feedback throughout the learning process in 3DVLEs. Savaskan Nowlan, Hartwick, and Arya (2018) made use of 3DVLE platform metrics to demonstrate how often and in which instances learners demonstrated *learning and thinking skills*, like complex problem solving (Dede, 2010). These metrics captured, for example, time spent in one area or time spent interacting with one feature, and were compared with teacher-recorded observations on the matrix (see Figure 7.1). The 3DVLE afforded increased opportunities for interaction, experiential learning, and learning by doing. Savaskan Nowlan et al. (2018) reported on the relationship between the metrics and the observation matrix, and how they mapped back onto the learning benefits. The observation matrix in combination with quantitative analytics, which measured the number of attempts and time on task, helped to account for and understand learning in these 3DVLE learning spaces and had benefits both internal to the classroom context and beyond.

Example 2: ePortfolio

Fox (2017) described the portfolio as a site for the collection of evidence of "learning and development over time" (p. 135). When ePortfolio practice "is done well", these socially integrated learning spaces afford opportunities for rich inquiry, reflection, and integration of learning (Hartwick, McCarroll, & Davidson, 2018). The literature touts ePortfolios as a high-impact practice (HIP) (Eynon & Gambino, 2017; Kuh, 2008) and as an integrative social pedagogy (Eynon & Gambino, 2017; Lewis, 2017). Further, benefits of ePortfolio practice have been described in terms of the opportunity for alternative assessment practices (Abrami & Barrett, 2005; Fox, 2017; Penny Light, Ittelson, & Chen, 2012), which stimulate deeper learning (see affordances of ePortfolios outlined below). Basically, ePortfolios not only provide a learning space for students to demonstrate mastery of learning outcomes, evidenced by submission of their work; they are, more importantly, a space that prompts ongoing review, reflection on learning, and self-awareness of language development over time.

Transdisciplinary partnerships

The ePortfolio learning space described here evolved through a shared interest in creating an online platform where students could demonstrate learning by providing evidence of learning through digital artifacts, such as text or audio entries, embedded links, and forms of multimedia. What began over six years ago in response to a call from the institution's Educational Development Centre (EDC) for teachers to pilot the ePortfolio in their courses culminated in a diverse partnership in which stakeholders shared a common goal for creating a rich pedagogical resource for teaching and learning. Rather than just a location for 'demonstrating learning', its potential to support ongoing reflection, self-awareness, goal setting, and learning became a focus for stakeholders.

Stakeholders included educational technology and instructional design experts, faculty from multiple departments, external community partners from the Scholarship of Teaching and Learning community, and the institution as a whole. One focus of the partnerships was the complexity of assessment. After the first year of piloting the ePortfolio, a Faculty Learning community was formed. This group set out to design a set of open educational rubrics based on five common categories (content, organization, professionalism, reflective thinking, and creative thinking). Faculty members who chose to use an ePortfolio tailored the rubric and categories to align with assignments and learning outcomes in their courses. Stakeholders shared a collective understanding of the value of the ePortfolio as an effective pedagogical resource. Through collaboration, research, and professional dissemination of findings, these partnerships, characterized by shared transdisciplinary expertise, have resulted in increased recognition of the value of the ePortfolio as a rich resource and a context for teaching and learning beyond the confines of a single course experience.

Detailed description of the ePortfolio learning space

The ePortfolio described herein is an online platform powered by Mahara (https://mahara.org), an open-source software discussed above, which resembles a webpage with multiple tabs and flexible layouts that allow a student to demonstrate their learning progress in a visually creative way. ePortfolios are intended to promote student-centred learning and provide students a personal online learning platform to "collect, select and reflect" (Clark & Eynon, 2009, p. 18) on their learning as they show evidence of achieving specific learning outcomes. In this learning context, students can use any combination of text, audio, and video files, and choose to embed an assortment of multimedia and open-source software like *Timeline* (https://timeline.knightlab.com/) and *Creatley* (https://creately.com/). These options help to personalize the learning experience and help students to integrate learning by making visible connections between course content, experiences, and learning outcomes. Meyer and Land (2006) cite a personal communication with P. Davies at the University of Staffordshire in 2002, who described the integrative learning process as first acquiring *bits of knowledge* in order to integrate the learning experience (p. 10). The bits of knowledge are readily available to the learner for integrating because of the ePortfolio affordances of *persistency* (i.e., 24/7 availability), *visibility* (e.g., multi-layered; multi-modal; multiple tabs, embedded clickable links, other embedded features), and *adaptability* (i.e., user flexibility in terms of manipulating content) (Hartwick, 2018) (Table 7.2). Students amass 'bits' over time and can later integrate them when reflecting about their own learning. Carefully designed reflective prompts will facilitate this integration of bits.

Table 7.2 Affordances and associated learning benefits of ePortfolios

Affordances of ePortfolios	*Learning benefits*
Persistency (persistent point of reference)	• Selection, collection, reflection • Self-assessment • Accessible feedback • Visible connections
Visibility (multi-layeredness)	• Investment of time and effort • Integrative learning • Frequent feedback and timely feedback
Adaptability (flexibility)	• Range of digital tools/media • Construct knowledge and create visual representations of learning • Demonstrate critical thinking and creativity

(Reprinted in part from Hartwick, 2018, p. 27)

Affordances

Much like the 3DVLE described above, an effective ePortfolio learning space includes systematic assessment task and activity design, which attend to the unique affordances of the space and allow for the assessment of student work over time, both informally and formally, in support of learning (cf. Turner & Purpura, 2016). While not normally referenced as affordances in the ePortfolio literature, some of the benefits of ePortfolios as social learning spaces include reflection, timely feedback, and integrated learning experiences, which we suggest are due to the affordances of the technology and the online space. In this chapter, we highlight *persistency*, *visibility*, and *adaptability*, which afford the learner a space to self-assess, reflect, and make visible connections, among other things. Hartwick (2018) posited that the affordance of persistency – the fact that the space is available 24/7 and is shareable – is one affordance that contributes to the social nature of the platform. It allows students to integrate and construct knowledge by making connections to other experiences visible (i.e., persistency), thereby providing an opportunity for frequent and timely feedback (i.e., visibility), which speaks to the benefits of formative assessment. Further, Hartwick, McCarroll, and Davidson (2018) explained how the highly visible and flexible nature (i.e., adaptability) of the ePortfolio can lead to students' investment of time and effort, allow for frequent and timely feedback, and prompt critical reflection using the tools and media at hand. Overall, the affordances of an ePortfolio help students to see and reflect on their learning over time – a much different perspective than is afforded by assessment as it has played out in traditional university courses. As a colleague once lamented after a week spent writing thoughtful commentary on final papers in a course, "Only ten of my students actually picked up their final papers – the rest are sitting in my office. It is sad to think that once the grade was out, the learning was no longer of interest". The ePortfolio does not let such thoughtful feedback go to waste. Its persistency, visibility, and adaptability support learning, self-reflection and self-awareness. It can also promote increased feelings of confidence and satisfaction with learning (Efklides, 2006) long after the completion of a course.

Reconsidered teaching practice

Eynon, Gambino, and Török's (2014) *Catalyst for Learning* framework includes five interconnected sectors: professional development, technology, scalability, outcomes assessment, and pedagogy. The pedagogy sector draws on a variety of socially informed perspectives of learning that stress how academic success is the result of meaningful reflection. The power of reflection in their framework is based largely on Dewey's (1896) understanding of reflection for learning, which he described as "a patchwork of disjointed parts" (p. 358).

Dewey argued that reflection is not solitary, but rather enriched through conversation and interaction with others. Further, reflection is not only a cognitive process, but involves attitudes that include others and self. Reflection is not willy-nilly, but rather it is systematic and descriptive and, in the context of teaching and learning languages, it draws out the learners' ability to integrate and connect lived experiences.

Generally, ePortfolio pedagogy sees learning as socially constructed and draws on many learning perspectives, such as constructivism (see Chapter 3), which is informed by social perspectives, and self-regulation, which is informed by cognitive perspectives. The power of reflection may transform student learning by making visible previously difficult and unrecognized connections (i.e., between 'bits' as discussed above), and lead to understanding of a subject or help students acquire confidence and skills. Such reflection allows a learner to come to terms with *threshold concepts*, which Meyer and Land (2006) (see Chapter 6) considered were "akin to a portal, opening up a new and previously inaccessible way of thinking about something" (p. 3) and evidenced in the transformational shifts in learning that occur over time, often arising from inquiry, reflection, and integration (Eynon, Gambino, & Török, 2014). Threshold concept theory seems highly applicable in relation to ePortfolio practice as the touted benefits of reflection include deep and integrative learning.

Hartwick et al. (2021) continue to investigate the use of ePortfolios in EAP to see how and if ePortfolios promote inquiry, reflection, and integration (IRI) – all socially constructed outcomes. As part of a larger project in which students used their ePortfolios to respond to a series of activities/tasks over the duration of a course, students were assigned three reflective prompts intermittently throughout the term. The prompts asked students to describe, explain, reflect, and provide evidence of learning in writing. It is expected that student responses will show evidence that ePortfolio pedagogy, when *done well*, creates opportunities for IRI.

Reconsidered assessment practice

Lewis (2017) argued that "identifying the learning purpose of an ePortfolio in the curriculum is fundamental to the design of authentic learning activities" (p. 73). We concur. We would add, however, that the designer must recognize the affordances, as identified above, and shift assessment practices accordingly. The question is, how do we shift our assessment practices to capture the rich learning benefits of this space?

Hartwick et al.'s (2021) study sought, among other things, to test a rating scale designed to assess evidence of *inquiry*, *reflection*, and *integration* (IRI), all socially constructed outcomes, in the students' reflective responses. This is an assessment practice *reconsidered* as the researchers and teachers moved away from assessing purely language constructed outcomes at a moment of time, like vocabulary, and looked for evidence of higher-order thinking like reflection and integration over time. For example, a student demonstrating evidence of successful reflection should be able to draw connections between personal experiences and/or apply experience to question course concepts. In developing descriptors for the Reflection category of the rating scale, the team drew from the open education resources described above that were created by an ePortfolio Faculty Learning community. Findings from this study could help teachers to develop and use reflective prompts that are designed with the affordances of the space in mind. The complexity of shifting assessment practices according to the context is articulated nicely by Lewis (2017): "The assumption that the ePortfolio is one discrete thing belies the complexity and potential of the technology to be used for both its tool and pedagogic purposes" (p. 73). On the other hand, there are those that have raised concerns that student privacy must be protected as such technologies could give rise to invasive practices (see Fox et al., 2022 for a discussion).

Example 3: open-source content creator (H5P)

The H5P examples described in the present chapter were designed as diagnostic workshops Hartwick and McCarroll (2019) and embedded in the course's LMS, which is the online platform that houses course content and digital tools (e.g., H5P). The beauty of H5P is that content can be easily shared and modified depending on the needs of the users. Further, content is highly interactive because of the ease with which different *content types* such as interactive video, audio recordings, quizzes, and flashcards can be incorporated in a seamless and interactive interface (cf. https://h5p.org/). For our purposes, we used the H5P content type called *Course Presentation*, as it allowed us to incorporate many of the other available content types, including interactive videos. While any research specific to H5P is sparse, the research on learning with interactive video (which shares similar qualities) shows that, when designed properly, interactive videos create meaningful learning opportunities and enhance engagement with course material (Chen, 2012). Hartwick and McCarroll surmised that, because of the multimodality and interactivity, H5Ps provided a motivating experience and active learning opportunity.

Transdisciplinary partnerships

H5P was first introduced to our institution about three years ago as a tool to promote interaction in online or blended learning contexts. Faculty from across the university were invited to learn, build, and pilot the tool in their courses. We drew expertise from language teachers, educational technologists, language assessment experts, platform developers, and CALL specialists – to name only a few. We shared a common goal, which was to support individual learners through interactive and rich learning experiences. As a community of stakeholders, we embarked on creating

H5P content unique to our own courses. In most cases, the content was designed to disseminate content or skills and included multiple opportunities for the learner to check their comprehension in a timely and risk-free manner. Often, faculty used the H5Ps to include an informal assessment mechanism so that learners could gauge their understanding at different time points throughout the term.

Detailed description of the H5P tool

Fox (2009) studied the impact of a decision to place students in different levels of an EAP program on the basis of external language proficiency test results (e.g., from TOEFL, IELTS), as opposed to a local, standardized language proficiency test (cf. O'Sullivan, 2016; Su et al., 2019) which had been aligned with course levels in the EAP program. This top-down policy decision created the need for systematic and innovative curricular change at the program level, because groups by level were no longer coherent. One of the recommendations from this study was to implement a post-admission diagnostic assessment and to design targeted, individual skill-based instruction.

The results prompted a second study (Fox & Hartwick, 2011), which demonstrated the importance of addressing sub-component skills, such as reading for the gist, by drilling down individual results on carefully designed diagnostic assessments. This study had the good fortune of employing four MA-level Teaching Assistants (TAs) to work in collaboration with the teacher in providing targeted skill-based instruction to small groups of EAP language learners who shared a common need for increased instruction in a sub-skill area. This approach was not sustainable beyond the study owing to the number of highly skilled TAs required at each level and for each group. However, in an effort to target individual needs, Hartwick and McCarroll (2019) have developed a series of level-appropriate, skill-based H5P workshops, for example, on paragraphing and reading academic texts. Following an early-term diagnostic, students are assigned specific targeted H5P workshops depending on their individual needs. An intensive, individualized, and targeted approach is sustainable thanks to the H5P learning space.

Affordances

Currently, there is little written specifically about H5P as a language learning tool, and so we refer to literature on interactive videos and commercial websites on H5P (Anderson, 2016; H5P, n.d.). Much like the ePortfolio literature, H5P does not explicitly use the term *affordance*; however, references to the many learning benefits of H5P and interactive video tutorials as teaching aids have been identified (Anderson, 2016). Hartwick and McCarroll (2019) reported on observed learning benefits afforded by the tool, such as opportunity for frequent and timely

Table 7.3 Affordances and associated learning benefits of H5P

Affordances of H5P	*Learning benefits*
Persistency (persistent point of reference)	• Self-regulated learning • Self-assessment • Frequent and timely feedback • Flipped learning
Adaptability (flexibility)	• Range of digital tools/media to embed • Overcoming the learning threshold

feedback and assessment (i.e., persistency, 24/7 availability), and the range of digital tools and media that can be embedded into the design of each H5P workshop (i.e., adaptability, flexibility). Following Hartwick's (2018) definition of an affordance and Evans, Pearce, Vitak, and Treem's (2017) three-step validation of an affordance, we mapped out reported and observed benefits to some of the earlier noted affordances of the ePortfolio, *persistency* (24/7) and *adaptability* (flexibility) (Table 7.3).

Owing to the affordance of *persistency*, the H5P interactive tool allowed students to navigate at their own pace and in a low-risk context. While engaging in the workshop, students get immediate feedback to embedded quiz questions, which helps them to self-assess, review material, and repeat the activity. Further, much like an interactive video used in online courses, the *adaptability* of H5P *Course Presentation* content type allows designers to embed multiple tools (i.e., quiz questions, videos, text, clickable links), thereby creating a multi-sensory and interactive workshop. The adaptability of H5P and the skill-based workshops explained below addressed the need to support a range of sub-skills and provided immediate feedback to the student in the form of embedded short-answer questions, mix and match, and other question types that allowed students immediate uptake as they could review material and retry the questions. Each H5P workshop culminated in an automatic grading and a systematic summary report on the final slide (cf., Fig. 7.2).

Reconsidered teaching practice

Recognizing the importance of diagnostic assessment in supporting the individual EAP student, Hartwick and McCarroll (2019) developed a series of online diagnostic assessments designed to measure reading, listening, vocabulary and grammar, writing, and citing/referencing at the intermediate and advanced levels of EAP. Diagnostic test items were designed specifically to drill down to sub-skills, such as reading for the gist and word form accuracy. Based on the diagnostic results, individual learner profiles were created to identify the learners' strengths and weaknesses across the five component sub-skill areas that were most in need of support. To compensate for the lack of TA classroom support

ADVANCED VOCABULARY	
Slide	Score/Total
Slide 5: Multiple tasks	3/7
Slide 7: Multiple tasks	4/7
Total score	7/15

Figure 7.2 H5P summary report example.
Screenshot by the authors

available (as in the study by Fox and Hartwick, 2011), Hartwick and McCarroll sought to maximize individualized student language support by creating a series of H5P skills-targeted, online workshops that students could complete at their own pace. These workshops were intentionally designed to target certain skills in a blended/flipped classroom delivery model, which means the workshops were available online for the students to work on at their own pace and at any time. The affordance of adaptability allowed for numerous integrations of content types within each H5P, making them highly meaningful and interactive.

Reconsidered assessment practice

Each H5P workshop provided an example of LOA in that they were designed by the teachers to address individual student needs and provided timely feedback through frequent and short quizzes that helped students check their understanding and review material at their own pace (Turner & Purpura, 2016). In the H5P example, formal assessment was merely complete or incomplete – six targeted workshops for a possible three points. The strength of assessment was based on the overall language learning context, wherein the workshops were designed to provide immediate feedback and a safe place for practicing skills. More importantly, these workshops were designed to help the *individual* student make visible connections about their own learning through reflections on their performance. In this case, three reflection prompts were designed, informed by the IRI framework (above), as students were asked to comment on how they had demonstrated critical integration and reflection in responding to the assessment tasks. Asking students to focus on their own individual skill development with H5P workshops, we anticipated that their ability to integrate experiences and reflect on their changed understanding would become evident. This moved away from measuring outcomes based on the accuracy and use of discrete language features and focused more on the learning processes, 21st Century learning and skills, and the ecological context within which learning took place.

Online learning spaces in changing teaching and learning contexts: a pandemic postscript

Taken together, the three examples of online learning spaces described above illustrated the effectiveness of technologically mediated approaches in online and blended teaching contexts, which were informed by social theories (e.g., affordance theory) and involved many transdisciplinary partnerships. However, these examples were drawn from a pre-pandemic, primarily face-to-face EAP teaching and learning context, in which online activities were an extension of the person-to-person classroom experience, with a teacher and her class in interaction within a physical classroom for a specified amount of time each week. As such, the teacher had flexibility in incorporating the technological resources she chose in relation to the needs of her students, to support and enhance their learning experiences. However, within the conditions imposed by the sudden shift to fully online classes as a result of the pandemic of 2020, teachers lost this flexibility.

> Below is Hartwick's reflection on how the sudden shift to fully online classes influenced her practice and understanding of online learning contexts. As a teacher she addressed the question: "How do I redesign and best accommodate my learners and support learning in a fully online learning course during a pandemic?" As a narrator, she reflects on how she responded to that question.

A teacher's reflection: perils and possibilities of online teaching and learning contexts in a pandemic world (narrated by Peggy Hartwick)

Hartwick's reflection on "How do I redesign and best accommodate my learners and support learning in a fully online learning course during a pandemic?"

The COVID-19 pandemic sent North American campuses into a frenzy and pushed forward the delivery of education online at an alarming pace. Because this push was sudden and unexpected, the need to *rethink* teaching and learning was urgent. Decisions had to be made quickly. In the moment, there was neither time to consider and reflect on the pedagogy that supported practice, nor was there time to systematically select and use digital technologies, within newly created online learning contexts, for teaching and learning, or assessing students. Prior to the pandemic, there was a *full* pedagogy to support such decisions – one that was informed by ongoing educational training, classroom experiences, and by empirical research on teaching and learning practices. There was also an extensive literature on classroom-based assessment (CBA) (e.g., Fox et al., 2022).

Teaching contexts shifted to online learning, dramatically and unexpectedly, in March 2020 – in the middle of preparing this chapter for inclusion in this book. Pandemic teaching contexts were anything but 'normal'. Many, indeed most, were unprepared, inexperienced, and unpracticed at the design and delivery of solely online language teaching and learning. Yet, what were our options? As a practiced researcher and experienced teacher in online and blended learning contexts, in this section I reflect on my experiences shifting from a face-to-face classroom – defined in space and time – to a fully online, partly synchronous and partly asynchronous context, which was undefined, mutable, emergent, and dynamic. It was not easy, nor ideal, as I missed my students' in-person presence most. In a face-to-face classroom, communities of learners emerge through interactive experiences; interactions are cued by body language and facial expressions and, classroom dynamics and personalities emerge organically. How do you build this in a fully online context wherein students are joining remotely from different time zones (e.g., China, Canada, Lebanon), with varying abilities and access to technologies, and within unique sociocultural and sociopolitical circumstances?

The move online was anything but seamless. While I considered myself experienced, from an online design, teaching, and research perspective, I found the challenges surprising and overwhelming. Despite efforts at implementing best practices, such as consistency and simplicity in delivery, what was most unexpected were issues of mental health, time spent on tasks, time spent designing the space, time spent on learning, and evolving assessment practices. Assessment practices that worked in the past no longer worked. My new mantra became, "Is it necessary? Is it worth it?"

In this reflection, I wanted to take stock of all the changes that were an outcome of the sudden move to a fully online context. One thing that I was not prepared for was the significantly high number of students and faculty struggling with mental health issues, such as loneliness, despair, fear, and isolation. These are barriers to learning, and I quickly recognized the importance of always taking these into account in my online classroom. While mental health issues existed in a pre-pandemic world, the pandemic itself accentuated these, and they became harder to address in an online classroom. This recognition profoundly reoriented my assessment expectations and practices, leading to a reduction in workload over time. For example, I completely dropped the ePortfolio research project in the second term despite the benefits reported above, because it was too much for my students to manage. The ePortfolio research project/assessment plan consisted of many small activity/assessment steps which elicited important ongoing formative feedback, but this depended on dedicated class time, which was no longer an option. In a fully online classroom, this practice was seen as "one more thing" students had to navigate technologically and so the merits of timely and consistent feedback were lost. The affordances of the ePortfolio as a dynamic, emergent interactive resource in a face-to-face classroom became a burden in the fully online context wherein more time was spent on troubleshooting than learning. Ask yourself first, "Is it necessary? Is it worth it?"

Time became a constant struggle. As teachers, we were now designing more than a lesson or course; we were designing an effective online learning context. This entailed trying to maximize the effectiveness of a LMS, such as Moodle, by selecting and integrating the most appropriate digital tools to best engage students, like chat forums. Our role shifted from being language teaching experts to novices in educational technology. This sudden shift necessitated exorbitant demands on time:

- creating a live trial of novel activities;
- designing visibly appealing digital spaces;
- selecting appropriate digital tools for promoting interaction;
- writing or recording clear, concise, and easily enacted tasks and instructions for online performance;
- accommodating individual and class needs by publishing and overriding pre-announced due dates and assignment details; and
- communicating such changes without causing a frenzy of email clarification requests.

It was not just the extra time spent on design, but the delivery took longer; everything seemed to take longer in a fully synchronous online context. For example, what may have taken half an hour in a face-to-face classroom now took as much as twice as long online because of unexpected technical issues and the constant need for clarification and feedback. This shift occurred suddenly, in what essentially became trial (and error) courses that were implemented without benefit of time, reflection, and evaluation of assessment practices which might best support learning in a fully online learning context.

Looking back now and from the vantage point of a year's experience, I recognize not only the perils but also the possibilities that have emerged and continue to emerge as I adjust my teaching practices and expectations in this evolving context. Nowhere has this been more evident than in my assessment practices. I am still learning, and below I list a few examples of how my practices changed in relation to the possibilities of online teaching contexts. For example, students:

- while mostly reticent about turning their cameras on, responded immediately to polls and chats (these became opportunities to check in);
- participated actively in breakout rooms (often complaining that there was not enough time);
- collaborated via shared note tools (such as Google Docs);

- demonstrated compassion and patience towards each other; and
- supported each other in navigating the task instructions and the tools.

Unexpectedly, the shared notes tool led to informal and spontaneous assessment and just-in-time learning opportunities that would not have emerged in the face-to-face classroom. In the online context, students generated responses in a dynamic collaborative writing surface that was visible to all and to which I could provide immediate spoken feedback, whereas in a face-to-face context students would have needed to participate individually with pen and paper, and it certainly would not have been possible for me to circulate and provide feedback to all. In another course, students shared in the responsibility of learning by negotiating assessment practice for a major project. In this instance, students (in breakout rooms) shared their understanding of an assignment and were able to then articulate the gaps clearly in their understanding of the project. As a result, students were engaged in the outcome of their learning and could direct the trajectory of their individual projects.

This pandemic teaching context has created an opportunity that may not otherwise have been possible – class sizes were smaller, and breakout rooms proved to be empowering, as the power relationship between the teacher and student was removed. Context had shifted, and so too did assessment practice in order to be flexible and fair.

Afterthoughts: what other social theories might have offered

The transdisciplinary initiatives described in this chapter included a diverse range of stakeholders, and drew on their richly varying insights, expertise, and experiences. While we shared a mutual interest in optimizing online learning contexts, the scope became larger along with the potential for innovation, because of the broader range of stakeholders. In keeping with the LOA framework, we demonstrated how three unique online learning spaces afforded opportunities for flexible and formative assessment. Our conceptualization of online teaching, learning, and assessment practices was shaped by social learning theories and emphasized "the contextual world as a whole" (van Lier, 2000, p. 259) and not just the individual and cognitive processes.

As discussed in Part I of this book, the theoretical perspectives we select to inform and interpret an empirical study simultaneously shape how we design it, the questions we ask, the data we collect for analysis, the presentation of our findings, and our interpretation of them. In the present chapter, we conceptualized and interpreted the findings of the studies summarized above through the lens of affordance theory (e.g., van Lier, 2000). However, we might have chosen other social theories to inform our research. For example, there has been an increasing application of *complex systems theory* (Larsen-Freeman & Cameron, 2008a,

2008b) (see also *complex dynamic/adaptive systems theory*) in research on social phenomena, particularly in studies focused on language development and language acquisition (e.g., Larsen-Freeman, 1997; Larsen-Freeman & Cameron, 2008a, 2008b; Nematizadeh & Wood, 2019). Complexity theory may be seen as an extension of affordance theory as both take "ecological approaches" that rest on "an analogy between complex ecological systems and human language using/learning systems" (Larsen-Freeman & Cameron, 2008b, p. 201).

Larsen-Freeman and Cameron (2008a) have provided a detailed account of complex systems theory along with a framework to guide research that is designed and informed by this theoretical perspective. They defined a *system* as "a set of components that interact in particular ways to produce some overall state or form at a particular point in time" (p. 26). Systems are comprised of *agents* – humans (acting as individuals or in groups) and nonhumans (e.g., objects, material, or conceptual artifacts) – which self-organize through actions and interactions with each other "across levels and timescales" (Larsen-Freeman & Cameron, 2008b, p. 200). Such agent-driven actions and interactions form a temporary, dynamic *web* of connections and interconnections. It is this mutable and evolving web at a moment in time that is the focus of research informed by this perspective: "Teasing out the relationships and describing their dynamics are key tasks of the researcher working from a complex systems perspective" (2008b, p. 203).

The use of complex systems theory has moved the focus away from cognitively informed views of "causality" to a focus "on co-adaptation and emergence" (Larsen-Freeman & Cameron, 2008b, p. 200). Because complexity theorists investigate social phenomena as complex, nonlinear, dynamic systems, "context is not seen as a backdrop, but rather as a complex system itself, connected to other complex systems, and variability in system behavior takes on increased importance" (p. 200).

Complexity theory (see also chaos theory, Larsen-Freeman, 1997) and complex systems theory are umbrella terms, which researchers have variously applied "as a frame of reference, heuristic, metaphor, or way of thinking – for analyzing complex adaptive systems" (Moss & Haertel, 2016, p. 197). This perspective would have been useful in the empirical studies summarized in this chapter. Adopting such a perspective would have necessitated a reconsideration of material and conceptual artifacts (e.g., computers, ePortfolios, 3DVLEs, online learning tasks, instructions, rubrics), as *agents* acting and interacting along with and in relation to *humans* (e.g., individual and groups of students; the teacher), and their *situatedness* (e.g., shared/unique virtual learning spaces; across town, around the world; social, cultural circumstances). From the perspective of complexity theory, "context includes the physical, social, cognitive, and cultural, and is not separable from the system" (Larsen-Freeman & Cameron, 2008b, p. 204). (See also models of *distributed cognition*, Chapter Three, in Hutchins, 1995a, 1995b.)

We might also have applied Actor Network Theory (ANT) (e.g., Callon, 1986; Latour, 1987, 2005) in our research on technologically mediated teaching, another perspective that is consistent with complex systems theory. See, for example, Addey, Maddox, and Zumbo (2020) for an example of ANT applied in a case study, which explored argument-based validation practices at play in an International Large-Scale Assessment (ILSA). Drawing on their transdisciplinary partnership, the three authors argue for the ANT notion of *assemblage* as "the way that unstable networks of human actors and material artefacts align temporarily to achieve shared goals" (2020, p. 590) within the diverse and variable systems/contexts of ILSA use and interpretation. Transdisciplinary partnerships were also essential to the research, development, and application of the three online learning spaces considered in this chapter. Taken together, these examples illustrated the benefits of collective, collaborative research undertaken by engaged partners who nonetheless reflect very different disciplinary and professional backgrounds. Further, the examples demonstrated the potential of social theories in informing, framing, and implementing research. Further, in teaching and learning contexts, the importance of the teacher's perspective as a critical partner in classroom-based research (cf. Poehner & Inbar-Lourie, 2020a) is illustrated by Hartwick's reflection above. What Hartwick's voice adds is the recognition that simply transferring classroom assessment practices to the online context without considering the affordances of each online space is perilous.

Acknowledgements

We would like to acknowledge the transdisciplinary input and collaboration from the following partners: Ali Arya, Allie Davidson, Ioana Dimitriu, Jen Gilbert, Shawn Graham, Sabina Hajizada, Beth Hughes, Eva Kartchava, Iryna Kozlova, Julie McCarroll, Samah Sabra, Nandini Sarma, Nuket Savaskan-Nowlan, Sarah Todd, and Rachelle Thibodeau.

Notes

1 learning management system is a software application or platform that contains learning content and digital tools designed to facilitate learning, for example, a discussion board or video lecture.

2 An ePortfolio is an electronically hosted space used in education to showcase students' work and learning progress through digitally enhanced or created artifacts (Hartwick, 2018).

Part III

Transdisciplinarity in practice

Moving the research agenda forward

8 Language assessment in the wild

Storying our transdisciplinary experiences

Janna Fox with Natasha Artemeva

In this final chapter, key themes developed throughout the book are related to short narratives of experience. These narratives recount transdisciplinary practices-in-process with the benefit of hindsight, and the coherence and clarity that comes from storying experience. Through these storied recollections of dialogue, actions, and interactions with collaborating transdisciplinary partners engaging in assessment research projects, the information, concepts, and discussion in Parts I and II of this book are linked to the "profitable confusion" (Paré, 2008, p. 20), navigable, negotiable "tension" (Messick, 1998, p. 38), and extraordinary potential of these dynamic, dialogic research spaces. If interpretations of assessment outcomes are to be meaningful, useful, and appropriate, the contexts within which they apply must be considered. Social theories – vast and varied as they are – provide useful, rival alternative perspectives and concomitant methodologies, which incorporate contextual diversity in considerations of validity. Language-centred readers and assessment-centred readers alike are encouraged to engage proactively, together, in transdisciplinary research (TR) projects, not only with researchers whose principal interest is language assessment, but with those who have the most to gain or lose in contexts of assessment use – where doors are opened or closed (or opening and closing) as a consequence of an assessment outcome.

> *If two ... theories sharing a common metaphorical perspective ... can engender the different-world phenomenon of investigators talking past one another, as we have seen, just imagine the potential babble when more disparate models are juxtaposed. Yet it is precisely such mutual confrontation of theoretical systems, especially in attempting to account for the same data, that opens their underlying scientific and value assumptions to public scrutiny and critique.*
>
> (Messick, 1989, pp. 61–62)

DOI: 10.4324/9781351184571-12

> *Like air or water, cultures and disciplines surround us; they are what we are in without knowing it. Cultures discipline us, and disciplines culture us. ... We see the strangeness of cultures and disciplines in others, but don't notice our own strangeness. The two lines of my thinking about disciplinarity and culture – intertwined and merged with each other. It proved – for me at least – a profitable confusion.*
>
> (Paré, 2008, p. 20)

> *The basic condition for all understanding requires one to test and risk one's convictions and prejudgments in and through an encounter with what is radically "other" and alien. To do this requires imagination and hermeneutical sensitivity ... Critical engaged dialogue requires opening of oneself to the full power of what the "other" is saying. Such an opening does not entail agreement but rather the to-and-fro play of dialogue. Otherwise dialogue degenerates into a self-deceptive monologue where one never risks testing one's prejudgments ... by exposing them to the sharpest and most penetrating questioning.*
>
> (Bernstein, 1998, p. 4)

Taking a closer look: transdisciplinary research (TR) practices-in-process

The title of this final chapter is an obvious reference to Hutchins' seminal book, *Cognition in the Wild* (1995a), and offers a closer look at transdisciplinary language assessment research in process – *in the wild* – in engagement with *others*, whose professional and workplace cultures, whose ways of thinking, doing, perceiving, and acting differ from those who have background and expertise in *language*, *assessment*, or *language assessment*. As Paré (2008) mused, such differences are particularly evident when we are working with research partners who bring alternative agendas, differing kinds of expertise, worldviews, and/or experiences to bear on collaborative projects. Readers who have worked in transdisciplinary research (TR) spaces will no doubt sympathize with a well-respected language testing colleague, who was collaborating on a large-scale testing project in the States and complained: "I can't get them to listen to me! I can't get them to understand why they shouldn't do what they seem determined to do with their test results". Language assessment research often occurs outside the bounds of disciplinary groupings, as was the case for this frustrated language testing colleague, who was seemingly unable to effectively communicate his concerns and influence the actions of his research partners. Elder (2021) provided insightful commentary on language testers in such situations, reflecting on *practices of engagement* with policy and decision makers. She called for more attention to be focused on the important roles played by language testers – who are sometimes effective, and sometimes not – in informing, influencing, intervening in, and mediating the consequences, actions, and decisions that result from assessment practices. This book was developed as a means of supporting informed engagement, dialogue, effective communication, and critical reflection in the complex *in-between spaces* (Gadamer, 1975, 2003) of such transdisciplinary assessment research (like those experienced by the language testing colleague and retrospectively reviewed by Elder in 2021).

Wicks and Reason (2009), writing from an action research perspective, might suggest that the language tester's communication problems may have begun at the outset of the project, at the very beginning of the research process, when the ground rules are set for co-researchers and the "communicative space" is shaped, that is, "in the way access is established, and ... how participants and co-researchers are engaged" (p. 243). From the alternative perspective of educational measurement, Moss (2016) might consider the language tester's concerns as further evidence that a *conceptual shift* is needed to focus concerted attention on the "uses of test scores", to evaluate and support "local capacity to use data well", and thereby increase "the value of tests for enhancing education practice" (p. 248). Such a conceptual shift would lead to a more *robust* agenda (Gibbons & Nowotny, 2001; Moss, 2016) in assessment validation research, more effectively address the uses of assessment data, and focus needed attention on the uptake and consequences of decisions and actions that are taken as a result of that data.

We have focused on the need to close *applicability gaps* (Lawrence, 2010) between two principal disciplinary communities with arguably the most to contribute to language assessment validation research, loosely defined as *assessment-centred* (e.g., psychology, measurement, psychometrics) and *language-centred* (e.g., discourse studies, linguistics, applied linguistics, language teaching, writing studies). However, such applicability gaps also occur *in the wild* – as assessment experts collaborate with and inform research partners in different professional and workplace contexts, characterized by different professional and workplace cultures, wherein partners collectively engage in assessment projects or initiatives. Arguably, transdisciplinary approaches, like those identified by Bernstein (1998), examined by Lawrence (2010), and defined by Pohl and Hirsch Hadorn (2007), are essential in addressing such applicability gaps. These in-between spaces would bring research partners with different backgrounds, experience, and knowledge together for the purpose of listening, questioning, discovering, understanding, reflecting, and learning from each other through mutual, respectful engagement. There is ample evidence from the history of validation efforts and debates that narrower (mono-disciplinary) approaches have been unable to adequately address *slippery* issues (Cole, 2003) in assessment, such as context (cf. Kvale, 1995) and consequences in assessment practices.

In support of such transdisciplinary approaches, the issue of context in assessment practices was examined through the underutilized perspectives afforded by an array of social theories in order to illuminate the benefits of the *beyond-a-discipline* opportunities that transdisciplinarity offers. Following Kemmis (2001/2006) and Wicks and

Reason (2009), transdisciplinarity can open up inclusive, *communicative spaces* in which collaborating research partners, both within and external to academia, contribute to inquiry processes. Stakeholders in contexts of assessment use (e.g., policy and decision makers, teachers, parents, test takers) often have the most *at stake*, along with critical insights to contribute as co-researchers (beyond their traditional role as participants). It is not surprising that TR approaches are often compared to long-standing traditions of participatory action research. As Herndl (2004) has demonstrated, and Wicks, Reason, and Bradbury (2008) explain,

> Action research is a family of practices of living inquiry that aims, in a great variety of ways, to link practice and ideas. ... It is not so much a methodology as an orientation to inquiry that seeks to create participative communities of inquiry in which qualities of engagement, curiosity and question posing are brought to bear on significant practical issues.
>
> (p. 1)

For decades, validation research practice has drawn on Messick's (1989) overarching theoretical conceptualization of validity (see Chapter 2). Validation research has been a central concern of assessment-centred communities, and Messick's definition of validity has been a magnet for ongoing discussion and debate. An enduring strength of Messick's (1989) seminal work on validity is his advice to consider alternative inquiry systems, worldviews, and methodologies in the accumulation of validation evidence in support of both the plausible, technical quality of an assessment practice, as well as its actual worth – the consequences, decisions, and actions that result from interpretations drawn from its use. He advocated for a Singerian approach in validation research (cf. Moss, 2018), wherein one inquiry system is applied to another in a recursive chain of iterative reflection, reconsideration, and action: "the Singerian inquirer, by taking recursive perspectives on problem representation transforms one mode of storytelling into another and tells stories not only about the other stories but about the other storytellers" (Messick, 1989, p. 32).

Like Cronbach (cf. 1988), Messick asserted the importance of alternative rival interpretations in arguments for validity. Messick's (1989) advice is explicit: an inquirer "starts with a set of other inquiry systems ... and applies any system recursively to another system, including itself". This approach, he argued, was an "exceptionally fertile source of methodological heuristics" and would ensure "improvement through successive approximation" (p. 32).

Messick's approach to validation requires alternative inquiry systems, diverse ways of studying inferences and actions, and multiple methodologies that investigate assessment practices from differing perspectives. However, on the one hand, in the main, assessment-centred communities have generally been informed by cognitive theories which have located cognition in the head of an individual and relied on quantitative approaches in validation research. On the other hand, language-centred communities have largely been informed by social theories, some of which are very helpful in conceptualizing *context*, by locating cognition in social practices (Lave, 1996). These two theoretical perspectives have informed language assessment validation research, but as indicated by the meta-review of the assessment literature reported in Chapter 4, the use of social theories to inform language assessment research continues to be limited, in spite of the usefulness of some socio-theoretical perspectives and differing methodological approaches in providing textured and clarifying validation evidence in contexts of assessment use. As a result, the problem of context in language assessment has not been adequately addressed. The issue is clearly articulated by Flyvbjerg (2001), who pointed out,

> The problem in the study of human activity is that every attempt at a context-free definition of an action, that is, a definition based on abstract rules or laws, will not necessarily accord with the pragmatic way an action is defined by the actors in a concrete social situation. (p. 42)

Arguably, the disciplinary expertise of *both* language-centred communities and assessment-centred communities is essential for a vigorous research agenda in language assessment. However, applicability gaps abound. Relevant extra-disciplinary perspectives, expertise, and experience are often overlooked, dismissed, or disregarded. And yet, increased sharing of expertise among disciplinary communities will serve the collective interests of all in addressing complex issues such as context and consequence in language assessment. The goal of such exchanges is not a reductive or artificial synthesis. Neither is it an impractical, utopian, or unrealistic vision of *how things ought to be*. Rather, as Bernstein so elegantly argued, a transdisciplinary approach creates potential to risk, test, listen, question, respect differences, and learn; to have an open "hermeneutical sensitivity" (1998, p. 4) to alternative worldviews and orientations.

Naming as rhetorical action: reconsidering community

Coe (1994) observed that "The act of naming is rhetorical. ... Even when we confine ourselves to the most concrete terms" (p. 187). In naming, he noted, we set a thing apart, "*sort* it ... *class*-ify it ... we direct our attention to salient characteristics (and thus deflect it from other characteristics)" (p. 187). At the outset of this book (Chapter 1) we acknowledged that our choice of the word *community* was problematic in identifying the shared disciplinary interests of groups of disciplines, fields, and sub-fields as language-centred or assessment-centred for purposes of argument, interpretability, and analysis. As Paré and Smart (1994) noted, by categorizing we have traded "a loss of reality for a gain in control" (p. 153). We may also have unintentionally provoked a negative response from readers and influential thinkers who have expressed dissatisfaction with the use of the term *community* (e.g., Gee, 2004; Fairclough, 1992; Kent, 1991; Scollon, 2001).[1] In 1994, Freedman and Medway observed that the "'term' community has lately become a contested notion on philosophic and political grounds" (1994, p. 7). The concerns identified by Freedman and Medway have a long history in the literature (e.g., Eraut, 2002; Harris, 1989; Willis et al., 2007). Prior (2003)[2] offered a particularly thorough discussion of the use of the word community in *community of practice* (CoP), discussing largely unacknowledged shifts in the evolution of its conceptualization, that is, from its Activity Theory base in Lave and Wenger (1991) to its "diverse set of anthropological and sociological references" (Prior, 2003, p. 10) in Wenger (1998). Prior (2003) argued that the widespread appropriation of a *catchy idea* like CoPs often obscures the "theoretical slipperiness" (p. 10) of such approaches. Prior warned against the use of such terms without acknowledging the theoretical grounds that support their use. He noted that "whatever terms we turn to will continue to slip ... unless we very consciously wrest them away and carefully stake out alternative theoretical grounds" (p. 20).

Along with our understanding of disciplines and disciplinary cultures (cf. Paré, 2008), and following Prior's (2003) advice, our choice of the term *community* refers to groups who share in common a "hermeneutical sensitivity" (Bernstein, 1998, p. 4) (aligned with particular worldviews, conceptual stances, and methodological approaches), which prompts their engagement in a particular range of "hermeneutic act[s]"; Fairclough, 1992, p. 427). At the risk of belabouring this point, the challenge of *naming* in the *in-between spaces* of transdisciplinary *conversations* (Gadamer, 2003) is not to be taken lightly. It is one of the reasons why it is so easy to talk *past one other* (Messick, 1989). This issue is highlighted here because naming – with a deep, collective understanding of each other's meanings and implications – is a critical issue in TR practice.[3]

Part I of this book provided selective background on the history and evolution of theoretical perspectives and research practices of assessment-centred and language-centred communities, and examined their contributions in relation to the social thread in language assessment research. In Part II, three empirical examples of language assessment research, each informed by differing social theories and undertaken with transdisciplinary co-researchers and partners, were provided as illustrations of TR in practice.

Chapter 5 offered an example of construct definition in high-stakes oral proficiency test development within the complex Language for Specific Purposes (LSP) context of radiotelephony communication between air traffic controllers and pilots. The study drew on the social theories of

English as a lingua franca (e.g., Jenkins et al., 2011), intercultural communication/awareness (e.g., Baker, 2011, 2017), and interactional competence (e.g., He & Young, 1998). This richly elaborated web of social theories framed the contributions of transdisciplinary stakeholder partners, who provided validation evidence for construct specification by drawing on their lived experience. In addition, the theory of distributed cognition (e.g., Hutchins, 1995a) helped to account for and understand communication practices within this professional aviation workplace context (the target language use domain) in order to sample them for an aural/oral proficiency test (the test domain) (Chapelle, 2021).

Chapter 6 examined the role of Rhetorical Genre Studies (RGS) (e.g., Bazerman, 1988; Freedman & Medway, 1994; Miller, 1984, 1994a, 1994b) in refining an analytic rating scale used in evaluating writing on a diagnostic assessment task. The task was part of a diagnostic assessment procedure, which was designed to identify entering engineering students in need of additional academic support at the beginning of their undergraduate program. The RGS lens engendered new insights, deepened understanding, generated meaningful discussion in rater training, and supported coherence and consistency. Further, incorporating the RGS perspective in writing assessment enhanced the link from a student's writing task performance to academic support tailored to meet an individual student's needs and increase the student's potential for success in the engineering program.

Chapter 7 described language teaching, learning, and assessment in online learning spaces through the socio-theoretical lens of *affordances* (Gibson, 1979/2015; Hartwick, 2018; van Lier, 2000). The chapter explored the benefits and challenges of three technologically mediated spaces (i.e., 3D Virtual Learning Environments, ePortfolios, and H5P tools in learning management systems) in teaching English for Academic Purposes. Within a *Framework of Learning-Oriented Assessment* (LOA) (Turner & Purpura, 2016) these online learning spaces created new opportunities for assessment in support of learning. Enactment was dependent upon the transdisciplinary collaboration of multiple partners who contributed differing knowledge, perspectives, skills, and experience while sharing the goal of improving the quality of teaching, learning, and assessment. The collaboration allowed for the development of novel and innovative classroom-based assessment procedures, but these were not without challenges in the fully online teaching context of the COVID-19 pandemic.

Taken together, the empirical studies in Part II illustrated the potential of transdisciplinary assessment research informed by social theories in pushing the validity agenda forward – approaches that are increasingly called for in the literature of both language-centred and assessment-centred communities (cf. Moss, 2016, 2018; Tardy, 2017; Zumbo, 2017) – and there is increasing evidence of their potential to generate new insights, deepen understanding, dialogue, and discussion. This is a productive way of moving forward, particularly as it relates to context (e.g., Addey, Maddox, & Zumbo, 2020; Deygers & Malone, 2019; Macqueen et al., 2019; Zumbo, 2017).

Having highlighted the importance and benefits of transdisciplinarity informed by selected social theories in addressing complex assessment issues throughout this book, it is important to acknowledge that TR spaces are inevitably more complex and can be challenging at times. Below, we share some of these challenges by recounting two transdisciplinary assessment research *experiences* which failed to achieve their envisioned potential. We compare these with another experience, which lived up to (and exceeded) expectations. Juxtaposing these accounts of TR in practice helps to highlight their complex nature and throws light on why they did or did not work. Recounting, reflecting on, and learning from such experiences help to clarify to a certain extent when and why transdisciplinarity may fail or succeed.

Beneficial interactions of social theories and transdisciplinary practices-in-process

The three transdisciplinary experiences considered here are examined through the lenses of two socio-theoretical perspectives that provided "powerful conceptual tool[s]" which helped us "to organize and understand" them (Freedman, 2006, p. 101): 1) Hutchins' (1995a, 1995b) *theory of distributed cognition* and 2) Wenger's (1998) early conceptualization of three dimensions of *communities of practice* (CoP) (see Chapter 3). Not all socio-theoretical perspectives, but many others, might have been chosen (as the other examples in this book suggest) to *unpack* the experiences recounted here. Taken together, the two socio-theoretical perspectives considered here helped us to clarify, better understand, and learn from these experiences.

Hutchins' (1995a, 1995b) theory of distributed cognition

As noted in Chapters 3 and 5, Hutchins investigated cognition *in action* within social and cultural contexts, arguing that "cultural practices are a key component of human cognition" (see http://pages.ucsd.edu/~ehutchins/). Hutchins' theory of distributed cognition views the cognitive properties of an individual as *systemic* properties; that is, as part of a system of such properties, which prompt and position individual awareness, recognition, and action in context. In his seminal book *Cognition in the wild* (1995a), he introduced this social theory of cognition through an example of the systematic *thinking-in-action,* or the collective cognition, that was distributed amongst the crew of a large navy vessel who averted a disaster at sea through their collective, collaborative actions and interactions. From the captain to the novice sailor, in keeping with their differentiated roles, each individual contributed intelligence, skill, and knowledge in the overall management of the emergency in order to save the ship. Hutchins recognized that our understanding of cognition is enhanced by moving researchers out of the *laboratory* (which takes a reductive, typically artificial view of cognition as an isolated and individual trait or phenomenon) and *into the wild*, by viewing cognition as a system, distributed across individuals, artifacts, time, and space, and manifested in the dynamic flow of action in context. In the narratives which are recounted in this chapter, Hutchins' notion of *distributed cognition* as cognition in the wild is applied to considerations of language assessment research experiences in three transdisciplinary assessment research projects.

Contested views of Wenger's (1998) communities of practice (CoPs)

The perspective afforded by *distributed cognition* is combined with another socio-theoretical perspective, *communities of practice* (Wenger, 1998), in storying and analyzing the transdisciplinary assessment research experiences which are recounted later in this chapter. As previously noted, a number of researchers (e.g., Gee, 2004; Prior, 2003; Scollon, 2001) have taken issue with the notion of *community* – particularly as it is used in communities of practice (CoPs). For example, Gee (2004)[4] viewed a CoP as a sometimes "fruitful" (p. 77) notion, but he rejected labelling a group of individuals as members or non-members of a community. Rather, he argued that researchers should "start with 'spaces' and not groups" (p. 78). His perspective is in keeping with that of Scollon's (2001) preference for a "nexus of practice" rather than the narrower and bounded notion of a *community* of practice. Scollon argued that discarding the "problematical" notion of community would better account for a more fluid, less homogenous and "unbounded" (p. 5) location for the engagement of diverse participants with differing backgrounds and expertise, who were simultaneously informed by their participation in other practices, situations, and contexts. Prior (2003) objected to the apparent simplification and reduction evident in discussions of CoPs. Following Goffman (1981), he identified such *community* spaces as "laminated or layered" (p. 13) (see also *nested*, in Chapters 5 and 6). He argued "there are no spaces where social histories of people, practices, artifacts, and institutions disappear"; neither are there spaces where "identities can be figured simply ... [as] just an engineer, just a student, just a teacher" (p. 14). These ideas were taken into account in our use of Wenger's (1998) explanation of a *community of practice*, which we viewed pragmatically as a useful unit of analysis.

Wenger's (1998) dimensions of a community of practice (CoP)

Wenger (1998) linked *practices* to *communities* through three constituent "dimensions of relation by which practice is the source of coherence of a community" (p. 72): 1) *mutual engagement*, 2) *joint enterprise*, and

3) *shared repertoire*. Taken together, these *constituent* dimensions comprise a *community of practice*.

He identified *mutual engagement* as negotiation amongst participating members who are invested in an outcome, participate actively in the process, and perceive their contributions are valued and meaningful (although their contributions may be diverse and varied and have differing degrees of influence). He viewed *joint enterprise* as essentially the negotiated outcome of members' engagement: the collectively agreed to "product" (p. 79) that emerges through the process of negotiation. Wenger (1998) explained that joint enterprise "is not just the stated goal but creates among participants relations of mutual accountability that become an integral part of the practice" (p. 78). Further, although the joint enterprise is mutually negotiated, it does not imply that all members agree or that all contributions equally influence the final outcome. Disagreement may lead to new recognitions, insights, and reflection. What is key is that the joint enterprise was mutually negotiated – in good faith. The third dimension by which practice becomes a source of community coherence is a *shared repertoire* of resources that support meaningful negotiation. A shared repertoire develops over time in the process of engaging in a joint enterprise and allows for meaningful, efficient, localized interaction. Such CoPs are located at the site or *nexus of practice* which may be bounded, as in the insurance company example discussed in Wenger (1998), or unbounded, as in Gee's (2000) notion of a *semiotic social space* or an *affinity space* (e.g., sites which attract gamers to a particular computer gaming site for a time). All sites are *laminated*, but lamination potentially figures more in bounded institutional or organizational settings where hierarchies of power in relation to practices come into play.

Like Freedman (2006), Wenger (1998) had highlighted the "practicality of theory". He pointed out that a theoretical perspective "is not a recipe, it does not tell you just what to do. Rather it acts as a guide about what to pay attention to, what difficulties to expect, and how to approach problems" (p. 9).

Understanding transdisciplinary practice-as-process through narratives of assessment design, development, and implementation

In sharing the three *narratives of experience* which follow, we have drawn on the tradition of *narrative inquiry*[5] which has been used by researchers across a broad array of disciplines (e.g., Polkinghorne, 1988; Potter & Wetherell, 1987 in psychology; Clandinin & Connelly, 2000 in education; or Gee, 1996, in sociolinguistics, discourse studies, and critical literacy). Connelly and Clandinin (2006) explain how such storied accounts inform the meaning and interpretation of experience:

> People shape their daily lives by stories of who they and others are and as they interpret their past in terms of these stories. Story, in the current idiom, is a portal through which a person enters the world and by which their experience of the world is interpreted and made personally meaningful. Narrative inquiry, the study of experience as story, then, is first and foremost a way of thinking about experience. (p. 479)

Storying TR experiences which occurred *in the wild* (outside familiar disciplinary research spaces) helped us to reflect on and learn from them. Sharing such experiences may help others to develop awareness, knowledge, and strategies in managing processes and practices within such complex TR spaces. As Clandinin and Rosiek (2007) pointed out, narrative accounts shed light "not only on individuals' experiences but also on the social, cultural, and institutional narratives within which individuals' experiences are constituted, shaped, expressed, and enacted" (pp. 42–43).

In storying these three transdisciplinary experiences, two additional differentiating features of such research contexts are identified, which have been helpful in understanding both their *lamination* and their dynamic trajectories over time: 1) the *latitude* of action, or the scope for experimentation, innovation, etc., that is afforded each participating research partner in a research project; and 2) the *magnitude* of influence that an individual researcher and/or the research team can exert in influencing the trajectory of a research project. These two concepts, along with the perspectives afforded by the two selected social theories of distributed cognition and CoPs, framed the narratives and their analysis and illuminated why two transdisciplinary projects did not live up to their full potential and the third exceeded expectations. Taken together, these *narratives of experience* are offered as *food for thought* and provide evidence of transdisciplinarity as it played out in process. As Bruner (2002) explained, "it is our narrative gift that gives us the power to make sense of things when they don't" (p. 28). (We would add that narratives also help us make sense of things when they *do*).

> Below are three narratives of assessment design, development, and implementation that provide examples of transdisciplinarity-in-process, *in the wild*, viewed in retrospect through the lenses afforded by time, reflection, and social theories. The first two transdisciplinary experiences are narrated by Janna Fox, who reflects on her role as a consultant in the contexts of complex and challenging large-scale assessment projects. The third experience is narrated by Janna Fox and Natasha Artemeva. The transdisciplinary partnerships recounted in the third narrative have prompted the writing of this book and illustrate the extraordinary potential of transdisciplinarity.

Three narratives of transdisciplinary assessment experiences

Context one. What is the construct? Law, policy, and power in transdisciplinary assessment (narrated by Janna Fox)

In transdisciplinary contexts such as assessment workplaces outside academia, where assessment expertise is drawn on (over years in some cases) to inform assessment practices, and where contributions to an assessment project involve acting as a technical expert or consultant (e.g., in test development, assessment reform, validation projects, curricular initiatives), a CoP (Wenger, 1998; cf. Wenger-Trayner & Wenger-Trayner, 2015; Wenger-Trayner, Fenton-O'Creevy, Hutchinson, Kubiak, & Wenger-Trayner, 2015) may form over time. However, it will differ greatly from the CoPs that provide a relatively stable ground for what is known, done, and valued by members of a disciplinary research team who choose to work together on a research project of interest to their shared disciplinary/academic communities. Conversely, when language testers engage in assessment projects *in the wild,* they typically join other diverse research partners (not of their own choosing), who have experiences, knowledge, beliefs, and expertise that differ considerably from their own. Although understanding this in the abstract is useful, as "forewarned is forearmed", encountering such diversity in practice while engaging in a project, can at times be a challenging experience (cf. Wicks & Reason, 2009).

At the beginning of the test development research project which is the focus of this first narrative account, I had just completed a consultancy as a member of a research team working on the development of new task prototypes for an oral proficiency test. In that project, the working group was able to shape the initial development of the new tasks, which promised to better represent meaningful, situated communication. The group was given complete freedom in developing a range of potential task prototypes, and the experience was invigorating, enlightening, and fully satisfying. The new task prototypes provided options for the initial redevelopment of a high-stakes test in the *Second Language Evaluation* (SLE) battery of the Public Service Commission of the Government of Canada. This battery of tests is administered to prospective and current federal government employees as part of Canada's national policy on bilingualism. The tests implement the policies inscribed in the *Official Languages Act(s)* (1969/1985/1988) and are consistent with the *Canadian Charter of Rights and Freedoms* (1982). They have the objectives of ensuring 1) that services of equally high quality are delivered to the public in the official languages of Canada, and 2) that both French speakers and English speakers have equal opportunities for employment and advancement in federal institutions.

After completing the consultancy, I agreed to join a TR team in progress, which was at that time redeveloping the controversial (cf. Bessette,

2005; McNamara & Roever, 2006; Nearing, 2020) *Test of Written Expression* (English/French), another high-stakes test in the SLE battery. Within the national, sociocultural, and political history of Canada, the role and relationships of French and English, and other languages (see the *Multiculturalism Act*, 1988, regarding the rights of linguistic minorities) have at times been flashpoints for conflict and tension. This explains in part why the *Official Languages Act(s)* (1969, 1988) have not been substantively altered since first enactment in the late 1960s, although there have been several amendments. As previously discussed, definitions and theoretical conceptualizations of language have undergone dramatic changes since the 1960s (see Chapter 3).

Over the past decades there has been "growing dissatisfaction with and concern about the tendency to view individuals acquiring a second language as aspirant, and for the most part, failed native speakers" (Leung & Valdés, 2019, p. 348). Recently, there has been mounting rejection of the notion of monolingual, native-speaker norms as the appropriate standard for bilingual language proficiency (cf. Turnbull & Dailey-O'Cain, 2009; Schissel & Arias, 2021). However, the *Official Languages Act(s)* dictated a monolingual, native-speaker standard in the classification of levels of bilingual proficiency, in keeping with linguistic descriptions that were current in the 1960s to 1980s. These linguistic descriptions are inscribed in law and policy documents. In accepting to work on the English team at initial stages of the redevelopment of the *Test of Written Expression*, I underestimated how much this narrowing of the construct by law would impact the scope or latitude of our research team's contributions to a new test.

Because the test was to be delivered in both English and French, the two versions needed to be as similar as possible and equated (i.e., of comparable difficulty) across the two languages. There was ongoing and productive interaction between the French and English development teams to achieve these goals. There were a number of positive outcomes of our *mutual engagement* (Wenger, 1998). For example, we built a corpus of commonly recurring communications across all government ministries; undertook corpus analysis to ascertain commonly recurring features; and developed a range of differing but recurring tasks involving written expression (scheduling, timetabling, responding in letters, filling in forms, writing memos, emails, etc.). We also engaged in *rhetorical-linguistic* genre analysis (Devitt, 2015). Swales (1990) identified genres in terms of their "communicative purpose" which

> is both a privileged criterion and one that operates to keep the scope of a genre as here conceived narrowly focused on comparable rhetorical action. In addition to purpose, exemplars of a genre exhibit various patterns of similarity in terms of structure, style, content and intended audience.
>
> (p. 58)

However, negotiations for a range of differing tasks, derived from the linguistic corpus analysis plus the Swalesian Rhetorical-linguistic genre analysis, failed to meet the requirements of government research partners, who were required to find the most efficient and practical means of administration, limit marking requirements, etc. Further, we were constrained in the provision of multiple tasks (e.g., timetables, agendas, schedules), because they would require additional accommodations for test takers who had visual or other challenges. In addition, and in spite of extensive discussions regarding method effects, given the cost of training, calibrating, and monitoring raters on an ongoing basis, and the inability to hire additional staff to carry this out over time, only multiple-choice item types were acceptable. Ultimately the *Test of Written Expression* was (as noted in the research literature, for example, Bessette, 2005; McNamara & Roever, 2006; Nearing, 2020), a test of the *recognition* of correct (monolingual) written expression, which non-native/second language (L2) speakers of English took in English to verify their level of English proficiency, and non-native/ L2 speakers of French took in French to verify their level of French proficiency. These tests were only required for bilingually designated positions.

Over the three years of the project, the transdisciplinary assessment research team became a community of practice (Wenger, 1998; Wenger-Trayner & Wenger-Trayner, 2015; Wenger-Trayner et al., 2015), at the level of our test development working group. Drawing on Wenger's (1998) three dimensions of a CoP (see also Chapter 3), the test development group was *mutually engaged.* All of the participating members (English and French linguists; English and French test developers/technical experts; government employees responsible for the test; experts in formatting and framing for software platforms; an accommodation specialist; public service employees; language teachers; former test takers; labour and protocol experts; textual and secretarial support workers; managers, etc.) within the test development working group contributed in good faith. Members were responsible, open to suggestions, inventive, and accountable to the group as a whole. I always felt that my contributions were valued, and I valued the contributions of the other members of the test development project group in turn. There were a number of disagreements, and even some tensions at times, particularly with regard to the weighting of different item types in negotiating test specifications. There were also challenges in working across languages and versions. However, such disagreements were resolved by negotiation, and the group was consistently productive and positive.

There was value in the testing expertise drawn on for the project. It was a *joint enterprise* which resulted in a collectively negotiated new and more useful "product" (Wenger, 1998, p. 79) (i.e., test(s)). There was, in my view, a strong sense of *mutual engagement and accountability* amongst the test developers and the government employees who were directly contributing to and responsible for the process of development. However, all of our work was directly shaped by largely unseen decision makers in the government hierarchy, and by existing laws, policy, and accepted practices.

We developed over time a shared *repertoire* of resources to support communication, negotiations, and increasing *coherence* over the years of the project, but at one level only: within the test development project group itself. But this level was *nested* (Maguire, 1994, 1997) (Chapters 5 and 6) or *laminated* (Goffman, 1981; Prior, 2003) within a surrounding culture and hierarchy, which influenced both the *latitude* we could exercise and the *magnitude* of the influence we might have on ultimate outcomes. Non-participating stakeholders ultimately exerted the most influence in defining the project's evolution and outcomes.

From the perspective of distributed cognition, Hutchins' (1995a) account of the relationship between the captain of a large navy vessel, his officers, and the many participating sailors onboard is apt in characterizing how I ultimately felt about my role as a test developer, engaged in developing this new proficiency test. Although there was general recognition of the critical role of language testing expertise in the project, how it influenced outcomes was limited in relation to the function it served in the hierarchy of functions that characterized the testing project as a whole. Hutchins' (1995a) analysis of the hierarchy of decision making and enactment, from captain to crew, provides a useful analogy for the power distribution in this test development project. As a TR space, its potential for innovation, initiative, or imagination was limited by the unequal distribution of power. From the outset, constraints related to roles, responsibility, and influence (cf. Wicks & Reason, 2008; Wicks, Reason, & Bradbury, 2008) narrowed the project's potential, given the legal and policy context within which it was situated.

The test development working group (CoP) was a time limited CoP at the "nexus of practices" (Scollon, 2001, p. 5), which was embedded within the enormous bureaucracy of a national government. As noted above, power was vested in the unseen decision makers within the government hierarchy from which the testing project had received its mandate. In addition to very limited latitude or scope for change, there was also very limited magnitude or power to influence it, given:

- the monolingual, native-speaker norms applied in *a priori* construct definition and written into law;
- non-negotiable policy with regard to monolingual evaluation standards,
- the need for simplicity in administration;
- requirements for practicality in the face of the high numbers of test takers requiring the test;
- efficiency requirements in reporting results as quickly and reliably as possible; and
- the absence of additional funding to recruit, train, and monitor raters on an ongoing basis to evaluate writing.

In spite of these constraints, there were some positive outcomes. The new versions of the test:

- increased domain representation and relevance because specifications were informed by an LSP construct (Douglas, 2000; Knoch & Macqueen, 2020), which meant that wherever possible and in keeping with general language knowledge, workplace language features were incorporated in test tasks/items (see, Chapter 5);
- were more representative of recurring texts, tasks, content, vocabulary, etc., due to corpus analysis and rhetorical-linguistic (Devitt, 2015; Swales, 1990) genre analysis;
- situated items within contextualized scenarios as testlets (grouping items/tasks in relation to situations, communicative events, and texts); and
- were accompanied by the development of a greatly improved website to support test taker preparation and language development.

However, the initial goal of the test development working group, namely to build a *Test of Written Expression* (as the name suggests), was not realized. No actual writing was elicited by the multiple-choice tasks and items. Only recognition-based responses were required as test takers chose the best answer amongst the item distractors. Focus was on assessing a test taker's knowledge and recognition of grammaticality, usage, meaning, wording, etc. operationalizing to a large extent dated conceptualizations of language (see Chapter 3 for an overview of evolving conceptualizations of language).

In the end, the new test was positioned to generate some *negative washback* (e.g., Nearing, 2020), just as the older test had done (Bessette, 2005; McNamara & Roever, 2006). It would unfortunately continue to contribute to the perceived "gap between the lofty goals of the *Official Languages Act* and the largely instrumental sense in which too many public servants view language training and testing" (Mitchell, 2005, p. 10). A report published by the Office of the Commissioner of Official Languages (2013) indicated that of a sample of 70 respondents surveyed from across Canada, 52 (74%) saw little relationship between passing the test and comfort using both English and French in their workplaces. The fundamental irony of this project was the fact that the *lofty goals* of the *Official Languages Acts* were manifested daily in the actions, communications, and interactions of the test development working group. Although the degree of bilingualism varied across members of the group, communication continually shifted from French to English and English to French; communications were fluent and easy; they were (as they typically are in bilingual environments) characterized by *code-switching* and *translanguaging* (Leung & Valdés, 2019): language choice was speaker- and purpose-specific (see also *translanguage* in Chapter 3). This dynamic, bilingual communicative environment did not interfere with the ultimate monolingual French or English test items/tasks produced for the test, but the items/tasks were produced in an enriched context of meaningful bilingual communication. The construct we had wanted to test was everywhere around us. Ironically, the test operationalized separate monolingual constructs rather than bilingual ones. If a bilingual construct were operationalized, there would be the need for only one test that would probe the *bilingual proficiency* of all test takers regardless of language background, instead of two tests of monolingual proficiency (with a French version administered only to English speakers and an English version administered only to French speakers), as is currently the case (see also Chapter 5).

Postscript

On reflection, the construct operationalized by the *Test of Written Expression* may have greater fidelity to the ways in which bilingual writing works in government offices than I had first thought. Years later, I asked a French-speaking manager, who was exempt from further bilingual testing, how often he wrote in English. He replied that it depended on the situation. He reported writing in English informally for *ordinary* communication, but if he needed to write something more substantive and complex, he would often call on an anglophone (i.e., English-speaking) colleague to work with him on a first draft. His response was similar to that of an English-speaking manager who was exempt from further bilingual proficiency testing in French. She also remarked that she would ask a francophone (i.e., French-speaking) colleague to draft some of her correspondence in French. Both reported that they needed to verify, revise, check, and review written correspondence in their second languages (much as the *Test of Written Expression* asked them to do). This was anecdotal evidence in support of the recognition of written expression construct that had been operationalized by the test.

However, this highly instrumental type of bilingualism is not in keeping with the goals for bilingualism promoted in policy. There is a will to address the issues related to the *Official Languages Act(s)*. On March 11, 2019 in honour of the fiftieth anniversary of the original *Official Languages Act*, the University of Ottawa hosted the Honourable Mélanie Joly, Minister of Tourism, Official Languages and la Francophonie, who announced a modernization project for the Act. Since that time, the pandemic has redirected government attention to other issues, but the most recent report from the Office of the Commissioner of Official Languages (2020–2021) reinforced the need to modernize the *Act*. In this report, the Commissioner highlighted the intention to update the *Official Languages Act(s)*, to ensure compliance across the government in employment practices, and to do more to promote both official languages across Canada. At the same time, MacCharles (2021) sees bilingual policies "on a collision course" with the multicultural and multilingual diversity of Canada's population. In reference to the requirements for federally hired jurists, she reported that "advocates of greater diversity say mandatory bilingualism will block many qualified candidates". From a testing perspective, the question remains whether two separate monolingual constructs or a bilingual construct will be mandated by proposed modernization initiatives.

Context two. Shifting partnerships in a transdisciplinary project (narrated by Janna Fox)

The second narrative of transdisciplinary assessment experience originated in the context of a national assessment reform agenda that was implemented in language and settlement programs for newly arrived immigrants and refugees in Canada. The program has the general aim of supporting "newcomers' successful settlement and integration so that they may participate and contribute in various aspects of Canadian life". (See Overview of the Settlement Program, available at www.canada.ca/en/immigration-refugees-citizenship/corporate/reports-statistics/evaluations/settlement-program.html#summary.)

At its inception, the strategic management of the assessment reform was undertaken by a group of national government employees who engaged in extensive research to investigate alternative assessment approaches. They examined assessment initiatives in other parts of the world which had been similarly motivated by interest in improving the quality of reception services (in settlement and language support) for newcomers. The objectives of the initiative were to:

- generate more core, system-wide consistency in *Language Instruction for Newcomers to Canada* (LINC) programs;
- encourage and support LINC teachers' use of the *Canadian Language Benchmarks* (CLBs) (a set of proficiency descriptors intended to serve as criteria to guide assessment of language proficiency development);
- support the development of task-based language teaching (TBLT) in LINC classes (connect TBLT to the CLB proficiency benchmarks as learning outcomes, and thereby build consistency in expectations and pedagogical experiences across programs);
- use assessment to support language learning; and, most importantly,
- develop adult language learners' self-awareness, realistic goal setting, self-assessment, and autonomy.

When I was first approached to act as a consultant on the project, I was heartened to learn of the engagement of other collaborating partners (e.g., LINC students, teachers, researchers, program developers, administrators) and the decision to use portfolio-based language assessment as the primary assessment strategy. I had been involved in other successful portfolio assessment approaches with adult language learners and had worked extensively with language teachers to support positive outcomes in these assessment initiatives. Further, the working group that was assembled included partners who were experienced in portfolio assessment within a number of LINC programs across Canada.

The project manager was a capable, long-serving, well-respected government employee who fully understood the potential of portfolio assessment approaches, as well as their challenges and perils. He was well connected to the government hierarchies who were funding the project, passionate about its potential, and articulate and persuasive with regard to the outcomes it would achieve. He was an expert in navigating potential obstacles to resource requests, knowledgeable about portfolio use, highly communicative, enthusiastic, and engaged. He motivated the collective enthusiasm of all the working group members assembled for the project.

In an initial meeting of the research team, drawing on the experiences of others who had used portfolio assessment in large-scale assessment initiatives, he shared his concerns regarding implementation. When a portfolio approach was introduced too quickly, without sufficient support for teachers and learners, the initiative could be undermined. Rule One was to build collective shared understanding across teachers *and* learners as to *why* the approach would serve their interests in facilitating language development. The teachers' commitment to the initiative was key. In order to engender commitment, they needed to clearly understand *why* portfolio assessment was a good choice and be provided with strategies, approaches, and resources to support their students' understanding as well. Rule Two was to use portfolios as dynamic collections of student work, as interactive sites for dialogue, discussion, reflection, and learning, which were anchored in evidence of students' development over time. The danger was that portfolios would become static receptacles or filing cabinets that housed documentation as evidence of achievement. Such portfolios ceased to be active and effective in informing teaching and supporting ongoing learning and could become burdens for teachers and students alike (Abdulhamid & Fox, 2020; Fox, 2014; Hargreaves, Earl, & Schmidt, 2002). In such cases, portfolios were often relegated to dusty shelves and only referred to when, by happenstance, someone asked about them, or if a teacher needed to provide evidence to account for a student's failure to pass a course or as justification for a student's move to a higher level in a program. Worse yet, they could become *portfolio prisons* (Hargreaves et al., 2002) which trapped students and teachers alike in their mechanical maintenance but did not engender active learning.

Members of the working group assumed different roles in implementation of the initiative. Two members of the working group had worked successfully with portfolios in their home provinces, and they and other colleagues developed workshops to introduce teachers to portfolio assessment and support their use as the locus of language learning, reflection, and language development. My role (along with several colleagues) was one of evaluation over time of:

- the impact and effectiveness of the workshops;
- changes in teachers' perceptions of the CLB, their knowledge and use of TBLT, and their use of portfolio assessment; and
- changes in students' reported levels of engagement, autonomy, and self-reflection.

The working group (i.e., the project manager and his colleagues, the workshop coordinators, the evaluation team, LINC program representatives, LINC teachers, etc.) met frequently. We were a lively group, interacting and supporting each other with a shared commitment to the project.

As noted previously, TR spaces are dynamic and emergent. They are subject to change, which may be unanticipated or misapprehended, sometimes because transdisciplinary stakeholders bring to an endeavour their own workplace cultures and taken-for-granted practices (cf. *lamination* in Prior, 2003; Scollon, 2001). Just after the first year of this three-year project, the Project Manager was promoted to a new position in the government. Turnover in government positions is frequent. Particularly capable employees are likely to seek new employment opportunities, and they are likely to be offered such opportunities at regular intervals. The Project Manager who had pulled together the transdisciplinary partners and had overseen initial engagement with the project was replaced by a very capable colleague. However, the new Project Manager had not previously been involved in the project. Moreover, an election overtook the initiative in mid-stream. All policy decisions were subject to review.

In August, at end of the first year of the project, many of the LINC teachers who were involved lost their positions as LINC programs were dramatically cut by the new government in advance of reorganization. The workshops from that point forward continued to focus on how to develop learning portfolios in relation to CLB criteria and task-based-language teaching, but there was no longer extensive discussion of *why* portfolio assessment was a useful approach in supporting language teaching and learning. As a result, the teachers who remained or were newly hired or rehired in September tended to focus on the mechanics of pulling a portfolio together – and the mechanics were complicated and at times daunting and discouraging. In a climate of cutbacks and instability, few teachers expressed concern that the portfolios were being used to covertly evaluate their teaching, not to support the learning of their students.

As part of the evaluation design, questionnaires were circulated to the teachers and their students at intervals over the three-year period. After three years of the project, of the 300+ LINC teachers who had participated in the first workshop (in year one), only ~40 had attended *all* of the workshops (over three years), and had responded to *all* of the questionnaires on their experiences with portfolio assessment. Although amongst the respondents the original goals of the project were by and large achieved (i.e., they reported increased systematic planning, task-based teaching, use of the CLB, and use of portfolio assessment), the attitudes in general toward portfolio assessment were not those which had been originally envisioned. At the very least, some LINC teachers began to see it as an unnecessary nuisance (cf. Fox, 2014). At its worst, it was a burden. Further, there was evidence of a significant policy shift in conceptualization of the portfolio: from a working/formative resource for teaching and learning to a showcase/summative repository of learning artifacts (Abdulhamid & Fox, 2020; Fox, 2014).

This transdisciplinary project had begun with fully engaged and knowledgeable partner collaborators, who:

- were jointly committed to and enthusiastic about the project;
- formed balanced, interactive, and productive relationships;
- freely exchanged expertise and perspectives; and
- were well-resourced and supported.

This project was initially very fertile ground for a new CoP, as it was characterized by the three dimensions Wenger (1998) identified which develop "coherence" (p. 72) in a community of practice. The research partners shared a strong mutual commitment to project outcomes; they were proactive, drawing on different kinds of expertise and experience, sharing and negotiating how best to proceed, with a strong sense of the ultimate "product" outcomes (what Wenger referred to as evidence of a "joint enterprise", p. 77). Partner contributions differed, as did their influence and impact within the group, but partners were accountable to each other and respected the decisions that were taken. All contributions were welcomed and valued. Further the "shared repertoire" (p. 82) of resources supporting the work of the research partners was substantial. There were physical resources (e.g., compensation for the time collaborating partners gave to the project; access to information; and the ongoing communication of the importance of the project in shaping language teaching and learning in LINC programs). More importantly, however, over the first year of the project, the research partners' joint engagement in the project "create[d] resources for negotiating meaning" (p. 82), and as the project moved forward, practices evolved that contributed to the groups' sense of coherence and its overall effectiveness. However, the situation dramatically changed with the loss of the critical research partner-manager and changes in policy directions.

The lesson to be learned from this experience is that the effectiveness of a transdisciplinary approach is directly dependent upon the quality and stability of the partnerships that sustain it. The essential foundation for TR – which is key to coherence and potential outcomes – is the mutual shared knowledge and understanding, "in the strongest possible light" (Bernstein, 1998, p. 4), of each participating partner. In this case, the sudden departure of the first Project Manager and changes in the taken-for-granted policies governing the working group fundamentally altered the trajectory of the project as a whole.

Once again, power was unequally distributed, and the hierarchy of decision making was distanced and external to the working group itself (Hutchins, 1995a). In such *laminated* spaces that are characterized by highly unequal distributions of power, the scope or latitude for innovation and imagination may remain open and flexible; but the magnitude or impact of innovation may be greatly lessened, given the policy context within which an assessment initiative is embedded (Abdulhamid & Fox, 2020; Fox, 2014). In retrospect, what the working group had taken for granted was that the new Project Manager had the same level of expertise and background knowledge in portfolio assessment as the original Project Manager. At the outset of the project, the original Project Manager had taken care to orient the assessment working group to the vision, purpose, and strategic directions of the assessment initiative. The depth of his knowledge of portfolio assessment initiatives and his experience within the external hierarchy that had mandated the initiative made him particularly effective in bridging gaps between layers of practice and policy external to the working group. His replacement did not have the benefit of this knowledge or experience. Considerable knowledge and expertise was shared within the working group itself, but *we did not take time* to orient the new Project Manager and develop his understanding of the vision and strategic approaches which we had developed over the first year of the project. In retrospect, his understanding of the project was critically important as he was communicating project concerns to decision makers outside the working group. As such, our means of bridging gaps that arose between the motivations and directions of the working group and external policy decisions in the initiative's implementation became problematic and gradually, the coherence of the working group was also undermined.

Context three. Transdisciplinarity at its best (narrated by Janna Fox and Natasha Artemeva)

Having presented two narratives of experience to illustrate challenging transdisciplinary contexts and circumstances, the final narrative highlights a project that exceeded all expectations.

Project initiation

In 2009, Janna proposed a diagnostic assessment procedure at an informal brown bag lunch meeting of Associate Deans, from business, engineering, science, arts, and social science, at a mid-sized Canadian university. She explained that a diagnostic assessment procedure, administered to entering first-year undergraduate students, could identify students who would potentially encounter challenges in meeting the demands of their university program and connect them with immediate academic support tailored to meet their individual needs. Such a procedure held the promise of increasing academic success and reducing attrition.

Shortly thereafter, Janna was contacted by the Associate Dean of Engineering, and plans were negotiated for the development of an engineering-specific diagnostic assessment.[6] Initial research was carried out within undergraduate engineering, and with university colleagues from New Zealand, who had developed the Diagnostic English Language Needs Assessment (DELNA) (e.g., Elder & von Randow, 2008). DELNA operationalized a construct of academic language proficiency and was used to assess all entering undergraduates regardless of degree program. The new diagnostic assessment procedure proposed for engineering was intended to operationalize an LSP construct (see Chapters 5 and 6), diagnose areas of need specific to undergraduate engineering, and provide effective, individualized academic support. By 2011 the new engineering diagnostic assessment was being administered to all entering, first-year undergraduates in engineering. It incorporated three of DELNA's computer-administered tasks; however, it became evident early in the project that the DELNA writing task was not providing a sufficiently *fine grain* of information to allow for tailored individual support relevant to the demands of engineering courses. Based on research with collaborating partners (e.g., engineering faculty, TAs, students, engineering communications instructors, practicing engineers), the focus in test development shifted to the design of engineering-specific writing tasks that could provide more useful information regarding an entering student's preparation for the engineering program.

Ongoing project development, 2011–2019

Although Janna and Natasha had been collaborating on numerous transdisciplinary projects from the early 1990s, in 2011 they formed a new TR partnership for the diagnostic assessment project. Natasha has an engineering degree, has worked as an engineer, and had engaged extensively on various engineering-related and other writing projects. She had developed the curriculum for and coordinated the Engineering Communications Courses which were taken by all engineering students as a degree requirement. Further, she had undertaken extensive research on engineering students' learning trajectories as they transitioned through academic to engineering workplaces.[7]

The transdisciplinary partnerships (see Chapter 6) that were forged at the beginning of the diagnostic assessment project remained integral to it and sustained it over time. Over the years many collaborating partners engaged in the project, including,

- administrators;
- professors;
- lab/course instructors in engineering;

- upper-year undergraduate and graduate students (in engineering, writing studies, teaching English as a second language (TESOL), language assessment);
- postdoctoral fellows;
- first- and second-year undergraduate students in engineering;
- engineering communications instructors;
- teaching assistants;
- coordinators; and
- other faculty who were teaching in the engineering program (e.g., from mathematics, physics, or chemistry, and who taught special courses for engineering students).

As the primary test developers, within applied linguistics and discourse studies (ALDS), Janna and Natasha had ongoing responsibility for conducting research to support:

- the technical quality of the assessment;
- train raters and monitor their consistency;
- develop learning profiles for individual engineering students;
- link profiles to recommended pedagogical intervention;
- meet on an ongoing basis with collaborating partners to exchange ideas and discuss issues; and
- conduct ongoing validation.

The Associate Dean in engineering had primary responsibility for coordinating the administration of the assessment and managing follow-up academic support within engineering.

There was active and ongoing engagement of research partners from different faculties, with different expertise, who contributed to validation research that improved the overall quality and usefulness of the assessment. Table 8.1 illustrates the components of the diagnostic assessment that was developed, and some of the academic risk factors that it addressed (see also Chapter 6).

An important spinoff of the diagnostic assessment procedure was the development of an engineering-specific Academic Support Centre, staffed jointly by exceptional students from the upper years of undergraduate engineering and by graduate student in ALDS, with backgrounds in writing studies, technical communications, teaching (e.g., TESOL/TESL, EAP, writing), and discourse studies. Engineering and ALDS staff worked jointly with first-year undergraduate engineering students (providing specific/targeted support for students identified by the diagnostic assessment as potentially at risk). Although specialized approaches were taken with students in need of academic support, the Centre was open to all entering, first-year engineering students. Use of the academic support offered by the Centre was voluntary – students were free to use it or not, regardless of their results on the diagnostic assessment (see Chapter 6).

Table 8.1 Diagnostic assessment procedure: components and risk factors

Components of the diagnostic assessment	*Risk factors*
Questionnaire (background, attitudes, self-assessment)	Transfers from other university programs; first in family to attend university; no contact with engineers or engineering; disinclined to build social networks, ask questions, or ask for clarification or help
Computerized tasks	
Academic vocabulary (DELNA)	Limited knowledge of word meaning/use in academic English [Significant predictor, in year one, of failure or withdrawal]
Reading (DELNA)	Limited proficiency in English
Writing tasks	
Graph interpretation task (embedded in first lecture and lab of required, introductory engineering course)	Did not follow instructions; misunderstood the task and/or engineering expectations [Significant predictor, in year one, of failure or withdrawal]
Email task (simulated co-op placement context)	Did not follow instructions; failure to understand the task, engineering expectations
Mathematics tasks (Engineering/ Mathematics task developers)	Issues with threshold knowledge; identification of curricular gaps in engineering program

Source: Adapted from Fox & Artemeva (April, 2018); Beynen & Fox (July, 2018)

This transdisciplinary project was enormously successful. The assessment became increasingly refined in identifying issues in a student's learning profile that might cause difficulty; interventions were individualized, and there was increasing evidence of the positive influence of early diagnosis and academic support in students' retention and success. The three dimensions of a CoP (Wenger, 1998; Wenger-Trayner & Wenger-Trayner, 2015; Wenger-Trayner et al., 2015) were evident. On the whole, CoP members shared common understandings, contributed enthusiastically, and engaged productively with one another. This was a joint enterprise and over time collaborating partners developed a "shared repertoire" (Wenger, 1998, p. 82) of resources to maintain and improve the quality of the project. Further, the joint participation of ALDS and engineering students in the Academic Support Centre was an ongoing source of evidence for improving the effectiveness of the assessment and the quality of pedagogical interventions. Although members of the CoP fluctuated over the years as student members graduated and new students/ members were mentored into the group, the collective understanding, experience, and practices built up by the core engineering and ALDS project members remained constant throughout.

During this TR project, the collaborating partners experienced the magic, excitement, and sense of fulfillment that such projects can produce.

The spinoff of the Centre to support engineering students' academic work is physical evidence of substantive institutional change that took place as an unanticipated positive consequence of the project. It has become a hub in engineering – a gathering place for the undergraduate student community. The collection of resources developed by the tutors in the Centre provide a rich repository of resources which has extended from tutors past to tutors present and is linked directly to the initial courses in the program. Aggregate feedback from the results of the diagnostic assessment identified gaps in students' preparation for engineering courses and was drawn on to inform curricular and course changes.

There was significant improvement in retention and overall academic success for those students who worked with tutors in the Centre. Of continuing concern were students who needed support (based on the diagnosis) but did not take advantage of the support that was offered to them (Fox & Artemeva, 2017). Uptake was the choice of the student (there were no penalties or requirements imposed). Knoch, Elder, and O'Hagan (2016) acknowledge similar concerns in other *voluntary uptake* post-admission diagnostic initiatives. However, over time the Centre increasingly attracted more students – both high-achieving students and students who were experiencing initial difficulties in their programs. Uptake gradually increased as the word spread about the usefulness of the Centre. At times the tutors working in the Academic Support Centre complained they were *too busy*, but this was ultimately more evidence of the success of the diagnostic assessment and follow-up support. Indeed, their *complaints* (and the Centre's obvious popularity and success) resulted in its renovation and expansion.

Over the years of the engineering diagnostic assessment project, there has been latitude for change, initiative, innovation, and growth, and the magnitude or power to influence changes has remained constant due to the mutual engagement of the TR partners.

What can we learn about transdisciplinarity from these three narratives of experience?

Although all research spaces are emergent, *laminated*, dynamic, and unstable to a degree, TR spaces (given their complexity) are markedly so. As illustrated by each of the three narratives of experience considered here, transdisciplinary projects often require a longer commitment of time and the continuity of a core number of partnerships is essential in maintaining and sustaining their quality. Prior to engaging in a TR project, it is useful to take stock of both *latitude* (i.e., the scope and potential for innovation in relation to the embeddedness of the project in hierarchies of power) and *magnitude* (i.e., the power of participant members and the research team to control or influence research trajectories). These notions have proved to be useful in unpacking experience in transdisciplinary projects, as have social theories such as distributed cognition, and communities of practice. Wenger's (1998) unit of analysis was helpful in relation to the other ideas that it has attracted, including Scollon's (2001) nexus of practice and Prior's (2003) explanation of lamination.

Narratives of experience are prominent in the curricular literature. It should not be surprising that we recommend resources from this literature (e.g., theories, methodologies, empirical research, expertise) as particularly useful for transdisciplinary assessment research projects (e.g., Clandinin & Connelly, 2000; Connelly & Clandinin, 2006). Validation and concerns for validity are fundamental in curriculum: much foundational work in conceptualizations of validity originated in program evaluation related to curricular reform agendas (e.g., Cronbach, 1988). The traditional *end-of-project/summative evaluation* of an initiative or existing program has been joined by *developmental or formative approaches* to program evaluation, in which evaluators engage in providing expertise and input *in process* to support the use-focused, ultimate success of an initiative. Although there are debates within program evaluation communities about such a change in the role of evaluators, and some view the narrower traditional role as appropriate and developmental approaches as "crossing the line" (see, Patton, 2012, p. 160 for a discussion of this debate), the array of perspectives, models for framing practice, and analytical approaches (e.g., questionnaires, checklists, communication gambits, strategic assessment grids, exercises) provide a remarkably useful resource for transdisciplinary initiatives. Further, as previously noted, the tradition of *action inquiry* shares much in common with transdisciplinary approaches to research and offers a wealth of information, strategies, and experience (e.g., Bradbury-Huang, 2015; Mertler, 2019; Reason & Bradbury, 2008) for navigating the "productive tension" (Moss & Haertel, 2016, p. 37) and "profitable confusion" (Paré, 2008, p. 20) of transdisciplinary assessment research – *in the wild*.

Toward a socially informed, transdisciplinary dialogue on context and validity

Recognition of the need to better address the role of context in assessment practices and concern for the disconnect between communities focused on *language* and on *assessment* motivated the publication of this book. We were guided by both Messick (1989) and Cronbach (1988), who voiced concerns for the consequences, actions, and decisions that result from assessment-in-use, *in context* – concerns that continue to be voiced today (cf. Moss, 2016, 2018; Turner, 2018). During the period when Messick and Cronbach were shaping what continue to be prevailing conceptualizations of validity, acerbic debates were raging between members of research communities over the merit and appropriacy of differing research approaches. At a philosophic or ideologic level, these approaches were considered incompatible. As discussed in Chapter 2, during the period labelled the *paradigm wars* (Gage, 1989), the most vociferous debates appeared to decline owing to: the rise of qualitative research approaches; movement away from the staunchly ideologic epistemological, and methodological stances of the warring research communities; and increasing acceptance of pragmatic, mixed methods approaches to research. However, as Bryman (2008) has pointed out, the paradigm wars may not have ended. The current situation may be more aptly described as an uneasy peace or "détente" (p. 23). For example, Bryman identified emerging trends toward new orthodoxies (e.g., prioritizing quantitative over qualitative findings in educational research, and removing qualitative research approaches from required university course offerings in psychology).

Notably, the 2017 editorial in the *International Journal of Qualitative Methods,* entitled "It's a New Year ... So let's stop the paradigm wars" (Given, 2017), provides an important commentary on the state-of-understanding of qualitative research practices. After many years of experience with qualitative research in academia, Given complained about the "general lack of awareness of qualitative research practices" (p. 1), and lamented the ongoing need for qualitative researchers to explain and defend their research decisions:

> While many of us descry the notion of the paradigm wars – and dismiss the simplistic notion that there is a qualitative "camp" and a quantitative camp on opposing sides of a great abyss – the casualties of this war continue to approach me at workshops, in classrooms, and in my office, looking for advice and support as they navigate the pathways to grant-writing, publishing, and career advancement.
>
> (p. 2)

It is our view that such trends, if they prevail, will again deter researchers from addressing complex assessment questions, such as the role of context in assessment validation practices, and undermine forward movement in language assessment research as a whole. The contervailing, emergent trend – the call for transdisciplinary dialogue and engagement – suggests a promising alternative, and one which we argue is in keeping with validity theory and validation practices.[8]

At the end of their academic careers, both Cronbach and Messick suggested how best to proceed. Cronbach (1988) argued for the ongoing identification and interrogation of *plausible rival* explanations for assessment outcomes. Messick (1998) expressed a similar hope that "multiple perspectives of interacting inquiry systems and exposure of the value bases of scientific models would facilitate convergent and discriminant arguments penetrating the theory-laden and value-laden character of particular data" (p. 36). Both advised "patience" (Cronbach, 1988, p. 14) and persistence, and warned of "tension" that would "need to be negotiated in validation practice" (Messick, 1998, p. 37). Moss (1998), in response, argued that Messick's view was fundamentally *dialectic* – "always open to other perspectives and critically reflexive in light of those challenges" (p. 55). Her prescient observations foretold the promise of the movement toward increased appreciation for, and understanding and application of alternative theories (e.g., social theories), TR agendas in validation, and methodological pluralism which, we argue, offer a better means of addressing the role of context in language assessment.

Disciplines are *freeing* in that they create a zone of comfort due to shared understandings, values, knowledge, cultures – but they are also constraining. They develop their own ways of doing, being, and sharing and have a tendency to conservative rather than innovative activity. Disciplines tend to *value* in relation to what is known and recognizable as having value within their communities. Stringent disciplinary perspectives and practices can impede interactions between disciplinary communities – even though the communities may share a common interest in a problem, and approaching that issue or problem from different perspectives might increase the potential for new understanding, knowledge, and innovation.

Many research opportunities are currently being overlooked because of narrower rather than broader perspectives. For example, at a higher education conference with the theme *Student success and the first-year experience*, a doctoral candidate in psychology questioned case study findings that were presented by a doctoral candidate in applied linguistics, asking, "What's the point, you only had two participants?" A professor of economics agreed with the student in psychology adding, "Right. You had to have at least ten participants for your study". The applied linguist replied somewhat defensively, "This was a longitudinal qualitative study. I interviewed and observed the two participants at intervals for four years. In applied linguistics there are many award-winning research articles that involve fewer than ten participants". The psychology student responded: "Whether you have ten or two, I still don't see the point. What can you possibly do with your findings?"

The exchange between these three academics illustrated for us the challenges posed by the practices that are engrained in disciplinary cultures. The three academics shared common interests in issues related to student success. Working together, they might have had a better chance of improving student success in first year – but that would require "openness, flexibility, and attention to the diversity and uncertainty in knowledge" (Weichselgartner & Truffer, 2015, p. 89).

Most would agree that student attrition in the first year of university is a big problem. Most would also agree with the aphorism that big, complex problems typically require big, *outside-the-box* thinking to resolve them. In the 1970s, the Apollo space program addressed the *big problem* of how to land humans on the moon and bring them safely back to earth by drawing on experts and expertise from exceptionally diverse disciplines. Although approximately 50% had backgrounds in engineering, 17 different engineering disciplines were listed in a 1985 report of the Personnel Evaluation and Analysis Office, NASA Headquarters (retrieved from www.history.nasa.gov/SP-4104/appb.htm). The other 50% were drawn from an extraordinary range of nearly 30 disciplines (e.g., agriculture, architecture, statistics, computer science, science, mathematics, physics, chemistry, biology, education, psychology, social sciences, communication, interdisciplinary studies, to name a few). They pulled together, overriding disciplinary differences in order to solve the many challenging and perplexing problems of travel in space.

Evidence of their effective teamwork in addressing complex problems related to the Apollo space missions is well documented for history, and a dramatization of the teamwork during an emergency incident is provided in the film *Apollo 13*. On the return flight from the moon, an oxygen tank exploded, damaging the capsule in which three astronauts were travelling. Because the capsule was losing both power and oxygen, in order to save the astronauts, the NASA team needed to solve the problem from the ground, using only items that were available to the astronauts in the spacecraft. If the film's account is correct, this amounted to three small cardboard boxes of random tubes, duct tape, astronauts' suits, etc. Under pressure of time, in a life-or-death situation, the team on the ground worked together and found a solution.

The issue of context in language assessment validation research is not manifested in a finite number of physical objects, manipulated by teams of experts with very little time, and with dramatic, immediate, life-or-death consequences. However, though less dramatic in the short term, the issue of the validity of inferences drawn from assessment outcomes is nonetheless of extraordinary consequence for those who have a stake in it. Assessment practices shape life trajectories, opportunities, or constraints; and the role of context in considerations of validity remains an undertheorized and underresolved problem that is particularly evident in language assessment validation.

Our point is this: big problems cannot be addressed by single disciplinary approaches alone – however richly informative these are within the boundaries of their disciplinary communities. Following Pohl and Hirsch Hadorn (2007),

> There is a need for TR [transdisciplinary research] when knowledge about a societally relevant problem field is uncertain, when the concrete nature of problems is disputed, and when there is a great deal at stake for those concerned by problems and involved in dealing with them.
>
> (p. 20)

Moss and Haertel (2016) stress the need for deeply collaborative and collective *transdisciplinary* approaches to address complex issues, questions, and problems (typically characteristic of social phenomena, processes, actions, and outcomes). We concur. The issue of context in language assessment validation research is one such problem. Collaboration begins with the acknowledgement of, and respect for, alternative worldviews, practices, and traditions; knowledge which activates curiosity; and a willingness to engage beyond the confines and comforts of what we know now and what we know how to do now, and an openess to the possibilities afforded by the alternative perspectives of others.

Looking back over the chapters in this book, we realized how often we used metaphors related to *light* in recounting TR orientations and experiences (e.g., *strongest possible light*, *highlight*, *illuminate*). This speaks to our foundational understanding of what transdisciplinary perspectives and social theories can contribute to validation by contextualizing assessment practices. Generating new *conversations* among knowledgeable and experienced colleagues within and outside academia and engaging in research together, in the *in-between* spaces of TR practice, promises to throw new light on complex problems and move our research agendas forward.

Notes

1 Gee (2004), Prior (2003), and Scollon (2001) have problematized the notion of communities of practice. Scollon preferred the less "problematical" concept of a "nexus of practice", which was "unbounded", unlike the notion of a *community*, and acknowledged that "most practices ... can be linked variably to different practices in different sites of engagement and among different participants" (p. 5).

2 Prior (2003) also provided an extensive discussion of the word *community* in the term *discourse community* (e.g., Swales 1988, 1990). Discourse communities have not been fully discussed in this book. Readers interested in discourse communities are referred to the work of Swales (1988, 1990, 2016), who originally defined discourse communities as "socio-rhetorical networks that form in order to work towards sets of common goals" (p. 8). This concept has been problematized and extensively reconsidered in the literature (Freedman & Medway, 1994; Prior, 2003). See particularly Swales' (2016, 2017) reflections on the concept of discourse communities, which he more recently described as "an old warhorse [that is] ... being brought back for active duty" (Swales, 2017), in a post entitled "The concept of discourse community: some recent personal history". The post is followed by the article "Reflections on the concept of discourse community/Le concept de communauté de discours: Quelques réflexions", *Composition Forum* 37 (Fall, 2017), available at http://compositionforum.com/issue/37/swales-retrospective.php.

3 Recent experience with a colleague from education highlighted again the issues of word choice in terms of the disciplinary socio-historical/sociocultural perspectives, associations, or collocations a word suggests. The colleague was opposed to using either *teachers* or *stakeholders* in a conference abstract, arguing passionately for *practitioners* instead. In her view, *stakeholder* carried with it the ideology of neoliberal agendas, and *teacher* was too reductive in relation to the hierarchy of power relationships inherent in educational institutions. Practitioner was her choice. As Bakhtin (1981b) famously noted, "Language is not a neutral medium that passes freely and easily into the private property of the speaker's intentions; it is populated – overpopulated – with

the intentions of others" (p. 294). The negotiation of the word *practitioner* in the conference abstract was yet another reminder of Bakhtin's observation.

4 Gee (2000) is particularly critical of Wenger's (1998) terminology and examples (see references in Wenger to *joint enterprise* and the use of an insurance company's employees/claims processors as an illustration). Gee argued that Wenger (1998) had unreflectively situated dimensions of a CoP within the ideologies, identities, and practices of global capitalistic agendas.

5 Within the tradition of narrative inquiry, storying experience is a means of making sense of it: a way of capturing it as a process, imposing coherence, and learning from it. It was interesting to reflect on the concerns we had for using this approach in the final chapter of this book. How would readers with backgrounds in measurement or psychometrics deal with these stories as data for analysis? We realized how far away from their dominant traditions of research these narratives of experience are. In writing a book that argues for transdisciplinarity, we decided this was a key turning point for us and for our intended readers. Would some simply put down the book at this point, consider it "*fluffy*", "*distracting*", or "*unhelpful*" (as some colleagues have suggested to us over the years), or would they read, reflect, keep an open mind, and take the chance that what others have valued in storying might offer more than was first expected?

6 We wish to thank Donald Russell, Professor/Associate Dean of Engineering, Carleton University, for his engagement as a research partner throughout the life of the diagnostic assessment project, and Malcolm Bibby, Professor/Dean of Engineering, Carleton University, who saw the potential of a diagnostic approach and whose initial support was the catalyst for its development.

7 As noted at the beginning of this book, we have collaborated on various TR projects for over 25 years, and that collaboration is culminating in the work undertaken for this book. We have reported widely on the diagnostic assessment project (e.g., Artemeva & Fox, 2010; Fox & Artemeva, 2017; Fox, Haggerty, & Artemeva, 2016), and other TR projects involving multiple research partners (e.g., Artemeva & Fox, 2011; Fox & Artemeva, 2011).

8 See Teddlie and Tashakkori (2010) for a discussion of alternative positions on the "*either-or*" traditional, paradigmatic conceptual stances of quantitative and qualitative practices. They argue for a "broad inquiry logic" and principled "methodological eclecticism" (p. 5). See also, Moss and Haertel, 2016, re. *engaging methodological pluralism*; and Niglas (2010): "from dichotomies to continua in philosophies and methodologies" (p. 216).

References

Abbott, A. D. (2001). *Chaos of disciplines*. Chicago, IL: University of Chicago Press.

Abdulhamid, N., & Fox, J. (2020). Portfolio Based Language Assessment (PBLA) in language instruction for newcomers to Canada (LINC) programs: Taking stock of teachers' experience. *Canadian Journal of Applied Linguistics/Revue canadienne de linguistique appliquée, 23*(2), 168–192. doi:10.37213/cjal.2020.31121

Abedi, J. (2004). The No Child Left Behind Act and English language learners: Assessment and accountability issues. *Educational Researcher, 33*(1), 4–14.

Abrami, P., & Barrett, H. (2005). Directions for research and development on electronic portfolios. *Canadian Journal of Learning and Technology/La revue canadienne de l'apprentissage et de la technologie, 31*(3). doi:10.21432/T2RK5K

Addey, C., Maddox, B., & Zumbo, B. D. (2020). Assembled validity: Rethinking Kane's argument-based approach in the context of International Large-Scale Assessments (ILSAs). *Assessment in Education: Principles, Policy & Practice, 27*(6), 588–606. doi:10.1080/0969594X.2020.1843136

Adler, G. (1885). *Umfang, methode und ziel der musikwissenschaft* [The scope, method, and aim of musicology]. Leipzig, Germany: Breitkopf und Härtel.

Alderson, J. C. (1991). Language testing in the 1990s: How far have we come? How much further have we to go? In A. Sarinee (Ed.), *Current developments in language testing. Anthology series 25* (pp. 1–26). Paper presented at the Regional Language Centre Seminar on Language Testing and Language Programme Evaluation (April 9–12, 1990); see FL 021 757. ED 365 145 [Eric Document].

Alderson, J. C. (1993). The state of language testing in the 1990s. In A. Huhta, K. Sajavaara, & S. Takala (Eds.), *Language testing: New openings* (pp. 1–19). Jyväskylä, Finland: University of Jyväskylä.

Alderson, J. C. (2011). The politics of aviation English testing. *Language Assessment Quarterly, 8*(4), 386–403. doi:10.1080/15434303.2011.622017

Alderson, J. C., & Wall, D. (1993). Does washback exist? *Applied Linguistics, 14*(2), 115–129.

Alderson, J. C., Brunfaut, T., & Harding, L. (2014). Towards a theory of diagnosis in second and foreign language assessment: Insights from professional practice across diverse fields. *Applied Linguistics, 36*(2), 236–260. doi:10.1093/applin/amt046

Allee, V. (2000). Knowledge networks and communities of practice. *OD Practitioner, 32(4)*. Retrieved from http://methodenpool.uni-koeln.de/communities/~%20OD%20Practitioner%20Online%20-%20Vol_%2032%20-%20No_%204%20(2000)%20~.htm

American Educational Research Association, American Psychological Association, and National Council on Measurement in Education. (1985). *Standards for educational and psychological testing*. Washington, DC: American Educational Research Association.

American Educational Research Association, American Psychological Association, and National Council on Measurement in Education. (1999). *Standards for educational and psychological testing*. Washington, DC: American Educational Research Association.

American Educational Research Association, American Psychological Association, and National Council on Measurement in Education. (2014). *Standards for educational and psychological testing*. Washington, DC: American Educational Research Association.

Anastasi, A. (1986). Evolving concepts of test validation. *Annual Review of Psychology, 37*, 1–15.

Anderson, T. (2016). Theories for learning with emerging technologies. In G. Veletsianos (Ed.), *Emergence and innovation in digital learning: Foundations and applications* (pp. 35–50). Edmonton, AB: Athabasca University Press.

Angoff, W. H. (1988). Validity: An evolving concept. In H. Wainer & H. Braun (Eds.), *Test validity* (pp. 9–13). Hillsdale, NJ: Lawrence Erlbaum.

Aragão, B. F. (2018). O uso de critérios autóctones no contexto aeronáutico: Contribuições para uma nova escala de proficiência para controladores de tráfego aéreo [The use of indigenous assessment criteria in the aeronautical context: Contributions to a new proficiency rating scale to air traffic controllers]. In M. V. R. Scaramucci, P. Tosqui-Lucks, & S. M. Damião (Eds.), *Pesquisas sobre Inglês Aeronáutico no Brasil* (pp. 243–269). Campinas, SP, Brazil: Pontes Editores.

Arias, A., & Schissel, J. L. (2021). How are multilingual communities of practice being considered in language assessment? A language ecology approach. *Journal of Multilingual Theories and Practices*, 2(2), 141–153.

Artemeva, N. (2004). Key concepts in rhetorical genre studies: An overview. *Discourse and Writing/Rédactologie, 20*(1), 3–38.

Artemeva, N. (2005). A time to speak, a time to act: A Rhetorical Genre Analysis of a novice engineer's calculated risk taking. *Journal of Business and Technical Communication, 19*(4), 389–421. doi:10.1177/1050651905278309

Artemeva, N. (2006). Approaches to learning genres: A bibliographical essay. In N. Artemeva & A. Freedman (Eds.), *Rhetorical genre studies and beyond* (pp. 9–99). Winnipeg, MB: Inkshed Publications.

Artemeva, N. (2008). Toward a unified theory of genre learning. *Journal of Business and Technical Communication* 22(2), 160–185. doi:10.1177/1050651907311925

Artemeva, N., & Fox, J. (2010). Awareness versus production: Probing students' antecedent genre knowledge. *Journal of Business and Technical Communication, 24*, 476–515. doi:10.1177/1050651910371302

Artemeva, N., & Fox, J. (2011). The writing's on the board: The global and the local in teaching undergraduate mathematics through chalk talk. *Written Communication, 28*, 345–379. doi:10.1177/0741088311419630

Artemeva, N., & Freedman, A. (2001). "Just the boys playing on computers": An Activity Theory analysis of differences in the cultures of two engineering firms. *Journal of Business and Technical Communication, 15*(2), 164–194.

Artemeva, N., & Freedman, A. (Eds). (2015). *Genres studies around the globe: Beyond the three traditions*. Edmonton, AB: Inkshed Publications.

Artemeva, N., Rachul, C., O'Brien, B., & Varpio, L. (2017). Situated learning in medical education. *Academic Medicine, 92*(1), 134–134.

Assessment Reform Group. (2002). *Assessment for learning: 10 principles*. London, UK: Assessment Reform Group. Retrieved from www.aaia.org.uk/storage/medialibrary/o_1d8j89n3u1n0u17u91fdd1m4418fh8.pdf.

Bachman, L. F. (1990). *Fundamental considerations in language testing*. Oxford, UK: Oxford University Press.

Bachman, L. F. (2007). What is the construct? The dialectic of abilities and contexts in defining constructs in language assessment. In J. Fox, et al. (Eds.), *Language testing reconsidered* (pp. 41–71). Ottawa, ON: Ottawa University Press.

Baker, W. (2011). Intercultural awareness: Modelling an understanding of cultures in intercultural communication through English as a lingua franca. *Language and Intercultural Communication, 11*(3), 197–214. doi:10.1080/14708477.2011.577779

Baker, W. (2012). From cultural awareness to intercultural awareness: Culture in ELT. *ELT Journal, 66*(1), 62–70. doi:10.1093/elt/ccr017

Baker, W. (2015). Culture and complexity through English as a lingua franca: Rethinking competences and pedagogy in ELT. *Journal of English as a Lingua Franca, 4*(1), 9–30. doi:10.1515/jelf-2015-0005

Baker, W. (2016). Culture and language in intercultural communication, English as a lingua franca and English language teaching: Points of convergence and conflict. In P. Holmes & F. Derwin (Eds.), *The cultural and intercultural dimensions of English as a lingua franca (1)* (pp. 70–89). Bristol, UK: Channel View Publications. https://ebookcentral.proquest.com

Baker, W. (2017). English as a lingua franca and intercultural communication. In J. Jenkins, W. Baker, & M. Dewey (Eds.), *The Routledge handbook of English as a lingua franca* (Chapter 2). London, UK: Routledge. https://ebookcentral.proquest.com

Bakhtin, M. M. (1981a). Forms of time and of the chronotope in the novel: Notes towards a historical poetics. In M. Holquist (Ed.), *The dialogic imagination: Four essays by M. M. Bakhtin* (C. Emerson & M. Holquist, Trans.) (pp. 84–258). Austin, TX: University of Texas Press.

Bakhtin, M. M. (1981b). Discourse in the novel. In M. Holquist (Ed.), *The dialogic imagination: Four essays by M. M. Bakhtin* (C. Emerson & M. Holquist, Trans.) (pp. 259–422). Austin, TX: University of Texas Press.

Bakhtin, M. M. (1986). The problem of speech genres. In C. Emerson & M. Holquist (Eds.) (V. W. McGee, Trans.), *Speech genres and other late essays* (pp. 60–102). Austin, TX: University of Texas Press. (Original work published 1979).

Balsiger, P. (2004). Supradisciplinary research practices: History, objectives and rationale. *Futures, 36*(4), 407–421. doi:10.1016/j.futures.2003.10.002

Bandura, A. (1977). *Social learning theory*. Englewood Cliffs, NJ: Prentice Hall.

Bandura, A. (1986). *Social foundations of thought and action: A social cognitive theory*. Englewood Cliffs, NJ: Prentice-Hall.

Barker, R. G. (1968). *Ecological psychology: Concepts and methods for studying the environment of human behavior*. Stanford, CA: Stanford University Press.

Bass, R. (2012). Disrupting ourselves: The problem of learning in higher education. *EDUCAUSE Review, 47*(2). Retrieved from https://net.educause.edu/i

Bawarshi, A. (2000). The genre function. *College English, 62*(3), 335–360.

Bawarshi, A. (2015). Accounting for genre performances: Why uptake matters. In N. Artemeva & A. Freedman (Eds.), *Genre studies around the globe: Beyond the three traditions* (pp. 186–206). Edmonton, AB: Inkshed Publications.

Bawarshi, A. S., & Reiff, M. J. (2010). *Genre: An introduction to history, theory, research, and pedagogy*. Parlor Press LLC and WAC Clearinghouse. Retrieved from https://wac.colostate.edu/docs/books/bawarshi_reiff/genre.pdf

Bazerman, C. (1982). Scientific writing as a social act: A review of the literature of the sociology of science. In P. V. Anderson, J. Brockman, & C. R. Miller (Eds.), *New essays in technical and scientific communication: Research, theory, and practice* (pp. 156–184). Farmingdale, NY: Baywood.

Bazerman, C. (1988). *Shaping written knowledge: The genre and activity of the experimental article in science*. Madison, WI: University of Wisconsin Press.

Bazerman, C. (1994a). Systems of genres and the enactment of social intentions. In A. Freedman & P. Medway (Eds.), *Genre and the new rhetoric* (pp. 79–101). London, UK: Taylor & Francis.

Bazerman, C. (1994b). *Constructing experience*. Carbondale and Edwardsville, IL: Southern Illinois University Press.

Bazerman, C. (2003). What is not institutionally visible does not count: The problem of making activity assessable, accountable, and plannable. In C. Bazerman & D. R. Russell (Eds.), *Writing selves/writing societies: Research from activity perspectives* (pp. 428–483). Fort Collins, CO: WAC Clearinghouse. doi:10.37514/PER-B.2003.2317

Beaufort, A. (2004). Developmental gains of a history major: A case for building a theory of disciplinary writing expertise. *Research in the Teaching of English, 39*(2),136–185.

Bhatia, V. K., Flowerdew, J., & Jones, R. H. (Eds.). (2008). *Advances in discourse studies*. London, UK: Routledge.

Becher, T., & Trowler, P. (2001). *Academic tribes and territories* (2nd ed.). Buckingham, UK: Society for Research into Higher Education and Open University Press.

Bennett, R. E. (2010). Cognitively based assessment of, for, and as learning (CBAL): A preliminary theory of action for summative and formative assessment. *Measurement: Interdisciplinary Research & Perspectives, 8*(2–3), 70–91. doi:10.1080/15366367.2010.508686

Berger, P. L., & Luckmann, T. (1966). *The social construction of reality*. London, UK: Penguin.

Berger, P. L., & Luckmann, T. (1967). *The social construction of reality. A treatise in the sociology of knowledge*. Harmondsworth, UK: Penguin Books.

Berkenkotter, C., & Huckin, T. N. (1993). Rethinking genre from a sociocognitive perspective. *Written communication, 10*(4), 475–509.

Berkenkotter, C., & Huckin, T. N. (1995). *Genre knowledge in disciplinary communication: Cognition/culture/power*. Mahwah, NJ: Lawrence Erlbaum Associates.

Bernstein, R. J. (1998). *The new constellation: The ethical-political horizons of Modernity/Postmodernity* (4th ed.). Cambridge, MA: MIT Press.

Bessette, J. (2005). Government French language training programs: Statutory civil servants' experiences (Unpublished master's thesis). University of Ottawa, Ottawa, ON.

Beynen, T., & Fox, J. (July, 2018) *Diagnostic assessment and the transition to university: Fostering success in university.* Paper presented at the conference of the International Test Commission (ITC), Montreal, PQ.

Biesta, G. (2010). Pragmatism and the philosophical foundations of mixed methods research. In A. Tashakkori & C. Teddlie (Eds.), *SAGE handbook of mixed methods in social and behavioral research* (pp. 95–118). Thousand Oaks, CA: SAGE.

Bieswanger, M. (2016). Aviation English: Two distinct specialized registers? In C. Schubert & C. Sanchez-Stockhammer (Eds.), *Variational text linguistics: Revisiting register in English* (pp. 67–85). Berlin, Germany: De Gruyter. Retrieved from https://ebookcentral.proquest.com

Biggs, J., & Tang, C. (2011). *Teaching for quality learning at university: What the student does* (4th ed). Maidenhead, UK: Open University Press.

Bingham, W. V. (1937). *Aptitudes and aptitude testing.* New York, NY. Harper.

Black, P., & Wiliam, D. (1998). Inside the black box: Raising standards through classroom assessment. *Phi Delta Kappan*, 92, 81–90. doi:10.1177/003172171009200119

Blake, R. J. (2008). *Brave new digital classroom: Technology and foreign language learning.* Washington, DC: Georgetown University Press.

Blin, F. (2016). The theory of affordances. In C. Caws & M.-.J Hamel (Eds.), *Language-learner computer interactions* (pp. 41–64). Philadelphia, PA: John Benjamins.

Borsboom, D. (2005). *Measuring the mind.* Cambridge, UK: Cambridge University Press.

Borsboom, D., & Markus, K. A. (2013). Truth and evidence in validity theory. *Journal of Educational Measurement*, *50*, 110–114.

Borsboom, D., Cramer, A. O. J., Keivit, R. A., Scholten, A. Z., & Franic, S. (2009). The end of construct validity. In R. W. Lissitz (Ed.), *The concept of validity: Revisions, new directions, and applications* (pp. 135–170). Charlotte, NC: Information Age.

Borsboom, D., Mellenbergh, G. J., & van Heerden, J. (2004). The concept of validity. *Psychological Review*, *111*, 1061–1071.

Bourdieu, P. (1991). *Language and symbolic power* (G. Raymond and M. Adamson, Trans.). Cambridge, MA: Harvard University Press.

Bradbury-Huang, H. (Ed.). (2015). *The SAGE handbook of action research.* London, UK: SAGE. Retrieved from https://ebookcentral-proquest-com.proxy.library.carleton.ca

Brandist, C. (1997). Bakhtin, Cassirer and symbolic forms. *Radical Philosophy*, *85*, 20–27.

Bransford, J. D., Brown, A. L., & Cocking, R. R. (2000). *How people learn: Brain, mind, experience, and school: Expanded edition.* Retrieved from www.nap.edu/openbook.php?record_id=9853

Britton, J., & Pradl, G. M. (1982). *Prospect and retrospect: Selected essays.* Montclair, NJ: Boynton/Cook Publishers.

Bronfenbrenner, U. (1979). *The ecology of human development: Experiments by nature and design.* Cambridge, MA: Harvard University Press.

Bronfenbrenner, U. (1994). Ecological models of human development. In T. Huston & T. N. Postlethwaith (Eds.), *International encyclopedia of education* (2nd ed., Vol. 3, pp. 1643–1647). New York, NY: Elsevier Science.

Bronfenbrenner, U., & Ceci, S. J. (1994). Nature-nurture reconceptualized in developmental perspective: A bioecological model. *Psychological Review, 101*(4), 568–586. doi:10.1037/0033-295X.101.4.568

Brooks, L. (2009). Interacting in pairs in a test of oral proficiency: Co-constructing a better performance. *Language Testing, 26*(3), 341–366. doi:10.1177/0265532209104666

Brooks, L., & Swain, M. (2014). Contextualizing performances: Comparing performances during TOEFL IBT™ and real-life academic speaking activities. *Language Assessment Quarterly, 11*(4), 353–373. doi:10.1080/15434303.2014.947532

Brown, A. (2003). Interviewer variation and the co-construction of speaking proficiency. *Language Testing, 20*, 1–25.

Brown, J. S., Collins, A., & Duguid, P. (1989). Situated cognition and the culture of learning. *Educational Researcher, 18*(1), 32–42. doi:10.3102/0013189X018001032

Brown, P., & Levinson, S. C. (1987). *Politeness: Some universals in language usage*. Cambridge, UK: Cambridge University Press.

Bruhn, J. G. (2000). Interdisciplinary research: A philosophy, art form, artifact or antidote? *Integrative Psychology and Behavioral Science, 35*, 58–66. doi:10.1007/BF02911166

Bruner, J. (1987). Prologue to the English edition. In R. W. Rieber & A. S. Carton (Eds.), *The collected works of L. S. Vygotsky* (pp. 1–16). Boston, MA: Springer.

Bruner, J. (2002). *Making stories: Law, literature, life*. Cambridge, MA: Harvard University Press.

Bruner, J. S., Goodnow, J., & Austin, G. A. (1956). *A study of thinking*. New York, NY: John Wiley & Sons.

Bryman, A. (2008). The end of the paradigm wars? In P. Alasuutan, L. Bickman, & J. Brannen (Eds.), *The SAGE handbook of social research methods* (pp. 12–25). London, UK: SAGE.

Bryman, A., & Teevan, J. J. (2005). *Social research methods*. Oxford, UK: Oxford University Press.

Bullock, N. (2015, Jun. 26). *Approach, content & method: Wider considerations in teaching English in the context of aeronautical communications* [Conference session]. ICAEA International Aviation English Forum, Warsaw, Poland.

Burgoon, J. K., & Hubbard, M. S. E. (2005). Cross-cultural and intercultural applications of expectancy violations theory and interaction adaptation theory. In W. B. Gudykunst (Ed.), *Theorizing about intercultural communication* (pp. 149–171). Thousand Oaks, CA: SAGE.

Burke, K. (1935). *Permanence and change, an anatomy of purpose*. Berkeley & Los Angeles, CA: University of California Press.

Butler, J. (1997). *The psychic life of power: Theories in subjection*. Stanford, CA: Stanford University Press.

Bygate, M., Skehan, P., & Swain, M. (Eds.). (2001). *Researching pedagogic tasks: Second language learning, teaching, and testing*. Harlow, UK: Pearson Longman.

Byram, M. (1997). *Teaching and assessing intercultural communicative competence*. Clevedon, UK: Multilingual Matters.

Byram, M., & Grundy, P. (2002). Context and culture in language teaching and learning. *Language, Culture, and Curriculum, 15*(3), 193–195.

Callon, M. (1986). Some elements of a sociology of translation: Domestication of the scallops and the fishermen of Saint-Brieuc Bay. In J. Law (Ed.), *Power, action and belief: A new sociology of knowledge? Sociological Review Monograph* 32 (pp. 196–233). London, UK: Routledge and Kegan Paul.

Cambridge University Press (n.d.). Context. In *The Cambridge dictionary*. Retrieved from https://dictionary.cambridge.org/dictionary/english/context

Camic, C., & Joas, H. (Eds.). (2004). *The dialogical turn: New roles for sociology in the postdisciplinary age: Essays in honor of Donald N. Levine*. Lanham, MD: Rowman Littlefield.

Camiciottoli, B. C., & Fortanet-Gómez, I. (2015). *Multimodal analysis in academic settings: From research to teaching*. London, UK: Routledge

Canadian Charter of Rights and Freedoms (1982). Part 1 of the Constitution Act, 1982, being Schedule B to the Canada Act 1982 (UK), 1982, c 11. Retrieved from https://canlii.ca/t/ldsx

Canagarajah, A. S. (1999). *Resisting linguistic imperialism in English teaching*. Oxford, UK: Oxford University Press.

Canagarajah, A. S. (2006). Changing communicative needs, revised assessment objectives: Testing English as an international language. *Language Assessment Quarterly, 3*(3), 229–42. doi:10.1207/s15434311laq0303_1

Canagarajah, A. S. (2007). Lingua franca English, multilingual communities, and language acquisition. *The Modern Language Journal, 91*, 923–939. doi:10.1111/j.1540-4781.2007.00678.x

Canagarajah, A. S. (2011). Codemeshing in academic writing: Identifying teachable strategies of translanguaging. *The Modern Language Journal, 95*(3), 401–417.

Caplan, N. A., & Johns, A. M. (Eds.). (2019). *Changing practices for the L2 writing classroom: Moving beyond the five-paragraph essay*. Ann Arbor, MI: University of Michigan Press.

Carbaugh, D. (2007). Cultural discourse analysis: Communication practices and intercultural encounters. *Journal of Intercultural Communication Research, 36*(3), 167–182. doi:10.1080/17475750701737090

Carroll, J. B. (1961). Fundamental considerations in testing for English proficiency of foreign students. In *Testing the English proficiency of foreign language students* (pp. 30–40). Washington, DC: Centre for Applied Linguistics.

Carroll, J. B. (1968). The psychology of language testing. In A. Davies (Ed.), *Language testing symposium: A psycholinguistic approach* (pp. 46–69). London, UK: Oxford University Press.

Chaiklin, S., & Lave, J. (Eds.). (1996). *Understanding practice: Perspectives on activity and context* (pp. 64–103). Cambridge, UK: Cambridge University Press.

Chalhoub-Deville, M. (2001). Task-based assessments: Characteristics and validity evidence. In M. Bygate, P. Skehan, & M. Swain (Eds.), *Researching pedagogic tasks: Second language learning, teaching and testing* (pp. 210–228). Harlow, UK: Longman.

Chalhoub-Deville, M. (2003). Second language interaction: Current perspectives and future trends. *Language Testing, 20*(4), 369–383. doi:10.1191/0265532203lt264oa

Chalhoub-Deville, M. (2016). Validity theory: Reform policies, accountability testing, and consequences. *Language Testing, 33*(4), 453–472.

Chalhoub-Deville, M., & Deville, C. (2005). A look back at and forward to what language testers measure. In E. Hinkel (Ed.), *Handbook of research in second language teaching and learning* (pp. 815–832). Mahwah, NJ: Lawrence Erlbaum Associates.

Chalhoub-Deville, M., & Tarone, E. (1996). Assessment measures for specific contexts of language use. Paper first presented at the 18th annual meeting of the American Association for Applied Linguistics (Chicago, IL, March 23–26, 1996). Report, ERIC documument (ED 401 721; FL 024 173). Retrieved from https://eric.ed.gov/?q=assessment+measures+for+specific+context+language+use&ft=on&id=ED401721

Chapelle, C. A. (2000). Is networked-based learning CALL? In M. Warschauer & R. Kern (Eds.), *Network-based language teaching: Concepts and practice* (pp. 204–228). New York, NY: Cambridge University Press.

Chapelle, C. A. (2009). The relationship between second language acquisition theory and Computer-Assisted Language Learning. *The Modern Language Journal, 93*(s1), 741–753. doi:10.1111/j.1540-4781.2009.00970.x

Chapelle, C. A. (2021). *Argument-based validation in testing and assessment.* Los Angeles, CA: SAGE.

Chapelle, C. A., Cotos, E., & Lee, J. (2015). Validity arguments for diagnostic assessment using automated writing evaluation. *Language Testing, 32*(3), 385–405.

Chapelle, C. A., Enright, M. K., & Jamieson, J. (2008). *Building a validity argument for the test of English as a foreign language.* New York, NY: Routledge.

Charmaz, K. (2006). *Constructing grounded theory: A practical guide through qualitative analysis*. Los Angeles, CA: SAGE.

Charmaz, K. (2014). *Constructing grounded theory* (2nd ed.). London, UK: SAGE.

Chatterji, M. (Ed.). (2013). *Validity and test use: An international dialogue on educational assessment, accountability, and equity.* Bingley, UK: Emerald Group.

Chen, Y. T. (2012). A study on interactive video-based learning system for learning courseware. *Research Journal of Applied Sciences, Engineering and Technology*, *4*(20), 4132–4137. Retrieved from https://maxwellsci.com/jp/abstract.php?jid=RJASET&no=224&abs=42

Cheng, L. (1997). How does washback influence teaching? Implications for Hong Kong. *Language and Education, 11*(1) 38–54.

Cheng, L. (2014). Consequences, impact, and washback. In A. J. Kunnan (Ed.), *The companion to language assessment: Evaluation, methodology and interdisciplinary themes (Vol. III, Part 9: Designing Evaluations)* (pp. 1130–1146). Chichester, UK: John Wiley & Sons. doi:10.1002/9781118411360.wbcla071

Cheng, L., & Fox, J. (2013). Review of doctoral research in language assessment in Canada (2006–2011). *Language Teaching: Surveys and Studies, 46*, 518–544. doi:10.1017/S0261444813000244

Cheng, L., & Fox, J. (2017). *Assessment for the language classroom.* London, UK: Palgrave Macmillan.

Cheng, L., Andrews, S., & Yu, Y. (2011). Impact and consequences of school-based assessment (SBA): Students' and parents' views of SBA in Hong Kong. *Language Testing, 28*(2), 221–249.

Cheng, L., Watanabe, Y., & Curtis (Eds.). (2004). *Washback in language testing: Research contexts and methods*. Mahwah, NJ: Lawrence Erlbaum.

Chomsky, N. (1957). *Syntactic structures*. The Hague, NL: Mouton.

Christ, T. W. (2010). Teaching mixed methods and action research: Pedagogical, practical, and evaluative consideration. In A. Tashakkori & C. Teddlie (Eds.), *SAGE handbook of mixed methods in social & behavioral research* (2nd ed., pp. 643–676). Thousand Oaks, CA: SAGE.

Churchman, C. W. (1971). *The design of inquiring systems: Basic concepts of system and organization*. New York, NY: Basic Books.

Cizek, G. J. (2012). Defining and distinguishing validity: Interpretations of score meaning and justifications of test use. *Psychological Methods*, *17*(1), 31–43. doi:10.1037/a0026975

Cizek, G. J. (2020). *Validity: An integrated approach to test score meaning and use*. New York, NY: Routledge.

Clandinin, D. J., & Connelly, F M. (2000). *Narrative inquiry: Experience and story in qualitative research*. San Francisco, CA: Jossey-Bass.

Clandinin, D. J., & Rosiek, J. (2007). Mapping a landscape of narrative inquiry. In D. J. Clandidn (Ed.), *Handbook of narrative inquiry: Mapping a methodology* (pp. 35–76). Thousand Oaks, CA: SAGE.

Clark, J. E., & Eynon, B. (2009). E-portfolios at 2.0 – Surveying the field. *Peer Review*, *11*(1), 18–23.

Coe, R. M. (1990). *Process, form, and substance: A rhetoric for advanced writers* (2nd ed.). Englewood Cliffs, NJ: Prentice Hall.

Coe, R. M. (1994). "An arousing and fulfillment of desires": The rhetoric of genre in the process era and beyond. In A. Freedman & P. Medway (Eds.), *Genre and the new rhetoric* (pp. 181–190). London, UK: Taylor Francis.

Coe, R., Lingard, L., & Teslenko, T. (2002). Genre, strategy, and *differance*: An introduction. In R. Coe, L. Lingard, & T. Teslenko (Eds.), *The rhetoric and ideology of genre: Strategies for stability and change* (pp. 1–10). Cresskill, NJ: Hampton Press.

Cogo, A. (2009). Accommodating difference in ELF conversations: A study of pragmatic strategies. In A. Mauranen & E. Ranta (Eds.), *English as a lingua franca: Studies and findings* (pp. 254–273). Newcastle upon Tyne, UK: Cambridge Scholars.

Cogo, A. (2015). English as a lingua franca. Descriptions, domains and applications. In H. Bowles & A. Cogo (Eds.), *International perspectives on English as a lingua franca: Pedagogical insights* (pp. 1–12). London, UK: Palgrave McMillan.

Cogo, A., & Dewey, M. (2006). Efficiency in ELF communication: From pragmatic motives to lexicogrammatical innovation. *Nordic Journal of English Studies 5*(2), 59–94. Retrieved from http://ub016045.ub.gu.se/ojs/index.php/njes/article/view/65/69

Cogo, A., & Dewey, M. (2012). *Analysing English as a lingua franca: A corpus-driven investigation*. London, UK: Continuum.

Cole, M. (1985). The zone of proximal development: Where culture and cognition create each other. In J. V. Wertz (Ed). *Culture, communication and cognition: Vygotskian perspectives* (pp. 146–161). Cambridge, UK: Cambridge University Press.

Cole, M. (1995). Socio-cultural-historical psychology: Some general remarks and a proposal for a new kind of cultural-genetic methodology. In J. V. Wertsch, P. del Río, & A. Alvarez (Eds.), *Sociocultural studies of mind* (pp. 187–214). Cambridge, UK: Cambridge University Press. doi:10.1017/CBO9781139174299.010

Cole, M. (2003, June 22–27). *Vygotsky and context. Where did the connection come from? and What difference does it make?* [Paper presentation]. Biennial conference of the International Society for Theoretical Psychology, June 22–27, Istanbul, Turkey. Retrieved from www.lchc.ucsd.edu/People/MCole/lsvcontext.htm

Cole, M., & Wertsch, J. V. (1996). Beyond the individual–social antinomy in discussions of Piaget and Vygotsky. *Human Development, 39*(5), 250–256.

Collins, A., Brown, J. S., & Newman, S. (1989). Cognitive apprenticeship: Teaching the crafts of reading, writing and mathematics. In L. B. Resnick (Ed.), *Knowing, learning, and instruction* (pp. 453–493). Hillsdale, NJ: Lawrence Erlbaum.

Common Core State Standards Initiative. (n.d.). Retrieved from www.corestandards.org.

Connelly, F. M., & Clandinin, D. J. (1990). Stories of experience and narrative inquiry. *Educational Researcher, 19*(5), 2–14. doi:10.2307/1176100

Connelly, F. M., & Clandinin, D. J. (2006). Narrative inquiry. In J. L. Green, G. Camilli, & P. Elmore (Eds.), *Handbook of complementary methods in education research* (3rd ed., pp. 477–487). Mahwah, NJ: Lawrence Erlbaum.

Cooper, M., & Holzman, M. (1989). *Writing as social action.* Portsmouth, NH: Boynton.

Coste, D., de Pietro, J., & Moore, D. (2012). Hymes and the palimpsest of communicative competence: A journey in language didactics. *Langage et société, 139*, 103–123. doi:10.3917/ls.139.0103

Creswell, J. W. (2015) *A concise introduction to mixed methods research.* Los Angeles, CA: SAGE.

Creswell, J. W., & Plano Clark, V. L. (2011). *Designing and conducting mixed methods research* (2nd ed.). Thousand Oaks, CA: SAGE.

Cronbach, L. J. (1971). Test validity. In R. L. Thorndike (Ed,), *Educational measurement* (2nd ed., pp. 443–507). Washington, DC: American Council on Education.

Cronbach, L. J. (1988). Five perspectives on validity argument. In H. Wainer & H. Braun (Eds.), *Test validity* (pp. 3–17). Hillsdale, NJ: Erlbaum.

Cronbach, L. J., & Gleser, G. C. (1965). *Psychological tests and personnel decisions*. Urbana, IL: University of Illinois Press.

Cronbach, L. J., & Meehl, P. E. (1955). Construct validity in psychological tests. *Psychological Bulletin, 52*, 281–302.

Crusan; R., & Ruecker, T. (2019). Standardized testing pressures and the temptation of the five-paragraph essay. In N. Caplan & A. Johns (Eds.), *Practices for the L2 writing classroom: Beyond the five-paragraph essay* (pp. 201–220). Ann Arbor, MI: University of Michigan Press.

Culpeper, J. (1996). Towards an anatomy of impoliteness. *Journal of Pragmatics, 25*, 349–367. doi:10.1016/0378-2166(95)00014-3

Curtis, A. (2017). *Methods and methodologies for language teaching*. London, UK: Palgrave Macmillan.

Cushing, S. T. (Ed.). (2017). *Corpus linguistics in language testing research* [Special issue]. *Language Testing, 34*(4).

da Costa, T. (2016). Between relevance systems and typification structures: Alfred Schutz on habitual possessions. *Phenomenology and Mind*, 6, 66–72. doi:10.13128/Phe_Mi-19552

Danermark, B., Ekström, M., Jakobsen, L., & Karlsson, J. C. (2002). *Explaining society: Critical realism in the social sciences*. London, UK: Routledge.

Dannels, D. P., & Martin, K. N. (2008). Critiquing critiques: A genre analysis of feedback across novice to expert design studios. *Journal of Business and Technical Communication, 22*(2), 135–159.

Davidson, F. & Lynch, B. K. (2002). *Testcraft: A teacher's guide to writing and using language test specifications*. New Haven, CT and London, UK: Yale University Press.

Davies, A. (1990). *Principles of language testing*. Cambridge, MA: Basil Blackwell.

Davies, A. (1991). *The native speaker in applied linguistics*. Edinburgh, UK: University of Edinburgh Press.

Davies, A. (2007). Assessing academic English language proficiency: 40+ years of UK language tests. In J. Fox et al. (Eds.), *Language Testing Reconsidered* (pp. 73–86). Ottawa, ON: University of Ottawa Press.

Deardorff, D. K. (2006). Identification and assessment of intercultural competence as a student outcome of internationalization. *Journal of Studies in Intercultural Education, 10*, 241–266. doi:10.1177/1028315306287002

Dede, C. (2010). Comparing frameworks for 21st Century Skills. In J. Bellanca & R. Brandt (Eds.), *21st Century Skills: Rethinking how students learn* (pp. 51–76). Bloomington, IN: Solution Tree Press.

Deville, C., & Chalhoub-Deville, M. (2006). Test score variability: Implications for reliability and validity. In M. Chalhoub-Deville, C. A. Chapelle, & P. Duff (Eds.), *Inference and generalizability in applied linguistics: Multiple research perspectives* (pp. 9–25). Amsterdam, Netherlands: John Benjamins.

Devitt, A. J. (2004). *Writing genres: Rhetorical philosophy & theory*. Carbondale, IL: Southern Illinois University Press.

Devitt, A. J. (2015). Genre performances: John Swales' Genre Analysis and rhetorical-linguistic genre studies. *Journal of English for Academic Purposes. 19*, 44–51. doi:10.1016/j.jeap.2015.05.008

Dewey, J. (1896). The reflex arc concept in psychology. *Psychological Review, 3*, 357–370.

Dewey, J. (1938). *Logic: The theory of inquiry*. New York, NY: Henry Holt & Company.

Dewey, J. (1941). Propositions, warranted assertibility, and truth. *Journal of Philosophy, 35*(7), 169–186.

Deygers, B., & Malone, M. (2019). Language assessment literacy in university admission policies, or the dialogue that isn't. *Language Testing, 36*(3), pp. 347–368. doi:10.1177/0265532219826390

Dias, P., Freedman, A., Medway, P., & Paré, A. (1999). *Worlds apart: Acting and writing in academic and workplace contexts*. London, UK: Routledge.

Doe, C. (2015). Student interpretations of diagnostic feedback. *Language Assessment Quarterly, 12*(1), 110–135.

Doody, S., & Artemeva, N. (2022). "Everything is in the lab book": Multimodal writing, activity, and genre analysis of symbolic mediation in medical physics. *Journal of Written Communication, 39*(1), doi:10.1177/07410883211051634

Dörnyei, Z. (2000). Motivation in action: Towards a process-oriented conceptualisation of student motivation. *British Journal of Educational Psychology, 70*(4), 519–538. doi:10.1348/000709900158281

Dörnyei, Z. (2009). Motivation, language identities and the L2 self: Future research directions. In *Motivation, language identity and the L2 self* (pp. 350–356). Bristol, UK: Multilingual Matters.

Douglas, D. (2000). *Assessing languages for specific purposes.* Cambridge, UK: Cambridge University Press.

Douglas, D. (2001). Language for Specific Purposes assessment criteria: Where do they come from? *Language Testing, 18*(2), 171–185. doi:10.1177/026553220101800204

Douglas, D. (2004). Assessing the language of international civil aviation: Issues of validity and impact. *Proceedings from the International Professional Communication Conference*, IEEE Professional Communication Society (pp. 248–252). Minneapolis, MN: IEEE.

Douglas, D. (2014). Nobody seems to speak English today: Enhancing assessment and training in aviation English. *Iranian Journal of Language Teaching Research, 2*(2), 1–12. Retrieved from http://ijltr.urmia.ac.ir/article_20410.html

Douglas, D. (Ed.). (2015). The Language Testing Research Colloquium and the International Language Testing Association: Beginnings. Retrieved from https://cdn.ymaws.com/www.iltaonline.com/resource/resmgr/docs/A_Short_History_of_LTRC.pdfl

Douglas, D. (2020). [Review of the book *Assessing English for Professional Purposes*, by U. Knoch & S. Macqueen]. *English for Specific Purposes, 59*, 42–44. doi:10.1016/j.esp.2020.04.001

Douglas, D., & Myers, R. K. (2000). Assessing the communication skills of veterinary students: Whose criteria? In A. Kunnan (Ed.), *Fairness in validation in language assessment* (pp. 60–81). Selected papers from the 19th Language Testing Research Colloquium. Studies in Language Testing 9. Cambridge, UK: Cambridge University Press.

Downing, S. M., & Haladyna, T. M. (2006). *Handbook of test development.* Mahwah, NJ: Lawrence Erlbaum.

Ducasse, A. M., & Brown, A. (2009). Assessing paired orals: Raters' orientation to interaction. *Language Testing, 26*(3), 423–443.

Duchesne, S., McMaugh, A., Bochner, S., & Krause, K.-L. (2013). *Educational psychology for learning and teaching* (4th ed.). South Melbourne, VIC: Cengage.

Durkheim, E. (1952). *Suicide: A study in sociology.* New York, NY: Free Press.

East, M. (2012). *Task based language teaching from the teachers' perspective: Insights from New Zealand.* Amsterdam, Netherlands: John Benjamins.

Efklides, A. (2006). Metacognition and affect: What can meta cognitive experiences tell us about the learning process? *Educational Research Review*, 1, 3–14. doi:10.1016/j.edurev.2005.11.00

Elbow, P. (1983). Embracing contraries in the teaching process. *College English, 45*(4), 327–339.

Elbow, P. (1998). *Writing without teachers.* New York, NY: Oxford University Press.

Elbow, P., & Belanoff, P. (1986). Portfolios as a substitute for proficiency examinations. *College Composition and Communication,* 37, 336–39. Retrieved from www.jstor.org/stable/358050

Elder, C. (1996). The effect of language background on "foreign" language test performance: The case of Chinese, Italian, and Modern Greek. *Language Learning, 46(*2), 233–282.

Elder, C. (2021, June 17). *Responding to policy imperatives: Can language testers do more?* [Keynote conference session: Distinguished Achievement Award lecture]. Language Testing Research Colloquium, online conference. Retrieved from https://nardoneconsulting.app.box.com/s/tbc18eju34umg6v6h2eg3wh1x9y9u3bk

Elder, C., & McNamara, T. F. (2016). The hunt for "indigenous criteria" in assessing communication in the physiotherapy workplace. *Language Testing, 33*(2), 153–174. doi:10.1177/0265532215607398

Elder, C., & von Randow, J. (2008). Exploring the utility of a web-based English language screening tool. *Language Assessment Quarterly, 5*(3), 173–194.

Elder, C., McNamara, T. F., & Congdon, P. (2003). Understanding Rasch measurement: Rasch techniques for detecting bias in performance assessments: An example comparing the performance of native and non-native speakers on a test of academic English. *Journal of Applied Measurement, 4*, 181–197.

Elder, C., McNamara, T. F., Kim, H., Pill, J., & Sato, T. (2017). Interrogating the construct of communicative competence in language assessment contexts: What the non-language specialist can tell us. *Language & Communication, 57*, 14–21. doi:10.1016/j.langcom.2016.12.005

Ellis, R. (1994). *The study of second language acquisition.* Oxford, UK: Oxford University Press.

Ellis, R. (2008). *The study of second language acquisition.* Oxford, UK: Oxford University Press.

Ellis, R. (2015). *Understanding second language acquisition.* Oxford, UK: Oxford University Press.

Elster, J. (2017). The temporal dimension of reflexivity: Linking reflexive orientations to the stock of knowledge. *Distinktion: Journal of Social Theory, 18*(3), 274–293.

Emery, H. J. (2014). Developments in LSP testing 30 years on? The case of aviation English. *Language Assessment Quarterly, 11*(2), 198–215. doi:10.1080/15434303.2014.894516

Engeström, Y. (1987). *Learning by expanding: An activity-theoretical approach to developmental research.* Helsinki, Finland: Orienta-Konsultit Oy.

Engeström, Y. (1996). Developmental studies of work as a testbench of activity theory: The case of primary care medical practice. In S. Chaiklin & J. Lave (Eds.), *Understanding practice: Perspectives on activity and context* (pp. 64–103). Cambridge, UK: Cambridge University Press.

Engeström, Y. (1999). Activity theory and individual and social transformation. In Y. Engestrom, R. Miettinen, & R.-L. Punamaki (Eds.), *Perspectives on activity theory* (pp. 19–38). Cambridge, UK: Cambridge University Press.

Engeström, Y. (2009). The future of activity theory: A rough draft. In A. Sannino, H. Daniels, & K. D. Gutiérrez (Eds.), *Learning and expanding with activity theory* (pp. 303–328). Cambridge, UK: Cambridge University Press.

Engeström, Y., & Miettinen, R. (1999). Activity theory: A well-kept secret. In Y. Engeström, R. Miettinen, & R.-L. Punamäki-Gitai (Eds.), *Perspectives on activity theory* (pp. 1–16). Cambridge, UK: Cambridge University Press.

Eraut, M. (2002). *Conceptual analysis and research questions: Do the concepts of "learning community" and "community of practice" provide added value?* Paper presented at the Annual Meeting of the American Educational Research Association (New Orleans, LA, April 1–5, 2002). ERIC EA 031 732

Estival, D. (2016). Aviation English: A linguistic description. In D. Estival, C. Farris, & B. Molesworth, *Aviation English: A lingua franca for pilots and air traffic controllers* (chapter 2). London, UK: Routledge. Retrieved from https://ebookcentral.proquest.com

Estival, D. (2018). What should we teach native speakers? In J. Roberts & D. Estival (Eds.), *The proceedings of the International Civil Aviation English Association (2018) Conference, Daytona Beach* (pp. 37–46). Retrieved from https://commons.erau.edu/icaea-workshop/2018/proceedings/1/

Estival, D., Farris, C., & Molesworth, B. (2016). *Aviation English: A lingua franca for pilots and air traffic controllers.* London, UK: Routledge. Retrieved from https://ebookcentral.proquest.com

Evans, S. K., Pearce, K. E., Vitak, J., & Treem, J. W. (2017). Explicating affordances: A conceptual framework for understanding affordances in communication research. *Journal of Computer-Mediated Communication, 22*(1), 35–52. doi:10.1111/jcc4.12180

Eynon, B., & Gambino, L. (2017). *High-impact ePortfolio practice: A catalyst for student, faculty, and institutional learning.* Sterling, VA: Stylus.

Eynon, B., & Gambino, L. (2018). *Catalys in action: Case studies of high impact ePortfolio practice.* Sterling, VA: Stylus.

Eynon, B., Gambino, L., & Török, J. (2014). *Reflection, integration, and ePortfolio pedagogy.* New York, NY: City University of New York. Retrieved from https://academicworks.cuny.edu/cgi/viewcontent.cgi?article=1026&context=nc_pubs

Faigley, L. (1995). Non-academic writing: The social perspective. In L. Odell & D. Goswami (Eds.), *Writing in non-academic settings* (pp. 233–248). New York, NY: Guilford Press.

Fairclough, N. (1992). The appropriacy of "appropriateness". In N. Fairclough (Ed.), *Critical language awareness* (pp. 33–56). London, UK: Longman.

Fairclough, N. (2003). *Analysing discourse: Textual analysis for social research.* London, UK: Routledge.

Fantini, A. E. (2000). A central concern: Developing intercultural communicative competence. *School for International Training Occasional Papers Series, Inaugural Issue*, 25–33. Retrieved from http://citeseerx.ist.psu.edu/viewdoc/download?doi=10.1.1.117.8512&rep=rep1&type=pdf#page=33

Farris, C. (2016). ICAO language proficiency requirements. In D. Estival, C. Farris, & B. Molesworth, *Aviation English: A lingua franca for pilots and air traffic controllers* (chapter 3). London, UK: Routledge. Retrieved from https://ebookcentral.proquest.com

Fields, R. E., Wright, P. C., Marti, P., & Palmonari, M. (1998). Air traffic control as a distributed cognitive system: A study of external representations. In *Proceedings of the 9th European Conference on Cognitive Ergonomics* (pp. 85–90). Rocquencourt, France.

Flores, N., & Schissel, J. L. (2014). Dynamic bilingualism as the norm: Envisioning a heteroglossic approach to standards-based reform. *TESOL Quarterly, 48*(3), 454–479. doi:10.1002/tesq.182

Flower, L. (1994). *The construction of negotiated meaning: A social cognitive theory of writing.* Carbondale, IL: Southern Illinois University Press.

Flower, L., & Hayes, J. R. (1981). A cognitive process theory of writing. *College Composition and Communication, 32*(4), 365–387.

Flower, L., & Hayes, J. (2009). The cognition of discovery: Defining a rhetorical problem. In S. Miller (Ed.), *The Norton book of composition studies* (pp. 467–478). New York, NY: W.W. Norton & Company.

Flyvbjerg, B. (2001). *Making social science matter: Why social inquiry fails and how it can succeed again.* Cambridge, MA: University Press.

Fogarty-Bourget, C. G., Artemeva, N., & Fox, J. (2019). Gestural silence: An engagement device in the multimodal genre of the chalk talk lecture. In C. Sancho Guinda (Ed.), *Engagement in professional genres* (pp. 177–195). Amsterdam: John Benjamins. doi.org/10.1075/pbns.301.15fog

Foucault, M. (1977). *Discipline and punish: The birth of the prison* (A. Sheridan, Trans.). London, UK: Allen Lane. (Original work published 1975)

Foucault, M. (1980). *Power/knowledge: Selected interviews and other writings, 1972–1977*. New York, NY: Pantheon Books.

Foucault, M. (1982). The subject and power. In H. L. Dreyfus & P. Rabinow (Eds.), *Michel Foucault: Beyond structuralism and hermeneutics* (pp. 208–26). Note: pp. 208–16 written in English by M. Foucault; pp. 216–26 L. Sawyer, Trans. Brighton, UK: Harvester Press.

Foucault, M. (1990). *The history of sexuality, Volume 3: The care of the self* (R. Hurley, Trans). New York, NY: Vintage Books/Random House. (Original work published 1976)

Foucault, M. (1997). The ethics of the concern for self as a practice of freedom. In P. Rabinow (Ed.), *Michel Foucault, Ethics: Subjectivity and truth (The essential works of Michel Foucault, 1954–1984, Vol. 1)* (pp. 281–302). London, UK: Allen Lane/Penguin.

Fox, J. (2001). *It's all about meaning: L2 test validation in and through the landscape of an evolving construct* (Unpublished doctoral thesis). McGill University, Montreal, QC.

Fox, J. (2003). From products to process: An ecological approach to bias detection. *International Journal of Testing, 3*(1), 21–48. doi:10.1207/S15327574IJT0301_2

Fox, J. (2004). Test decisions over time: Tracking validity. *Language Testing, 21*(4), 437–465.

Fox, J. (2005a). Revisiting the storied landscape of language policy impact over time: A case of successful educational reform. *Curriculum Inquiry, 35*(3), 261–293.

Fox, J. (2005b). Re-thinking second language (L2) admission requirements: Problems with language-residency criteria and the need for language assessment and support. *Language Assessment Quarterly*, *2*(2), 85–115.

Fox, J. (2009). Moderating top-down policy impact and supporting EAP curricular renewal: Exploring the potential of diagnostic assessment. *Journal of English for Academic Purposes, 8*(1), 26–42.

Fox, J. (2014). Portfolio based language assessment (PBLA) in Canadian immigrant language training: Have we got it wrong? [Special research symposium issue]. *Contact, 40*(2), 68–83.

Fox, J. (Ed.) (2015). *Trends and issues in language assessment in Canada* [Special issue]. *Language Assessment Quarterly, 12*(1).

Fox, J. (2017). Alternative assessment/Portfolio assessment. In E. Shohamy, I. Or, & S. May (Eds.), *Language testing and assessment: Encyclopedia of language and education* (3rd ed., pp. 101–117). New York, NY: Springer. Retrieved from www.springer.com/us/bok/9783319022604

Fox, J. (2021). Perspectives on the multilingual turn in assessment: Constructs and consequences in context. *Journal of Multilingual Theories and Practices, 2*(2), 310–319.

Fox, J., & Artemeva, N. (2011). The cinematic art of teaching university mathematics: Chalk talk as embodied practice. *Multimodal Communication, 1*(1), 83–103.

Fox, J., & Artemeva, N. (2017). From diagnosis toward academic support: Developing a disciplinary, ESP-based writing task and rubric to identify the needs of entering undergraduate engineering students. *ESP Today, 5*(2), 148–171.

Fox, J., & Artemeva, N. (April, 2018). *Progress report: The diagnostic assessment of entering undergraduate engineering students.* Presentation for the Faculty of Engineering, Carleton University, Ottawa, ON.

Fox, J., & Cheng, L. (2007). Did we take the same test? Differing accounts of the Ontario Secondary School Literacy Test by first and second language test-takers. *Assessment in Education, 14*(1), 9–26.

Fox, J., & Hartwick, P. (2011). Taking a diagnostic turn: Reinventing the portfolio in EAP classrooms. In D. Tsagari and I. Csepes (Eds.), *Language testing and evaluation: Classroom-based language assessment* (pp. 47–61). Frankfurt, Germany: Peter Lang.

Fox, J., Abdulhamid, N., & Turner, C. (2022). Classroom based assessment. In G. Fulcher & L. Harding (Eds.), *Routledge handbook on testing* (pp. 119–135). London/New York: Routledge.

Fox, J., Haggerty, J., & Artemeva, N. (2016). Mitigating risk: The impact of a diagnostic assessment procedure on the first-year experience in engineering. In J. Read (Ed.), *Post-admission language assessment of university students* (pp. 43–65). Cham, Switzerland: Springer.

Fox, J., von Randow, J., & Volkov, A. (2016). Identifying students at-risk through post-entry diagnostic assessment: An Australasian approach takes root in a Canadian university. In V. Aryadoust, & J. Fox (Eds.), *Trends in language assessment research and practice: The view from the Middle East and Pacific Rim* (pp. 266–285). Newcastle upon Tyne, UK: Cambridge Scholars.

Franks, D., Dale, P., Hindmarsh, R., Fellows, C., Buckridge, M., & Cybinski, P. (2007). Interdisciplinary foundations: Reflecting on interdisciplinarity and three decades of teaching and research at Griffith University, Australia. *Studies in Higher Education, 32*(2), pp. 167–185.

Freadman, A. (1994). Anyone for tennis? In A Freedman & P. Medway (Eds). *Genre and the new rhetoric* (pp. 43–66.) London, UK: Taylor & Francis.

Frederiksen, N. (1984). The real test bias: Influences of testing on teaching and learning. *American Psychologist, 39*, 193–202.

Freedman, A. (2006). Interaction between theory and research: RGS and a study of students and professionals working "in computers". In N. Artemeva & A. Freedman (Eds.), *Rhetorical genre studies and beyond* (pp. 101–120). Winnipeg, MB: Inkshed Publications.

Freedman, A., & Adam, C. (1996). Learning to Write Professionally: "Situated Learning" and the Transition from University to Professional Discourse. *Journal of Business and Technical Communication, 10*(4), 395–427.

Freedman, A., & Medway, P. (1994). Locating genre studies: Antecedents and prospects. In A. Freedman & P. Medway (Eds.), *Genre and the new rhetoric* (pp. 1–20). London, UK: Taylor & Francis.

Friginal, E., Mathews, E., & Roberts, J. (2020). *English in global aviation: Context, research, and pedagogy*. London, UK/New York, NY: Bloomsbury Academic.

Frow, J. (2005). *Genre.* London, UK: Routledge. doi:10.4324/9780203962619

Fulcher, G. (1996). Does thick description lead to smart tests? A data-based approach to rating scale construction. *Language Testing, 13*(2), 208–238. doi:10.1177/026553229601300205

Fulcher, G. (2003). *Testing second language speaking*. Harlow, UK: Pearson.

Fulcher, G. (2013). Philosophy and language testing. In A. Kunnan (Ed.), *The companion to language assessment, volume III. Evaluation, methodology, and interdisciplinary themes. Part 12*. (pp. 1–19). Hoboken, NJ: Wiley. doi:10.1002/9781118411360.wbcla032

Fulcher, G. (2015). Context and inference in language testing. In J. King (Ed.), *The dynamic interplay between context and the language learner* (pp. 225–241). New York, NY: Palgrave-Macmillan.

Fulcher, G. (2021, June 16). *Validity worlds and values*. [Keynote conference session: Samuel J. Messick Memorial Lecture]. Language Testing Research Colloquium. Conference program. Retrieved from https://nardoneconsulting.app.box.com/s/tbc18eju34umg6v6h2eg3wh1x9y9u3bk

Fulcher, G., & Davidson, F. (2007). *Language testing and assessment: An advanced resource book*. London, UK: Routledge.

Fulcher, G., & Davidson, F. (2009). Test architecture, test retrofit. *Language Testing, 26*(1), 123–144. doi:10.1177/0265532208097339

Fuhrer, U. (1996). Behaviour setting analysis of situated learning: The case of newcomers. In S. Chaiklin & J. Lave (Eds.), *Understanding practice: Perspectives on activity and context* (pp. 179–211). Cambridge, UK: Cambridge University Press.

Gadamer, H. G. (1975). *Truth and method* (Sheed and Ward Ltd., Trans.). New York, NY: Seabury Press.

Gadamer, H. G. (2003). *Truth and method* (2nd ed., J. Weinsheimer & D. Marshall, Trans.). New York, NY: Continuum. (Original work published 1989)

Gafni, N. (2016). Comments on implementing validity theory. *Assessment in Education: Principles, Policy & Practice, 23*(2), 284–286, doi:10.1080/0969594X.2015.1111195

Gage, N. L. (1989). The paradigm wars and their aftermath: A historical sketch of research on teaching since 1989. *Educational Researcher, 18*(7), pp. 4–10. doi:10.3102/0013189X018007004

Galaczi, E. D. (2008). Peer–peer interaction in a speaking test: The case of the First Certificate in English examination. *Language Assessment Quarterly, 5*(2), 89–119. doi:10.1080/15434300801934702

Galaczi, E. D. (2014). Interactional competence across proficiency levels: How do learners manage interaction in paired speaking tests? *Applied Linguistics, 35*(5), 553–574. doi:10.1093/applin/amt017

Galaczi, E. D., & Taylor, L. (2018). Interactional competence: Conceptualisations, operationalisations, and outstanding questions. *Language Assessment Quarterly, 15*(3), 219–236. doi:10.1080/15434303.2018.1453816

Gallois, C., Ogay, T., & Giles, H. (2005). Communication accommodation theory. In W. B. Gudykunst (Ed.), *Theorizing about intercultural communication* (pp. 121–148). Thousand Oaks, CA: SAGE.

Garcia, A. C. M. (2015). *What do ICAO language proficiency test developers and raters have to say about the ICAO language proficiency requirements 12 years after their publication? A qualitative study exploring experienced professionals' opinions*. (Unpublished master's thesis). Lancaster University, Lancaster, UK.

Garcia, A. C. M., & Fox, J. (2020). Contexts and constructs: Implications for the testing of listening in pilots' communication with air traffic controllers. *The Especialist, 41*(4), 1–33. doi:10.23925/2318-7115.2020v41i4a4

Gardner, R. C. (1988). The socio-educational model of second language learning: Assumptions, findings, and issues. *Language Learning, 38*, 101–126.

Gardner, R. C. & Lambert, W. (1972). *Attitudes and motivation in second language learning*. Rowley, MA: Newbury House.

Garrett, P. B., & Baquedano-López, P. (2002). Language socialization: Reproduction and continuity, transformation and change. *Annual Review of Anthropology, 31*, 339–361. doi:10.1146/annurev.anthro.31.040402.085352

Garrison, D. R., Anderson, T., & Archer, W. (2000). Critical inquiry in a text-based environment: Computer conferencing in higher education. *The Internet and Higher Education*, *2*(2–3), 87–105.

Gass, S. M., & Selinker, L. (2008). *Second language acquisition: An introductory course*. New York, NY: Routledge.

Gee, J. P. (1990). *Social linguistics and literacies: Ideology in discourses*. London, UK: Palmer House.

Gee, J. P. (1996). *Social linguistics and literacies: Ideology in discourses* (2nd ed.). London, UK: Falmer Press.

Gee, J. P. (2000). New people in new worlds: Networks, the new capitalism, and schools. In B. Cope & M. Kalantizis (Eds.), *Multiliteracies: Literacy learning and the design of social futures* (pp. 92–105). London, UK: Routledge.

Gee, J. P. (2004). *Situated language and learning: A critique of traditional schooling*. New York, NY: Routledge.

Gee, J. P. (2008). Learning and situated domains: A social and situated account. In M. Prinsloo & M. Baynham (Eds.), *Literacies, global and local* (pp. 137–149). Amsterdam, Netherlands: John Benjamins.

Gibbons, M., & Nowotny, H. (2001). The potential of transdisciplinarity. In J. Thompson Klein, W. Grossenbacher-Mansuy, R. Haberli, A. Bill, R. W. Scholz, & M. Welti (Eds.), *Transdisciplinarity: Joint problem solving among science, technology, and society* (pp. 67–80). Basel, Switzerland: Springer.

Gibson, J. J. (1966). *The senses considered as perceptual systems*. Boston, MA: Houghton-Mifflin.

Gibson, J. J. (1979/2015). *The ecological approach to visual perception* (classic ed.). London, UK: Routledge. doi:/10.4324/9781315740218

Giltrow, J. (2002). *Academic writing: Writing and reading across the disciplines* (3rd ed.). Peterborough, ON: Broadview Press.

Giorgi, A. (2009). *The descriptive phenomenological method in psychology: Husserlian approach*. Pittsburgh, PA: Duquesne University Press.

Given, L. (2017). It's a new year . . . so let's stop the paradigm wars. *International Journal of Qualitative Methods, 16*(1–2). doi:10.1177/1609406917692647

Goettlich, A. (2011). Power and powerlessness: Alfred Schutz's theory of relevance and its possible impact on a sociological analysis of power. *Civitas: Revista de Ciências Sociais, 11*(3), 491–508.

Goffman, E. (1981). *Forms of talk*. Philadelphia, PA: University of Pennsylvania Press.

Gray, R. (2021). Multimodality in the classroom presentation genre: Findings from a study of Turkish psychology undergraduate talks. *System, 99*, 1–14. doi:10.1016/j.system.2021.102522

Green, A. (2007). *IELTS washback in context: Preparation for academic writing in higher education*. Cambridge, UK: Cambridge University Press.

Greene, J. C., & Caracelli, V. J. (1997). Defining and describing the paradigm issue in mixed-method evaluation. *New Directions for Evaluation, 74*(3), 5–17.

Guba, E. G., & Lincoln, Y. S. (1989). *Fourth generation evaluation.* Thousand Oaks, CA: SAGE.

Gudykunst, W. B. (Ed.). (2005a). *Theorizing about intercultural communication.* Thousand Oaks, CA: SAGE.

Gudykunst, W. B. (2005b). An anxiety/uncertainty management (AUM) theory of effective communication. In W. B. Gudykunst (Ed.), *Theorizing about intercultural communication* (pp. 281–322). Thousand Oaks, CA: SAGE.

Guilford, J. P. (1946). New standards for test evaluation. *Educational & Psychological Measurement, 6*, 427–438.

H5P. (n.d.). *H5P*. Retrieved from https://h5p.org/

H5P Vocabulary workshop (n.d.). H5P Sample from course. H5P attribution 4.0 International (CC BY 4.0). Retrieved from https://culearn.carleton.ca/moodle/mod/hvp/view.php?id=2060667

Haas, C. (1994). Learning to read biology: One student's rhetorical development in college. *Written Communication, 11*(1), 43–84.

Hall, J. K. (1993). The role of oral practices in the accomplishment of our everyday lives: The sociocultural dimension of interaction with implications for the learning of another language. *Applied Linguistics, 14*(2), 145–166. doi:10.1093/applin/14.2.145

Hall, J. K. (1995). (Re)creating our worlds with words: A sociohistorical perspective of face-to-face interaction. *Applied Linguistics, 16*(2), 206–232. doi:10.1093/applin/16.2.206

Hall, J. K. (1999). A prosaics of interaction: The development of interactional competence in another language. In E. Hinkel (Ed.), *Culture in second language teaching and learning* (pp. 137–151). New York, NY: Cambridge University Press.

Halliday, M. A. K. (1973). *Explorations in the functions of language.* London, UK: Edward Arnold.

Halliday, M. A. K. (1978). *Language as social semiotic: The social interpretation of language and meaning.* Baltimore, MD: University Park Press,

Halliday, M. A. K. (1994). *An introduction to functional grammar* (2nd ed.). London, UK: Edward Arnold.

Halliday, M. A. K. (1999). The notion of "context" in language education. In M. Ghadessy (Ed.), *Text and context in functional linguistics* (pp. 1–24). Amsterdam, Netherlands: John Benjamins.

Halliday, M. A. K., & Hasan, R. (1989). *Language, context, and text: Aspects of language in a social-semiotic perspective.* Oxford, UK: Oxford University Press.

Hamp-Lyons, L. (Ed.) (1991). *Assessing second language writing in academic contexts.* Norwood, NJ: Ablex.

Hamp-Lyons, L. (2000). Social, professional, and individual responsibility in language testing. *System* 28(4), 579–98. doi:10.1016/S0346-251X(00)00039-7

Hamp-Lyons, L., & Condon, W. (2000). *Assessing the portfolio: Principles for practice, theory, and research.* Cresskill, NJ: Hampton.

Hanks, W. F. (1987). Discourse genres in a theory of practice. *American Ethnologist, 14*(4), 668–692.

Harding, L. (2015). Adaptability and ELF communication: The next steps for communicative language testing? In J. Mader, & Z. Urkun (Eds.), *Language testing: Current trends and future needs.* IATEFL TEASIG.

Harding, L., & Brunfaut, T. (2020). Trajectories of language assessment literacy in a teacher–researcher partnership: Locating elements of praxis through narrative inquiry. In M. E. Poehner & O. Inbar-Lourie (Eds.), *Toward a reconceptualization of second language classroom assessment: Praxis and researcher–teacher partnerships* (pp. 23–41). Cham, Switzerland: Springer. doi:10.1007/978-3-030-35081-9

Harding, L., & McNamara, T. F. (2017). Language assessment: The challenge of ELF. In J. Jenkins, W. Baker, & M. Dewey (Eds.), *The Routledge Handbook of English as a Lingua Franca* (Chapter 45). London, UK: Routledge. Retrieved from https://ebookcentral.proquest.com

Harding, L., Alderson, J. C., & Brunfaut, T. (2015). Diagnostic assessment of reading and listening in a second or foreign language: Elaborating on diagnostic principles. *Language Testing, 32*(3), 317–336. doi:10.1177/0265532214564505

Hargreaves, A., Earl, L., & Schmidt, M. (2002). Perspectives on Alternative Assessment Reform. *American Educational Research Journal, 39*(1), 69–95. doi:10.3102/00028312039001069

Harris, J. (1989). The idea of community in the study of writing. *College Composition and Communication, 40*(1), 11–22.

Hartwick, P. L. (2018). *Exploring the affordances of online learning environments: 3DVLEs and ePortfolios in second language learning and teaching* (Unpublished doctoral dissertation). Carleton University, Ontario, ON. Retrieved from https://curve.carleton.ca/263f2dc2-ba83-4895-9ae5-ba6059ad3112

Hartwick, P., & McCarroll, J. (2019). *Targeting student needs by shifting to a blended approach* [Conference presentation]. TESL Canada Conference, December 5–6, Toronto, ON. www.teslontario.org/tesl-ontario-2019-conference

Hartwick, P., & Savaskan Nowlan, N. (2018). Integrating virtual spaces: Connecting affordances of 3D virtual learning environments to design for twenty-first century learning. In Y. Qian (Ed.), *Integrating multi-user virtual environments in modern classrooms* (pp. 111–136). Hershey, PA: IGI Global.

Hartwick, P., McCarroll, J., & Davidson, A. (2018). What is ePortfolio "done well"? A case of course-level analysis. In B. Eynon & L. Gambino (Eds.), *Catalyst in action: Case studies of high-impact ePortfolio practice* (pp. 184–196). Sterling, VA: Stylus.

Hartwick, P., McCarroll, J., & Davidson, A. (2021). *Exploring inquiry, reflection, and integration through the use of ePortfolio*. (Unpublished manuscript.) Faculty of Arts and Social Science, Carleton University, Ottawa, ON.

Hashemi, M., & Babaii, E. (2013). Mixed methods research: Toward new research designs in applied linguistics. *The Modern Language Journal, 97*(4), 828–852. doi:10.1111/j.1540-4781.2013.12049.x

Hazrati, A. (2015). Intercultural communication and discourse analysis: The case of Aviation English. *Procedia – Social and Behavioral Sciences, 192*, 244–251. doi:10.1016/j.sbspro.2015.06.035

He, A., & Young, R. (1998). Language proficiency interviews: A discourse approach. In R. E. Young & A. W. He (Eds.), *Talking and testing: Discourse approaches to the assessment of oral proficiency* (pp. 1–24). Amsterdam, Netherlands: John Benjamins.

Helmreich, R. L. (1994). Anatomy of a system accident: The crash of Avianca Flight 052. *International Journal of Aviation Psychology, 4*, 265–284. doi:10.1207/s15327108ijap0403_4

Helmreich, R. L., & Merritt, A. C. (1998). *Culture at work: National, organizational, and professional influences*. London, UK: Ashgate.

Henricksen, K. (2003). *A framework for context-aware pervasive computing applications* (Unpublished doctoral dissertation). University of Queensland, Queensland, QLD.

Herndl, C. G. (2004). Introduction to the Special Issue: The legacy of critique and the promise of practice. *Journal of Business and Technical Communication, 18*(1), 3–8. doi:10.1177/1050651903258143

Herndl, C. G., & Brown, S. C. (Eds.). (1996). *Green culture: Environmental rhetoric in contemporary America*. Madison, WI: University of Wisconsin Press.

Herndl, C. G., & Wilson, G. (2007. Reflections on field research and professional practice. *Journal of Business and Technical Communication, 22*(2), 2160225.

Herndl, C. G., Goodwin, J., Honeycutt, L., Wilson, G., Graham, S. S., & Niedergeses, D. (2011). Talking sustainability: Identification and division in an Iowa community. *Journal of Sustainable Agriculture, 35*(4), 436–461, doi:10.1080/10440046.2011.562068

Hirch, R. (2020). An interview with Dr. John Read. *Language Assessment Quarterly, 17*(2), 204–215. doi:10.1080/15434303.2020.1730842

Hofstede, G. (1991). *Cultures and organizations: Software of the mind*. London, UK: McGraw-Hill.

Hollan, J., Hutchins, E., & Kirsh, D. (2000). Distributed cognition: Toward a new foundation for human–computer interaction research. *ACM Transactions on Computer–Human Interaction, 7*(2), 174–196. doi:10.1145/353485.353487

Holliday, A. (2005). *The struggle to teach English as an international language*. Oxford, UK: Oxford University Press.

Holt Rinehart Winston. (1974). Context. In *Winston Canadian dictionary for schools* (p. 126).

Hongwen, C. (2020). Distinguishing language ability from the context in an EFL speaking test. In G. J. Ockey & B. A. Green (Eds.), *Another generation of fundamental considerations in language assessment* (pp. 201–219). Singapore: Springer.

Hubbard, P., & Levy, M. (2016). Theory in computer-assisted language learning research and practice. In F. Farr & L. Murray (Eds.), *The Routledge handbook of language learning and technology* (pp. 24–38). London, UK: Routledge. doi:10.4324/9781315657899

Hubley, A. M., & Zumbo, B. D. (2011). Validity and the consequences of test interpretation and use. *Social Indicators Research, 103*(2), 219–230.

Hughes, A. (1989). *Testing for language teachers*. Cambridge, UK: Cambridge University Press.

Huhta, A., Kalaja, P., & Pitkänen-Huhta, A. (2006). Discursive construction of a high-stakes test: The many faces of a test-taker. *Language Testing, 12*(3), 326–350. doi:10.1191/0265532206lt331oa

Hunt, R. (1994). Traffic in genres: In classrooms and out. In A. Freedman & P. Medway (Eds.), *Genre and the new rhetoric* (pp. 211–230). London, UK: Taylor Francis.

Husserl, E. (1989). *The crisis of European sciences and transcendental phenomenology. An introduction to phenomenological philosophy*. (D. Carr, Trans.). Evanston, IL: Northwestern University Press. (Original work published 1936)

Hutchins, E. (1995a). *Cognition in the Wild*. Cambridge, MA: MIT Press.

Hutchins, E. (1995b). How a cockpit remembers its speeds. *Cognitive Science, 19*, 265–288. doi:10.1016/0364-0213(95)90020-9

Hutchins, E., & Klausen, T. (1996). Distributed cognition in an airline cockpit. In Y. Engeström & D. Middleton (Eds.), *Cognition and communication at work*. Cambridge, MA: Cambridge University Press.

Hymes, D. H. (1972). On communicative competence. In J. B. Pride & J. Holmes (Eds.) *Sociolinguistics: Selected readings* (pp. 269–293). Harmondsworth, UK: Penguin.

Hynes, G. (2014). Bakhtinian dialogism. In D. Coghlan & M. Brydon-Miller (Eds.), *The SAGE encyclopedia of action research* (pp. 73–75). Thousand Oaks, CA: SAGE.

H5P. (n.d.). *H5P*. Retrieved from https://h5p.org/

H5P Vocabulary Workshop. (n.d.). H5P Sample from course. H5P attribution 4.0 International (CC BY 4.0). Retrieved from https://culearn.carleton.ca/moodle/mod/hvp/view.php?id=2060667

ICAO. (2007a). *Manual of radiotelephony (Doc 9432)* (4th ed.). Montreal, QC: International Civil Aviation Organization.

ICAO. (2007b). *Procedures for air navigation services – Air traffic management (Doc 4444)* (15th ed.). Montreal, QC: International Civil Aviation Organization.

ICAO. (2010). *Manual on the implementation of ICAO language proficiency requirements (Doc 9835)* (2nd ed.). Montreal, QC: International Civil Aviation Organization.

ICAO. (2014). *Annex 10 to the Convention on International Civil Aviation – Aeronautical Telecommunications – Volume II, communication procedures including those with PANS status* (6th ed.). Montreal, QC: International Civil Aviation Organization.

ICAO. (2020). *Annex 1 to the Convention on International Civil Aviation – Personnel licensing* (13th ed.). Montreal, QC: International Civil Aviation Organization.

Inbar-Lourie, O. (2008). Constructing a language assessment knowledge base: A focus on language assessment courses. *Language Testing, 25*: 385–402. doi:10.1177/0265532208090158

Intemann, F. (2008). "Taipei ground, confirm your last transmission was in English . . .?" An analysis of aviation English as a world language. In C. Gnutzmann & F. Intemann (Eds.), *The globalization of English and the English language classroom* (2nd ed.) (pp. 71–88). Tübingen, Germany: Narr.

Ivanič, R. (1998). *Writing and identity: The discoursal construction of identity in academic writing*. Amsterdam, Netherlands: John Benjamins.

Jacoby, S., & McNamara, T. F. (1999). Locating competence. *English for Specific Purposes, 18*(3), 213–241. doi:10.1016/S0889-4906(97)00053-7

Jacoby, S., & Ochs, E. (1995). Co-construction: An introduction. *Research on Social Interaction, 28*(3), 171–183. doi:10.1207/s15327973rlsi2803_1

James, W. (1907). *Pragmatism: A new name for some old ways of thinking*. New York, NY: Longman Green and Co.

James, W. (1996). Pragmatism: A new name for some old ways of thinking. In W. James, *Pragmatism and the meaning of truth* (pp. 1–166). Cambridge, MA: Harvard University Press. (Original work published in 1907).

Jamieson, K. M. H. (1975). Antecedent genre as rhetorical constraint. *Quarterly Journal of Speech, 61*, 406–415.

Jenkins, J. (2000). *The phonology of English as an international language.* Oxford, UK: Oxford University Press.

Jenkins, J. (2002). A sociolinguistically based, empirically researched pronunciation syllabus for English as an International Language. *Applied Linguistics, 23*(1), 83–103. doi:10.1093/applin/23.1.83

Jenkins, J. (2006). The spread of English as an international language: A testing time for testers. *ELT Journal, 60*(1), 42–50. doi:10.1093/elt/cci080

Jenkins, J. (2007). *English as a lingua franca: Attitude and identity.* Oxford, UK: Oxford University Press.

Jenkins, J., Cogo, A., & Dewey, M. (2011). Review of developments in research into English as lingua franca. *Language Teaching, 44*(3), 281–315. doi:10.1017/S0261444811000115

Johnson, B., & Gray, R. (2010). A history of the philosophical and theoretical issues for mixed methods research. In A. Tashakkori & C. Teddlie (Eds.), *SAGE handbook of mixed methods in social and behavioral research* (pp. 69–94). Los Angeles, CA: SAGE.

Kachru, B. (1992). World Englishes: Approaches, issues and resources. *Language Teaching, 25*(1), 1–14. doi:10.1017/S0261444800006583

Kalaja, P., & Pitkänen-Huhta, A. (2018). ALR special issue: Visual methods in applied language studies. *Applied Linguistics Review, 9* (2–3), 157–176. doi:10.1515/applirev-2017-0005

Kane, M. T. (1990). *Generalizing criterion-related validity evidence for certification requirements across situations and specialty areas.* ACT Research Report (ERIC Number: ED337463).

Kane, M. T. (1992). An argument-based approach to validity. *Psychological Bulletin, 112*(3), 272–235. doi:10.1037/0033-2909.112.3.527

Kane, M. T. (2006). Validation. In R. L. Brennan (Ed.), *Educational measurement* (4th ed., pp. 17–64). Westport, CT: American Council on Education and Praeger Publishers.

Kane, M. T. (2008). Terminology, emphasis, and utility in validation: Comments on Lissitz and Samuelsen. *Educational Researcher, 37*(2), 76–82.

Kane, M. T. (2010). Validity and fairness. *Language Testing, 27*(2), 177–182. doi:10.1177/0265532209349467

Kane, M. T. (2012). What the bar examination must achieve: Three perspectives. *The Bar Examiner, 81*(3), 1–15.

Kane, M. T. (2013a). Validity and fairness in the testing of individuals. In M. Chatterji (Ed.), *Validity and test use: An international dialogue on educational assessment accountability, and equity* (pp. 17–53). Bingley, UK: Emerald Group.

Kane, M. T. (2013b). Validating the interpretations and uses of test scores. *Journal of Educational Measurement, 50*(1), 1–73. doi:10.1111/jedm.12000

Kane, M. T. (2013c). The argument-based approach to validation. *School Psychology Review, 42*(4), p. 448–457. doi:10.1080/02796015.2013.12087465

Kane, M. T. (2016). Explicating validity. *Assessment in Education: Principles, Policy & Practice, 23*(2), 198–211. doi:10.1080/0969594X.2015.1060192

Kane, M. T., Crooks, T., & Cohen, A. (1999). Validating measures of performance. *Educational Measurement: Issues and Practice, 18*(2), 5–17.

Kaplan-Rakowski, R., & Gruber, A. (2019). Low-immersion versus high-immersion virtual reality: Definitions, classification, and examples with a foreign language focus. In *Innovation in Language Learning Conference Proceedings 2019* (pp. 552–555). Florence, Italy: Pixel.

Kaptelinin, V., & Nardi, B. A. (2006). *Acting with technology: Activity theory and interaction design*. Cambridge, MA: MIT Press.

Karlqvist, A. (1999). Going beyond disciplines: The meanings of interdisciplinarity. *Policy Sciences, 32*(4), 379–383.

Kaur, J. (2009). Pre-empting problems of understanding in English as a lingua franca. In A. Mauranen & E. Ranta (Eds.), *English as a lingua franca: Studies and findings* (pp. 107–123). Newcastle upon Tyne, UK: Cambridge Scholars.

Kecskes, I. (2014). *Intercultural pragmatics*. Oxford Scholarship Online. doi:10.1093/acprof:oso/9780199892655.001.0001

Kemmis, S. (2001/2006). Exploring the relevance of critical theory for action research: Emancipatory action research in the footsteps of Jürgen Habermas. In P. Reason & H. Bradbury (Eds), *Handbook of action research: Participative inquiry and practice* (pp. 91–102). London, UK: SAGE. [Also published in P. Reason & H. Bradbury (Eds.). (2006). *Handbook of action research: Concise paperback edition* (pp. 94–105). London: SAGE]

Kempf, A. (2016). *The pedagogy of standardized testing: The radical impacts of educational standardization in the US and Canada*. New York, NY: Palgrave.

Kent, T. (1991). On the very idea of a discourse community. *College Composition and Communication, 42*, 349–363.

Kim, H. (2012). *Exploring the construct of aviation communication: A critique of the ICAO language proficiency policy* (Unpublished doctoral thesis). University of Melbourne, Melbourne, VIC.

Kim, H. (2013). Exploring the construct of radiotelephony communication: A critique of the ICAO English testing policy from the perspective of Korean aviation experts. *Papers in Language Testing and Assessment, 2*(2), 103–10. Retrieved from www.altaanz.org/uploads/5/9/0/8/5908292/6_kim.pdf

Kim, H. (2018). What constitutes professional communication in aviation: Is language proficiency enough for testing purposes? *Language Testing, 35*(3), 403–426. doi:10.1177/0265532218758127

Kim, H., & Elder, C. (2009). Understanding Aviation English as a lingua franca. *Australian Review of Applied Linguistics, 32*(3), 23.1–23.17. doi:10.2104/aral0923.

Kim, H., & Elder, C. (2015). Interrogating the construct of aviation English: Feedback from test takers in Korea. *Language Testing, 32*(2), 129–149. doi:10.1177/0265532214544394

Kim, K. K., & Berard, T. (2009). Typification in society and social science: The continuing relevance of Schutz's social phenomenology. *Human Studies, 32*(3), 263–289.

Kim, M. (2001). Detecting DIF across the different language groups in a speaking test. *Language Testing, 18*(1), 89–114.

Kim, M. (2005). Culture-based conversational constraints theory. In W. B. Gudykunst (Ed.), *Theorizing about intercultural communication* (pp. 93–117). Thousand Oaks, CA: SAGE.

Kirschner, S. R., & Martin, J. (Eds.). (2010). *The sociocultural turn in psychology: The contextual emergence of mind and self*. New York, NY: Columbia University Press.

Kirshner, D., & Whitson, J. A. (Eds.) (1997). *Situated cognition: Social, semiotic, and psychological perspectives*. Mahwah, NJ: Lawrence Earlbaum.

Klein, J. T. (1990). *Interdisciplinarity: History, theory, practice*. Detroit, MI: Wayne State University Press.

Klein, J. T. (2007). Interdisciplinary approaches in social science research. In W. Outhwaite & S. P. Turner (Eds.), *The SAGE handbook of social science methodology* (pp. 32–50). London, UK: SAGE.

Klein, J. T., & Newell, W. (1998). Advancing interdisciplinary studies. In W. H. Newell (Ed.), *Interdisciplinarity: Essays from the literature* (pp. 3 – 22). New York, NY: College Entrance Examination Board.

Knoch, U. (2014). Using subject specialists to validate an ESP rating scale: The case of the International Civil Aviation Organization (ICAO) rating scale. *English for Specific Purposes, 33*, 77–86. doi:10.1016/j.esp.2013.08.002

Knoch, U., & Macqueen, S. (2016). Language assessment for the workplace. In D. Tsagari & J. Banerjee (Eds.), *Handbook of second language assessment* (chapter 18). Berlin, Germany: De Gruyter, Inc. Retrieved from https://ebookcentral.proquest.com

Knoch, U., & Macqueen, S. (2020). *Assessing English for professional purposes*. New York, NY: Routledge.

Knoch, U., Elder, C., & O'Hagan, S. (2016). Examing the validity of a post-entry screening tool embedded in a specific policy contex. In J. Read (Ed.), *Post-admission language assessment of university students* (pp. 23–42). Cham, Switzerland: Springer.

Kolb, D. A. (1984). *Experiential learning: Experience as the source of learning and development*. Englewood Cliffs, NJ: Prentice Hall.

Krahn, G. L., Holn, M. F., & Kime, C. (1995). Incorporating qualitative approaches into clinical child psychology research. *Journal of Clinical Child Psychology, 24*, 204–213.

Kramsch, C. J. (1986). From language proficiency to interactional competence. *The Modern Language Journal, 70*(4), 366–372. doi:10.1111/j.1540-4781.1986.tb05291.x

Kramsch, C. J. (1993). *Context and culture in language teaching*. Oxford, UK: Oxford University Press.

Kress, G. (2012, March 15). What is a mode? Interview at the University of London [Video]. YouTube. www.youtube.com/watch?v=kJ2gz_OQHhI

Kress, G., & Van Leeuwen, T. (2001). *Multimodal discourse: The modes and media of contemporary communication*. London, UK: Arnold Publishers.

Kuh, G. (2008). *High impact practices: What they are, who has access to them, and why they matter*. Retrieved from www.aacu.org/leap/hip.cfm

Kuhn, T. S. (1962). *The structure of scientific revolutions*. Chicago, IL: University of Chicago Press.

Kuhn, T. S. (1970). *The structure of scientific revolutions* (enlarged 2nd ed.). Chicago, IL: University of Chicago Press.

Kunnan, A. J. (Ed.). (1998). *Validation in language assessment*. Mahwah, NJ: Lawrence Erlbaum.

Kunnan, A. J. (1990). DIF in native language and gender groups in an ESL placement test. *TESOL Quarterly, 24*, 741–746.

Kunnan, A. J. (2018). *Evaluating language assessments*. New York, NY: Routledge.

Kvale, S. (1989). To validate is to question. In S. Kvale (Ed.), *Issues of validity in qualitative research* (pp. 73–92). Lund, Sweden: Studentlitteratur.

Kvale, S. (1995). The social construction of validity. *Qualitative Inquiry, 1*(1), 19–40.

Kvale, S. (1996). Examinations re-examined: Certification of students or certification of knowledge. In S. Chaiklin & J. Lave (Eds.), *Understanding practice: Perspectives on activity and context* (pp. 215–240). Cambridge, UK: Cambridge University Press.

Lado, R. (1961). *Language testing: The construction and use of foreign language tests*. London, UK: Longman.

Lado, R. (1964). *Language teaching: A scientific approach*. London, UK: McGraw Hill.

Lakatos, I. (1970). Falsification and the methodology of scientific research programs. In I. Lakatos & A. Musgrave (Eds.), *Criticism and the growth of knowledge* (pp. 91–195). New York, NY: Cambridge University Press.

Lam, D. M. K. (2018). What counts as "responding"? Contingency on previous speaker contribution as a feature of interactional competence. *Language Testing, 35*(3), 377–401. doi:10.1177/0265532218758126

Lamont, M., & Molnár, V. (2002). The study of boundaries in the social sciences. *Annual Review of Sociology*, 28(1), 167–195. doi:10.1146/annurev.soc.28.110601.141107

Lantolf, J. P. (2000). (Ed.). *Sociocultural theory and second language learning*. Oxford, UK: Oxford University Press.

Lantolf, J. P., & Appel, G. (Eds.). (1994). *Vygoskian approach to second language research*. Oxford, UK: Oxford University Press.

Lantolf, J. P., & Inbar-Lourie, O. (2020). T*oward a reconceptualization of second language classroom assessment: Praxis and researcher–teacher partnerships*. Cham, Switzerland: Springer.

Lantolf, J. P., & Poehner, M. E. (2011). Dynamic assessment in the classroom: Vygotskian praxis for second language development. *Language Teaching Research, 15*(1), 11–33.

Lantolf, J. P., & Poehner, M. E. (2014). *Sociocultural theory and the pedagogical imperative in L2 education. Vygotskian praxis and the research/practice divide*. London, UK: Routledge. doi:10.4324/9780203813850

Lantolf, J. P., & Thorne, S. L. (2007). *Sociocultural theory and the genesis of second language development*. Oxford, UK: Oxford University Press.

Larsen-Freeman, D. (1997). Chaos/complexity science and second language acquisition. *Applied Linguistics, 18*(2), 141–165. doi:10.1093/applin/18.2.141

Larsen-Freeman, D., & Cameron L. (2008a). *Complex systems and applied linguistics*. Oxford, UK: Oxford University Press

Larsen Freeman, D., & Cameron, L. (2008b). Research methodology on language development from a Complex Systems perspective. *The Modern Language Journal, 92*(2), 200–213. doi:10.1111/j.1540-4781.2008.00714.x

Latour, B. (1987). *Science in action*. Milton Keynes, UK: Open University Press.

Latour, B. (2005). *Reassembling the social: An introduction to actor–network theory*. New York, NY: Oxford University Press.

Lave, J. (1977). Tailor-made experiments and evaluating the intellectual consequences of apprenticeship training. *The Quarterly Newsletter of the Institute for Comparative Human Development, 1*, 1–3.

Lave, J. (1988). *Cognition in practice*. Boston, MA: Cambridge.

Lave, J. (1996). The practice of learning. In S. Chaiklin & J. Lave (Eds.), *Understanding practice: Perspectives on activity and context* (pp. 3–31). Cambridge, UK: Cambridge University Press.

Lave, J., & Wenger, E. (1991). *Situated learning: Legitimate peripheral participation*. Cambridge, UK: Cambridge University Press.

Law, J. (Ed.). (1991). *A sociology of monsters: Essays on power, technology, and domination.* London, UK: Routledge.

Lawrence, R. J. (2010). Deciphering interdisciplinary and transdisciplinary contributions. *Transdisciplinary Journal of Engineering and Science, 2*(1), 125–130.

Lazaraton, A. (1995). Qualitative research in Applied Linguistics: A progress report. *TESOL Quarterly, 29*(3), 455–472.

Lazaraton, A. (2005). Quantitative research methods. In E. Hinkel (Ed.), *Handbook of research in second language teaching and learning* (pp. 209–224). Mahwah, NJ: Lawrence Erlbaum.

Lazaraton, A., & Taylor, L. (2007). In J. Fox, M. Wesche, D. Bayliss, L. Cheng, C. Turner, & C. Doe (Eds.), *Language testing reconsidered* (pp. 113–129). Ottawa, ON: University of Ottawa Press.

Lea, M. R., & Street, B. V. (1998). Student writing in higher education: An academic literacies approach. *Studies in Higher Education, 23*(2), 157–172.

Leman, M. (2007a). *Embodied music cognition and mediation technology.* Cambridge, MA: MIT Press.

Leman, M. (2007b). *Transdisciplinary music research at the cross-roads: Tendencies, perspectives, and opportunities.* Retrieved from www.ufmg.br/ieat/wp-content/uploads/2015/06/Marc_Leman-Transdisciplinary-music-research-at-the-cross-roads-tendencies-perspectives-and-opportunities.pdf [Texto presented as a result of participation in the FUNDEP/IEAT Chair Program, July 30 to August 17, 2007]

Lemke, J. L. (1995). *Textual politics: Discourse and social dynamics.* London, UK: Taylor & Francis.

Lenz, A. S., & Wester, K. L. (2017). Development and evaluation of assessments for counseling professionals. *Measurement and Evaluation in Counselling and Development, 50*, 201–209.

Leont'ev, A. N. (1981). The problem ofactivity in psychology. In J. V. Wertsch (Ed.), *The concept of activity in Soviet psychology* (pp. 37–71). Armonk, NY: Sharpe.

Leung, C. (2004). Developing formative teacher assessment: Knowledge, practice, and change. *Language Assessment Quarterly, 1*, 19–41. doi:10.1207/s15434311laq0101_3

Leung, C. (2005). English as an additional language policy: Issues of inclusive access and language learning in the mainstream. *Prospect, 20*(1), 95–113.

Leung, C., & Mohan, B. (2004). Teacher formative assessment and talk in classroom contexts: Assessment as discourse and assessment of discourse. *Language Testing, 21*, 335–359.

Leung, C., & Valdés, G. (2019). Translanguaging and the transdisciplinary framework for language teaching and learning in a multilingual world. *The Modern Language Journal, 103*(2), 348–370. doi:10.1111/modl.12568

Lewis, L. (2017). ePortofolio as pedagogy: Threshold concepts for curriculum design. *E-Learning and Digital Media 14*(1–2), 72–85. doi:10:1177/2042753017694497

Lewkowicz, J. (1997). The integrated testing of a second language. In C. Clapham & D. Corson (Eds.), *Encyclopedia of language and education, vol. 7: Language testing and assessment* (pp. 121–130). Dordrecht, Netherlands: Kluwer Academic.

Liddicoat, A. (2010). Applied Linguistics in its disciplinary context. Australian *Review of Applied Linguistics, 33*(2), pp. 14.1–14.7. doi:10.2104/aral1014

Lincoln, Y. S., & Guba, E. G. (1985). *Naturalistic inquiry*. Beverly Hills, CA: SAGE.

Lissitz, R. W., & Samuelsen, K. (2007). A suggested change in terminology and emphasis regarding validity and education. *Educational Researcher, 36*, 437–448.

Little, D. (2020). Plurilingualism, learner autonomy and constructive alignment: A vision for university language centres in the 21st century. *Language Learning in Higher Education, 10*(2), 271–286.

Lortie, D. C. (1975). *Schoolteacher: A sociological study*, Chicago, IL: University of Chicago Press.

Lunsford, S. (2002). Contextualizing Toulmin's model in the writing classroom: A case study. *Written Communication, 19*(1), 109–174.

Lynch, B. (2001). Rethinking assessment from a critical perspective. *Language Testing, 18*, 351–72.

MacCharles, T. (2021). Diversity is on a collision course with bilingualism at Canada's top court. *Toronto Star*, March 6. Retrieved from www.thestar.com/politics/federal/2021/03/06/

Macqueen, S., Knoch, U., Wigglesworth, G., Nordlinger, R., Singer, R., McNamara, T. F., & Brickle, R. (2019). The impact of national standardized literacy and numeracy testing on children and teaching staff in remote Australian Indigenous communities. *Language Testing, 36*(2), 265–287. doi:10.1177/0265532218775758

Madaus, G., & Kellaghan, T. (1992). Curriculum evaluation and assessment. In P. W. Jackson (Ed.), *Handbook on research on curriculum* (pp. 119–154). New York, NY: Macmillan.

Maddox, B. (2014). Globalising assessment: An ethnography of literacy assessment, camels and fast food in the Mongolian Gobi. *Comparative Education, 50*(4), 474–489.

Maddox, B. (2015). The neglected situation: Assessment performance and interaction in context. *Assessment in Education: Principles, Policy and Practice, 22*(4), 427–443. doi:10.1080/0969594X.2015.1026246

Maddox, B., & Zumbo, B. D. (2017). Observing testing situations: Validation as jazz. In B. D. Zumbo & A. M. Hubley (Eds.), *Understanding and investigating response processes in validation research* (pp. 179–192). Cham, Switzerland: Springer.

Maguire, M. (1994). Cultural stances informing storytelling among bilingual children in Quebec. *Comparative Education Review, 38*(1), 115–143.

Maguire, M. (1997). Shared and negotiated territories: The socio-cultural embeddedness of children's acts of meaning. In A. Filer, A. Pollard, & D. Thiessen (Eds.), *Children and their curriculum: The perspectives of primary and elementary school children* (pp. 51–80). London, UK: Routledge.

Malinowski, B. (1923). Supplement 1: The problem of meaning in primitive languages. In E. A. Ogden & I. A. Richards (Eds.), *The meaning of meaning* (pp. 296–336). New York, NY: Harcourt, Brace & World.

Malinowski, B. (1935). *Coral gardens and their magic: A study of the methods of tilling the soil and of agricultural rites in the Trobriand Islands* (Vol. II). London, UK: Allen & Unwin.

Markus, K. A. (1998). Science, measurement, and validity: Is completion of Samuel Messick's synthesis possible? *Social Indicators Research, 45*(1–3), 7–34.

Markus, K. A., & Borsboom, D. (2013). *Frontiers of test validity theory: Measurement, causation, and meaning*. New York, NY: Routledge.

Matusov, E. (2007). In search of 'the appropriate' unit of analysis for sociocultural research. *Culture & Psychology, 13*(3), 307–333.

Mauranen, A. (2009). Chunking in ELF: expressions for managing interaction. *Intercultural Pragmatics,* 6(2), 217–233.

Mauranen, A. (2012). *Exploring ELF: Academic English shaped by non-native speakers.* Cambridge, UK: Cambridge University Press.

Mauranen, A. (2017). Conceptualizing ELF. In J. Jenkins, W. Baker, & M. Dewey (Eds.), *The Routledge handbook of English as a lingua franca* (Chapter 1). London, UK: Taylor & Francis Group. Retrieved from https://ebookcentral.proquest.com

Maxwell, J. A., & Miller, B. A. (2008). Categorizing and connecting strategies in qualitative data analysis. In S. N. Hesse-Biber & P. Leavy (Eds.), *Handbook of emergent methods* (pp. 461–477). New York, NY: Guilford Press.

May, L. (2011). *Interaction in a paired speaking test: The rater's perspective.* Frankfurt am Main, Germany: Peter Lang.

May, L., Nakatsuhara, F., Lam, D., & Galaczi, E. D. (2020). Developing tools for learning oriented assessment of interactional competence: Bridging theory and practice. *Language Testing, 37*(2), 165–186. doi:10.1177/0265532219879044

May, S. (Ed.). (2014). *The multilingual turn: Implications for SLA, TESOL, and bilingual education.* Abingdon, UK: Routledge.

McCarroll, J., & Hartwick, P. (2019, December). *Targeting student needs by shifting to a blended approach.* Paper presented at the conference of Teachers of English as a Second Language (TESL) Ontario, Toronto, ON.

McDermott, R. P. (1996). The acquisition of a child by a learning disability. In S. Chaiklin & J. Lave (Eds.), *Understanding practice: Perspectives on activity and context* (pp. 269–305). Cambridge, UK: Cambridge University Press.

McGuire, W. J. (1983). A contextualist theory of knowledge: Its implications for innovation and reform in psychological research. *Advances in Experimental Social Psychology, 16,* 1–47. doi:10.1016/S0065-2601(08)60393-7

McLeod, M. (2012). *Looking for an ounce of prevention: The potential for diagnostic assessment in academic acculturation* [Unpublished master's thesis]. Carleton University, Ottawa, ON.

McMillan, J. H., & Schumacher, S. (2010). *Research in education: Evidence-based inquiry* (7th ed.). Boston, MA: Pearson.

McMullen, L. M. (2011). A discursive analysis of Teresa's protocol: Enhancing oneself, diminishing others. In F. J. Wertz, K. Charmaz, L. M. McMullen, R. Josselson, R. Anderson, & E. McSpadden (Eds.), *Five ways of doing qualitative analysis: Phenomenological psychology, grounded theory, discourse analysis, narrative research, and intuitive inquiry* (pp. 205–223). New York, NY: Guilford Press.

McNamara, T. F. (1995). Modelling performances: Opening Pandora's box. *Applied Linguistics, 16*(2), 159–175.

McNamara, T. F. (1997). "Interaction" in second language performance assessment: Whose performance? *Applied Linguistics, 18*(4), 446–466. doi:10.1093/applin/18.4.446

McNamara, T. F. (2007). Language testing: A question of context. In J. Fox et al. (Eds.), *Language testing reconsidered* (pp. 131–137). Ottawa, ON: University of Ottawa Press.

McNamara, T. F. (2008). The social-political and power dimensions of tests. In E. Shohamy and N. H. Hornberger (Eds.), *Encyclopedia of language and education, vol. 7: Language testing and assessment* (2nd ed., pp. 415–427). Dordrecht, Netherlands: Springer.

McNamara, T. F. (2011). Managing learning: Authority and language assessment. *Language Teaching, 44*(4), 500–515. doi:10.1017/S0261444811000073

McNamara, T. F. (2012). English as lingua franca: The challenge for language testing. *Journal of English as a Lingua Franca, 1*(1), 199–202. doi:10.1515/jelf-2012-0013

McNamara, T. F. (2014). 30 years on – evolution or revolution? *Language Assessment Quarterly, 11*(2), 226–232. doi:10.1080/15434303.2014.895830

McNamara, T. F., & Roever, C. (2006). *Language testing: The social dimension.* Oxford, UK: Oxford University Press.

McNamara, T. F., Knoch, U., & Fan, J. (2019). *Fairness, justice, and language assessment.* Oxford, UK: Oxford University Press.

Mellow, J. D. (2002). Toward principled eclecticism in language teaching: The two-dimensional model and the centring principle. *TESL-EJ, 5*(4), 1–18.

Mendes-Flohr, P. (Ed.). (2015). *Dialogue as a trans-disciplinary concept: Martin Buber's philosophy of dialogue and its contemporary reception.* Berlin, Germany: De Gruyter. Retrieved from www.jstor.org/stable/j.ctvbj7kb3

Merriam-Webster. (n.d.). Context. In *Merriam-Webster.com dictionary.* Retrieved from www.merriam-webster.com/dictionary/context

Merritt, A. C. (2000). Culture in the cockpit: Do Hofstede's dimensions replicate? *Journal of Cross-Cultural Psychology, 31*(3), 283–301. doi:10.1177/0022022100031003001

Merritt, A. C., & Helmreich, R. L. (1996). Human factors on the flight deck: The influence of national culture. *Journal of Cross-Cultural Psychology, 27*, 5–24. doi:10.1177/0022022196271001

Mertler, C. A. (2019). *The Wiley handbook of action research in education.* Hoboken, NJ: Wiley Blackwell.

Messick, S. (1980). Test validity and the ethics of assessment. *American Psychologist, 35*, 1012–1027.

Messick, S. (1988). The once and future issues of validity. Assessing the meaning and consequences of measurement. In H. Wainer & H. Braun (Eds.), *Test validity* (pp. 33–45). Hillsdale, NJ: Lawrence Erlbaum.

Messick, S. (1989). Validity. In R. L. Linn (Ed.), *Educational measurement* (3rd ed., pp. 13–103). Phoenix, AZ: American Council on Education and Oryx Press.

Messick, S. (1994). The interplay of evidence and consequences in the validation of performance assessments. *Educational Researcher, 23*(2), 13–24. doi:10.3102/0013189X023002013

Messick, S. (1995a). Validity of psychological assessment. Validation of inferences from persons' responses and performance as scientific inquiry into score meaning. *American Psychologist, 50*(9), 474–479. doi:10.1037/0003-066X.50.9.741

Messick, S. (1995b). Standards of validity and the validity of standards in performance assessment. *Educational Measurement: Issues and Practice, 14*(4), 5–8. doi:10.1111/j.1745-3992.1995.tb00881.x

Messick, S. (1996). Validity and washback in language testing. *ETS Research Report Series* (pp. 1–18). doi:10.1002/j.2333-8504.1996.tb01695.x

Messick, S. (1998). Test validity: A matter of consequences. *Social Indicators Research, 45*, 35–44.

Meyer, J. H. F. (2010). Helping our students: Learning, metalearning, and threshold concepts. In J. Christensen Hughes & J. Mighty (Eds.), *Taking stock: Research on teaching and learning in higher education* (pp. 191–213). Kingston, ON: McGill-Queen's University Press.

Meyer, J. H. F., & Land, R. (2003). Threshold concepts and troublesome knowledge: Linkages to ways of thinking and practising. In C. Rust (Ed.), *Improving student learning: Theory and practice ten years on* (pp 412–424). Oxford, UK: Oxford Centre for Staff and Learning Development.

Meyer, J. H. F., & Land, R. (2005). Threshold concepts and troublesome knowledge (2); Epistemological considerations and a conceptual framework for teaching and learning. *Higher Education, 49*(3), 373–388.

Meyer, J. H. F., & Land, R. (Eds.). (2006). *Overcoming barriers to student understanding: Threshold concepts and troublesome knowledge*. London, UK: Routledge.

Meyer, J. H. F., Land, R., & Baille, C. (Eds.). (2010). *Threshold concepts and transformational learning*. Rotterdam, Netherlands: Sense Publishers.

Michell, M., & Davison, C. (2020). Bringing the teacher back in: Toward L2 assessment praxis in English as an additional language education. In M. E. Poehner & O. Inbar-Lourie (Eds.), *Toward a reconceptualization of second language classroom assessment: Praxis and researcher–teacher partnerships* (pp. 61–81). Cham, Switzerland: Springer. doi:10.1007/978-3-030-35081-9

Miller, C. R. (1984). Genre as social action. *Quarterly Journal of Speech, 70*(2), 151–167.

Miller, C. R. (1992). Kairos in the rhetoric of science. In S. P. Witte, N. Nakadate, & R. D. Cherry (Eds.). *A rhetoric of doing: Essays on written discourse in honor of James L. Kinneavy* (pp. 310–327). Carbondale, IL: Southern Illinois University Press.

Miller, C. R. (1994a). Rhetorical community: The cultural basis of genre. In A. Freedman & P. Medway (Eds.), *Genre and the new rhetoric* (pp. 67–78). London, UK: Taylor & Francis.

Miller, C. R. (1994b). Genre as social action. In A. Freedman & P. Medway (Eds.), *Genre and the new rhetoric* (pp. 23–42). London, UK: Taylor & Francis.

Miller, C. R. (2015). "Genre as social action" (1984), revisited 30 years later (2014). *Letras & Letras, 31*(3), 56–72. Retrieved from www.seer.ufu.br/index.php/letraseletras/article/download/30580/16706

Miller, C. R., & Devitt, A. J. (Eds.). (2019). *Landmark essays on rhetorical genre studies*. London, UK: Routledge.

Miller, C. R., & Kelly, A. R. (Ed.). (2017). *Emerging genres in new media environments*. Cham, Switzerland: Springer.

Miller, G. A. (1956). The magical number seven, plus or minus two: Some limits on our capacity for processing information. *Psychological Review, 63*(2), 81–97.

Mislevy, R. (2009). Validity from the perspective of model-based reasoning. In R. W. Lissitz (Ed.), *The concept of validity* (pp. 83–108). Charlotte, NC: Information Age.

Mitchell, J. R. (2005). *Toward a new vision for language training in the Public Service: A discussion paper prepared for the ADM Working Group*. Ottawa, ON: Public Service Human Resource Management Agency of Canada.

Moder, C. L. (2013). Aviation English. In B. Paltridge & S. Starfield (Eds.), *The handbook of English for specific purposes* (pp. 227–242). Malden, MA: Wiley Blackwell.

Moder, C. L., & Halleck, G. B. (2009). Planes, politics and oral proficiency: Testing international air traffic controllers. *Australian Review of Applied Linguistics, 32*(3), 25.1–25.16. Retrieved from https://benjamins.com/catalog/aral.32.3

Moeini, R. (2020). *Cognitive evidence for construct validity of the IELTS Reading Comprehension Module: Content analysis, test taking processes and experts' accounts* [Unpublished doctoral dissertation]. Carleton University, Ottawa, ON.

Moeller, A. J., Creswell, W., & Saville, N. (Eds.). (2016). *Second language assessment and mixed methods research.* Cambridge, UK: Cambridge University Press.

Monteiro, A. L. T. (2016, March). *Pilot–air traffic controller interactions and intercultural communicative competence: An issue for non-native speakers alone?* Poster session presented at the 11th Annual Graduate Symposium of the Society of Applied Linguistics and Discourse Studies, Carleton University, Ottawa, ON.

Monteiro, A. L. T. (2017, March). *Aviation international radiotelephony communications: An interdisciplinary approach to construct definition in a specific occupational domain.* Poster session presented at the 12th Annual Graduate Symposium of the Society of Applied Linguistics and Discourse Studies, Carleton University, Ottawa, ON.

Monteiro. A. L. T. (2019). *Reconsidering the measurement of proficiency in pilot and air traffic controller radiotelephony communication: From construct definition to task design* [Unpublished doctoral dissertation]. Carleton University, Ottawa, ON.

Monteiro, A. L. T., & Bullock, N. (2020). A broader view of communicative competence for aeronautical communications: Implications for teaching and high-stakes testing. *The Especialist*, 41(3), 1–29. doi:10.23925/2318-7115.2020v41i3a4

Morgan, D. (2007). Paradigms lost and pragmatism regained: Methodological implications of combining qualitative and quantitative methods. *Journal of Mixed Methods Research, 1*(1), 48–76.

Moss, P. A. (1994). Can there be validity without reliability? *Educational Researcher*, *23*(2), 5–12. doi:10.3102/0013189X023002005

Moss, P. A. (1998). Recovering a dialectical view of rationality. *Social Indicators Research, 45*, 55–67.

Moss, P. A. (2013). Validity in action: Lessons from studies of data use. *Journal of Educational Measurement, 50*(1), 91–98.

Moss, P. A. (2016). Shifting the focus of validity for test use. *Assessment in Education: Principles, Policy & Practice, 23*(2), 236–251. doi:10.1080/0969594X.2015.1072085

Moss, P. A. (2018). *Evolving our knowledge infrastructures in measurement: Recovering Messick's Singerian approach to inquiry.* [Keynote conference session: Samuel J. Messick Memorial Lecture]. Language Testing Research Colloquium, July 5, Auckland, New Zealand.

Moss, P. A., & Haertel, E. H. (2016). Engaging methodological pluralism. In D. Gitomer & C. Bell (Eds.), *Handbook of research on teaching* (5th ed., pp. 127–247). Washington, DC: AERA.

Moss, P. A., Phillips, D. C., Erickson, F. D., Floden, R. E., Lather, P. A., & Schneider, B. L. (2009). *Learning from our differences: A dialogue across perspectives on quality in education research. Educational Researcher, 38*(7), 501–517. doi:10.3102/0013189X09348351

Multiculturalism Act (1988). Ottawa, ON: Government of Canada.

Nakatsuhara, F. (2013). *The co-construction of conversation in group oral tests.* Frankfurt am Main, Germany: Peter Lang.

Nearing, E. (2020). *The Government of Canada's Second Language Evaluation, Test of Written Expression: Exploring validity* [Unpublished master's thesis]. Carleton University, Ottawa, ON.

Nematizadeh, S., & Wood, D. (2019). Willingness to communicate and second language speech fluency: An investigation of affective and cognitive dynamics. *The Canadian Modern Language Review, 75*(3), pp. 197–215. doi:10.3138/cmlr.2017-0146

Newton, P. E. (2012). Clarifying the consensus definition of validity. *Measurement, 10*, 1–29.

Newton, P. E., & Baird, J. (2016). The great validity debate. *Assessment in Education: Principles, Policy & Practice, 23*(2), 173–177. doi:10.1080/0969594X.2016.1172871

Newton, P. E., & Shaw, S. D. (2014). *Validity in educational and psychological assessment.* London, UK: SAGE.

Newton, P. E., & Shaw, D. S. (2016). Disagreement over the best way to use the word "validity" and options for reaching consensus. *Assessment in Education: Principles, Policy & Practice 23*(2), 178–197. doi:10.1080/0969594X.2015.1037241

Nicolescu, B. (2006). Transdisciplinarity: Past, present and future. In B. Haverkort & C. Reijntjes (Eds.), *Moving worldviews: Reshaping sciences, policies and practices for endogenous sustainable development* (pp. 142–166). Leusden, Netherlands: COMPAS Editions.

Niglas, K. (2010). The multidimensional model of research methodology: An integrated set of continua. In A. Tashakkori & C. Teddlie (Eds.), *SAGE handbook of mixed methods in social & behavioral research* (pp. 215–236). Thousand Oaks, CA: SAGE.

Nocetti, A. M, Chacón, C., Chizrella, C., & Erbetta, E. (2017). Interdisciplinary pedagogical actions to optimize engineering undergraduate written production. In C. Vargas-Sierra (Ed.), *Professional and academic discourse: An interdisciplinary perspective. Proceedings of the 8th International Conference of the Spanish Society for Applied Linguistics AESLA 2016, v. 2*, 127–137.

No Child Left Behind Act of 2001, P.L. 107-110, 20 U.S.C. § 6319 (2002). Common Core State Standards (n.d.). Retrieved from www.corestandards.org.

Norton, B. (2000). *Identity and language learning: Gender, ethnicity and educational change.* London, UK: Longman.

Norton, J. (2013). Performing identities in speaking tests: Co-construction revisited. *Language Assessment Quarterly, 10*(3), 309–330.

Norton, B., & Stein, P. (1998). Why the "Monkeys Passage" bombed: Tests, genres and teaching. In A. Kunnan (Ed.), *Validation in language assessment* (pp. 231–249). Mahwah, NJ: Lawrence Earlbaum.

Oakley, A. (1999). Paradigm wars: some thoughts on a personal and public trajectory. *International Journal of Social Science Research Methodology, 2*(3), 247–254.

Office of the Commissioner of Official Languages (2013). *Challenges: The new environment for language training in the federal public service.* Ottawa, ON: Minister of Public Works and Government Services Canada.

Office of the Commissioner of Official Languages (2020–2021). *Annual Report 2020 –2021.* Ottawa, ON: Minister of Public Works and Government Services

Canada. Retrieved from www.clo-ocol.gc.ca/en/publications/annual-reports/2020-2021

Official Languages Act(s) (1969/1985/1988). *Official Languages Act* 1969, repealed and replaced by *Official Languages Act*, RSC 1985, c 31 (4th Supp), [Amended in 1988, See *Official Languages Act* 1988, c38, assented to 28th July, 1988]. Retrieved from https://laws-lois.justice.gc.ca/eng/acts/o-3.01/FullText.html.html

Omaggio Hadley, A. (1993). *Teaching language in context* (2nd ed.). Boston, MA: Heinle & Heinle.

Organisation for Economic Co-operation and Development. (1972). *Problems of teaching and research in universities*. Paris, France: OECD.

Ortega, L. (2013). SLA for the 21st century: Disciplinary progress, transdisciplinary relevance, and the bi/multilingual turn. *Language Learning*, *63*(Supplement 2019), 1–24. doi:10.1111/j.1467-9922.2012.00735.x

Ortega, L. (2014). Ways forward for a bi/multicultural turn in SLA. In S. May (Ed.), *The multilingual turn. Implications for SLA, TESOL, and bilingual education* (pp. 32–53). New York, NY: Routledge.

O'Sullivan, B. (2014). Adapting tests to the local context. Paper presented at the 2nd New Directions in English Language Assessment Conference, September 29. Meiji Kinenkan, Japan. Power point slides available at www.britishcouncil.jp/sites/default/files/new-directions-powerpoint-barry-osullivan.pdf.

O'Sullivan, B. (2016). Adapting tests to the local context. *New directions in language assessment, special edition of the JASELE Journal* (pp. 145–158). Tokyo, Japan: Japan Society of English Language Education & the British Council.

Oxford University Press. (1974). Context. In A. S. Hornby with A. P Cowie (Eds.), *Oxford advanced learner's dictionary of current English* (3rd ed., p. 184).

Oxford University Press. (2005). Context. In *Oxford dictionary of philosophy*. Retrieved from https://books.google.ca/books?hl=en&lr=&id=5wTQtwB1NdgC&oi=fnd&pg=PR5&dq=Oxford+Dictionary+of+Philosophy+definitions+of+context&ots=Zc_R-amF-B&sig=U26m8mXmdPNvyk3KWlOnCFas1wo#v=onepage&q=Oxford%20Dictionary%20of%20Philosophy%20definitions%20of%20context&f=false

Pape, C. (2016). Husserl, Bakhtin, and the other I. Or: Mikhail M. Bakhtin – a Husserlian? Horizon. *Феноменологические исследования*, *5*(2), 271–289.

Paré, A. (2008). Interdisciplinarity: Rhetoric, reasonable accommodation, and the Toto effect. In H. Graves & R. Graves (Eds.), *Interdisciplinarity: Thinking and writing beyond borders: Proceedings from the 2008 Conference of the Canadian Association of Teachers of Technical Writing* (pp. 17–30). Edmonton, AB: Inkshed Publications.

Paré, A., & Smart, G. (1994). Observing genres in action: Towards a research methodology. In A. Freedman & P. Medway (Eds.), *Genre and the new rhetoric* (pp. 146–154). London, UK: Taylor & Francis.

Patton, M. Q. (2012). *Essentials of utilization-focused evaluation*. Thousand Oaks, CA: SAGE.

Penny Light, T., Ittelson, J. C., & Chen, H. L. (2012). *Documenting learning with ePortfolios: A guide for college instructors* (1st ed.). San Francisco, CA: Jossey-Bass.

Perelman, C., & Olbrechts-Tyteca, L. (1958). *Traité de l'argumentation: La nouvelle rhétorique*. Paris, France: Presses Universitaires de France.

Perelman, C., & Olbrechts-Tyteca, L. (1969). The new rhetoric: A treatise on argumentation. (J. Wilkinson & P. Weaver, Trans.). Notre Dame, IN: University of Notre Dame Press.

Personnel Evaluation and Analysis Office (1985). Report (the Apollo space program). NASA Headquarters. Retrieved from www.history.nasa.gov/SP-4104/appb.htm

Phillipson, R. (1992). *Linguistic imperialism*. Oxford, UK: Oxford University Press.

Piaget, J. (1972). L'épistémologie des relations interdisciplinaires. In L. Apostel, G. Berger, A. Briggs, & G. Michau, *L'interdisciplinarité: problèmes d'enseignement et de recherche dans les universités* (pp 131–144). Paris, France: OCDE. Retrieved from http://pascal-francis.inist.fr/vibad/index.php?action=getRecordDetail&idt=13228486

Pill, J. (2016). Drawing on indigenous criteria for more authentic assessment in a specific purpose language test: Health professionals interacting with patients. *Language Testing, 33*(2), 175–193. doi:10.1177/0265532215607400

Pitzl, M.-L. (2005). Non-understanding in English as a lingua franca: Examples from a business context. *Vienna English Working Papers, 14*(2), 50–71.

Plough, I., Banerjee, J., & Iwashita, N. (2018). Interactional competence: Genie out of the bottle. Language *Testing, 35*(3), 427–445. doi:10.1177/0265532218772325

Poehner, M. E. (2008). Both sides of the conversation: The interplay between mediation and learner reciprocity in Dynamic Assessment. In J. P. Lantolf & M. E. Poehner (Eds.), *Sociocultural theory and the teaching of second languages* (pp. 33–56). London: Equinox.

Poehner, M. E., & Inbar-Lourie, O. (Eds.). (2020a). *Toward a reconceptualization of second language classroom assessment: Praxis and researcher–teacher partnerships*. Cham, Switzerland: Springer. doi:10.1007/978-3-030-35081-9

Poehner, M. E., & Inbar-Lourie, O. (2020b). An epistemology of action for understanding and change in L2 classroom assessment: The case for Praxis. In M. E. Poehner & O. Inbar-Lourie (Eds.), *Toward a reconceptualization of second language assessment: Praxis and researcher–teacher partnerships*. (pp. 1–20). Cham, Switzerland: Springer. doi:10.1007/978-3-030-35081-9

Pohl, C., & Hirsch Hadorn, G. (2007). *Principles for designing transdisciplinary research*. Bern, Switzerland: Swiss Academies of Arts and Sciences. Retrieved from www.oekom.de/_files_media/titel/leseproben/9783865810465.pdf

Pohl, C., & Hirsch Hadorn, G. (2008). Core terms in transdisciplinary research. In G. Hirsch Hadorn, H. Hoffmann-Riem, S. Biber-Klemm, W. Grossenbacher-Mansuy, D. Joye, C. Pohl, U. Wiesmann, & E. Zemp (Eds.), *Handbook of transdisciplinary research* (pp. 427–432). Dordrecht, Netherlands: Springer Science + Business Media.

Polkinghorne, D. (1988). *Narrative knowing and the human sciences*. Albany, NY: SUNY Press.

Poole, B. (1998). Bakhtin and Cassirer: The philosophical origins of Bakhtin's carnival messianism. *The South Atlantic Quarterly, 97*(3/4), 537–78.

Popham, W. J. (1997). Consequential validity: Right concern–wrong concept. *Educational Measurement: Issues and Practice, 16*(2), 9–13. doi:10.1111/j.1745-3992.1997.tb00586.x

Potter, J. (2003). Discursive analysis and discursive psychology. In P. M. Camic, J. E. Rhodes, & L. Yardley (Eds.), *Qualitative research in psychology:*

Expanding perspectives in methodology and design (pp. 73–94). Washington, DC: American Psychological Association.

Potter, J., & Wetherell, M. (1987). *Discourse and social psychology: Beyond attitudes and behaviours*. London, UK: SAGE.

Prior, P. (1991). Contextualizing writing and response in a graduate seminar. *Written Communication, 8*, 267–310.

Prior, P. (2003, March 24). Are communities of practice really an alternative to discourse communities? Paper presented at the Conference of the American Association of Applied Linguistics (AAAL).

Prior, P., Solberg, J., Berry, P., Bellwoar, H., Chewning, B., Lunsford, K. J., Rohan, K., Roozen, M., Sheridan-Rabideau, P., Shipka, J., Van Ittersum, D. I., & Walker, J. R. (2007). Re-situating and re-mediating the Canons: A cultural-historical remapping of rhetorical activity. *Kairos, 11*(3). Retrieved from https://technorhetoric.net/11.3/topoi/prior-et-al/core/core.pdf

Purpura, J. E., & Turner, C. E. (forthcoming). *Learning-oriented assessment in language classrooms: Using assessment to gauge and promote language learning*. London, UK: Taylor & Francis.

Ragan, P. (2004). Cross cultural communication in aviation. *Proceedings of the 14th European Symposium on Language for Special Purposes*. Guildford, UK.

Rea-Dickins, P. (2006). Currents and eddies in the discourse of assessment: A learning-focused interpretation. *International Journal of Applied Linguistics, 16*(2), 163–188.

Rea-Dickins, P., & Gardner, S. (2000). Snares and silver bullets: Disentangling the construct of formative assessment. *Language Testing, 17*, 215–243.

Read, J. (Ed.). (2016). *Post-admission language assessment of university students*. Cham, Switzerland: Springer.

Read, J., & Knoch, U. (2009). Clearing the air: Applied linguistic perspectives on aviation communication. *Australian Review of Applied Linguistics, 32*(3), 21.1–21.11. Retrieved from https://benjamins.com/catalog/aral.32.3

Reason, P., & Bradbury, H. (Eds.) (2008). *The SAGE handbook of action research* (2nd ed.). London, UK: SAGE. Retrieved from www-doi-org.proxy.library.carleton.ca/10.4135/9781848

Reeves, S., Albert, M., Kuper, A., & Hodges, B. D. (2008). Why use theories in qualitative research? *British Medical Journal, 337*, 631–634. doi:10.1136/bmj.a949

Reichardt, C. S., & Rallis, S. F. (1994). The qualitative–quantitative debate: New perspectives. *New Directions for Program Evaluation, 61*, 1–98.

Richards, K. (2009). Trends in qualitative research in language teaching since 2000. *Language Teaching, 42*(2), 147–180.

Roever, C., & Kasper, G. (2018). Speaking in turns and sequences: Interactional competence as a target construct in testing speaking. *Language Testing, 35*(3), 331–355. doi:10.1177/0265532218758128

Rogoff, B. (1990). *Apprenticeship in thinking: Cognitive development in social context*. Oxford, UK: Oxford University Press.

Rorty, R. (1982). *The consequences of pragmatism. Essays, 1972–1980*. Minneapolis, MN: University of Minnesota Press.

Rossman, G., & Wilson, B. (1985). Numbers and words: Combining quantitative and qualitative methods in a single large scale evaluation study. *Evaluation Review, 9*, 627–643.

Russell, D. R. (1993). Vygotsky, Dewey, & externalism: Beyond the student/discipline dichotomy. *Journal of Advanced Composition, 13*, 172–195.

Russell, D. R. (1997). Rethinking genre in school and society: An activity theory analysis. *Written Communication, 14*(4), 504–554. doi:10.1177/0741088397014004004

Russell, D. R. (2013). Contradictions regarding teaching and writing (or writing to learn) in the disciplines: What we have learned in the USA. *Revista de Docencia Universitaria. REDU, 11* (1), 161–181. Retrieved from https://dialnet.unirioja.es/descarga/articulo/4243905.pdf

Saldaña, J. (2009). *The coding manual for qualitative researchers.* Los Angeles, CA: SAGE.

Samuda, V. (2001). Guiding relationships between form and meaning during task performance: The role of the teacher. In M. Bygate, P. Skehan, & M. Swain (Eds.), *Researching pedagogic tasks: Second language learning, teaching, and testing* (pp. 119–140). Harlow, UK: Pearson Education.

Sandler, S. (2015). A strange kind of Kantian: Bakhtin's reinterpretation of Kant and the Marburg School. *Studies in East European Thought, 67*(3), 165–182.

Savaskan Nowlan, N., Hartwick, P., and Arya, A. (2018). Skill assessment in virtual learning environments, *2018 IEEE International Conference on Computational Intelligence and Virtual Environments for Measurement Systems and Applications (CIVEMSA), Ottawa, ON, 2018*, pp. 1–6. doi: 10.1109/CIVEMSA.2018.8439968

Savignon, S. J. (1991). Communicative language teaching: State of the art. *TESOL Quarterly, 25*(2), 261–277. doi:10.2307/3587463

Savin-Baden, M. (2008). *Learning spaces: Creating opportunities for knowledge creation in academic life.* New York, NY: McGraw Hill.

Schiffrin, D. (1990). The management of a co-operative self during argument: The role of opinions and stories. In A. D. Grimshaw (Ed.), *Conflict talk* (pp. 241–59). Cambridge, UK: Cambridge University Press.

Schissel, J. (2019). *Social consequences of testing for language-minoritized bilinguals in the United States.* Bristol, UK: Multilingual Matters.

Schissel, J., & Arias, A. (Eds.). (2021). Special issue: On assessment innovations in multilingual contexts. *Journal of Multilingual Theory and Practice,* 2(2), 141–319.

Schryer, C. F. (1993). Records as genre. *Written Communication, 10* (2), 200–234.

Schutz, A. (1946). The well-informed citizen: An essay on the social distribution of knowledge. *Social Research, 13*(4), 463–478.

Schutz, A. (1966). *Collected papers, vol. III: Studies in phenomenological philosophy.* The Hague, Netherlands: Martinus Nijhoff.

Schutz, A. (1967). *The phenomenology of the social world.* Evanston, IL: Northwestern University Press.

Schutz, A. [1942–55] (1982). *Collected papers I: The problem of social reality.* Hague, Netherlands: Martinus Nijhoff.

Schutz, A., & Luckmann, T. (1973). *The Structures of the Life-World* (R. M. Zaner & T. Engelhardt, Trans.). Evanston, IL and London, UK: Northwestern University Press and Heinemann.

Schryer, C. F. (1993). Records as genre. *Written Communication, 10*(2), 200–234.

Schryer, C. F., & Spoel, P. (2005). Genre theory, health-care discourse, and professional identity formation. *Journal of Business and Technical Communication, 19*(3), 249–278.

Schryer, C. F., Lingard, L., & Spafford, M. M. (2005). Techne or artful science and the genre of case presentations in healthcare settings. *Communication Monographs,* 72(2), 234–260.

Schwandt, T. A. (1994). Constructivist, interpretivist approaches to human inquiry. In N. K. Denzin & Y. S. Lincoln (Eds.), *Handbook of qualitative research* (pp. 118–137). Thousand Oaks, CA: SAGE.

Schwandt, T. A. (1997). *Qualitative inquiry: A dictionary of terms*. Thousand Oaks, CA: SAGE.

Scollon, R. (2001). *Mediated discourse: The nexus of practice*. London, UK: Routledge.

Scollon, R., & Scollon, S. B. K. (2001). *Intercultural communication: A discourse approach*. Malden, MA: Blackwell.

Seidlhofer, B. (2001). Closing a conceptual gap: The case for a description of English as a lingua franca. *International Journal of Applied Linguistics, 11*(2), 133–158. doi:10.1111/1473-4192.00011

Seidlhofer, B. (2004). Research perspectives on teaching English as a lingua franca. *Annual Review of Applied Linguistics 24*, 209–239. doi:10.1017/S0267190504000145

Seidlhofer, B. (2009). Accommodation and the idiom principle in English as a lingua franca. *Intercultural Pragmatics,* 6(2), 195–215. doi:10.1515/IPRG.2009.011

Seidlhofer, B. (2011). *Understanding English as a lingua franca*. Oxford, UK: Oxford University Press.

Shapere, D. (1964). The structure of scientific revolutions. [Review of the book *The structure of scientific revolutions*, by T. S. Kuhn]. *The Philosophical Review, 73*(3), 383–394.

Shepard, L. (2016). Evaluating test validity: Reprise and progress. *Assessment in Education: Principles, Policy & Practice, 23*(2), 268–280.

Shohamy, E. (1997). Testing methods, testing consequences: Are they ethical? Are they fair? *Language Testing, 14*(3), 340–349.

Shohamy, E. (1998). Critical language testing and beyond. *Studies in Educational Evaluation, 24*, 331–345.

Shohamy, E. (2001). *Language policy: Hidden agendas and new approaches*. London, UK: Routledge.

Shohamy, E. (2006). *The power of tests: A critical perspective on the uses of language tests*. London, UK: Pearson.

Shohamy, E. (2007). Tests as power tools: Looking back, looking forward. In J. Fox, M. Wesche, D. Bayliss, L. Cheng, C. E. Turner, & C. Doe (Eds.), *Language testing reconsidered* (pp. 141–152). Ottawa, ON: University of Ottawa Press.

Shohamy, E. (2011). Assessing multilingual competencies: Adopting construct valid assessment policies. *The Modern Language Journal, 95*, 417–429. doi:10. 1111/i.1540-4781.2011.01210.x

Shohamy, E. (2016). Critical language testing. In E. Shohamy, I. Or, & S. May (Eds.), *Language testing and assessment. Encyclopedia of language and education* (3rd ed.). Cham, Switzerland: Springer. doi:10.1007/978-3-319-02326-7_26-1

Shohamy, E. (2017). ELF and critical language testing. In J. Jenkins, W. Baker, & M. Dewey (Eds.), *The Routledge handbook of English as a lingua franca* (Chapter 46). London, UK: Routledge. doi:10.4324/9781315717173

Shohamy, E. (2018). Critical language testing and English lingua franca: How can one help the other? In K. Murata (Ed.), *English-medium instruction from an English as a lingua franca perspective*. doi:10.4324/9781351184335

Singer, E. A. Jr. (1959). *Experience and reflection*. (C.W. Churchman, Ed.). Philadelphia, PA: University of Pennsylvania Press.

Skehan, P. (1998). *A cognitive approach to language learning*. Oxford, UK: Oxford University Press.

Skehan, P. (2001). Tasks and language performance assessment. In M. Bygate, P. Skehan, & M. Swain (Eds.), *Researching pedagogic tasks: Second language learning, teaching and testing* (pp. 167–185). Harlow, UK: Pearson Longman.

Skinner, B. F. (1957). *Verbal behaviour*. New York, NY: Appleton-Century-Crofts.

Smart, G. (2008). Ethnographic-based discourse analysis: Uses, issues and prospects. In V. K. Bhatia, J. Flowerdew, & R. H. Jones (Eds.), *Advances in discourse studies* (pp. 56–66). London, UK: Routledge.

Smythe, S., Hill, C., MacDonald, M., Dagenais, D., Sinclair, N., & Toohey, K. (2017). *Disrupting boundaries in education and research*. Cambridge, UK: Cambridge University Press.

Solano-Flores, G., & Trumbull, E. (2003). Examining language in context: The need for new research and practices paradigms in the testing of English-language learners. *Educational Researcher, 32*(2), 3–13.

Somerville, M., & Rapport, D. (Eds.). (2000). *Transdisciplinarity: Recreating integrated knowledge*. Oxford, UK: ELOSS.

Spinuzzi, C., & Guile, D. (2019, July). Fourth-generation activity theory: An integrative literature review and implications for professional communication. In *2019 IEEE International Professional Communication Conference (ProComm)* (pp. 37–45). IEEE.

Spolsky, B. (1967). Do they know enough English? In D. Wigglesworth (Ed.), *ATESL Selected Conference Papers*. Washington, DC: NAFSA Studies and Papers, English Language Series.

Spolsky, B. (1981). Some ethical questions about language testing. *Practice and Problems in Language Testing, 1*, 5–21.

Spolsky, B. (1984). The uses of language tests: An ethical envoi. In C. Rivera (Ed.), *Placement procedures in bilingual education: Education and policy issues* (pp. 3–7). Clevedon, UK: Multilingual Matters.

Spolsky, B. (1995). *Measured words*. Malden, MA: Blackwell.

Spolsky, B. (2009). Editor's introduction. *Annual Review of Applied Linguistics, 29*, vii–xii.

St. Amant, K. (2013). Culture and rhetorical expectations: A perspective for technical communicators. *Communication & Language at Work, 2(2)*, 33–40.

Stenhouse, M. (1975). *An introduction to curriculum research and development*. London, UK: Heinemann.

Stetsenko, A., & Arievitch, I. M. (2004). The self in cultural-historical activity theory: Reclaiming the unity of social and individual dimensions of human development. *Theory & Psychology, 14*(4), 475–503.

Stetsenko, A., & Arievitch, I. M. (2010). Cultural-historical activity theory: Foundational worldview and major principles. In S. R. Kirschner & J. Martin (Eds.), *The sociocultural turn in psychology: The contextual emergence of mind and self* (pp. 231–253). New York, NY: Columbia University Press. Retrieved from www.jstor.org/stable/10.7312/kirs14838

Stoller, A. (2015). Taylorism and the logic of learning outcomes. *Journal of Curriculum Studies, 47*(3), 317–333.

Stone, J., & Zumbo, B. D. (2016). Validity as a pragmatist project: A global concern with local application. In V. Aryadoust & J. Fox (Eds.), *Trends in language assessment research and practice* (pp. 555–573). Newcastle upon Tyne, UK: Cambridge Scholars.

Strike, K. (2006). The ethics of educational research. In J. L. Green, G. Camilli, & P. B. Elmore (Eds.), *Handbook of complementary methods in education research* (pp. 57–73). Washington, DC: American Educational Research Association.

Su, L. I.-W., Weir, C. J., & Wu, J. R. W. (Eds.). (2019). *English language proficiency testing in Asia: A new paradigm bridging global and local contexts.* London, UK: Routledge. doi:10.4324/9781351254021

Sussex, R., & Curtis, A. (2018). Introduction. In A. Curtis, & R. Sussex (Eds.), *Intercultural communication in Asia: Education, language and values* (pp. 1–18) Cham, Switzerland: Springer.

Swain, M. (2000). The output hypothesis and beyond: Mediating acquisition through collaborative dialogue. In J. Lantolf (Ed.), *Sociocultural theory and second language learning* (pp. 97–114). Oxford, UK: Oxford University Press.

Swain, M., & Lapkin, S. (2013). A Vygotskian sociocultural perspective on immersion education: The L1/L2 debate. *Annual Review of Applied Linguistics, 20*, 199–212. doi:10.1075/jicb.1.1.05swa

Swain, M., Kinnear, P., & Steinman, L. (2010). *Sociocultural theory in second language education: An introduction through narratives.* Bristol, UK: Multilingual Matters.

Swales, J. M. (1988). Discourse communities, genres and English as an international language. *World Englishes, 7*(2), 211–220.

Swales, J. M. (1990). *Genre analysis: English in academic and research settings.* Cambridge, UK: Cambridge University Press.

Swales, J. M. (1993). Genre and engagement. *Revue belge de philologie et d'histoire, 71*, 687–698.

Swales, J. M. (1998). Textography: Toward a contextualization of written academic discourse. *Research on Language and Social Interaction, 31*(1), 109–121.

Swales, J. M. (2016). Reflections on the concept of discourse community. *ASp. La revue du GERAS, 69*, 7–19.

Swales, J. M. (2017). The concept of discourse community: Some recent personal history; Reflections on the concept of discourse community/Le concept de communauté de discours: Quelques réflexions. *Composition Forum, 37.* Retrieved from http://compositionforum.com/issue/37/swales-retrospective.php

Takala, S., & Kaftandjieva, F. (2000). Test fairness: A DIF analysis of an L2 vocabulary test. *Language Testing, 17*(3), 323–340. doi:10.1177/026553220001700303

Tardy, C. M. (2009). *Building genre knowledge.* West Lafayette, IN: Parlor Press.

Tardy, C. M. (2012). A rhetorical genre theory perspective on L2 writing development. In R. Manchoìn (Ed.), *L2 writing development: Multiple perspectives* (pp. 165–190). Boston, MA: Walter de Gruyter.

Tardy, C. M. (2017). Crossing, or creating, divides? A plea for transdisciplinary scholarship. In B. Horner & L. Tetreault (Eds.), *Crossing divides: Exploring translingual writing pedagogies and programs* (pp. 181–189). Logan, UT: Utah State University Press.

Tardy, C. M. (2019). Is the five-paragraph essay a genre? In N. A. Caplan & A. M. Johns (Eds.), *Changing practices for the L2 writing classroom: Moving beyond the five-paragraph essay* (pp. 14–41). Ann Arbor, MI: University of Michigan Press.

Tashakkori, A., & Teddlie, C. (Eds.). (2010). *SAGE handbook of mixed methods in social & behavioral research* (2nd ed.). Los Angeles, CA: SAGE.

Taylor, L. (2005). Using qualitative research methods in test development and validation. *Research Notes, 21* (August), 2–4. Cambridge, UK: University of Cambridge ESOL Examinations

Teddlie, C., & Tashakkori, A. (2010). Overview of contemporary issues in mixed methods research. In A. Tashakkori & C. Teddlie (Eds.), *SAGE handbook of mixed methods in social & behavioral research* (pp. 1–41). Thousand Oaks, CA: SAGE.

Ting-Toomey, S. (2005). The matrix of face: An updated face-negotiation theory. In W. B. Gudykunst (Ed.), *Theorizing about intercultural communication* (pp. 71–92). Thousand Oaks, CA: SAGE.

Tinto, V. (1993). Leaving college: Rethinking the causes and cures of student attrition (2nd. ed.). Chicago, IL: Chicago University Press.

Tolman, E. C. (1948). Cognitive maps in rats and men. *Psychological Review, 55*, 189–208.

Tosqui-Lucks, P., & Silva, A. L. B. C. (2020). Da elaboração de um glossário colaborativo à discussão sobre os termos inglês para aviação e inglês aeronáutico. [From writing a collaborative glossary to discussing the terms "aviation English" and "aeronautical English"]. *Estudos Linguísticos, 48*(4), 97–116. doi:10.21165/el.v49i1.2561

Toulmin, S. E. (1958). *The uses of argument.* Cambridge, UK: Cambridge University Press.

Toulmin, S. E. (1969). Concepts and the explanation of human behaviour. In T. Mischel (Ed.), *Human action: Conceptual and empirical issues* (pp. 71–104). New York, NY: Academic Press.

Toulmin, S. E. (1972). *Human understanding* (vol 1). Princeton, NJ: Princeton University Press.

Toulmin, S. E. (1990). *Cosmopolis: The hidden agenda of modernity.* Chicago, IL: University of Chicago Press.

Tucker, W. T. (1965). Max Weber's "Verstehen". *The Sociological Quarterly,* 6(2), 157–165.

Turnbull, M., & Dailey-O'Cain, J. (2009). *First language use in second and foreign language learning.* Bristol, UK: Multilingual Matters.

Turner, C. E. (2000). Listening to the voices of rating scale developers: Identifying salient features for second language performance assessment. *Canadian Modern Language Review, 56*(1), 555–584.

Turner, C. E. (2009). Examining washback in second language education contexts: A high stakes provincial exam and the teacher factor in classroom practice in Quebec secondary schools. *International Journal on Pedagogies and Learning, 5*(1), 103–123. doi:10.5172/ijpl.5.1.103

Turner, C. E. (2012). Classroom assessment. In G. Fulcher & F. Davidson (Eds.), *The Routledge handbook of language testing* (pp. 65–78). New York, NY: Routledge.

Turner, C. E. (2014). Mixed methods research. In A. J. Kunnan (Ed.), *The companion to language assessment* (pp. 1403–1417). Chichester, UK: John Wiley & Sons. doi:10.1002/9781118411360.wbcla142

Turner, C. E. (2018, July 6). *The methodological evolution in language testing/assessment research and the role of community: A personal view* [Conference session: The Distinguished Achievement Award Lecture]. Language Testing Research Colloquium, July 6, Auckland, New Zealand.

Turner, C. E., & Purpura, J. E. (2016). Learning-oriented assessment in the classroom. In D. Tsagari & J. Banerjee (Eds.). *Handbook of second language assessment* (pp. 255–273). Berlin, Germany: DeGruyter Mouton.

Turner, C. E., & Upshur, J. A. (2002). Rating scales derived from student samples: Effects of the scale maker and the student sample on scale content and student scores. *TESOL Quarterly, 36*(1), 49–70.

Tynjälä, P., & Gijbels, D. (2012). Changing world: Changing pedagogy. In P. Tynjälä, M. Stenström, & M. Saarnivaara (Eds.), *Transitions and transformations in learning and education* (pp. 205–222). Dordrecht, Netherlands: Springer.

van den Branden, K. (Ed.). (2006). *Task-based language education: From theory to practice.* Cambridge, UK: Cambridge University Press.

van Lier, L. (1989). Reeling, writhing, drawling, stretching, and fainting in coils: Oral proficiency interviews as conversation. *TESOL Quarterly, 23*(3), 489–508. doi:10.2307/3586922

van Lier, L. (2000). From input to affordance: Social-interactive learning from an ecological perspective. In J. R. Lantolf (Ed.), *Sociocultural theory and second language learning* (pp. 245–259). Oxford, UK: Oxford University Press.

Van Eemeren, F. H. (1995). A world of difference: The rich state of argumentation theory. *Informal Logic, 17*(2), 144–158.

Van Eemeren, F. H., Grootendorst, R., & Kruiger, T. (2019). *Handbook of argumentation theory: A critical survey of classical backgrounds and modern studies* (Vol. 7). Berlin, Germany: Walter de Gruyter.

Vogt, W. P. (2007). *Quantitative research methods for professionals.* Boston, MA: Pearson.

Vygotsky, L. S. (1978). *Mind in society: The development of higher psychological processes* (M. Cole, V. John-Steiner, S. Scribner, & E. Soubennan, Eds.). Cambridge, MA: Harvard University Press.

Vygotsky, L. S. (1987). *The collected works of L. S. Vygotsky, Vol. 1. Problems of general psychology* (R. W. Rieber & A. S. Carton, Eds.). New York, NY: Plenum Press.

Vygotsky, L. S. (2003a). Umstvennoe razvitie detey v procese obuchenia [Mental development of children in the course of education]. In *L. S. Vygotsky, Psikhologia razvitia rebenka* [Psychological development of a child] (pp. 327–505). Moscow: EKSMO. (Original work published in 1935)

Vygotsky, L. S. (2003b). Mishlenie i rech' [Thinking and speech]. In L. S. Vygotsky, *Psikhologia razvitia cheloveka* [Psychology of human development] (pp. 664–1019). Moscow: Smisl EKSMO. (Original work published in 1934)

Vygotsky, L. S. (2012a). *Thought and language* (pp. 13–59). Cambridge, MA: The MIT Press. (Original work published in 1934)

Vygotsky, L. S. (2012b). *The collected works of LS Vygotsky: The fundamentals of defectology (abnormal psychology and learning disabilities*). Berlin, Germany: Springer Science & Business Media.

Wagner, H. R. (1970). *Introduction.* In A. Schutz, *Alfred Schutz on phenomenology and social relations* (Vol. 360, pp. 1–50) (H. R. Wagner, Ed.). Chicago, IL: University of Chicago Press.

Wall, D. (1997). Impact and washback in language testing. In C. Clapham and D. Corson (eds.), *Encyclopedia of language and education* (pp. 291–302). Dordorecht, Netherlands: Kluwer Academic.

Walters, F. S. (2022). Ethics and fairness. In G. Fulcher & L Harding (Eds.), *The Routledge handbook of language testing* (2nd ed., pp. 563–577). London, UK & New York, NY: Routledge.

Wasserman, S., & Faust, K. (1997). *Social network analysis: Methods and applications*. Cambridge, UK: Cambridge University Press.

Weber, M. (2019). *Economy and society: a new translation*. (K. Tribe, Trans.). Cambridge, MA & London, UK: Harvard University Press. Kindle edition. (Original work published in 1922)

Weichselgartner, J., & Truffer, B. (2015). From knowledge co-production to transdisciplinary research: Lessons from the quest to produce socially robust knowledge. In B. Werlen (Ed.), *Global sustainability* (pp. 89–106). Cham, Switzerland: Springer. https://doi-org.proxy.library.carleton.ca/10.1007/978-3-319-16477-9_5

Weideman, A. (2012). Validation and validity beyond Messick. *Per Linguam*, *28*(2), 1–14. doi:10.5785/28-2-526

Weir, C. J. (1993). *Understanding and developing language tests*. New York, NY: Prentice-Hall.

Weir, C. J. (2005). *Language testing and validation: An evidence-based approach*. Basingstoke, UK: Palgrave Macmillan.

Weir, C. J. (2019). Global, local, or "glocal": Alternative pathways in English language test provision [Abstract]. In L. I.-W. Su, C. J. Weir, & J. R. W. Wu (Eds.), *English language proficiency testing in Asia: A new paradigm bridging global and local contexts*. London, UK: Routledge. doi:10.4324/9781351254021

Wells, G. (1981). Language as interaction. In G. Wells (Ed.), *Learning through interaction: The study of language development* (pp. 22–72). Cambridge, UK: Cambridge University Press.

Wenger, E. (1998). *Communities of practice: learning, meaning, and identity*. Cambridge, UK: Cambridge University Press.

Wenger-Trayner, E., & Wenger-Trayner, B. (2015). *Introduction to communities of practice*. Retrieved from https://wenger-trayner.com/introduction-to-communities-of-practice/

Wenger-Trayner, E., Fenton-O'Creevy, M., Hutchinson, S., Kubiak, C., & Wenger-Trayner, B. (Eds.). (2015). *Learning in landscapes of practice: Boundaries, identity, and knowledgeability in practice-based learning*. London, UK/ New York, NY: Routledge.

Wertsch, J. V. (1993). *Voices of the mind: Sociocultural approach to mediated action*. Cambridge, MA: Harvard University Press.

Wertz, F. J. (2011). The qualitative revolution and psychology: Science, politics, and ethics. *The Humanistic Psychologist*, *39*, 77–104.

Wertz, F. J., Charmaz, K., McMullen, L. M., Josselson, R., Anderson, R., & McSpadden, E. (Eds.). (2011). *Five ways of doing qualitative analysis: Phenomenological psychology, grounded theory, discourse analysis, narrative research, and intuitive inquiry*. New York, NY: Guilford Press.

White, R.V. (1988). *The ELT curriculum: Design, innovation and management*. Oxford, UK: Basil Blackwell.

Wicks, P. G., & Reason, P. (2009). Initiating action research: Challenges and paradoxes of opening communicative space. *Action Research*, *7*(3), 243–262. doi:10.1177/1476750309336715

Wicks, P. G., Reason, P., & Bradbury, H. (2008). Living inquiry: Personal, political and philosophical groundings for action research practice. In P. Reason & H. Bradbury (Eds.), *The SAGE handbook of action research* (2nd ed., pp. 1–15). Los Angeles, CA: SAGE. Retrieved from www-doi-org.proxy.library.carleton.ca/10.4135/978184

Widdowson, H. G. (2003). *Defining issues in English language teaching*. Oxford, UK: Oxford University Press.

Wiggins, G., & McTighe, J. (2005). *Understanding by design* (2nd ed.). Alexandria, VA: Association for Supervision and Curriculum Development.

Williams, R. (1976). *Keywords: A vocabulary of culture and society*. London, UK: Fontana/Croom Helm.

Willis, K., Daly, J., Kealy, M., Small, R., Koutroulis, G., Green, J., Gibbs, L., & Thomas, S. (2007). The essential role of social theory in qualitative public health research. *Australian and New Zealand Journal of Public Health, 31*(5), 438–443.

Woods, D. (1996). *Teacher cognition in language teaching: Beliefs, decision-making, and classroom-practice*. Cambridge, UK: Cambridge Applied Linguistics.

Wyman, L., Marlow, P., Andrew, C. F., Miller, G., Nicholai, C. R., & Rearden, Y. N. (2010). High stakes testing, bilingual education and language endangerment: A Yup'ik example. *International Journal of Bilingual Education and Bilingualism,13*(6), 701–721. doi:10.1080/13670050903410931

Yallow, E. S., & Popham, W. J. (1983). Content validity at the crossroads. *Educational Researcher, 12*(8), 10–15.

Yates, J. A., & Orlikowski, W. (2007). The PowerPoint presentation and its corollaries: How genres shape communicative action in organizations. In M. Zachary & C. Thralls (Eds.), *Communicative practices in workplaces and the professions: Cultural perspectives on the regulation of discourse and organizations* (p. 67–92). Amityville, NY: Baywood.

Youn, S. J. (2020). Managing proposal sequences in role-play assessment: Validity evidence of interactional competence across levels. *Language Testing, 37*(1) 76–106. doi:10.1177/0265532219860077

Young, R. (2000, March). *Interactional competence: Challenges for validity*. Paper presented at the Annual Meeting of the American Association for Applied Linguistics, Vancouver, BC, Canada. Retrieved from https://eric.ed.gov/?id=ED444361

Young, R. (2006). Series editor's foreword. In T. F. McNamara & C. Roever, *Language testing: The social dimension* (pp. xi–xiv). Malden, MA: Blackwell.

Young, R. (2008). *Language and interaction: An advanced resource book*. London, UK: Routledge.

Young, R. (2011). Interactional competence in language learning, teaching and testing. In E. Hinkel (Ed.), *Handbook of research in second language teaching and learning* (Vol. 2, pp. 426–443). New York, NY: Routledge.

Young, R., & He, A. W. (1998). *Talking and testing: Discourse approaches to the assessment of oral proficiency*. Amsterdam, Netherlands: John Benjamins.

Young, R., & Miller, E. R. (2004). Learning as changing participation: Discourse roles in ESL writing conferences. *The Modern Language Journal 88*(4), 519–535.

Zhu, H. (2016). Identifying research paradigms. In Zhu Hua (Ed.), *Research methods in intercultural communication: A practical guide*. Hoboken, NJ: John Wiley & Sons. doi:10.1002/9781119166283.ch1

Zumbo, B. D. (1998). Opening remarks to the special issue on validity theory and the methods used in validation: Perspectives from the social and behavioral sciences. *Social Indicators Research 45*, 1–3.

Zumbo, B. D. (2014). What role does, and should, the test Standards play outside of the United States of America? Special issue: The AERA/APA/NCME Standards for Educational and Psychological Testing. *Educational Measurement: Issues and Practice, 33*(4), 31–33. doi:10.1111/emip.12052

Zumbo, B. D. (2017). Trending away from routine procedures, towards an ecologically informed "in vivo" view of validation practices. *Measurement: Interdisciplinary Research and Perspectives,15*(3–4), 137–139. doi:10.1080/15366367.2017.1404367

Zumbo, B. D., & Chan, E. K. H. (Eds.). (2014). *Validity and validation in social, behavioral, and health sciences*. New York, NY: Springer.

Zumbo, B. D., & Hubley, A. (2017). *Understanding and investigating response processes in validation research*. Cham, Switzerland: Springer.

Index

Note: Page numbers in *italics* indicate figures and in **bold** indicate tables on the corresponding pages